THE *CHANGING FACE*
OF COMMUNISM
IN EASTERN EUROPE

THE *CHANGING FACE* OF COMMUNISM
IN EASTERN EUROPE

Edited by PETER A. TOMA

Collaborating Authors

Vernon V. Aspaturian   George Klein

Donald D. Dalgleish   Bennett Kovrig

Stephen Fischer-Galati   Nicholas C. Pano

Joseph R. Fiszman   Marin V. Pundeff

Wolfgang Klaiber   Jan F. Triska

THE UNIVERSITY OF ARIZONA PRESS

Tucson, Arizona

THE UNIVERSITY OF ARIZONA PRESS

. . . intellectual freedom is essential to human society—freedom to obtain and distribute information, freedom for open-minded and unfearing debate and freedom from pressure by officialdom and prejudices. Such a trinity of freedom of thought is the only guarantee against an infection of people by mass myths, which . . . can be transformed into bloody dictatorship. [It] . . . is the only guarantee of the feasibility of a scientific, democratic approach to politics, economy, and culture.

ANDREI D. SAKHAROV, 1968

Contents

Foreword

Many teachers in the United States interpret events of recent years in Eastern Europe and in Southeast Asia as part of a conspiracy representing a monolithic world Communist movement. Old cliches about Communism are often applied to new situations, and students are frequently given the impression that Communism is a totally rigid, ideologically controlled movement. On the other hand, there are a few teachers whose information and conclusions about Eastern European countries, in particular, reflect attitudes of confusion, indifference, and alienation. Furthermore, educators need to become aware of new methods of teaching about Communism. These new methods are cross-disciplinary and rely on the inductive approach in the inquiry method.

In independent studies authors W. E. Lambert, O. Klineberg, Robert Hess, and Judith Torney, among others, in surveys of attitudes among American youth have found American children very high in the degree of their liking for people of different countries. Yet, the majority of children at grades four, six, and eight expressed the belief that the "Communists want to take over our country" and that "we can never rest as long as there are any Communists in our country." At the same time the majority of children at all grades believed that it is the Soviet leaders rather than the people who are the enemies of the United States.

Having been taught the ideal of citizen participation in government, friendliness on an individualized-international scale sounds plausible and ideal to most of the youth, but is naive and stands in the way of developing realistic perceptions about international relations. It may also cause strong disillusionment when American youth discovers that the world is not made up of Soviets and Chinese who can be converted to democracy by acts of personal friendliness.

Similar distortions and oversimplifications of realities exist among many high school and college students. Consequently there is a manifest need to improve the teaching of international affairs and, in particular, the teaching about Communism in all schools.

In 1969, the United States Office of Education funded eight summer institutes in the field of international affairs. One of these was at the University of Arizona. The Arizona Institute on "The Changing Face of Communism in Eastern Europe" was the only advanced study on Communism offered under the Education Professions Development Act. It was designed for secondary school social studies teachers who demonstrated the greatest need for inservice instruction about Communism. Out of 1,100 applicants, only 28 were selected to participate in the intensive integrated multidisciplinary program.

Although the University of Arizona Institute had no commitment to the U.S. Office of Education to produce the present volume on Eastern Europe, we welcome it as a significant contribution to the cognitive area of knowledge about Communism in a diverse Eastern Europe. As the book demonstrates, the Institute not only improved the professional competence of the participants in the cognitive area but also was a model for inservice instruction about Communism. Most of the presentations given in the Institute are incorporated in this book. They represent an up-to-date analysis of the major developments in eight Eastern European countries and their relations with the Soviet Union and the West at the opening of the 1970s.

CHARLES R. FOSTER
U.S. Office of Education

Preface

The aim of this volume is to analyze the significant changes which have occurred in Albania, Bulgaria, Czechoslovakia, East Germany, Hungary, Poland, Rumania, and Yugoslavia and the impact of these changes on their relations with the USSR and the West. Throughout the book, the authors point out that it is not only deceptive but unscholarly to lump together the eight socialist countries of Europe into one geographic region governed by uniform political rules. Pluralism in Europe is as strong in east Europe as it is in west. De-Stalinization, which led to desatellitization, transformed Soviet utopianism into de-ideologized national Communism and in the late sixties caused a direct threat to Soviet hegemony in several parts of Europe. Thus the determination of Kremlin leaders to regain their control over the Warsaw-Pact countries induced the USSR to reestablish some old but unpopular means of foreign policy. Regardless of whether the Soviet Union maintains these tactics or not, there are some critics who believe that the lack of intellectual leadership, the application of Stalinesque methods, and the revival of cold war diplomacy have produced fear and paralysis which may ultimately lead the Soviet Communist system tottering toward death.

Some critics who are more optimistic, however, feel that the future leadership in the USSR—a product of the post-Stalinist era—may be more perceptive to the needs of modernization at home and thus develop a more flexible policy toward the countries of Communist Europe. Since forecasting or predicting was not our objective in this volume, we leave projections into the future entirely up to the reader.

This volume is a result of an Education Professions Development Act Institute in International Affairs held during the summer of 1969 at the

University of Arizona under the auspices of the United States Office of Education. The various chapters were orally presented to participants of the Institute. As editor, I have tried to make only changes concerned with style and clarity. Each contributor assumes responsibility for his own content.

It is a great pleasure to acknowledge the original contributions of the chapter authors and to recognize the other lecturers in the Institute: Reginald Barr, R. V. Burks, Mirko Bruner, Merlyn Gubser, Dragan Kavran, Frederick Kellogg, J. G. Oswald, Jaroslav Pribyl, Jan Skaloud, and Paul Zinner. Many thanks also to my colleagues and administrators at the University of Arizona for their moral support, and special thanks to HEW for financial support.

I am also grateful to my graduate students, Edgar Zaharia and Kimball Gaines, for their time and effort in the Institute and to Betty Powell for her administrative assistance. Andrew Elias was kind enough to assist me with the compilation of aggregate data for the country profiles. Finally, I would like to express my gratitude to Karen Thure and Marshall Townsend of the University of Arizona Press for their valuable suggestions and able guidance.

PETER A. TOMA

About the Authors

VERNON V. ASPATURIAN contributes to this volume as research professor of political science and director of the Slavic and Soviet Language and Area Center at Pennsylvania State University. He specializes in international politics, comparative foreign policy, and Soviet politics and foreign policy. The author of *The Union Republics in Soviet Diplomacy* and *The Soviet Union in the World Communist System,* and the co-author of *Modern Political Systems: Europe,* and of *Foreign Policy in World Politics,* he has contributed chapters to several other books, and his articles have appeared in many scholarly journals. He has held numerous fellowships and consultantships, has been a research associate at the Washington Center for Foreign Policy Research, and has held visiting appointments at Columbia, Hopkins, and UCLA, and a Smith-Mundt Professorship in Geneva.

DONALD D. DALGLEISH specializes in comparative political systems of Central and Eastern Europe. His publications include a book, *Die Nazi "Vergangenheit" im Diensten des Kommunismus* "1971," a contribution to the *Handbook of Historical Concepts,* and articles in scholarly journals. In 1962 Professor Dalgleish became assistant professor of political science at Arizona State University, and in 1966, he was visiting professor at the University of Colorado.

STEPHEN FISCHER-GALATI is author of *Ottoman Imperialism and German Protestantism, 1521–1555; New Rumania: From People's Democracy to Socialist Republic;* and *The Socialist Republic of Rumania.* He is editor of the book *Eastern Europe in the Sixties and Rumania,* and has contributed many articles to scholarly journals, becoming editor of *East European Quarterly* in 1966. He has held many fellowships and consultantships with the Ford Foundation, American Council of Learned Societies, the Library of Congress, and the U.S. Department of State. Professor Fischer-Galati has been a research associate of the Russian Research Center at Harvard University and a visiting professor at Indiana University. At the time of this study he was professor of history and director of the Center for East European Affairs at the University of Colorado.

JOSEPH R. FISZMAN has held numerous fellowships and consultantships with the U.S. Department of Labor, the United Steelworkers' Union, and the Oregon State Department of Education. His career includes the editing of the book *The American Political Arena,* membership on the editorial board of *Western Political Quarterly,* and the publication of many scholarly articles. In 1968 he became associate professor of political science at the University of Oregon and one year later became acting director of the Institute of Comparative Experimental Research on Behavioral Systems .there.

WOLFGANG KLAIBER, after serving as research coordinator in the Foreign Policy Research Institute at the University of Pennsylvania, became a staff member of the International and Social Studies Division, Institute for Defense Analyses, Arlington, Virginia. The author of several scholarly articles, he has been on the editorial board of ORBIS.

GEORGE KLEIN became associate professor of political science and chairman of Slavic studies at Western Michigan University after serving as assistant professor of political science at the University of Illinois from 1956–58. He has published in scholarly journals and contributed to books in his field of specialization, the contemporary political systems of Eastern Europe. Professor Klein has been the recipient of several grants to study abroad.

BENNETT KOVRIG, author of the book *The Hungarian People's Republic,* became assistant professor of political science at the University of Toronto in 1968. A specialist in the economic political systems of Eastern Europe, he has been a Canadian National Defense Fellow.

NICHOLAS C. PANO is author of *The People's Republic of Albania* and of several articles in scholarly journals. His career also includes membership on the editorial board of *The Journal of Developing Areas* and work as an abstractor for *Historical Abstracts.* Concentrating on modern Eastern Europe and Soviet Russia, he contributes to this volume as assistant professor of history at Western Illinois University.

MARIN V. PUNDEFF, specialist in modern Balkan history and Marxist historiography, has written *Bulgaria: A Bibliographic Guide,* edited the book *History in the USSR,* contributed chapters to several other books, and published numerous scholarly articles. He has held several fellowships and consultantships. Professor Pundeff has taken leave from his post as professor of history at San Fernando Valley State College to serve as visiting professor at the University of Colorado, UCLA, and USC.

PETER A. TOMA, author of *The Politics of Food for Peace* and co-editor of *Basic Issues in International Relations,* has contributed chapters to several textbooks and written articles for numerous scholarly journals. As a specialist in contemporary political systems of Eastern Europe and the USSR, and in sociopolitical change, he has become secretary-treasurer of the Western Slavic Association and director of an EPDA Institute in International Affairs. He has held a Haynes and a Social Science Foundation Fellowship and a consultantship with AID/FFP. In 1970 he went on leave from his post of professor of government at the University of Arizona to lecture in the National War College.

JAN F. TRISKA writes from the vantage point of professor of political science and director of studies of the Communist system at the Institute of Political Studies, Stanford University. Focusing on contemporary political system of Eastern Europe and the USSR, he is the co-author of *Soviet Foreign Policy; A Calendar of Soviet Treaties, 1917–1957; The Theory, Law, and Policy of Soviet Treaties;* and *The Law of International Waterways,* and is editor of the books *Communist Party-States; Constitutions of Communist Party-States;* and *Soviet Communism: Programs and Rules.* He also has published articles in several scholarly journals. Professor Triska has held fellowships at the Harvard Russian Research Center and the Hoover Institution as well as consultantships with the Stanford Research Institute and the Office of Navy Research. He has been on the executive council of the American Society of International Law and president of the Far Western Slavic Conference.

1
Introduction
Peter A. Toma

1. Introduction

Peter A. Toma

In the late 1940s, it was appropriate to refer to the Kremlin as the center of world Communism, dominating the entire world Communist movement. At that time the Communist world was known as a monolithic entity equipped with satellites and controlled by the rigid doctrinal teachings of Stalinism. Moscow's neighbors to the west—all the way to Berlin and Belgrade—represented a solid Soviet bloc in Europe. Scholars who followed the geopolitical school of thought identified this contiguous region as Communist Eastern Europe. There was strong evidence to support their claim: uniformity in coersive one-party rule, Soviet-imposed command economy, an ideological straitjacket, and Kremlin supervision through the Cominform.

Within the framework of the cold war, Eastern Europe (which included not only Poland, Czechoslovakia, Rumania, Bulgaria, Albania, Yugoslavia, and Hungary but East Germany as well) became popularly known as a Soviet sphere of influence. The oversimplification of world problems, due to ideological differences, led to the acceptance of the idea that all of these countries were similar and that they represented an extension of Soviet power in Europe. This stereotyped notion prevailed in the United States and elsewhere long after Stalin's death. Although the Soviet-Yugoslav split in June 1948 created a serious crack in Stalin's monolithic machinery, it was not until 1956 (after the abolition of the Cominform and the Hungarian revolt) that most American scholars accepted the idea that the Communist world had ceased to be a monolithic entity—that the differences among the socialist countries of Eastern Europe were far greater than the similarities. Nevertheless, Eastern Europe continued and still continues to be identified with international

Communism and Soviet power. For this reason alone, the German Democratic Republic (which is not, geographically speaking, part of Eastern Europe) as well as Yugoslavia and Albania (which are not, politically speaking, under the Soviet sphere of influence) are discussed here as components of the once Iron Curtain region of Eastern Europe.

As the following chapters reveal, however, there is no regional entity called Eastern Europe. Soviet efforts to integrate nations into one regional unit have not been successful in geographic areas which have a disparaged economy, a long tradition of religious, linguistic, and cultural differences, and a strong aspiration for national independence. National sovereignty, no matter how defined, is stronger today in Eastern Europe than international Communism. Consequently, what we are witnessing now is disintegration rather than integration of Communist Eastern Europe. This process seems to be a natural result of the impact of Soviet utopian ideology on East European nations—it reflects the myths and realities in the Soviet mirror.

Mutation of Soviet Ideology

Present-day ideological symbols in the Soviet Union are mutations of Marxian, Leninist, Stalinist, Khrushchevist, Brezhnevist, and other concepts, which represent "realities" that started with a myth more than fifty years ago. As Sidney Hook correctly points out, Marxism never existed in Soviet Russia. Therefore, Marxian concepts, which were introduced to the Soviet Union by Lenin, Stalin, Khrushchev, Brezhnev, and others, became myths that stimulated action. Since men everywhere react to symbols with real behavior, in the USSR citizens reacted to Marxian symbols by gradually adopting Bolshevism. As self-professed Marxists, Lenin, Stalin, Khrushchev, Brezhnev, and other Bolsheviks considered themselves part of an international proletarian movement. Thus Communist ideology became a symbolic means of communication among the members of this movement, and, as such, it was dynamic enough to accommodate new realities based upon old myths, which in the West very often appeared to be contradictions in values.

Ideological mutation of Marxian concepts leads some scholars and politicians to believe that Communist ideology is dead. While certain aspects of Communist ideology (for example, class struggle and internationalism and the law of uneven economic and political development) have lost their appeal, it is presumptuous to argue that Communist ideology is dead. It is still a useful tool of "fraternal communication," despite the fallacy of several of its predictive "laws," such as the law of the inevitability of world Communism. Communist symbolism is an effective instrument of Soviet foreign policy garnished with ideological greens. It has produced conditions which really exist, although these symbols originated with a myth called Marxism.

Since Soviet interpretations of realities vary drastically with the leaders of the Soviet state, a sudden reversal in the selection of values (through which realities are interpreted) by these statesmen can cause both confusion and distrust among the followers, which, in turn, can trigger a social, cultural, and even a political and economic upheaval in the society. This seems to be the case in the Soviet Union today because of Khrushchev's de-Stalinization policy and the limits imposed on this policy by the Kremlin leaders who replaced him.

Khrushchev's de-Stalinization policy was not so much a tactical device —which made his transition to power a popular counterpart of the despised Stalinist cult and therefore a means of liberalization in the Soviet Union—as it was a consequence of the discovery of new weapons systems which made most of Stalin's concepts obsolete. This new discovery was the development of thermonuclear weapons and their delivery system, which altered the Stalinist concepts of class struggle, the unevenness of economic and political developments of capitalism, and the Stalinist concept of labor theory of value.

In the period prior to the invention of nuclear weapons, the Kremlin leaders believed that wars were unavoidable under imperialism because the unevenness of economic and political development of the individual countries lead to a sharpening of the conflicts in the imperialist camp. After war, according to Stalin, follow revolutions, depression, fascism, and then, to complete the cycle, again war, revolutions, depression, and so on. Peaceful coexistence in this cycle was nothing but a period of respite. Since the development of thermonuclear weapons, however, Stalin's (and for that matter Lenin's) law of uneven economic and political developments leading to war is obsolete by Soviet admission. Under such conditions, thermonuclear war would be the outcome and not the continuation of policy because it would have lost its characteristics of being a political means for resolving conflicts between states. For most participants, such a war would mark the end of policy. This new development also applies to the Soviet thesis of the unavoidability of the transition to Communism for all mankind. Thus the transition of mankind to Communism is not an inescapable need, as Lenin, Stalin, and others have argued, but merely one of the possibilities of development.

Khrushchev, who had no choice but to accept this new reality, devised the concept of peaceful coexistence and peaceful transition to socialism. Under Khrushchev, peaceful coexistence was no longer a period of respite, as it was under Stalin and Lenin. On the contrary, Khrushchev equated peaceful coexistence with the principle of rejection of war as a means for settlement of disputes among states. It was based on the principle of trust, economic and cultural cooperation, and on the principle of mutual respect for interests, territorial integrity, and sovereignty. It was based on the principle of non-interference in the domestic affairs of states and recognition of the right of each nation to settle independently its own affairs. The application of the Khrushchevist concept of peaceful coexistence led many Communists to believe that the abolition of capitalism would come about not as a result of war with Communist countries, but as a result of the maturing stage of development of capitalism.

Thus the impact of the development of thermonuclear weapons on Soviet policy-making under Khrushchev was so profound that it unleashed a social mobilization of unprecedented magnitude—not only in the Soviet Union, but in Eastern Europe as well.

Social Mobilization versus Stalinist Tradition

The political regimes erected by Stalin after World War II functioned under a trinity known as despotism, terror, and utopia. Despotism was the body and soul of the ruling Communist parties. Despotism thrived on the maxim which stated, one will, one leader. Therefore the conflict between despotism and the doctrinal primacy of the party was always resolved by terror. Like Stalin, the East European despots employed the secret police not only to dominate but also to terrorize the party. Through terror the Stalinist dictators were able to prevent the organization of elites, and through utopianism they made use of command economy as inspiration for the masses. The key factor, however, which kept Stalinism in Eastern Europe alive was the availability of terror. During this period, the regimes were afraid of the universal hostility of the populations, and thus they proceeded to control these societies by the systematic use of terror.

Once terror began to decline, at different times in different countries, the parties lost in their importance, the dictators were absorbed into elites, the populations were provided with increased material incentives (more consumers' goods), and political socialization was extended to a larger strata. The regimes now needed the loyalty and support of the masses to make the new system of economic efficiency work. Consequently, the de-Stalinizing regimes of Eastern Europe appealed to national feelings, promised greater material rewards (an increase in the living standards), made concessions in the field of individual rights (greater freedom of expression and travel), and permitted more non-party people to take part in the political process.

Since the Stalinist social, economic, and psychological commitments in Eastern European countries were eroded or broken immediately after Stalin's death, and because people in Eastern Europe were yearning for new patterns of socialization and behavior while Stalin was still alive, social mobilization for a legitimate socialist state without terror was a successful policy even before the advent of thermonuclear weapons. There is no doubt, however, that it was the threat of these weapons that reinforced the social mobilization policy of Khrushchev and his followers. The area in which the impact of social mobilization was felt most was the field of economics.

The Stalinization of Eastern Europe, with the exception of Yugoslavia, caused a hundred million Europeans to fall ten or more years behind the standard of living of their western neighbors. The primary cause for this decline in the standard of living was Stalin's decision to impose a Soviet economic system on Soviet satellites. The inherent inefficiencies of this system began to show up as soon as the shifting of manpower from agriculture to industry and the mobilization of women for work were completed. The national goal was simply to produce goods, regardless of quality or marketability. The East European factories consumed a lot of resources for which they produced only statistics. When Stalin died, Communist Eastern Europe found itself using more and more capital to get the same increase in output. The elite suddenly began to realize that the economic road upon which they originally embarked was leading nowhere; that there is a limit to progress in a command economy operated from one center. Thus, after Stalin's death, several East European economists and farsighted party leaders—encouraged by events in the USSR—took a new look at their economic conditions and decided to seek new opportunities for the modernization of their national economies. Modernization, however, required the replacement of the rule by coercion with the rule by consent and loyalty of the governed. Fortunately for many East Europeans, this transition to non-coercive methods was also a policy espoused by N. S. Khrushchev under his principle of competitive peaceful coexistence. All but Albania and Rumania accepted Khrushchev's dictate and thus de-Stalinization à la Soviet style became an official policy in the larger part of Eastern Europe.

In some countries (Poland and Hungary) de-Stalinization started in the middle-fifties—in others (East Germany, Bulgaria, and Czechoslovakia) not until the middle-sixties. The plan for de-Stalinization was similar in all five East European countries. Its chief components were an appeal to the national interest, democratization of the one-party system, and the promise to improve the living standards. Since de-Stalinization for Khrushchev also meant economic integration of the Comecon countries under Soviet auspices, Albania and Rumania once more rebuffed the Soviet plan. Thus, Khrushchev's de-Stalinization attempts in these two countries caused a desatellitization process which resulted in Albania and Rumania taking independent roads to socialism. But in Yugoslavia, where de-Stalinization was an official policy while Stalin was alive, desatellitization was accomplished suddenly and all at once. While de-Stalinization threatened the existence of the Soviet dictatorship from inside, desatellitization threatened the Soviet dictatorship from the outside. Hence, both movements have come to be considered dangerous and intolerable by the Kremlin. The Brezhnev doctrine of limited sovereignty, although vague, makes this point quite explicit.

The Independent Road to Socialism and Limited Sovereignty

One recent profound change that led to confusion and the alienation of many followers of Soviet ideology was the redefining of the concept of the independent road to socialism. Titoism, which from 1948 to 1953 represented one of the greatest sins under Communism, became, after the Moscow meeting in November 1957, an accepted ideological tenet —first under Khrushchev and then under Brezhnev. Independent roads to socialism in Eastern Europe were a Kremlin concession for obtaining satellite support against Peking. Most East European countries took full advantage of this situation; they sought and received more independence from Moscow. Because of Rumania's go-it-alone foreign policy and because of Czechoslovakia's threat to become completely independent from Moscow in 1968, the Soviet concept of sovereignty of socialist nations was reinterpreted once more; but this time so as to resemble neo-Stalinism.

The new doctrine of the "socialist community" (*obshchina*) negated the Khrushchevist doctrine of "socialist commonwealth" (*sodruzhestvo*). The latter was built on the basis of equality, national independence and sovereignty, and noninterference in each other's affairs. The theory of "socialist community," published in Moscow's *Pravda* on September 26, 1968, is similar, but noninterference has been dropped. It is based on the notion that the laws and legal norms are subordinated to the laws of class struggle and to the law of social development. It follows the maxim that any decisions peoples of socialist countries adopt must not inflict damage to socialism in their country. The question is, who decides when and where to act? Does "communal sovereignty" supersede "national sovereignty"? Which are the countries in the "socialist community"? Answers to these questions will determine whether the new Soviet doctrine of limited sovereignty is simply a temporary restraint on growing nationalism in Eastern Europe or a permanent instrument of Soviet foreign policy aiming to restore and maintain Soviet control over Eastern Europe.

It appears that during the short Khrushchevist period of de-Stalinization in Eastern Europe, social mobilization—initiated by the USSR— changed the Communist man into an economic man who, in the eyes of the dogmatists, threatened the very existence of socialism. Although modernization and economic efficiency were, and still are, among the primary goals of the socialist countries of Eastern Europe, the ruling elites have been cautious not to sacrifice "socialism" for economic achievement. Most East European countries favor one type of economic reform or another—so does the USSR. The questions are those of how to prevent the erosion of the power of the party and how to prevent the totalitarian society from becoming a pluralistic one.

Just as Khrushchev in his day experimented with methods of de-Stalinization, Brezhnev today is experimenting with methods of repression. Whatever the outcome of these experiments, one thing appears to be certain: there can be no return to Stalinist despotism, terror, and utopia. The use of automation and modernization in the USSR supports this hypothesis. The old Marxian thesis that manual labor creates most of the wealth in the world has been disproved by the latest developments in automation. Recognition of this fact by the Soviet elite led to a new theory of labor value which gave the "specialist" a much more favorable position in the society of toilers than "the party bureaucrat." Competitiveness with capitalism is a constant reminder to the Soviet economic planners to accept innovation and modernization in their economy, even if it resembles capitalism. And what is good for Moscow must also be good for the Comecon countries, even if it means growing nationalism in Eastern Europe.

National Communism in Eastern Europe is a complex movement encompassing many features of national development. In the economic area, several East European countries have ambitious plans for economic reforms which are designed to improve their standards of living through a more flexible "market-socialism," and, if necessary, to effect certain political and social changes which would permit the enjoyment of greater personal freedom by more citizens. To this end, central programming of production has been replaced by direct bargaining between enterprises; central allocation of investment has been replaced by self-financing; the rationing system has been abolished, and a market for the means of production has been established; enterprise incentives have been changed in favor of profit maximization; centrally fixed wages have been replaced by a link between wages and enterprise profit; and the administrative price system has been replaced by a market price system. Although the details vary from country to country, the aim of these reforms is the same everywhere: to equip the ruling elites with new methods of economic knowhow which would afford them greater economic progress and smoother economic control. Thus, the programs are directed, on the one hand, against the stubborn, unimaginative, and backward *apparatchiki,* whose doctrinaire interpretations of the socialist economy can mean only central planning; and, on the other, against the indolent, unskilled, and uneducated members of the socialist societies, whose interest in the socialist economy is equated only with social benefits.

In the political area, most East European countries are seeking liberalization not for liberalization's sake but as a prerequisite to modernization. So far the greatest gains of political liberalization have been recorded in countries where the economic reforms have been most effective. In such countries the citizens may now criticize the regime's bureaucratic shortcomings; produce political satires and other plays criticizing the regime; enjoy access to some Western publications, radio and television; and in some cases even travel in non-socialist countries. In several instances East European nations may enter into commercial, cultural, and diplomatic relations with Western or nonaligned nations without Moscow's approval. Nevertheless, most East European countries are still firmly welded to Moscow, especially through the Warsaw Pact and the Comecon structure. The question is, can official relations among governments, parties, and their auxiliary organizations—which are outwardly oriented (that is, oriented toward Moscow)—negate the feelings and attitudes expressed in unofficial relations among the citizens of East European countries—which are inwardly (egocentrically) oriented? For example, the relations among the governments and parties of the Soviet Union, Poland, and East Germany are very friendly, but the relations among the citizens of the three countries are far from being friendly. Similar relations prevail among the Czechs, Slovaks, Hungarians, and Russians.

The Mosaic of Eastern Europe

Ever since social mobilization came into being in Eastern Europe, there has been an expansion of the politically relevant strata of the population, which has brought about mounting pressures for economic and political changes. Since the regimes want to modernize without pluralization, and the peoples desire modernization without totalitarism, political tension between the two groups has become unavoidable. Similarly, it can be hypothesized that the greater the success of modernization without totalitarianism in an East European country, the greater the likelihood of Soviet intervention. Thus it is possible that there is a designated limit established by the ruling elites for modernization with pluralization beyond which a Comecon country cannot venture.

Can the Communist elites, willingly or unwillingly, afford to turn the clock back on modernization? Perhaps so, for a short time, but not for long. The technological gap between the two halves of Europe, as Professor R. V. Burks points out, is constantly widening rather than narrowing. Sooner or later the Kremlin leaders will have to solve the dilemma as to whether to permit East European countries to modernize even at the expense of greater independence, or to impose restraints— military if necessary—in order to keep Eastern Europe under Soviet mandate, regardless of what happens to their economy. Which course the Soviet Union will follow depends very much on the future internal developments in the USSR. One thing is clear, however: as we enter the seventies, the Soviet Union and all East European states (except Albania) are engaged in some kind of economic reform, which is designed to provide greater efficiency in their countries. These reforms vary from Yugoslavia, which is following a major liberal program, to Rumania with a conservative mini-reform. Between these two extremes are the reforms of Hungary, Czechoslovakia, East Germany, Poland, and Bulgaria. All of them are different; they follow the national characteristics of each country. What separates one reform from another is the degree of risk-taking by the government and party in the achievement of efficiency. In Yugoslavia, for example, the elite is willing to take a much greater risk for the achievement of efficiency through de-Stalinization of the decision-making process than the elite in Rumania. The risk-taking is greater in Hungary than it is in Czechoslovakia, but it is smaller in East Germany and Bulgaria than it is in Czechoslovakia. In Poland risk-taking is greater than in Rumania, but smaller than in Bulgaria. The following chapters demonstrate this paradigm quite well.

2

The Socialist Republic
of Rumania

Stephen Fischer-Galati

Country Profile: THE SOCIALIST REPUBLIC OF RUMANIA

Head of State: Nicolae Ceausescu, Chairman of the Council of State
Premier: Ion Gheorghe Maurer, Chairman of the Council of Ministers
General Secretary, Central Committee, Rumanian Communist Party:
  Nicolae Ceausescu

Party Membership (1968): 1,800,000[1]
Armed Forces (1969): 193,000 (Army: 170,000; Navy: 8,000; Air Force:
  15,000)[2]
Population: Mid-1968: 19,721,000 (Bucharest: 1,431,993)[3]
Area: 237,500 square kilometers (91,699 square miles)
Population Density: 83 per square kilometer (215 per square mile)
Birth Rate (1968): 26.7 per thousand[3]
Death Rate (1968): 9.6 per thousand[3]
Divorce Rate (1968): 0.2 per thousand[3]
Gross Material Product (1968): 170.1 billion lei ($28.4 billion at official
  rate)[4]
National Income by Sectors (1968):[5]
  Industry: 54.2%
  Construction: 9.2%
  Agriculture: 26.2%
  Transportation and Communications: 4.3%
  Trade: 3.5%
  Other: 2.6%
Foreign Trade by Area (1968):[6]
  Socialist Countries (including USSR): 55.2%
  USSR: 28.7%
  Non-Socialist countries: 44.8%

Foreign Trade by Commodity (1968):[7]	Export	Import
Machinery, capital goods	21.3%	46.7%
Industrial consumer goods	14.4%	6.2%
Raw materials, semi-finished products	50.2%	44.4%
Comestibles	14.1%	2.7%

SOURCES:
1. U.S. Department of State, Bureau of Intelligence and Research, *World Strength of Communist Party Organizations* (Washington, D.C.: U.S. Government Printing Office, 1969), p. 59.
2. *The Military Balance 1969–1970* (London: The Institute for Strategic Studies, 1969), p. 14.
3. *Anuarul Statistic al Republicii Socialiste Romania 1969* (Bucharest, 1969), pp. 65–69.
4. Based on the dollar figure in *The Military Balance 1969–1970,* p. 14 and the official exchange rate (rather than 9.4 lei = $1.00).
5. *Anuarul Statistic al Republicii Socialiste Romania 1969,* p. 106.
6. *Ibid.,* pp. 545–49.
7. *Ibid.,* pp. 551–53.

2. The Socialist Republic of Rumania

Stephen Fischer-Galati

In April 1964 the Central Committee of the Rumanian Workers' Party issued the "Statement on the Stand of the Rumanian Workers' Party Concerning the Problems of the World Communist and Working-Class Movement."[1] That document has been regarded in the history of the Rumanian Communist movement as a declaration of independence from Soviet Communism and the Soviet Union.

The "Statement" is indeed far-reaching. It addresses itself primarily to the sovereign rights of nation-states. In essence, these rights are proclaimed to be inviolate. In the case of Rumania, the threat to national sovereignty comes from the Soviet Union which, according to the "Statement," has abandoned the norms of Marxism-Leninism guiding relations among members of the international Communist movement. The Soviet Union and, by implication the Communist Party of the Soviet Union (CPSU), have consistently abused their doctrinal and political powers to interfere in the internal affairs of fraternal parties and states, to impose their will and men with a view to reducing these parties and states to satellites of the Kremlin. Such actions are inadmissable but may be condoned in cases of emergency, such as existed at the end of World War II. According to the Rumanian Communist Party (RCP) they are, however, intolerable and extremely dangerous to the international Communist movement at a time when the triumph of socialism over capitalism is inevitable.

Divested of the dialectics of Marxism-Leninism, the Rumanian declaration states, in effect, that despite the interference in Rumanian internal affairs exercised by the Kremlin after the country's "liberation from facsism" in August 1944, Communist Rumania has been able to

[15]

develop its own "road to socialism" and become a respectable member of the "socialist camp" and of the international community as a whole. To safeguard these gains and Rumania's status as a nation state, the RCP and the Rumanian state are determined to resist any and all attempts by the Soviet Union and the CPSU to arrest or redirect the national Rumanian effort in a manner detrimental to the national interest.

Of immediate concern to the Rumanians was the Sino-Soviet conflict, and it was for that reason that the Statement was primarily devoted to the question of Communist unity. On paper the Rumanians deplored the controversy as a manifestation alien to the spirit of Marxism-Leninism and contributory to the strengthening of the forces of Western imperialism. In reality, the Rumanians were vitally concerned by the danger of polarization of the international Communist movement into a Russian and a Chinese camp, a situation that would enhance the likelihood of Russian interference in Rumanian affairs. In other words, the future of Rumania and of the Rumanian party depended on the containment of Soviet imperialism, on the reduction of the CPSU to the status of one among equals in the international Communist movement, and on the acceptance by the Soviet Union of the principles of equality of the members of the socialist camp and of the inviolability of the sovereign rights of Communist nation-states.

Inasmuch as the very same questions were raised in June 1969 by the Rumanian delegation attending the International Conference of Communist and Workers' Parties in Moscow,[2] it is relevant for the purposes of this study to ascertain the reasons for the Rumanian Communists' concern with these problems in 1964 and 1969 in terms of the evolution of the RCP and the Rumanian state, first during the twenty years preceding the Statement of 1964 and then during the five momentous years following that declaration of independence.

The Source of Friction Between Moscow and Bucharest

It is still a matter of dispute as to whether the safeguarding of the gains achieved by Rumania in the postwar years under the direction of the Rumanian Workers' Party (RWP) was the primary motivation of the authors of the Statement or whether the political survival of those authors dictated their action of April 1964. It is by no means certain that the "building of socialism" in Rumania would have been possible without Soviet "interference" in Rumanian affairs after World War II. And it is certain that without such interference Communist rule could not have been established in postwar Rumania.[3] It is also difficult to ascertain the extent to which Soviet plans for the "socialist transformation" of Rumania differed from autochthonous Rumanian plans for the attainment of that goal during the years following Rumania's "liberation." What is clear, however, is that by 1964 a seemingly irreconcilable split had occurred between the Rumanian and Soviet leaderships involving the limits of independent action by the Rumanians in socialist construction.[4]

The roots of the political conflict between Moscow and Bucharest are deep. They may be traced to World War II. But they were originally and for a long time thereafter only peripherally related to the construction of socialism as such. The initial issue, which recurred at frequent intervals, was that of selection by the Kremlin of the leaders of other Communist parties.

In Rumania the Communist movement was arrested at an early date by the regime in power and by popular apathy or hostility toward Communist dogma and associations. The Rumanian Communist Party was established in 1921 and was outlawed three years later.[5] During the brief period of legal existence it was identified with non-Rumanian interests. Officially it was branded a creature of Moscow designed to subvert the Rumanian national state and the genuine interests of the Rumanian working class. These accusations were largely true and also effective. The Communist movement was controlled by Moscow and was subservient to it. Its goal was revolution for the benefit of the traditional enemy of Rumania, Russia, and for the subservient leadership of the Rumanian Communist Party. That leadership consisted primarily of non-Rumanians, mostly Jewish intellectuals unidentified with the Rumanian worker. In a country with a long tradition of anti-Semitism and suspicion of Russia and of Communism, the discrediting of the Communist movement as a "Judaeo-Russian conspiracy" was a relatively easy task.

Whether the anti-Russian and anti-Semitic elements inherent in governmental propaganda were shared by the few representatives of the Rumanian working class who belonged to the party during its periods of legal and illegal existence is difficult to determine. In all likelihood, the workers and their leaders in the RCP must have been aware of the constant purges ordered by Moscow and its non-Rumanian and non-proletarian agents in the organization and of the leadership's indifference to the workers' cause and representation in the upper echelons of the party. The Kremlin's lack of concern for the fate of the leaders of the only genuine expression of revolutionary discontent recorded in interwar Rumania—the so-called Grivita Strike of the railway men in 1933—must also have been evident to the participants in the rebellion. It was certainly evident to the leaders of the strike, headed by Gheorghe Gheorghiu-Dej himself, who were incarcerated and left to languish in jail while non-proletarian leaders of the RCP, headed by Ana Pauker, were provided sanctuary in Moscow through bilateral extradition agreements between Soviet Russia and the Rumanian "fascist" regime against whom Gheorghiu-Dej and his followers had rebelled. It is possible that the ill feeling toward Moscow had somewhat abated in the later thirties when the Kremlin found it advantageous to encourage "Popular Front" movements in Europe.[6] In Rumania the Popular Front incorporated Communist activities and representatives of minor agrarian and intellectual groupings of which the most important was the Plowmen's Front headed by Petru Groza. In this process of identification of proletarian, intellectual, and agrarian interests and of Soviet and Rumanian concerns for peace, prosperity, and democracy, an unusual degree of mobility within the RCP was afforded to young Rumanian Communists identifiable with the ostensible goals of the Popular Front. The non-Rumanian leaders of the RCP were temporarily relegated to less conspicuous posts —frequently in the so-called "Rumanian Bureau," which directed Rumanian affairs from Moscow—while Rumanians emerged, at least pro forma, as the leaders of the Rumanian organization.

The possible consequences of tactical shifts are unpredictable. Since World War II terminated the experiment, all consequences of the tactical shifts written in the RCP cannot be evaluated. We do know, however, that some of the changes in party tactics resulted in the jailing of most of the young Rumanian leaders, including Nicolae Ceausescu, and the concentration of Rumanian-related Communist activities in Moscow. Thus, the Rumanian Communists were in "fascist" jails, while Rumanian-speaking Jewish, Hungarian, Ukrainian, and other non-Rumanian Communists were manning the Rumanian Bureau in Moscow. The incarcerated Rumanians were aware of this situation and reacted accordingly at the right time.

Early in 1944, as the Soviet forces were moving toward Rumania, the jailed Rumanian Communists, led by Gheorghiu-Dej, assumed unilateral control of the Rumanian Communist organization.[7] The coup whereby Gheorghiu-Dej became the party's First Secretary was designed to ensure Rumanian representation in the postwar period of inevitable Communist power. It was not directed against Moscow, on whose support the future of Rumanian Communism depended, but against the non-Rumanian members of the Moscow bureau, who threatened to assume total command of the Communist movement in Rumania. Gheorghiu-Dej and his associates were persuaded that the Kremlin needed the support of the Rumanian working class and working peasantry to secure control over "liberated" Rumania and that such support could best be secured through Rumanian Communists of proletarian origin rather than through Jewish and other non-Rumanian intellectuals and *apparatchiks*. To this extent Gheorghiu-Dej was correct, for indeed the Soviets, upon "liberating" Rumania in August 1944, found it expedient to seek legitimacy for Communism through the spontaneous identification of the interests of the Rumanian masses with the progressive Rumanian forces led by Gheorghiu-Dej and Petru Groza. The Popular Front was de facto revived in 1945 according to the formulas of the thirties. The reconstituted Communist Party—RWP—which became the instrument for the attainment of the Soviet goal of transforming Rumania into a faithful Communist client state was, however, controlled by the Kremlin through its most faithful agents—the non-Rumanian members of the Moscow bureau. There was friction between the Rumanian contingent and the so-called Moscovites in terms of leadership within the RWP but not in terms of subservience to Moscow or over domestic and foreign policies. On these fundamental issues all leaders of the Rumanian Communist movement took orders from the Kremlin.

Gheorghiu-Dej: Stalin's Disciple

Internally, the socialist transformation of the country was assigned priority as early as 1945. In October of that year, the first postwar conference of the Rumanian Workers' Party outlined the plans for socialist industrialization and general socialist construction ostensibly on the basis of the experience of the Soviet Union and factors unique to Rumania and the RWP.[8] The only specific Rumanian factor was the omission of any plans for agricultural collectivization, but that was an omission based purely on political considerations. In the struggle with the anti-Communist forces in Rumania, which included the majority of the peasantry, it would have been fatal for the Kremlin and its Rumanian Communist allies to mention socialization in agriculture. Gheorghiu-Dej's commitment to the continuation of private property in agriculture was dictated by Moscow and endorsed by Ana Pauker. If anything, he was more persuaded of the need for eventual collectivization than the Moscovites.

Nor is there any evidence that Gheorghiu-Dej was less in favor of complying with subsequent Russian directives for the Communization of Rumania than were Ana Pauker and her associates. He took full credit for the onerous Soviet-Rumanian economic and political agreements signed after the conclusion of the Peace Treaty and the establishment of the Rumanian People's Republic in 1947, agreements which reduced Rumania to the position of a colonial dependency of Moscow. Similarly, he took credit for the inauguration of industrial planning in 1948, for the decision to collectivize agriculture in 1949, and for all the draconic measures directed against actual and potential opponents to the Moscow-directed Communization of Rumania.[9] Indeed, to retain the position of General Secretary of the party and consolidate his own power in the Rumanian Communist movement, Gheorghiu-Dej became the most abject servant of Stalin in Eastern Europe, outdoing in the process the Kremlin's non-Rumanian representatives, Ana Pauker and her long-time associates in the Moscow bureau. His success was not based on his efforts to carry out the socialist transformation of Rumania in accordance with Rumania's "objective conditions" (in juxtaposition to Soviet Russia's) but rather to render them compatible with Stalin's goals for Rumania. And it was on the basis of these qualifications for survival and success that Gheorghiu-Dej was able to gradually undermine the power of the representatives of the Moscow bureau in the Rumanian Party and eventually, with Stalin's acknowledgment, to purge his principal opponents and assume control of the organization in 1952 as Stalin's man in Rumania.[10]

It is also noteworthy that between 1945 and 1952 Gheorghiu-Dej faithfully followed the blueprint for Rumania's isolation from the international community outside the Soviet bloc. Rumania nullified existing agreements and traditional ties with France, Italy, and the West in general and outdid other Communist states in the virulence of its denunciation of Western "imperialism." She terrorized all known to have had contacts with the West before World War II. Total subservience to Russia was the price which Gheorghiu-Dej was more than willing to pay for power in satellite Rumania.

In recording his victory over his internal rivals in the name of pure Stalinism, Gheorghiu-Dej stressed the gains obtained by the country through the unflinching execution of the Russian blueprint for the Communization of Rumania. The record of achievement was quite remarkable, testifying to the validity of the "Stalinist road to socialism" which he had pursued.[11] In practical terms, Gheorghiu-Dej had destroyed the economic power of the "bourgeois-landlord" class (including the *"kulaks"*), had eradicated all manifestations of "bourgeois-nationalism," and above all had established the bases for economic modernization. Industrial production was nearly three times greater in 1952 than in 1938; the size of the working class had expanded from 750,000 to 1,000,000 in the same period; the village was slowly disintegrating with accelerated migration into urban centers. The principal drawback to more rapid expansion was the opposition of the peasantry, and even of industrial workers, to the dogmatism of the planners and the inadequate system of remuneration, but these negative attitudes were controllable by Gheorghiu-Dej's perfected instruments of repression. Such other limitations upon further progress as exclusive dependence on the Soviet bloc for trade and technological knowhow were appreciated by the rulers of Communist Rumania. They were, however, relegated to a position subordinate to maintenance in power of the Gheorghiu-Dej regime. Nor did the regime ignore the fact that, despite its professions of devotion to the cause of socialist construction in Rumania, it was regarded by the population as an instrument of the Kremlin. In fact, the hatred of the Rumanian people for the Rumanian Communists was outdone only by their hatred for Stalin's Communist Russia.

It would therefore be difficult to ascribe the changes which occurred in Rumania after the death of Stalin in 1953 primarily to Gheorghiu-Dej's realization of the inadequacies of Stalin's formulas for socialist construction in Rumania. Rather, the economic and political measures adopted by Gheorghiu-Dej after Stalin's death, which have been identified as Rumanian as opposed to Soviet Russian, reflected a concern for his own political survival in the post-Stalinist period, when his rule was challenged both from within and from without Rumania.[12] Gheorghiu-Dej, between the spring of 1953 and the final defeat of his internal opponents in the summer of 1957, introduced no basic changes in his mode of Stalinist rule in Rumania. There were no departures from rigid planning, no toleration of any deviations that could be in any way detrimental to Stalinist principles and practices. Such progress as was attained in these years was directly connected with the struggle for power which started in Rumania, as elsewhere in the Soviet bloc, after Stalin's death. In Rumania it concentrated on the attempts of reformists first to limit Gheorghiu's powers and eventually to remove the Rumanian Stalinist from power altogether. By 1954, that segment of the RWP was seeking at least tacit support from Khrushchev. By 1955, Khrushchev and the "progressive" elements in the RWP were identified as enemies of Gheorghiu-Dej by the Rumanian ruling elite, and the search for independence from anti-Stalinist forces, internal and external, became an integral part of Gheorghiu-Dej's raison d'état.

It is to Gheorghiu-Dej's credit that he realized the threat to his position during the early stages of the contest for power in the Kremlin. His conviction that Stalinism could not be continued in its pure form in the Soviet Union led him to the formulation of a defensive political theory whereby Stalin's principles were applicable to less developed countries than the USSR albeit in terms of the "objective conditions" pertinent to socialist construction in those countries. In the case of Rumania he, Gheorghiu-Dej, would apply Stalinism to Rumanian conditions: he would be the formulator and director of a "Rumanian road to socialism" as the experienced leader of the Rumanian Communist Party and infallible diagnostician of Rumanian realities.[13] Gheorghiu-Dejism, as it evolved after Stalin's death, was Rumanian Stalinism in juxtaposition to variations of Communism not applicable to Rumania, such as Khrushchevism, Titoism, and Maoism. As the threat to his power increased with the evolution of Khrushchevism in the Soviet Union and the growing determination of Khrushchev and his sympathizers in the Rumanian Communist movement to replace Gheorghiu-Dej as an unrepented Stalinist, the would-be victim devised ingenious alternatives to dependence on the Soviet Union and evolved methods for counteracting the "liberalization" efforts of his rivals in the party. And in the process he did evolve a "Rumanian road to socialism."

The Rumanian Road to Socialism

In internal affairs Gheorghiu-Dej undertook few innovations that could in any way be regarded as determined by specific Rumanian conditions. Thus, the "New Course," whereby the redistribution of planned economic allocations was reshuffled to ensure the improvement of agricultural production and the supply of consumer goods, was not a purely Rumanian phenomenon.[14] In fact, the "New Course" was adopted throughout the Soviet bloc on the initiative of Stalin's successors in the Kremlin. Nevertheless, Gheorghiu-Dej took full credit for the measures adopted in 1953 by characterizing the economic changes as achievements of his own rule which would not have been possible had the "deviations" and "heresies" of the deposed Moscovites not been uncovered and punished. Subsequent adjustments in prices, wages, and delivery quotas by peasants—which occurred periodically between 1953 and 1957—were also attributed to his understanding of Rumanian conditions and his unflinching concern with the well-being of the inhabitants of Rumania. It is noteworthy, however, that the essential plans for economic development adopted prior to 1953 as well as the Five-Year Plan adopted in 1955 showed no flexibility in terms of the attainment of rapid industrialization and collectivization of agriculture. Moreover, the economic machinery and the general structure of the RWP and the government remained intact. Similarly, there was no change in attitude toward the "class struggle," no attempt to relax the pressures directed against the "class enemy," no desire to moderate the rigid enforcement of the principles of "socialist realism" in arts and letters. Gheorghiu-Dejism stood for Stalinist paternalism exercised, however, for the benefit of the Rumanian people and the Rumanian state.

The emphasis on matters Rumanian was ultimately caused by the "internationalists" at home and abroad who invoked the principles of

Khrushchevism as the dogma valid for the post-Stalinist period. It is clear that the Rumanian leaders feared Khrushchev more than their rivals in the party. It is known that Gheorghiu-Dej was particularly alarmed by Khrushchev's insistence on separation of the functions and leadership of the party and the state in Rumania, as elsewhere in the bloc, in 1954. Gheorghiu regarded the Kremlin's demand as overt interference in the internal affairs of the RWP designed to break the power of the Rumanian Stalinists, but he was unable to resist its implementation. Consequently, Gheorghiu-Dej and his associates directed their efforts toward nullifying the effect of this externally ordered change by purging all potential competitors for power who did not enjoy the direct support of the Kremlin and by keeping at bay Moscow's actual protégés headed by Miron Constantinescu.[15] And, as reassurance against further hostile actions from Moscow, Gheorghiu-Dej sought from as early as 1954 the support of Communist China.[16]

In the last analysis Gheorghiu's understanding, or at least sensing, of the incompatibilities between Khrushchev's road to socialism and Mao's was his crowning political achievement. Even though his reasons for opposing Khrushchev's aims and policies toward the West and within the socialist world differed from Mao's, Gheorghiu-Dej realized that the enunciation of the doctrine of "national roads to socialism," even in the limited context of the Rumanian, coincided with the Chinese basic desire for equality in the socialist camp. His echoing of the Chinese slogans and pronunciamentos in 1954, with emphasis on the rights of individual members of the camp, gained in intensity in 1955 and particularly in 1956 after Khrushchev's views on Stalinism became clear and Russia's aims were unequivocally defined at the Twentieth Congress of the CPSU.[17] The insistence on the correctness of Gheorghiu-Dejism gained validity in October 1956 when Gheorghiu-Dej could point out the stability of Rumania during the Hungarian Revolution in contrast to the turmoil generated by Khrushchevism in Hungary, Poland, and elsewhere. By 1957, Gheorghiu-Dej and Mao Tse-tung were united in their defense of the validity of "individual roads to socialism" and in their de facto rejection of the tenets of Khrushchev's internationalism and anti-Stalinism.

However, neither the Rumanian nor the Chinese leaders counted on Khrushchev's resiliency and his determination to pursue Khrushchevism at all cost. Khrushchev's victory over the anti-party group headed by the Stalinists in the Kremlin in July 1957 had a profound effect in Rumania since the Rumanian Khrushchevists launched a concurrent attack on the Rumanian Stalinists headed by Gheorghiu-Dej. Unlike the outcome in Moscow, Miron Constantinescu and his supporters were ousted by

Gheorghiu-Dej's forces, with a resultant exacerbation of the conflict between the Rumanian Stalinists and the Khrushchevites in Rumania and the Kremlin as well.[18] In July 1957, Gheorghiu-Dej found it necessary to implement his "Rumanian road to socialism" in a manner that would ensure his political survival, as he knew full well that reconciliation with Khrushchev was unlikely. Thus, at that time the character of Gheorghiu-Dejism was redefined, and the blueprint of socialist construction in Rumania was altered in accordance with the ultimate political consideration, the continuation in power of Gheorghiu-Dej and his team.

It was in late 1957 and particularly in 1958 that the Rumanian leadership decided to rebuild economic bridges with the West and to prevent economic strangulation by the Soviet Union. It was in 1958 that the Rumanian leadership strengthened ties with a growingly anti-Soviet Chinese leadership with a view to removing Soviet military presence in Rumania and blocking the Kremlin from exerting extreme political pressures against the Gheorghiu-Dej regime. Finally, it was also in 1958 that Gheorghiu-Dej sought to secure the support of all Rumanians for the construction of socialism à la *roumaine* by placing allegiance to the Rumanian Communist—and by inference—national cause above internationalist considerations.[19]

Rumanian Economic Independence

Students of Rumanian Communism and of Communist Rumania have tended to attach extreme significance to the economic policies of the Rumanian regime, particularly to the dispute between Rumania and the Soviet Union (and Soviet Russia's loyal East European partners) on matters pertaining to economic integration under the Council for Mutual Economic Aid (Comecon).[20] It is true that the Comecon issue was dominant in Russo-Rumanian relations in the late fifties and early sixties, but the economic controversy merely reflected the fundamental political dispute between the two parties and states. Khrushchev's imperialism was more sophisticated than Stalin's, as evidenced *inter alia* in the field of economic integration through Comecon and military integration through the instrumentality of the Warsaw Pact. In both instances the Kremlin sought to retain political and economic control over the East European bloc as a whole without the necessity of interfering constantly and unilaterally in the internal affairs of individual members. It is believed that the Rumanian leaders were restive with respect to Soviet Russia's economic policies within the bloc before they started voicing objections to those policies in 1958. Their silence was motivated by caution determined by the overriding desire to remove Soviet troops from Rumanian soil.[21] This was achieved by supporting collective military action by members of the Warsaw Pact on the basis of collaboration by the individual military organizations of the member nations.

The principle of implied equality of all members was supported by Communist China as well, and at a crucial meeting of the Warsaw Pact held in May 1958 the Rumanians and the Chinese demanded the implementation of that principle through withdrawal of Russian troops from Rumania. For reasons generic to the Sino-Soviet conflict more than because of Soviet largess toward its partners, Khrushchev agreed reluctantly to withdraw Russia's forces in July. This action permitted Gheorghiu-Dej and his associates to implement plans for the reduction of Rumanian economic dependence on Soviet Russia which had been sketched as early as 1955.[22]

Economic independence was to be gained through the Rumanization of the industrialization of the country. In practical terms it meant the replacement of key managerial and technical personnel of non-Rumanian origin and unproven loyalty to Gheorghiu-Dej by loyal Rumanian Communists and a committing of the economic effort to the development of a socialist Rumania rather than of a second-rate member of Comecon. The formal commitment to a Rumanian course of economic development was made in November 1958 and met with immediate resistance by Moscow and her faithful partners.[23] Because Soviet Russia, East Germany, and Czechoslovakia ranked themselves as economically developed countries in contrast to underdeveloped Rumania, they insisted on relegating Rumania to the role of producer of raw materials for the advanced industrial nations of Comecon. The Rumanians' response was to turn to the West and the uncommitted nations of Asia and the Middle East for loans, markets, and materials, all for the purpose of "constructing socialism" in Rumania for Rumania.[24] By 1960, the Rumanians had secured both markets and financial and technical assistance from non-Communist nations to the extent that allowed them to formulate long-range plans for economic development despite Russian opposition to the tempo and character of Rumania's modernization.

At the Third Congress of the RWP in 1960, Gheorghiu-Dej could cite the doubling of Rumania's industrial production during the preceding five years and the diversification of Rumania's partners in foreign trade.[25] Whereas in 1957 external economic relations were almost exclusively with the Soviet bloc and a few members of the Communist camp in Asia, in 1960 trade with West Germany, France, England, Italy, and other capitalist countries amounted to over one-half of Rumania's total trade with the USSR and exceeded the total volume of Rumania's trade with the other members of Comecon. Moreover, Gheorghiu-Dej gave every indication of accelerating that trend in future years with a view to eradicating Rumania's relative backwardness and bringing the country to the level of advanced socialist states.

Socialist Patriotism

Significant too is the fact that after 1958 the Rumanian Communist leaders sought increasingly greater identification of their goals with those of the Rumanian nation. Although unwilling to "liberalize" the regime for fear of resurgence of pent-up "bourgeois-nationalism," with its profound anti-Communist orientation, they were ready to rehabilitate all discredited Rumanian intellectuals who could further the cause of the RWP.[26] "Socialist patriotism" did in fact become a substitute for "bourgeois-nationalism" after 1958 and a euphemism for "Communist nationalism" as opposed to Soviet imperialism. As all decisions of the party were ostensibly made for the benefit of the people and of the country, Gheorghiu-Dejism gradually became synonymous with the attainment of the historic goals of the Rumanian people: a Rumania for the Rumanians. This equation was not formally made by 1960, but it was discernible by that time.

The courage of the Rumanian leadership after 1958 and particularly the translation of their essentially anti-Russian policies into positive anti-Russian, independent actions was ultimately a function of their evaluation of the possibility of Russian intervention in Rumania, by military or political means, subsequent to the withdrawal of the Soviet armed forces from Rumania. And that possibility, in turn, was regarded as a function of the international situation in general and of the Sino-Soviet conflict in particular.

Khrushchev's policy of peaceful coexistence with the West provided Rumania with the opportunity to pursue a similar policy with the implicit sanction of Moscow. However, the Rumanian Stalinist regime was somewhat apprehensive about expanding the scope of peaceful coexistence beyond economic relations as it was fearful of the effects of a genuine rapprochement with the West. Not only would the rapprochement provide the Kremlin with an excuse for retaliation against Rumania, but it might also encourage the educated Rumanians, traditionally pro-Western, to seek liberalization at home.[27] Besides, such recurrent crises as the U-2 Incident, that of Berlin, and the incipient confrontation between the United States and the Soviet Union over Cuba served as deterrents to "adventurism."

By contrast, the Sino-Soviet conflict provided the best opportunities for securing the Rumanian road to socialism, while paving that road with Western assistance. The overt confrontation between the Soviet and

Chinese parties which occurred at the close of the Rumanian Party's congress in June 1960, and which could not be resolved at the Moscow conference of Communist and workers' parties in December of that year, was fully exploited by Gheorghiu-Dej.[28] While ostensibly favoring, with minor reservations, the Moscow line, he underlined the Chinese thesis of equality of all members of the socialist camp and the need for maintaining the unity of the international Communist movement. In this manner he hoped to keep the Kremlin at bay without alienating Peking. Khrushchev's need for unity of the camp during the Berlin Crisis of 1961 and the Cuban Confrontation of 1962 gave Bucharest time to expand economic relations with the West but, more significantly, to strengthen its economic and political ties with China in the name of socialist unity. When Khrushchev's "adventurism" met with failure in Cuba and was roundly condemned by Peking, Gheorghiu-Dej understood that the "objective conditions" favored further emancipation from Moscow's clutches. This time his move was to seek acceptance of Rumania's plans for unrestricted and multilateral industrialization, so opposed by Soviet Russia and her partners in Comecon, as reaffirmation of the economic and political independence of all partners in Comecon and all members of the socialist camp.

Moscow refused to accept Rumania's position on these matters but was paralyzed into temporary inaction by the Cuban fiasco. Whereupon Gheorghiu-Dej decided to reap the optimum benefits from this impasse through consolidation of Rumania's ties with Moscow opponents to the east and west. The tactic was the adoption of a neutralist position in the Sino-Soviet and East-West conflicts in the name of the accepted Soviet doctrines of "peaceful coexistence" and "unity of the socialist camp." On the basis of assurances of closer economic ties secured from the West and of political support obtained from Peking, Gheorghiu-Dej formally denounced Soviet Russia's economic and, by inference, political imperialism in March 1963.[29] At that time the Rumanians condemned Moscow's persistence in relegating Rumania to the rank of a second-rate member of Comecon and of violating the rights of sovereign members of the socialist camp.

The Statement of March 1963 was in effect a declaration of independence from satelliteship but not a rejection of the principle of interdependence of members of the Soviet bloc and of the socialist community as a whole. It left the door open to reconciliation of differences on the basis of firm political guarantees from Moscow. It was Khrushchev's rejection of Rumania's political demands, not of the economic, that led to a further redefinition of the Rumanian position and corollary adjustments in Rumania's internal and external policies.

The New Course

The most crucial period of change in the history of Rumanian Communism and of Communist Rumania was the year that started in the spring of 1963 and ended in the spring of 1964. It was during that period that Gheorghiu-Dej sought the nation's total support for his Rumanian policies, now clearly directed against the Soviet Union. National reconciliation and total identification between the interests of the party and the historic Rumanian traditions and aspirations became an integral part of Gheorghiu-Dejism. The class struggle was ended with the release of political prisoners and the integration of all Rumanians, regardless of social origin or previous political conviction, into the process of socialist construction. Cultural ties with the West were reestablished concurrently with intensification of economic and technological relations. The history of Rumania was rewritten with emphasis on the achievements of the nation and the national struggle for independence. References to Soviet imperialism, including Stalin's, with emphasis on the seizure of the Rumanian province of Bessarabia by imperial and Communist Russia reappeared. The production of consumer goods rose, and the construction of apartment buildings throughout Rumania was accelerated. Western businessmen and technical specialists flocked into the country, and the borders were opened to foreign visitors and to those Rumanians who had settled in the West after World War II who wished to visit friends and relatives. And, as the calculated risk inherent in this rapprochement with the West and the Rumanian people proved to be less risky than originally assumed, controlled Westernization and "liberalization" were pursued with greater energy in 1964.

Nevertheless, Gheorghiu-Dej and his close associates were persuaded that reliance on the West was dangerous ideologically and strategically. Therefore the political effort was directed toward maximal exploitation of the insoluble Sino-Soviet conflict. The tactic adopted in the spring of 1963 was that of strict neutrality with a view to acting as an "honest broker" between the two Communist giants. That opportunity came in the winter when Khrushchev acceded to the Rumanians' suggestion to act as mediators between Moscow and Peking. The timing, however, was not of Bucharest's choice but imposed by the Kremlin. Khrushchev, who was staking his political career on the restoration of the unity of the Communist camp under Moscow's supremacy, sought a showdown with Mao Tse-tung and his friends and allies. Such a showdown would have been fatal to the Rumanians and had to be averted. Therefore, the "neutral" Rumanians, with the support of members of the camp who for differing reasons wished to avoid a split in the international Communist movement, secured the Kremlin's consent to attempt mediation in Peking. If they had any expectations of success, which is indeed doubtful, such expectations were frustrated by the adamant opposition of both Mao and Khrushchev to any meaningful compromise. The failure of the mission merely strengthened Khrushchev's determination to expel the Chinese from the socialist camp and bring the Rumanians back into line. The Statement of April 1964 was Gheorghiu-Dej's reply to the threat of restoration of Soviet hegemony in the bloc and the camp.

The Statement of April 1964 did not usher in a radically new era for Rumania or the Rumanian Communist movement. It did preclude the possibility of reconciliation between Khrushchev and Gheorghiu-Dej which, if anything, increased the likelihood of greater pressure on the Rumanian regime from Moscow. In fact, until his fall from power in October 1964, the Soviet leader intensified his efforts to arrest Rumania's independent course. Aside from threatening Gheorghiu-Dej with military action, he encouraged his Hungarian allies to reopen, albeit discreetly, questions related to the treatment of the Hungarian population of Transylvania with obvious implications for the status of that disputed province.[30] The Rumanians' reaction was one of caution. Gheorghiu-Dej chose to restate Rumania's rights as a sovereign country and pursue the domestic and foreign policies with which he had been identified for some time before April 1964. There were no dramatic changes, no attempts to innovate either at home or abroad. On the other hand, the basic domestic and foreign policies pursued in 1963 were carried out without retrenchment. Nor did these policies change after the establishment of the Brezhnev-Kosygin regime in the Soviet Union. The cautious but determined Gheorghiu-Dej was carefully examining the "objective conditions" created by Khrushchev's downfall.

It is possible that he would have tried to capitalize on the change of leadership in Moscow to secure firm guarantees from the Kremlin for Rumania's sovereign rights had it not been for the intensification of the crisis in Vietnam after the November elections in the United States. The confrontation between the leader of the "imperialist" West and a fellow Communist nation restricted the implementation of the doctrine of peaceful coexistence, at least to the extent to which it allowed the Rumanians to rely on the West for political leverage against the Kremlin. According to its own doctrine, Rumania was a loyal member of the socialist camp, and that loyalty took precedence over coexistence with "imperialist aggressors." And this dilemma could not be solved during Gheorghiu-Dej's lifetime. He died in March 1965 shortly after the bombing of North Vietnam had transformed the conflict in Southeast Asia into a war between the United States and North Vietnam. Significant changes in Rumania proper and in the country's foreign relations were, however, to occur almost immediately after the change in leadership in Bucharest. With the advent to power of Nicolae Ceausescu and the delineation of the policies of the Brezhnev-Kosygin tandem, the Rumanian independent course was altered both in form and in substance.

The Ceausescu Era

Ceausescu formalized and legalized Rumania's and the Rumanian party's legitimacy, independence, and sovereignty. These steps were taken in rapid succession. First the name of the party was changed from Rumanian Workers' Party to Rumanian Communist Party (RCP), indicative of both equal status with the Soviet party and of the historic legitimacy of the Rumanian Communist movement and its organization. Next, the country's name was changed from Rumanian People's Republic to Socialist Republic of Rumania, symbolic of equality with the "advanced" socialist states of the camp. Finally, a new constitution mirroring the "objective Rumanian conditions" of 1965—primarily independence as a sovereign national state—replaced that of 1952.[31]

There was little originality or innovation in these basic documents, which were ratified by a party congress in July. The party statutes were basically unchanged from those in force during Gheorghiu-Dej's lifetime.[32] Such changes as were made concerned the streamlining of the apparatus for increased administrative efficiency. The Constitution of 1965 differed from that of 1952 only to the extent to which all allusions to dependence on the Soviet Union were eliminated and replaced by declarations of inviolability of national sovereign rights.[33] The descriptive document otherwise recorded the few changes which had occurred in the governmental structure since 1952. But the explanatory statements provided by Ceausescu at the party congress were in the form of commitments to the continuation of the policies and completion of the goals set by the party in the past. In Ceausescu's view, the aim of his rule was the attainment of the historic goals of the RCP and people—independence and prosperity.[34] In practical terms, defense against Soviet imperialism was assigned priority.

Ceausescu's commitments were far-reaching and unequivocal. They were also hazardous, as history since 1965 has proven. The leaders of the Soviet Union declared their hostility to Ceausescu's plans and actions from their very initiation. In September 1965, the Kremlin wrested a statement of renunciation of Rumania's implicit claims to Bessarabia, allegedly by threatening to reopen the Transylvanian question.[35] Subsequently, by withholding delivery of committed materials and equipment the Soviet regime applied economic pressure with a view to retarding the attainment of Rumania's economic goals. Most importantly, the Kremlin used the Warsaw Pact as a weapon of intimidation. The possibility of reentrance of Soviet troops into Rumania under the guise of maneuvers by Warsaw-Pact forces represented a peril to Ceausescu's regime and to Rumania's independence. At the same time the Soviet leaders sought to ostracize Rumania from bloc activities and thus isolate her until such time as reintegration on Soviet Russia's terms could be forced upon a chastened Rumanian regime.

Ceausescu's reaction to these pressure tactics was measured, at least until 1967. The caution was dictated by the escalation of the Vietnamese War and by the growing isolation and alienation of Communist China. The loss of political leverage resulting from these international factors could be compensated only by mobilizing the nation for the supreme national effort of building socialism in the fatherland and defending the country's gains against all enemies. Internal consolidation stressed nationalism and total identification of the party's and the nation's goals but did not involve modernization of the governmental and administrative structure or any lessening of the RCP's total control over all aspects of political, cultural, and economic life. It did, however, entail the removal of all restrictions on freedom of intellectual expression—as long as the literary, historic, and artistic productions emphasized the historic link between party and nation—and the encouragement of scientific and technological exchanges with the West.[36]

The execution of the ambitious plans for socialist construction calling for a fifty percent increase in industrial production and one hundred percent increase in agricultural production by 1970, however, required foreign capital, machinery, and trade. Pursuant to Rumania's policy of disengagement from Comecon and to Soviet Russia's of using foreign trade as an instrument for exerting political pressure on Rumania, Ceausescu's regime expanded the scope of its economic relations with the West. The most significant change was the near doubling of Rumania's foreign trade with the West European capitalist countries, most notably with West Germany.[37] By 1967, the volume of trade with Germany was second only to that with the Soviet Union.

Ceausescu's Foreign Policy

Rumania's foreign relations until 1967 reflected the "objective international conditions" for securing the country's independence. While paying lip service to the traditional formulas of coexistence and unity of the camp, the Rumanian leaders were seeking security in the doctrine of European unity. That doctrine, according to Ceausescu, was designed to eliminate the vestiges of World War II and establish a Europe of socialist and capitalist states united in the common goal of peace in Europe.[38] This Rumanian version of General De Gaulle's "Europe from the Urals to the Atlantic" coincided superficially with the views on European security advocated by the Warsaw Pact. Ceausescu, like De Gaulle and Brezhnev, asked for the liquidation of both the Warsaw Pact and NATO upon establishment of a European security system. Unlike them, however, Ceausescu was more concerned with the abolition of the Warsaw Pact and the containment of Russian imperialism than with NATO and American presence in Europe. The first action derived from the doctrine of European unity was the establishment of formal diplomatic relations with West Germany in January 1967.

That decision has been regarded as an act of defiance of Moscow and of East Germany and Poland, whose opposition to the diplomatic recognition of Bonn was well known to Bucharest. It has also been regarded as the beginning of an era of increased hostility between Rumania and the Soviet Union and its faithful allies in Eastern Europe. The Rumanian decision was apparently designed to precipitate Germany's recognition by other members of the bloc with a view to preventing the Kremlin from imposing its views on European unity on the members of the Warsaw Pact and on the European Communist movement as a whole. The Kremlin had in fact planned the summoning of a pan-European conference of Communist parties before the recognition of West Germany by Rumania and did summon one for April 1967, shortly after the Rumanian action. The Soviets had also thwarted repeated attempts made by Bucharest in 1966 to seek acceptance of its views on the equality of rights of all members of the bloc in economic, military, and political affairs and adoption of its ideas on the development of regional "zones of peace" as preliminary to a general pan-European accommodation. The Rumanians' suspicion of Soviet intentions was borne out by the Kremlin-sponsored conference held in Karlovy-Vary, as scheduled. To the Soviets, European security meant consolidation of Soviet control over the European Communist movement in general and the East European party-states in particular.

The Rumanians' criticism of the meeting, which they themselves had boycotted, was directed against the Soviet "tendency to impose on one party a certain orientation or a certain method for the solution of problems" and was justified in terms of each party's "inalienable right" to determine its line and political aims.[39] They were joined in this condemnation of Soviet actions and aims by other dissident parties and party-states such as the Yugoslav, Italian, and French, which allowed the Rumanians to assume the posture of the champion of the equality of rights of all Communist parties, European and non-European. These basic positions with respect to European security and the rights of Communist parties and party-states supplemented previous formulations of Rumanian foreign policy. Altogether, that policy, as restated in 1967, advocated the maintenance of peaceful relations among all sovereign states, regardless of their social, and political orientation, and was directed against Soviet Russia's growing determination to reimpose hegemony in the bloc and the camp. Thus, by the spring of 1967, a collision course had been charted by the USSR which Rumania was trying to circumvent by all means at its command without, however, retreating from Ceausescu's own basic orientation.

After the spring of 1967, and until the invasion of Czechoslovakia in the summer of 1968, the Rumanian regime pursued a policy of fortification of its domestic and foreign positions. In Rumania it concentrated on the adoption of new forms of administrative and institutional organization. Ostensibly these changes were made for the sake of accelerating the "consolidation of socialist construction" in Rumania, for removing all barriers to the optimum mobilization of the nation's resources for the attainment of that ultimate goal. In reality the several measures taken in 1967 and 1968 were expressly designed to secure broad popular support for Ceausescu's policies of national self-defense against the USSR. The fundamental measures delineated at the Conference of the Rumanian Communist Party of December 1967 were neither innovative nor radical in scope.[40] The decentralization of economic planning and direction of economic activities, which passed for scientific reform, was political rather than scientific in inspiration. Actual control of all economic activities remained, as before, in the hands of the party bureaucracy in Bucharest. Even the fiscal and monetary policies adopted or ratified by the conference, characterized by increases in the cost of rents and services, in income taxes and fees, and in restructuring of the wage and salary scales could be criticized in terms of their economic rationale. The accompanying administrative-territorial reorganization into a system of counties—such as existed before 1944—with the very restoration of the pre-World War II nomenclature of individual counties was motivated by the need for identification with an acceptable historical past at least as much as by the given reasons of administrative and economic efficiency.

Related reforms in the educational system whereby the school system of the twenties and thirties was reintroduced at the expense of Soviet prototypes adopted after World War II were also more nationalist than scientific in motivation. Nevertheless, Ceausescu's assumption of the role of restorer of traditional Rumanian values and leader of a modernized socialist Rumania imparted a new image to Rumanian Communism. His rule became even more popular when he took it upon himself to "humanize" and "liberalize" the oppressive aspects of Gheorghiu-Dej-ism. The revamping of the penal code through elimination of oppressive features in criminal definition and punishment; the destitution of officials identified with Soviet-type police methods; and above all the condemna-tion of the impropriety of the "Stalinist" undemocratic methods used by Gheorghiu-Dej, even including rehabilitation of victims of Gheorghiu-Dej's purges, which were announced and implemented at the congress or shortly thereafter; provided the ingredients for successful mobilization of the nation under Ceausescu's leadership.[41]

National unity was indeed required for the maintenance of a position of strength toward the Soviet Union and its conservative allies, particu-larly after the establishment of the Dubcek regime in Czechoslovakia. The Rumanian leadership was not sanguine about the Kremlin's con-doning "liberalization" anywhere in the bloc to the extent to which it could not control that process or to which that process would frustrate Moscow's determination to consolidate its hegemony in the bloc and camp. The several consultative meetings of members of the bloc held in 1967 after Karlovy-Vary were characterized by increased rigidity in Moscow's demands for conformity to its wishes, ostensibly to counteract German revanchism, American imperialism, and, after the defeat of the Arabs by Israel in June, international Zionism. The warnings addressed to these inimical forces and, by implication, to Communist nations and parties deviating from the Moscow line, were clearly understood by Bucharest. Rumania was particularly vulnerable to criticism because of her economic and political ties with West Germany, her refusal to condemn Israel, and her resistance to Soviet dictates in the socialist camp through maintenance of a neutral position in the Sino-Soviet conflict and of a position of leadership of parties and party-states opposed to the restoration of Soviet hegemony in the Communist world. On the basis of that experience and of continuing Soviet economic pressure on Bucharest, Ceausescu increased his search for safeguards after January 1968, fearful and suspicious as he was of the Kremlin's ultimate motives. Outwardly he merely strengthened existing ties with the West, China, and Yugoslavia, but these relations assumed an overt strategic character.[42]

A series of strategy meetings on how to cope with Soviet Russia's unification drive was held with Tito. The level of foreign trade ex-changes with West Germany was raised, particularly in the area of German exports that would facilitate the development of a Rumanian arms industry. More explicit commitments to European unity and secu-rity were given to De Gaulle during a state visit by the general in the spring of 1968. Restoration of political and economic links to China, which had been criticized during the Maoist cultural revolution, was sought by Bucharest, apparently with a modicum of success. One or another of these relationships was invoked and dramatized as the occasion arose in 1968, always in the framework of the Rumanian doctrines pertaining to national sovereignty, unity of the socialist camp, peaceful coexistence, European security, and all other instruments available to maintain Rumania's independence. Thus, at the Budapest Conference of February 1968, convened by the Kremlin to seek restoration of Communist unity at the expense of the dissidents led by China, the Rumanians staged a walkout ostensibly as the protector of the interest of the absent Chinese and of all parties and states opposed to Soviet-imposed hegemony. At a subsequent meeting of Warsaw Pact nations held in Bulgaria, the Rumanians refused to sign a declaration endorsing Moscow's view on non-proliferation of nuclear weapons on the grounds that those views, if implemented, would provide a basis for interference in the internal affairs of non-nuclear states. The Rumanians also refused to join in any Warsaw Pact maneuvers or decisions that would infringe upon the sovereign rights of member nations.

All these acts reflected fear of intervention by the Soviet Union in dissident countries under the aegis of supra-national instruments like the Comecon or the Warsaw Pact and in the name of socialist unity. By early summer, Rumania was in fact mobilized for total resistance to the Soviet Union and its faithful allies, who were at the time exerting direct military pressure on Czechoslovakia, having already isolated Rumania from their councils and consultations on matters pertaining to the bloc. The invasion of Czechoslovakia in August found the Rumanians ready to resist militarily any expansion of their allies' military action into Rumania. Ceausescu, posing as the latest of Rumania's historic heroes who fought for the maintenance of the integrity of the fatherland, rallied the nation in the moment of truth when a Soviet-led invasion of Rumania appeared imminent in late August and early September.[43]

Soviet Russia's failure to invade Rumania, whether determined by Moscow's own strategic considerations, by Rumania's determination to resist militarily, by President Johnson's warning to the Kremlin, or by any, all, or none of these factors, was interpreted by the Rumanian leadership as a victory for the Rumanian party and people, as a vindication of the validity and viability of the Rumanian course. In the aftermath of the Czechoslovak crisis, the Rumanian regime has reaffirmed the correctness of its policies, internal and external, and has carried them out with only slight tactical deviations from the norms previously established by Gheorghiu-Dej and Ceausescu.

The Tenth Party Congress

The internal policies have remained unchanged. National unity and national commitment to the completion of socialist construction are the fundamental tenets of the all-powerful party and state. The Tenth Congress of the RCP, held in August 1969, reconfirmed the basic goals of the regime and drew up even more elaborate plans for acceleration of Rumania's modernization to bring the country to the level of advanced countries of the West.[44] Rumania's foreign policy has also remained essentially unaltered. It is true that Rumania has been a more active participant in the councils and conferences of the socialist bloc held after August 1968. Bucharest has attended all meetings of the Comecon and of the Warsaw Pact and has pledged continuing allegiance to these bodies. However, it was able to oppose the holding of maneuvers on Rumanian soil by Warsaw Pact forces and has not intensified the level of economic exchange with its partners in the Comecon. Relations with the Soviet Union, as such, have become more civil but apparently not closer. Even if Rumania has agreed to support the repeated Soviet calls for a European security conference, it has steadfastly refused to abide by the Brezhnev doctrine, which it continues to regard as incompatible with the country's inalienable sovereign rights. It has also opposed the Kremlin's attempts to reestablish hegemony in the "socialist community" through international conferences of Communist parties and states such as that held in Moscow in June 1969. In fact, at Moscow, the Rumanians were the principal opponents to the acceptance of Soviet formulas for restoration of the unity of the socialist camp, the principal defenders of China's rights to self-determination, and the vigorous proponents of their own rights to make the independent decisions inherent in Rumania's status as a sovereign, independent nation-state.[45] And these fundamental positions were restated during the Tenth Congress of the RCP and at the plenary session of the party's Central Committee held a few months later, in December 1969.[46]

Ceausescu has also continued to strengthen Rumania's relations with Yugoslavia, in common opposition to Soviet imperialism, and to consolidate relations with China and Israel despite obvious Soviet dissatisfaction with these moves. The Rumanian regime is relentlessly pursuing the well-established policies of building bridges to the West with the result that the country's economic dependence on the Soviet bloc declined further in 1969 while its economy continued to prosper.[47] Following the dramatic visit of President Nixon to Rumania in August of that year, Premier Maurer visited England in November, and state visits to Rumania by political and economic leaders of West Germany, Austria, and the Netherlands were recorded on the busy diplomatic calendar of the Rumanian Socialist Republic in the summer and fall of 1969.

Thus, by exploiting the dilemmas caused to the Kremlin by Peking's policies, the difficulties in Czechoslovakia and the corollary Soviet desire for relaxation of East-West tensions, Rumania has readopted the strategic formulas incorporated in the Statement of 1964. It relies on the West and China to safeguard its own interests against the Soviet Union and to consolidate and expand the gains achieved in Rumania through implementation of Ceausescu's plans for socialism.

3

Poland —
Continuity and Change

Joseph R. Fiszman

Country Profile: THE POLISH PEOPLE'S REPUBLIC

Head of State: Marshal Marian Spychalski, Chairman of the State Council
Premier: Jozef Cyrankiewicz, Chairman of the Council of Ministers
First Secretary, Central Committee Polish United Workers' Party:
  Wladyslaw Gomulka

Party Membership (1968): 2,030,068[1]
Armed Forces (1969): 275,000 (Army: 185,000; Navy: 20,000; Air Force:
  70,000)[2]
Population: End of 1968: 32,426,000 (Warsaw: 1,279,000)[3]
Area: 312,700 square kilometers (126,733 square miles)[4]
Population Density: 104 per square mile, 269 per square kilometer
Birth Rate (1968): 16.2 per thousand[5]
Death Rate (1968): 7.6 per thousand[5]
Divorce Rate (1968): 0.91 per thousand[6]
Gross Material Product (1968): 1,742.8 billion zloty ($109.5 billion at
  official rate)[7]
National Income Total (1968): 648.9 zloty ($40.8 billion at official rate)[7]
National Income by Sectors (1968):[7]
  Industry: 52.6%
  Construction: 9.6%
  Agriculture: 21.7%
  Transportation and Communications: 5.9%
  Trade: 8.7%
  Other: 1.5%
Foreign Trade by Area (1968):[8]
  Socialist countries (including USSR): 65.1%
  USSR: 35.4%
  Non-socialist countries: 34.9%

Foreign Trade by Commodity (1968):[9]	Export	Import
Machinery, capital goods	37.0%	35.9%
Industrial consumer goods	15.9%	5.7%
Raw materials, semi-finished products	33.1%	47.1%
Comestibles	14.0%	11.3%

SOURCES:
1. U.S. Department of State, Bureau of Intelligence and Research, *World Strength of Communist Party Organizations* (Washington, D.C.: U.S. Government Printing Office, 1969), p. 59.
2. *The Military Balance 1969–1970* (London: The Institute for Strategic Studies, 1969), pp. 13–14.
3. Glowny Urzad Statystyczny, *Rocznik Statystyczny 1969* (Warsaw, 1969), pp. 24–25.
4. *Ibid.,* p. 609.
5. *Ibid.,* p. 51.
6. *Ibid.,* p. 57.
7. *Ibid.,* p. 89.
8. *Ibid.,* pp. 363–64.
9. *Ibid.,* p. 360.

3. Poland — Continuity and Change

Joseph R. Fiszman

Poland is a country of contrasts. Some of the contrasts are visible even to the most casual observers: modern jets streaking over a pastoral landscape; horsedrawn carts competing with automobiles on modern highways as well as on cobblestone roads built by Napoleon's soldiers; highrise apartments and modern industrial plants existing in the vicinity of unpaved, muddy streets, hand-plowed fields, and ruins and rubble from World War II. Streets are overhung with slogans extolling the wisdom of the party, the "eternal" teaching of Marx and Lenin, and protesting American aggression in Vietnam; they are the same streets on which traffic is halted to allow the passing of a slow-moving, cross-carrying, hymn-chanting religious procession. Funerals of old revolutionary veterans are accompanied by bands playing medleys of old revolutionary songs and the "Internationale" and by Catholic priests fingering beads and whispering prayers, the former assigned to the funeral by the party or by the deceased's organization, the latter requested by the family.

Poland is also a country in transition: it is in the process of transformation from a romantic tradition of gentry-induced cultural styles, of chivalry, cavalry charges and romantic death, to a political system of international "realism," of commitment to industrialization and labor, to a formal ideology of scientific materialism and Communism.

The old and the new coexist and also conflict. The broad sociopolitical culture still stresses the prestige models of the past as well as past values and norms: leisure, the "good life," appreciation of poetry, gallantry, and good manners; the new political system emphasizes labor, loyalty, and discipline, the language of the latest bureaucratic memorandum. The sociopolitical culture accords an honorable place to the church and the priest; the political system is centered around the United Polish Workers' Party (UPWP) and rests upon the devotion of the sociopolitical activists, members of the new intelligentsia who have often emerged—despite great odds—from the ranks of the working class or the peasantry and who jealously guard their newly gained authority and feel grateful to the system.

Both the old and the new, the still-persisting vestiges of the past as well as the authority of the new order, represent reality, and the symbols of both bear the mark of legitimacy. Relatively few citizens of People's Poland are members of the party, but many have made peace with reality, perceive their government as lawful and legal, and accept the order of authority as binding. And regardless of its official orientation, they see the republic as a continuation of their statehood, another chapter in their more than thousand-year history, and, as such, deserving of their loyalty. Some, while in disagreement with the official policies and ideological orientation of the government, nevertheless acknowledge the leadership's patriotism, and the leaders, in turn, attempt to project an image of themselves as bearers of a national idea in keeping with tradition, and in doing so create in the minds of the populace an identity of the present with the past. Thus, the "socialist Pole" may be thought of as the "patriotic Pole."

World War II began in Poland, and the occupation which followed the defeat of September 1939 lasted almost six years. That occupation was the last link in a historical chain of suffering, but a link surpassing all others in depth of despair. The campaign of September 1939, which saw Polish cavalry pitted against German armored divisions, marked not only the rude awakening of the Poles to the raw facts of a technological age by tearing them from the placidity and complacency of nineteenth century romanticism in the midst of the twentieth century, but it also brought them face to face with many a political and economic reality whose existence many Poles had long denied. The aftermath of that experience is felt to this day. The scars of the last war are visible not only in ruins, in altered state boundaries, and in the development of People's Poland—but the experience of war and occupation continues to live in the memory of many and in the new folklore, the literature, films, and the arts. The war has changed the ethnic composition of society: whereas before World War II Poland was a multi-national state, after the war it became homogeneous. The territories populated by Ukrainians and Belorussians were ceded to the Soviet Union, Germans were expelled or emigrated voluntarily; towns which prior to World War II were totally Jewish have radically changed their character. The slaughter of the Jews and the mass migration of the Jewish survivors after the war also meant that Poles who, in keeping with impoverished gentry tradition, abhorred mercantilism and trade as something less than noble had to fill traditionally middle-class positions in the economy, positions traditionally occupied by Jews, who were now prevented from bureaucratic or industrial employment.

As a consequence of war, shifts in occupations, border adjustments, population movements, as well as a lower birthrate (in itself the product of changing values and culture patterns), Poland in 1969 had a population 2,349,000 less than it had in the last year before the outbreak of World War II (32,500,000 in 1969 as compared to 34,849,000 in 1938). Twenty years after the war Warsaw, the capital of the republic, had—despite absorption within its boundaries of many far outlying areas—36,000 less residents than it had at the war's outbreak in 1939.

Perpetuation of traditional patterns and the frequent synthesis of the old and the new not only make Poland a country in flux, but they also lend the country a characteristic quite distinguished from other East European people's democracies. While religious and loyal to the Catholic Church, the Poles, it seems, never have allowed religion to penetrate individual consciousness deeply enough to affect personal behavior and attitudes towards one's fellow man. The identification the Pole feels with the church is a collective identification, a sense of membership in a group. For this reason the Poles distinguish various relationships with the church in terms of the individual's varying degrees of belief as well as practice—"believing and practicing," "nonbelieving but practicing," "believing but not practicing," "nonbelieving and nonpracticing." The girl, for example, who is lavish with her charms and favors toward men will frequently think of herself as a good Catholic and attend mass and confession without undue qualms.

Similarly, while traditionally highly politicized, political battles often take the form of verbal contests but do not penetrate the personal behavioral styles of the combatants and stop short, if at all possible, of physical violence. Thus, for example, one can find crosses and pictures of the Madonna in the homes of highly placed party officials whose children attend communion, and those criticized for political deviation will in some cases be kept on as members of the party's Central Committee. Poles who have left the United Polish Workers' Party in protest against what they felt was nonfulfillment of the liberal promises of October 1956—if of sufficient social prominence—continue to occupy their old prestigious apartments, to publish books and articles, and to be considered as part of the broad social elite. When a prominent Polish writer, after years in exile, returned to the homeland with U.S. citizenship, he was accused of transmitting anti-government information to his daughter abroad and jailed as a result: the First Secretary of the UPWP personally pleaded with him to appeal for clemency. But prior to 1956, under the Stalinist regime, when the First Secretary, Wladyslaw Gomulka, and the present Chief of the State Council, Marshal Marian Spychalski, were jailed and tortured, they were never tried and sentenced to death as were other political leaders in Hungary and Czechoslovakia.

One important explanation for such a pattern is the sense of solidarity permeating the elite—an elite which regardless of actual class origin of individual members is linked to the impoverished gentry which tradition-ally was at the helm and which has permeated much of Polish social, cultural, and political life. The traditional gentry prestige models are still in vogue, although titles have been formally abolished. The traditional gentry has put its stamp on the nongentry classes, and the latter have strived to assimilate old gentry styles and patterns. The urban intelligent-sia was traditionally recruited from the impoverished gentry, and so was much of the leadership of the conflicting sociopolitical movements, including those of the Left. Moreover, being impoverished and economi-cally rootless, members of the old gentry could accept many of the ethical premises of the new system and find these compatible with their own traditional moral values and prejudices (for example, the aforemen-tioned dislike for mercantilism and money-making). However, the per-sistence of gentry prestige models means that leisure and the ability to "enjoy oneself"—traditional gentry values—are socially more important than hard work, that knowledge of French and Latin and a humanistic education are still cherished more highly and pursued more avidly than the acquisition of economically more functional skills, and that the symbols of an aristocratically class-oriented society, including the stress on titles, are still prevalent despite adherence to a formal ideology of classlessness. To be sure, the titles are no longer related to noble birth, but those which do exist ("doctor," "professor," "chairman," "direc-tor," and so forth) not only carry prestige for the title holder, but such prestige is also transmitted to his spouse who, in turn, is referred to by such appellations as "Madame Professor." Yet, while having influenced the whole of Polish society and having claimed leadership of that society as a right due it by virtue of tradition as well as its education, the intelligentsia has remained clannishly introspective, snobbish, and aloof from the masses and has transmitted these characteristics to those who —despite great odds—have reached the ranks of the intelligentsia and the elite from nongentry background.[1]

As with prestige models continued from the past, many aspects of the economy and authority relations are traditional. The system of state intervention in the economy is not a feature which developed with the emergence of the people's democracy. Prior to World War II, under the presocialist regime, the state had a monopoly on such things as all public transportation, alcohol, tobacco, matches, and salt mining. While the content of the authority-symbol has changed and the White Polish Eagle, the symbol of the state, has lost its crown, the respect and homage accorded these symbols are traditional. The policeman (presently officially referred to as militiaman) is still spoken of as *"panie wladzo"* ("Mr. Authority")—and also traditional is the mild fun poked at that authority, a fun-poking not contradictory, however, to the respect and homage paid to it.

The end of World War II saw not only the emergence of People's Poland and the coming to power of the Left but also a shift of national boundaries. Having to cede its territories on the east to the Soviet Union, Poland has expanded on the west and in the north, having incorporated territories which belonged to a defeated Germany. The shift of boundaries brought about a greater level of urbanization and industrialization since the eastern territories were in the main agricultural and forest lands. The end of the war brought about both an external migration of non-Polish ethnic elements and an internal migration of Poles induced by need to settle the newly acquired lands. Rural families found themselves in large cities facing the problems of adjustment.

The internal migration was further accelerated in 1952 when large-scale collectivization was introduced into the countryside, and although the movement from the village to the city decreased after 1956, when collectivization was made optional, it was estimated in 1965 that on the average about one million Poles change their permanent residence annually.[2] The bulk of interior migration continues to be from village to urban area and is again increasing (especially since 1962), although the rural economy is stabilized, and in many respects village life is materially easier than life in the cities, especially in view of chronic housing shortages in the large centers. Nevertheless, for a society in which generations of families have lived in the same rural setting, the migratory stream is not only reflective of profound cultural and social change but, at the same time, is cause for many deep social, cultural, and economic transformations. Suffice it to point out that whereas in 1931 40 percent of the population lived on nonagricultural incomes, the percentage was 52.9 in 1950 and 61.6 in 1960.[3] Moreover, most of the peasants, once they decide to leave the village, do not settle in small- or medium-sized towns which could alleviate the problems of resettlement and adjustment but instead move to the capital city of Warsaw or to other big cities such as Bialystock and Wroclaw. Even the city of Lodz (known as the Polish

Manchester because of its textile industry), which shows the smallest ratio of peasant immigrants, attracted nine newcomers from the villages per one thousand old settlers during the first quarter of 1966 alone.[4]

The problem thus becomes further compounded: not only must the peasant newcomer to the city become socialized to the new urban environment, not only must he become "retooled" in terms of his economic skills but, like the traditional city dweller and those left behind in the rural areas, he must somehow adjust himself to the new sociopolitical system and its demands and expectations. Whereas in the village the peasant was close to kin and neighbor, while he could find sustenance for the perpetuation of traditional values in the proximity of the Catholic Church and the parish priest, he is often alone in the city— floating, as it were, exposed more sharply to conflicting values and styles, to conflicting signals emanating from the church (more impersonal in the city than in the village and more formally institutionalized), on the one hand, and from the political system and the party and its organizational network, on the other.

The Political Culture and the System

The Catholic Church and the gentry (*szlachta*) have placed strong imprints on Polish culture and Polish mass consciousness. The struggle, therefore, for transformation and for the development of a socialist society (and for the assurance of its endurance and security) must by necessity include the cultural front. It is the culture and its organization which gives rise to individual personality and to individual behavior. In normative terms, the aim of socialism is to create social, economic, and cultural conditions which would enable the individual to transcend, to sublimate, his self-centered concerns for personal welfare, gains, and pleasures for the sake of a higher and collectivistic purpose. The attainment of this goal, however, is hindered by both persistence of traditional cultural and social patterns and styles, and the possibilities realistically available, as well as by the allocation priorities given to the various activities and sectors on the wide front of system-building. Thus, although the system's planners and leaders are aware of the importance of education and culture and are indeed concerned over their prospects, they are faced with conflicting interest pressures and the need to evaluate which is more important: the investment of scarce resources in industry, the machinery of administration, the organization of the military, or the advancement of culture and education.

As in nonsocialist systems, given such decision-making conditions wrought with conflicting tugs and pulls, given the available alternatives and the limited resources, education and culture also tend to lose out in

Poland, despite official pronouncements on the importance of the latter and contrary to the general impression in the West that socialist systems do indeed allocate generously towards culture and education. Thus, for example, the construction of schools lags behind construction of new industrial plants, the salaries of elementary and secondary school teachers are behind salaries received by those employed in industry or governmental administration or the military (although the prestige of teachers is higher than that of the latter), and the low priority accorded investments in culture affects even the quality of radio and television programming. A writer on the staff of the Warsaw weekly *Kultura* once estimated that although the gastronomical establishments featuring "culture" charge an additional fifteen percent to the consumer, they remit only two percent to the institution in charge of culture organization—thus, in effect, instead of gastronomy supporting culture the reverse is taking place.[5]

Yet, as indicated, those employed in culture and education enjoy high levels of social esteem—an esteem far exceeding their income in comparison with others. Polish sociologists consequently draw the conclusion that within a socialist society the prestige hierarchy is less related to income hierarchy than in capitalist, profit-oriented societies. However, as Adam Sarapata points out, it is not so much income per se but rather the *source of income* which determines the gap between the prestige and income scales.[6] And here, from this vantage point, it appears that what affects the low coincidence between income and prestige is not so much acceptance on the part of the population of a socialist moral ethos but rather the traditional prestige patterns reflecting a gentry-related system of values. That is, income flows to those engaged in the private sector of the economy and these, in addition to small farmers, are private entrepreneurs engaged in occupations which were traditionally of low prestige value (craftsmen, artisans, small-scale tradesmen, and shopkeepers). Shopkeepers especially bear a social stigma since in prewar Poland this was traditionally the occupation of the Jewish minority, and this role in the mercantile economy (an occupation which presumably involves calculating, counting, and profit-making) was below the dignity of the "honorable," gentry-oriented Pole. In the days of the rich, landed gentry, each landowner kept his "own" Jew as a concessionaire dispensing liquor to the peasants in the gentry-owned village. The *szlachcic* spent his time in the exclusive resorts of the West but collected his rent both from the peasant and the concessionaire and despised both—the peasant because of his origin and lack of culture and the Jew for his concern over income and money and for his being "different." However, the gentry morality which "looked down" at money-making is very much similar to the contempt for money-making and profit which grows out of the socialist moral code—thus, in this respect at least, the traditional cultural and social pattern matches the socialist value system.

When we look at the income and prestige scale of those engaged in the *public sector* of the economy we see that here, too, although the general level of income is lower than that prevailing within the private economic sector, the relationship between income and prestige does not coincide. Thus, the gap between a teacher's income and his prestige is the widest with the weight in the direction of high prestige, whereas in the case of members of the governmental cabinet, policemen, army officers, and office supervisors the gap between income and prestige varies from medium to low with the weight in favor of income.[7] Yet some of these occupations such as cabinet member and army officer were traditionally of high prestige as well as relatively high income. What occurred, however, is that members of the governmental cabinet as well as professional army officers came to be recruited (or came to be perceived as recruited) from the traditionally lower socio-economic strata, and thus those in these occupations carry low prestige by virtue of their traditionally lower-class background.

Consequently, rather than the socialist moral ethos determining cultural and social attitudes, it would seem that tradition still holds sway. And indeed, according to studies conducted by Wlodzimierz Wesolowski and others, the intelligentsia still occupies the top position on the prestige scale followed by highly skilled, trained workers—with the last place on the scale occupied by the unskilled, uneducated proletariat.

Yet there are visible changes brought about by the revolution. When people speak of "the party," they mean the United Polish Workers' Party, which prior to World War II was known as the Polish Communist

TABLE 1

Occupational Group Hierarchy According to Social Prestige

Occupational Group	Median Points
Intelligentsia	1.74
Skilled Technicians	2.33
Private Economic Sector Occupations	2.81
White Collar	3.17
Unskilled Labor	4.06

NOTE: Median point scale is as follows: 1 = very high; 2 = high; 3 = medium; 4 = low; 5 = very low. Table taken from Wlodzimierz Wesolowski, "Changes in the Class Structure in Poland," in *Empirical Sociology in Poland,* ed. by the Institute of Philosophy and Sociology, Polish Academy of Sciences (Warsaw: PWN [Polish Scientific Publishers], 1966), p. 34.

Party, and was insignificant in membership numbers as well as illegal. People acknowledge the position of the party today as a fact of life. The tomb of the unknown soldier, which features an eternal flame and a military honor guard standing duty day and night—as it did before the Communists came to power—extols on the commemorative tablet battles different in nature from the battles remembered in the past. Whereas before World War II these tablets memorialized the exploits of Pilsudski's legionnaires and his First Brigade as well as the battles of 1920 against the young Soviet state, they now speak of the battles of the Spanish civil war in which many Poles fought on the side of the loyalists (despite the opposition of their government), the battles of World War II, especially those in which Polish Army units fought alongside the Soviet Red Army (Lenino, the storming of Berlin, etc.).

Electricity has reached the countryside, and so has radio and even television—radio at least in the form of a communal loudspeaker attached to a pole in the center of the village. "Houses of culture," operated by the local National Councils, have sprung up in small towns and even in villages, along with recreational centers and clubs operated by the Union of Socialist Youth, the Union of Rural Youth, and other sociopolitical organizations. While potent and influential, the Catholic Church is no longer the physical center of a town's or village's social attention on a day off work. Yet the youth which frequents the clubs and the houses of culture also attends church services, and Sunday, the day of the week when the whole family has the most free time and the only day the family has some opportunity for "togetherness," is usually spent "on longer morning or afternoon sleep as well as on church service."[8]

Villages and small towns enjoying Houses of culture, electricity, radio and even television lack, however, modern sewage systems and indoor toilet facilities; not infrequently, water is still carted in buckets from a centrally located well or pump. Despite recreation centers and clubs, youths dancing to the tunes of "big beat," boys roving the countryside on motorcycles imported from Czechoslovakia, and girls putting their hair up in rollers, there is a lack of that aspect of culture which one usually associates with bodily hygiene. Alongside a poetry of sensitivity and depth, a graphic art movement which has produced outstanding works, and avant-garde films, there is drunkenness, churlishness, and "hooliganism." In a country which prides itself on numerous art treasures and one of the most imposing opera houses in the world, in a country which economically and technically assists many "underdeveloped" countries in Africa, the Middle East and Latin America, only

36.8 percent of the working-class households have a tub or a shower and only 45.7 percent can boast of a simple indoor toilet.

Traditionally socialist ethics view negotiated matrimony as a product of an exploitive socio-economic system, a residue of feudalism and capitalism which treats the object of the matrimonial bargain as chattel, depriving at least one of the "partners" of human dignity, the exercise of free will, and love—and thus is to be condemned. However, many newspapers prominently feature matrimonial advertisements in which those who advertise stress as their attributes economic security and respectability—middle-class, petty, bourgeois values—and they seek in their future marriage partner old-fashioned virginity and virtues (no divorcees need apply, no smokers, and so forth).[9] Yet fifteen percent of the total expenditure on food is spent on alcohol, with the expenditure on such basic staples of the Polish diet as bread and all other wheat and flour products two percent lower. Only meat and dairy products (both expensive) commanded a higher portion from the average family food budget than alcohol. But at the same time, the official moral code is puritanical in character, and in provincial small towns girls in miniskirts are looked upon askance. While the eradication of class distinctions is proclaimed as the system's goal, such distinctions are perpetuated both formally and informally, although they are not necessarily related to economic income, as mentioned, but rather to the source of income, to education, life styles, and so forth—perpetuating a stratification pattern growing out of the impoverished gentry's social code. Similarly, the traditional gentry values are perpetuated in attitudes towards work, especially manual labor, as well as in attitudes towards leisure. There is a great deal of snobbism, with the peasantry being the most frequent and most prominent recipient of social disdain.

The mixture of traditionalism and modernity, of traditional national Catholic moral values and of secularized patterns brought about by industrialization, urbanization, and the sociopolitical revolution, has not left untouched the institution of the family. Thus, during the period 1958–64, 66.0 percent of the respondents in a national survey expressed themselves in favor of birth control and rational family planning.[10] Yet, at the same time, women desirous of abortion will go to private medical practitioners (who do a thriving business on abortions and venereal disease treatment) rather than to the public health clinic, where they can receive attention at no cost, simply because in the latter they would have to place their "problem" on official record and confide to the public health nurse or receptionist with other patients waiting in line and listening. Although in the aforementioned survey two-thirds of the re-spondents expressed themselves in favor of divorce—a solution to marital difficulties traditionally condemned by the church—in another survey 30.2 percent of education students age eighteen to nineteen, 36.4 percent of students age twenty to twenty-two, and 21.7 percent of students age twenty-three to twenty-eight agreed with the statement that "premarital virginity is testimony to the moral purity of a girl, and certainly the most decisive factor in consideration for marriage," and, similarly, 38.5 percent of the eighteen to nineteen year olds, 35.0 percent of the twenty to twenty-two year olds, and 46.7 percent of the twenty-three to twenty-eight year olds agreed that "marriage should be inviolate and even in the most difficult situations one should not resort to divorce."[11] The ratio of student-respondents accepting the traditional role of the woman in the family as one limited to the care of children and household and denying her the right to compete as an equal in the economic marketplace followed similar patterns. Significantly, the statement favoring female equality found less approval among female students than among males.[12]

What is surprising is that young Poles, while born into the new system, susceptible to the influences of "modernity," and fully educated in the new "socialist" school, are more responsive to some of the values of traditional morality and more attracted to the appeals of the church than persons of older age, who find themselves perhaps more pressured by social and economic necessities and thus are more accommodating to the demands of the political system. Older persons, especially among the intelligentsia, remember the church not only as the symbol of nationhood—often the only available symbol during periods of partition of the country by non-Catholic powers of the East and West—but also as a force of conservatism, frequently allied with political reaction. Younger people, on the other hand, see the Catholic Church today as a symbol of resistance to a reality with which they are often in disagreement, since it departs from the normative premises and ideological promises with which their socialist education has inculcated them. In addition, younger people, less sensitive to the need for economic security, less exposed to socio-economic pressures, find it easier to manifest their dissatisfactions. They, unlike their elders, are less sensitized to possible repercussions and have lesser responsibilities (for family and so forth). Moreover, many young persons find the endless exhortations for socialist morality and the endless lessons on ideology boring, and the system's efforts to socialize the young may therefore be counterproductive. Consequently, while on the symbolic and verbal level there is indeed a great deal of stress on "socialist morality" and "productivity," on the level of actual behavior there is a persistence of traditionalism, or else an acceptance of a shallow modernity which expresses itself in a desire for personal

comforts and gadgets—and the trappings of a technological culture—
but which has very little relation to the strict moral code of either
Catholicism or socialism. Similarly, while there is talk of work, there is a
great deal of shirking from hard labor and a desire to find a secure niche
within the economy, one which would demand the least exertion. As one
writer comments:

Many persons treat solid work as a mark of conservatism, and careless
"light" work as a mark of modernity, and public opinion by-and-large seems
to approve of such attitude. The person who has really worked, as expected,
during all of the 7 or 8 hours of the work day is often considered to be a
maniac or a harmless fool.[13]

As in other societies undergoing rapid change, in Poland juvenile
delinquency is a problem. The same youth which look to the church for
moral sustenance use in their speech a "lingo" in which casual references
to sex and toilet-related functions are commonplace, and their attitude
towards love and courtship has lost the romantic aura it held for
previous generations of Poles. Older tradition-oriented moralists blame
the changes in youth's behavior on "modernity" and on industrialization;
the ideology-oriented guardians of morality discern in these relaxed
patterns of conduct the influence of foreign cultural patterns, particularly of "Americanism." "Americanism" is perceived as the ultimate in
technological culture but, at the same time, as dehumanized, since it
presumably is lacking in "feeling," tradition, and warmth in interper-
sonal relations. The youth, or certain segments of the youth, do indeed
look curiously towards the West and are fascinated not only by Western,
and particularly American, technical innovations but also by Western
U.S. attire (including blue jeans and cowboy boots), as well as by jazz.
This fascination with things foreign has penetrated even the ranks of the
village youth, so much so that Madame Mira Ziminska was forced to
complain that she has given up attempts at recruitment of young rural
talent for her world-famous folk dance ensemble, "Mazowsze," because
young village people have fallen "victim" to foreign mannerisms and
rock-and-roll, apparently beyond redemption.[14]

The events of early spring 1968, during which Polish youth, especially
of institutions of higher learning in the big cities, in response to the
events in neighboring Czechoslovakia but directly as a result of the
banning of *Forefathers* (*Dziady*), a classic Polish drama by Adam
Mickiewicz, took to the streets and occupied school buildings, emphasized the failure of the schools and the broad network of youth organizations to socialize the young to the demands, expectations, and styles of
the system. Activists of the Union of Socialist Youth blamed their failure

on the noncooperative attitude of school administrators and teachers, who, in turn, claimed lack of time, lack of facilities, lack of precise character development guidelines, and inability to meet the various and often conflicting systemic demands and expectations made on them (for example, subject-matter education and sociopolitical activism). The failure to adequately socialize the youth, especially its most privileged segment, those of the institutions of higher learning and the secondary schools, was in turn, attributed to the social background and class imbalance prevailing within the student population. It was pointed out, quite correctly, that, although the intelligentsia represents about six percent of the adult labor force, their children are disproportionately over-represented in the institutions of learning of traditional prestige, both secondary and higher, and this over-representation increases with the prestige of a given institution. That is, the classes and groups of traditional social privilege continue to garnish privileges under the new system, and because of their easier access to the institutions of learning —graduation from which provides one with a claimant's ticket to position and status—they perpetuate themselves in the favored positions at the top of the social ladder. The demand was subsequently advanced that greater access to institutions of learning must be given to youth of working-class and peasant background, presumably more loyal and reliable from the point of view of the system. It was further maintained that among the most privileged and the least loyal were the children of intelligentsia parents who are not "fully Polonized," a clear allusion to the remnants of the once-substantial Jewish population wiped out in the holocaust of World War II, and, particularly, to the remnants of the Jewish intelligentsia, a disproportionate number of whom were members of the prewar Polish Communist Party and occupied leadership positions.

The political leadership thus attempted to mobilize public mass senti-ment, especially the sentiment of the working class and the peasantry, against the intelligentsia and the few remaining Poles of Jewish descent —the first, traditional targets of mass animosity (envy mixed with respect); the second, traditional targets of Polish national hostility, born of centuries of national and religious prejudice but also mixed with economic envy. The system thus tried to marshal the *twin forces of class animosity and traditional national-religious prejudice*. While the first was in accord with traditional ideological and Marxist premises, the second appeal was totally alien to it, although quite in keeping with past cultural patterns. Moreover, since the students participating in the student pro-tests referred sympathetically to the Czechoslovak experiments in liber-alization, it was easy for the leadership to appeal to traditional anti-

Czechoslovak sentiments as well (a sentiment born again out of envy and contempt—envy because Czechoslovaks are seen as more technologically developed, and contempt because, instead of displaying the traditional Polish élan for the romantic and honorable death, the Czechoslovaks traditionally were accommodative to superior outside force and, in the process of accommodation, have preserved intact their ancient cities and treasures). But by linking the Polish students with the liberal reforms in Prague, the "alien" Jews, and the intelligentsia, the leadership further tried to portray the unrest of March 1968 as inspired by culturally foreign and hostile elements. In doing so, it appealed to ingrained nationalistic and basically conservative, parochial, and culturally introspective sentiments which view everything foreign with suspicion, as if threatening the security of both the system and of traditional values and authority patterns.

While, however, it was rather simple for the regime to intimidate the remaining Jews (even those who had left the fold of the Jewish community but were suddenly reminded of their long-forgotten Jewish heritage) and to encourage them to renounce their Polish citizenship in exchange for exit visas pointedly limited for travel to Israel only (with which these Poles of Jewish descent had little in common), it is much harder to change the educational pattern which favored the traditional intelligentsia classes. (See tables 2 and 3.)

As indicated, first entrance to and then graduation from a university or similar institution of higher learning provides one with access to a profession and with status and prestige (but not necessarily with commensurate income which, while important, seems to be of less importance than social prestige to the honor and esteem-oriented Pole, attuned as he is to the still-prevailing values and conditions of the impoverished gentry). However, entry to a university is blocked if one does not possess a Certificate of Maturity (*Matura*), signifying graduation from a secondary school of general education. This certificate not only opens possibilities for entering the portals of higher education (and all that may follow) but it also, if the graduate is a male and called into military service, opens doors to obtaining officer's rank, thus further acknowledging his elite status by placing him in a command-giving position over those less privileged.

Before the war and before the establishment of People's Poland, secondary education was obtainable in both private and public schools. The first were economically prohibitive to most, the second were by-and-large limited to sons and daughters of the bureaucracy, professional officers corps, or the exceptionally gifted among the lower classes. Under

TABLE 2

Class Background of University Students in Poland, 1965–66

Class Background	No. of Students	Percent
Working Class	10,470	26.1
Peasantry	5,631	14.1
Intelligentsia	21,347	53.3
Self-Employed Artisans/Craftsmen	2,028	5.1
Other	578	1.4
Total	40,054	100.0

SOURCE: Glowny Urzad Statystyczny, *Rocznik Statystyczny Szkolnictwa: 1944/45–1966/67* (Warsaw: 1967), p. 434.

TABLE 3

Socio-economic Class Background of Students in Prestigious Schools (Lycea) of General Education in Poland, 1964–65

Class Background	No. of Students	Percent
Working Class	106,515	26.3
Peasantry	74,115	18.3
Intelligentsia	174,555	43.1
Self-Employed Artisans/Craftsmen	28,350	7.0
Agricultural Workers	4,455	1.1
Other	17,010	4.2
Total	405,000	100.0

SOURCE: Glowny Urzad Statystyczny (GUS), *Statystyka Szkolnictwa: Szkolnictwo Ogolnoksztalcace: Opieka nad dziecmi i mlodzieza, 1964/65 i 1965/66* (Warsaw: 1966), No. 4.

the revised prewar constitution only *Matura* holders could vote and be elected to the upper house of parliament (the senate), only they could become officers, and only *Matura*-holding females could marry members of the professional officers corps. Given such tradition, the clamor for entry into schools of secondary general education (as distinguished from vocational education) is great. However, the process of selection begins virtually at the end of the seventh grade of elementary school when the pupil is faced with the alternative of either proceeding to the academically oriented eighth grade, entering vocational training, or joining the unskilled labor force. Many village schools lack even a seventh grade, and the educational level of the elementary schools of the rural areas or provincial small towns is generally lower than that of the large metropolitan areas. Consequently, as a result of inferior primary education, children of peasants and rural residents find themselves unable to com-

pete with city-bred children in the entrance examinations to the secondary schools, even if they get that far.

Moreover, despite the formal stress on education, economic priorities
are such that less is allocated to education than to other branches of
governmental activities and, in addition, since a great deal of initiative in
the area of establishing educational resources is left to the local National
Councils and their own economic resources, youth in economically
disadvantaged areas, or in localities where the authorities have a lesser
appreciation of education, are left in an unfavorable competitive position. As a rule, secondary schools exist only in larger localities, and
those in provincial towns are to serve wider districts. Yet, again due to
non-educationally related priorities, the schools lack both busses to serve
students in outlying areas and dormitories to accommodate those beyond
commuting distance, provided they are otherwise eligible for secondary
general education. Furthermore, the youth of peasant background often
cannot be spared from their farm work, from helping their families, and
even those who somehow reach the city or town-based secondary school
of general education find themselves in a socially disadvantaged position,
since their rural style marks them as different, and they are seen as
"uncultured." The life of the city school is often quite bewildering to
them. There is also some evidence that even within the large cities
elementary schools located in general intelligentsia districts are superior
to those in working-class neighborhoods. Thus, *while the enrollment
flow, because of the persistence of traditional value patterns, is in the
direction of an education which might lead to social prestige and professional status, this flow is blocked to youth of traditionally lower-class
background by a system which is stacked in favor of traditional privilege
and abetted by decisions which prevent allocation of adequate resources
in the direction of equalizing educational opportunities.*

Special preferential entrance credits for youth of working-class or
peasant background have been in existence, on and off, for some time,
and, once admitted, youth of such background receives priorities in the
awarding of stipends, fellowships, and scholarships. Yet, while these
preferences and priorities have increased the number of working-class
and peasant youth within the general student population (especially as
compared with the situation which prevailed prior to World War II),
they have failed to alter the pattern of enrollment, especially in schools
of prestige, which continues to lean heavily toward predominance of the
intelligentsia. If the political leadership hopes to create a more favorable
climate for itself by pushing ahead youth of working-class and peasant
background on the assumption that these might be more loyal and less

unruly than youth of intelligentsia background, its effort might be counterproductive, especially in terms of maximizing commitment to the
system's ideological values and goals. There is evidence that the *youth of
intelligentsia background when challenging authority do so precisely
from the standpoint and the premises of the ideology, to which they
appear to be generally more receptive than the youth of working-class
background, and much more so than those of peasant background.* If the
church stands in opposition to the party, it is rather significant that
*students of peasant and working-class background overshadow those of
intelligentsia background—of all "prestigious" institutions of higher
learning—only at theological academies* (see Table 4). Moreover, if one
is to judge commitment to official ideology by level of commitment to
the opposing philosophical outlook of religion, it would appear from
research conducted among teachers in Poland at two different time
periods by Dr. Mikolaj Kozakiewicz and by this writer that while
persons of peasant and rural origins *express* greater allegiance to the
church than either persons of working-class or intelligentsia background,
it is the religiously oriented among those of working-class background
who, in the fervor of their commitment as judged by actual church
attendance, exceed either of the two other groups.[15]

If anything, it is persons of intelligentsia background, many of them
descended from the impoverished gentry, who have entered People's
Poland propertyless and imbued with the values and norms of a tradition
which calls for romantic honor, which, while almost feudal in character,
is also anticapitalist; who have a disdain for moneymaking, for profit,
and for all the other values of the middle class and the bourgeoisie; who
have nothing to lose from the nationalization of private capital and can
embrace emotionally and intellectually the ideational symbols of the
political revolution. On the other hand, the peasant clings to his land—
given to him by the land reform of the initial period following the
establishment of the People's Democracy, later collectivized but still
later through the upheaval of October 1956 brought back to him—and
the worker dreams of economic betterment and a better existential lot
for his children. The impoverished gentry and intelligentsia, though,
dream of national greatness, the rebuilding of the cities from the war's
devastation, the enrichment of the national culture, and is desirous of
maintaining its own leadership position in the process—a position to
which it traditionally has felt entitled. And, for its part, those in charge
of the new system have been quite willing to accord traditional social
prominence to the intelligentsia and to those of gentry background,
utilizing the skills at the disposal of these groups, so long as those so

TABLE 4
Socio-economic Class Background of Students in Various Prestigious Institutions of Higher Learning in Poland, 1965–66

Socio-economic Class Background of Students

Type of Academic Institutions	Workers		Peasants		Intelligentsia		Independent Artisans		Others	
	Number	Percent	Number	Percent	Number	Percent	Number	Percent	Number	Percent
Universities	10,470	26.1	5,631	14.1	21,347	53.3	2,028	5.1	578	1.4
Higher Technical Schools	18,831	29.7	7,481	15.0	25,432	51.0	1,763	3.5	409	.8
Higher Agricultural Schools	3,412	20.5	5,643	33.9	6,711	40.3	756	4.5	128	.8
Higher Economic Schools	3,278	33.6	1,783	18.3	4,215	43.2	385	3.9	95	1.0
Higher Pedagogic Schools	2,575	35.6	1,512	20.9	2,784	38.5	309	4.3	55	.7
Medical Academies	5,240	23.7	3,193	14.4	12,377	55.9	1,032	4.7	279	1.3
Higher Physical Education Schools	699	32.4	231	10.7	1,101	50.9	117	5.4	14	.6
Higher Art Schools	863	20.9	315	7.6	2,703	65.5	244	5.9	5	.1
Theological Academies	94	27.8	154	45.6	68	20.1	17	5.0	5	1.5

SOURCE: Glowny Urzad Statystyczny, *Rocznik Statystyczny Szkolnictwa 1944/45–1966/67* (Warsaw: 1967), pp. 434–35.

honored and used will serve with loyalty and accept the basic policy premises of the system, including that which calls for friendship with the powerful eastern neighbor. As Czeslaw Milosz points out:

. . . when I was working for the "People's Democracy," my origins caused me no trouble at all. On the contrary, my superiors viewed them very favorably . . . The real demons for them were the defenders of private initiative, the entrepreneurs, whether in trade, industry, or agriculture. By exterminating the acquisitive instinct, they believed that mankind could be raised to a higher level. On this point, they and I were in perfect accord—an accord that went deeper than any rationale, growing as it did out of an inborn aversion to counting, measuring, and weighing, activities that symbolized the unclean. There is really nothing more antibourgeois than certain segments of the intelligentsia who are defenseless when it comes to money. They retain a medieval disgust for usury because private capitalism never rubbed off on them. My superiors, not necessarily realizing it, professed an ideology strongly marked by the atavistic resentments of impoverished noblemen, those begetters of revolution in literature and politics.[16]

However, once the system becomes settled and secure, once its plans and priority allocations begin to depart from the original premises and promises, once it develops its own bureaucracy, and, in power, begins to attract the old middle class and the old bureaucrats—the mainstay of preceding regimes—and once these begin to openly envy and compete for authority with the traditional "children of privilege," the latter feel threatened, esthetically disgusted by the new petty bourgeois style ("the nouveau riche with a bureaucratic mind," as one Polish writer refers to the new political elite), and, consequently, they become sensitized to the departure from the original idealistic slogans which has taken place. That is, the old slogans remain in force but only to legitimize a rather prosaic, bureaucratized, drab, and primarily authority-oriented reality. The intelligentsia and those of the old impoverished gentry, although they have embraced the new system, do, however, continue to speak foreign languages, read foreign literature, vacation in the West, enjoy avant-garde art, experiment in extramarital sex, maintain contacts with friends and relatives in the West (many of them political exiles), flaunt their good breeding and social grace, and "look down" at those in authority, including those of working-class or peasant background who have made good, despite many odds, through the acquisition of an education. The latter are seen by the traditional intelligentsia as "churls with diplomas."[17]

What develops, consequently, is a clash of cultural styles and interests, a struggle in defense of established position, in which those in formal political and administrative authority turn to the working class and the peasantry, whose members are considered more reliable, more loyal, because they are more parochial, conservative, and nationalistic, without flights of fancy and without dreams of vacations in Paris. Workers and peasants may be grateful for whatever improvements have come their way, for whatever opportunities their children may enjoy, as compared with what was available to them in the past. They, like the new bureaucrats in authority, although trying to emulate the aristocratic style, are envious of the old intelligentsia and their children, whom they perceive as being social "parasites" enjoying the "good life" of students at the expense of the labor and the sweat of the masses. Their attitude is similar to that of the hard-working American taxpayer who turns periodically against school budgets and "eggheads"—whenever and wherever he has a chance—seeing in the schools and in the intellectual community fountainheads of cultural differentness which he resents, especially since he feels that his hard-earned dollar maintains it in style.

In Poland, these forces joined hands, and these sentiments emerged to the fore in March 1968, pitting the party and governmental bureaucracy allied with the nationalistic proletariat, the peasantry, and the provincial middle class, as well as the traditional guardians of national and religious moral purity, against "not completely Polonized" citizens of Jewish descent; intellectuals who felt increasingly alienated by parochialism, provincialism, and the cultural styles they traditionally detested; and their children, the students of intelligentsia background. What was at stake in the contest was not ideology or the proper interpretation of ideology or policy but rather authority—and in defense of their authority the leaders of the system turned for assistance to the traditionally authority-oriented segments of society, rallying them against those who still insisted on adhering to and referring to the ideational moral code of socialism. *In this contest the ideals of socialism had to surrender to authority exercised in the name of socialism.* In addition to the intellectuals and Jews (officially labeled as "Zionists" since the new anti-Semitism required legitimization in ideological terms), the authority tried to rally public sentiment against those in the nonagricultural private sector of the economy, the so-called "privateers" (*priwaciarze*), whose incomes set them aside from the rest of the population dependent on the public economic sector and from poor private farmers, making them, in fact, objects of envy.

Economics and Politics

A Polish citizen in his late sixties has survived a series of wars and upheavals in the course of attaining this "ripe old age." A war in 1905 followed by a revolution and a reaction which engulfed the entire Czarist empire of which east-central Poland was a part; World War I, occupation and starvation, civil disorder; a war (1920) with the young Soviet Republic which saw Polish troops deep in the Ukraine and Belorussia —victories which turned into defeat and brought the Red Army to the banks of the Vistula; uneasy peace of the late thirties; World War II and almost six years of occupation, starvation, destruction and slaughter; uprisings, persecution, and partisan warfare which continued in the woods and forests long after the war was officially over; Stalinism; and the liberalizing revolt of 1956. In 1950 persons sixty years of age or over constituted only seven percent of the population.

Although the great bulk of the population is young, many still carry memories of the holocaust either personally experienced or assimilated through tales repeatedly narrated. Yet, life is becoming normalized. Due to a system of public health care in which preventive medicine plays a significant role, due to paid vacations, rest homes, and sanatoria, more Poles now enter their sixties—despite the shattering experiences of the past—than ever before. It is estimated that by 1970 the number of persons sixty years of age or older will be thirteen percent. However, the life of the older retired citizen of People's Poland is not an easy one. Wages in the public sector of the economy are small in relation to prices on the consumer market, and retirement pensions are even lower—normally averaging about seventy-five percent of the pensioner's last salary up to a given amount, plus a bonus in some cases. He is entitled to earn some additional post-retirement income, but if such income exceeds a certain set norm, he stands to forfeit his pension. Some retired persons become involved in small private trade or small private cottage industry, keeping their earnings hidden from official eyes. The life of older people in Poland is, in fact, extremely difficult, and for the most part they become a financial burden to their children, whose earnings are also limited.

The elaborate welfare and health system is primarily geared for the benefit of the young and productive. The number of old-age homes is small, while that of sanatoria and vacation resorts is rather large—maintained by the trade unions, civic organizations, and enterprises, and supported by the state. The distribution of vacation benefits is uneven, reflecting at once the needs of the economy in relation to the availability of skilled manpower as well as traditional patterns of privilege. Thus, for example, a manual worker is entitled to twelve days vacation time after one year of uninterrupted employment, while a white-collar worker receives one full month vacation after one year of work and may request to take fourteen days off—an advance on his month vacation—after only half a year's employment. However, there are other types of leave, including leave of absence with pay for educational purposes, especially if such education would enhance the individual's job qualifications.

Those engaged in private trade or industry as well as private hothouse cultivation (especially of flowers and produce for export) constitute an economic elite whose style of consumption sets them markedly apart from the rest of the population. The resthome of the independent (private) artisans' and craftsmen's association in the mountain resort of Zakopane, for example, is indeed an imposing affair, featuring a kidney-shaped swimming pool and a large parking lot always filled with expensive foreign-made automobiles, as well as a bar. Private artisans and craftsmen are able to enjoy an evening out at a night club in a hotel catering to foreign tourists and can purchase their daily meat and dairy products (superior in quality to those available to the public-at-large in the regular shops) from the "black market" at high prices. The lot of those engaged in the public sector of the economy is much harder, and their incomes lag behind the prices of consumer goods, especially for such items as clothing and appliances.

The major problem is housing, since the country still suffers from the destruction brought about by World War II despite the feverish rebuilding efforts of the first postwar years. Much of that reconstruction fever, however, centered on the restoration of national monuments and shrines, including churches—partially because proponents of the new system felt compelled to show its links to the traditional past—and, later, the construction effort became centered on the development of new industrial plants, public buildings, and the like. As a result, individual housing needs still remain unfilled, and people are forced to move into apartment buildings before they are actually completed. Also, since many of the new highrise apartment dwellings in the cities were erected under accelerated conditions, they began to show structural defects after only a few years. Nevertheless, the need for housing and construction places those employed in that industry at the top of the income scale within the public economic sector, followed by persons engaged in public administration, including justice. Thus, for example, the average income in the construction industry in 1965 was 2,356 zlotys a month, and in public administration it was 2,178 zlotys a month. The average wage for industrial workers, other than construction, was 2,175 zlotys a month. By comparison, the average wage in education, science and culture was only 1,780 zlotys; in trade, 1,699 zlotys; in state and collectivized agriculture, 1,618; and in health and welfare, 1,543. Persons engaged in forestry received 1,471 zlotys a month.

To be sure, the low-paid state farmer or forester has the advantage of living close to the soil, and the medical practitioner can supplement his meager income from public health service by a more lucrative private practice. Likewise, within the educational establishment those active in *higher* education averaged (in 1965) 3,202 zlotys a month, and they, too, are able to individually further increase their incomes (through writing, research, and such). However, the average salary that year for a kindergarten teacher whose abilities to supplement income are limited was only 1,393 zlotys a month and that of a public health nurse was about the same. A custodian in a kindergarten averaged only 824 zlotys a month, and one in higher education, 1,246. Moreover, the kindergarten teacher and the public health nurse, being classed as members of intelligentsia professions, were not entitled to some of the privileges available to higher-earning workers or peasants (for example, preference with respect to dormitory space for their children of secondary school age). To better understand the general low level of salaries in the public sector of the economy, it should be remembered that in 1963 a ready-made men's woolen suit was 1,890 zlotys (more than the monthly salary of an elementary school teacher), a bed mattress was 2,150 zlotys (about the same as the average monthly salary of a person employed in public administration, including justice), a small refrigerator was 3,000 zlotys—exceeding the average monthly salary of a person in the relatively highly paid construction industry. The industrial worker, whose average monthly income in 1965 was 2,175 zlotys a month, could purchase in any one month that year either slightly more than 54 kilos of pork meat, 20.5 liters of vodka, less than fourteen men's poplin shirts, exactly twenty-nine cotton shirts, or seven pairs of mass-produced women's shoes. However, the average income was closer to that of an elementary school teacher than that of a relatively favored industrial worker. On the other hand, rentals (if available) were cheap, and so was the price of services.

But, as indicated, the Pole does not live by bread alone—social prestige and status is of equal, if not greater, importance to him. It is therefore noteworthy that among the occupations whose income exceeded social prestige were (in order of the income-prestige gap): private shopkeepers, private tailors, members of the governmental cabinet of ministers, private locksmiths, unskilled construction workers, lawyers, policemen, army officers, priests, office supervisors, and small farmers. Among the occupations where prestige exceeded income were (in order of the gap): teachers, nurses, university professors, medical doctors, mechanical engineers, agronomists, railway conductors, office cleaners, airplane pilots, accountants, office clerks, factory foremen, typists, and journalists. Only in the case of skilled steelworkers, machinists, and unskilled workers did the income coincide with respective prestige ratings.[18]

Because of the generally low salaries, many of those whose jobs would enable them to do so are only too eager to travel on business, alone or as members of delegations, and thus be entitled to a per diem (*dieta*), which, if used frugally, could indeed constitute a substantial supplementary income.

Despite low income, the aspiration horizon of many Poles, especially of working-class or peasant background, is on the increase, if not for themselves at least for their offspring. Poland is currently undergoing a process of "rising expectations" similar to that observed among other societies in a state of revolution and change. The general educational level is on the increase, especially among the young, electricity has reached the villages, and many rural elements have been absorbed into the cities and into industry. At the same time, industry has penetrated the rural areas, often offering the peasant opportunities for combined industrial and agricultural occupations (as in the area of Plock, where giant petrochemical facilities have been established). In 1969, nine hundred thousand small farm-owners were permanently employed in nonagricultural pursuits.[19] In fact, the rate of industry-related employment opportunities exceeded the level of available skill or even literacy, especially among the older Poles—a result of war, occupation, and interrupted or previously unavailable schooling. Much of the system's political success will hinge upon its ability to deliver on its stated or implied promises—many growing out of its own ideological orientation —that is, the extent to which it will be able to meet the tide of rising expectations, both for economic improvement and for status, of the traditionally lower classes.

The road towards meeting such expectations is full of obstacles related to matters of existing conflict between industrial managers and central economic planners, to Poland's ability to produce in volume as well as in quality, and to her capacity to enter into the competitive foreign-trade market—outside the Comecon with its guaranteed quota system—and to earn much-needed foreign exchange, hard currency. However, the problems of the economy are closely knit to problems of politics, and decisions in both realms are dependent upon each other. Thus, for example, many of Poland's foreign trade activities, including foreign aid and technical assistance to "underdeveloped" countries (the latter, an activity it can ill afford both for reasons of economic cost and because it diverts resources and rare skilled manpower from local needs) are undertaken for the sake of international prestige, or under Soviet pressure, or because of some other considerations. It seems that in confrontations between education and economic-industrial interests, the needs of the latter win out, while in confrontations between politics and the needs of the economy, the interests of politics take the upper hand.

Power and Authority

The country is administratively divided into seventeen major districts (*wojewodztwos*) plus five major metropolitan areas of *wojewodztwo* status (Warsaw, Lodz, Cracow, Poznan, and Wroclaw). The *wojewodztwos* are further divided into administrative units designated as *powiats,* equivalent to counties in the United States. In addition to the regular *powiats,* some cities have *powiat* status of their own. Until 1950 the *wojewodztwos* were headed by governors (*wojewodas*) appointed by the central authorities. In that year the posts of *wojewoda* were abolished in favor of elected National Councils. Similarly, National Councils as governing organs were established on each lower administrative level, including that of the village (*gromada*), where in previous years the elder (*starosta*) reigned supreme. Elected, the members of the National Councils are usually prominent citizens of the area, representing the various parties and groups of the Front of National Unity. The chairman or vice-chairman in a large urban center is usually a member of the Democratic Alliance (*Stronnictwo Demokratyczne*), the political-functional representative group of the economic middle class. Similarly, within rural districts and *gromadas* the chairman or vice-chairman of the National Council would be a local member of the United People's Alliance (*Zjednoczone Stronnictwo Ludowe*). That is, because of the system's need to maintain the appearance of "popular frontism" and "consensus," posts to leading organs on all administrative levels are distributed with the aid of a "key" (*klucz*), which calls for so many minor party representatives (while assuring a dominant role to the United Polish Workers' Party). This, in turn, enables many persons of ambition to build for themselves *power bases precisely because of their nonmembership in the ruling party.*

On each level the National Council (NC) is divided into functional committees, commissions, and departments—each with its own bureaucratic staff—to handle such matters as education and culture and economic development. These functional committees and departments are responsible to corresponding functional organs of the NC's of higher administrative level as well as to their own National Council. A *wojewodztwo* NC department on education and culture would be subordinated to the Ministry of Education and/or the Ministry of Culture of the central Council of Ministers as well as to its own NC. At the same time, however, the ruling party on each administrative level maintains equivalent functional committees and commissions, and a *wojewodztwo* NC department on education and culture, while taking administrative signals from the Ministry of Education, will also be politically sensitive to the signals emanating from the *wojewodztwo* United Polish Workers' Party Central Committee's Commission on Education and Science. While the UPWP provides policy guidelines, the government-related ministries provide machinery for execution of these guidelines. This does not mean, however, that the administrative bureaucracy, including that of the National Council, has no discretion of its own. It is known that the implementation of policy does in itself involve a great deal of political decision-making leeway.

The National Councils will vary in size, depending upon locality, from 150 members (for a city such as Warsaw) to 15 members (for a *gromada*). While in principle the work of the NC's is coordinated with the plans and policies of the central authorities (both administrative and party), they are expected to develop their own budget and allocation priorities. They must develop the local economic supportive base for education, health, and welfare through the development of economic enterprises and cooperatives which do not come directly under the jurisdiction of the central state authorities. Within large cities various districts, neighborhoods, street blocks, or even large apartment houses may have their own National Councils, which help provide neighborhood self-management, and these councils will either take care of the maintenance of buildings, streets, and the cultural needs of the residents —or appeal to the NC's of higher level in order to secure needed services. In this way, local government is brought down to the citizen's home and involves him in at least some aspects of the operations of the system.

As indicated, while formally subordinated to the central authorities and central planners, the local National Councils and their own functional bureaucracy have a great deal of discretion. Such discretion may work to cancel out the intent of the central planners, and there are many examples of cases of *deliberate lack* of coordination and administrative orchestration, as it were. In the Tatra mountain resort city of Zakopane, for example, the City National Council, committed to the preservation of Zakopane as a year-round sport and tourist center, successfully circumvented efforts of the Central Resort Management Bureau and the Ministry of Municipal Economy, as well as of the corresponding organs of the *wojewodztwo* NC, to convert Zakopane into a health and convalescence spa by simply pre-empting the building sites desired by the central authorities for its own municipal uses.[20]

Formally the highest constitutional authority of the Polish People's Republic is vested in the unicameral parliament, the *Sejm*. The first post-World War II *Sejm* was convened in 1947, inheriting the function which between 1944 and 1946 was in the hands of a countrywide National Council. The memory of the class character of the Senate of the immediate pre-World War II years, the thirties, was a contributing factor in the decision not to revive the upper house of parliament in 1947. However, the present *Sejm* does not resemble in terms of its composition or behavior the earlier *Sejms* either. Although, as said, it formally represents the highest authority of the Republic, it serves, in fact, merely as legitimizer of laws and policies submitted to it by the Council of Ministers which, in turn, is attuned to the directive signals from the United Polish Workers' Party leadership. In 1960 the number of deputies was fixed at 460, elected for four-year terms. It is a body of mixed political and economic interest representation—the latter by design. Alongside the formal political-party organizations, representation is also accorded to "non-party" functional interest groups. However, if class is to be judged by the occupation of the deputies, the intelligentsia constitutes the dominant social strata and, as in the institutions of education, is over-represented. On the other hand, the working class and the peasantry are under-represented, although these classes constitute the bulk of the population, and the *Sejm,* as the government and the ruling party, claims to speak on their behalf. (See Table 5.) What is also evident from Table 5 is the dominant role of the industrial management interests and of the administrative bureaucracy—the interest of the latter is represented by in addition to "administrators," many of the formally non-administrative occupational identifications. Although workers constitute one of the two single largest occupational groups, they, significantly, share this status with the industrial management elite.

A comparison between the political party and organizational composition of the *Sejm* deputies of the constitutional *Sejm* (1947–52)—since this was the *Sejm* that adapted the Constitution of the People's Republic on July 22, 1952—with that of 1961–65, reveals not only the strengthening of the position of the political organization of the Left but, perhaps more significantly, the extent to which the Communist component of the alliance has overshadowed its socialist partner, although the latter had come to the 1948 merger Congress with greater strength and a longer tradition in Polish politics. (See Table 6.) Of the various non-United Polish Workers' Party groups—both formally political and non-political—the Catholic *Znak* is the most independent and is more or less representative of the liberal Catholic intellectual elite. This group has emerged as a result of the liberalization brought about by the Poles in October 1956 and the short-lived alliance between Gomulka and Cardinal Wyszynski, between the party and the church. In opposition to *Znak*

TABLE 5

Composition of 1961–65 Sejm (Parliament)
By Sex, Direct Functional Interest, and Occupation

	Number	Percentage
By Sex		
Male	400	87.0
Female	60	13.0
Total	460	100.0
By Direct Functional Interest		
Industry	124	26.9
Administration	111	24.1
Agriculture	87	18.9
Education and Science	79	17.2
Literature and the Media	22	4.8
Health and Welfare	15	3.3
Youth/Students	12	2.6
Military	5	1.1
Private Economic Sector	5	1.1
Total	460	100.0
By Occupation		
Workers	62	13.5
Engineers/Technicians	62	13.5
Peasants/Farmers	59	12.7
Teachers	54	11.7
Economists	44	9.6
Lawyers	33	7.2
Agronomists/Agricultural Engineers	28	6.1
Administrators	28	6.1
University Professors/Scientists	25	5.4
Writers and Journalists	22	4.8
Physicians, Nurses, etc.	15	3.3
Students	12	2.6
Independent Artisans/Craftsmen	5	1.1
Military Officers	5	1.1
Others	6	1.3
Total	460	100.0

SOURCE: Based on material contained in *Polska Ludowa: Slownik encyklopedyczny* (Warsaw: Wiedza Powszechna, 1965), pp. 329–32.

is the Catholic lay group, *Pax,* which consists of some of the most nationalistic and radically conservative elements of prewar Poland but which now attempts to synthesize, as it were, the orthodoxies of both the Catholic Church and the UPWP, religion and ideology, in addition to expounding values of cultural and national conservatism in the name of patriotism. This group operates an extensive Catholic lay press, both daily and periodical, publishes books, and operates a chain of stores ("Veritas") dealing in religious articles and in the purchase of gold and jewelry. In the aftermath of the disturbances of March 1968, the *Pax*

TABLE 6

Political Party and Organizational Affiliations
of Sejm (Parliament) Deputies, 1947–52 and 1961–65

	Number	Percentage
1947–52 Sejm		
Polish Socialist Party (PPS)	116	26.4
Polish Workers' Party—Communists (PPR)	114	26.0
People's Alliance (SL)	109	24.8
Democratic Alliance (SD)	41	9.3
Polish People's Alliance (PSL)	24	5.5
Polish People's Alliance "Nowe Wyzwolenie"	17	3.9
Labor Alliance (SP)	15	3.4
Catholic	3	.7
Total	439	100.0
1961–1965 Sejm		
United Polish Workers' Party (PPR-PPS merger)	256	55.6
United People's Alliance (SL, PSL, PSL-NW merger)	117	25.4
Democratic Alliance (SD)	39	8.5
Union of Rural Youth	6	1.3
Catholic "Znak"	5	1.1
Union of Socialist Youth	5	1.1
Independent Craft Associations	5	1.1
Christian Social Association	3	.7
Pax	3	.7
Union of Polish Scouting	1	.2
Other "nonpartisan" (representing occupa-tional/professional and civic associations)	20	4.3
Total	460	100.0

SOURCE: Based on material contained in *Polska Ludowa: Slownik encyklopedyczny* (Warsaw: Wiedza Powszechna, 1965), pp. 329–32.

group—in alliance with conservative elements of the UPWP—often took the initiative to spearhead the drive against such groups as "alienated intellectuals" and "Zionists." Similarly, after the Polish government, following the lead of the Soviet Union, broke off relations with Israel after that country's victory over the Arabs in the Six-Day War of June 1967, *Pax,* either having been given the "green light" or having sensed a permissive atmosphere, was the first to stage violent demonstrations of an anti-Jewish nature.

Nevertheless, it would be a mistake to assume that the *Sejm,* aside from the *Znak* deputies, is a wholly pliable body in the hands of the government and the party leadership. Voices of discontent or even protest are sometimes heard from the *Sejm* chambers, especially from deputies who feel the interests of the functional groups they represent threatened. Moreover, *Sejm* deputies who serve on various specialized *Sejm* commissions (for example, education and science, light industry) are in a position to affect policy in certain areas and to influence the character of policy implementation, especially on issues less crucial in nature, involving low levels of controversy, and on which the ruling party is ambiguous or undecided.

The system is, of course, supported by an extensive apparatus of coercion consisting of the internal security forces and the regular armed forces. Poles traditionally have admired dash and uniforms and parades, and the military organization is perceived by many as being neither Communist nor anti-Communist but primarily Polish and loyal to the fatherland. Soldiers and officers take pride in their epaulets and other trappings of rank and status. New folk songs extolling army life were added to those of long ago. If the professional army officer does not enjoy the high social prestige of his predecessor of the interwar period, it is only because the new professional army officer is (or is perceived to be) a son of the peasantry or the working class, whereas his forerunner was generally identified with the impoverished aristocracy. However, the new Army of People's Poland attempts to link itself to past Polish military tradition and the heroic exploits of Polish arms. Still with one foot in a pre-industrial, pre-technological age, the Pole takes great pride in his Army, modernized and mechanized as it is, equipped with sophisticated weaponry—a far cry from the cavalry-dominated army which faced the German armored divisions in September 1939 and was drowned in the blood of its horses and men on the banks of the Brda and Vistula rivers, the Mazovian Plain, in the defense of Warsaw. The contemporary Polish Army consists of four armored divisions, nine motorized, and one airborne division, and commands a peacetime component of 215,000 men, in addition to 45,000 troops in the militarized Internal Security Corps and Border Guards with their own armored units. The Air Force consists of another 50,000 and is well equipped with planes and ground-to-air missiles. The Polish Navy presently consists of five destroyers, eight submarines, minesweepers, landing vessels and other maritime material, and commands a personnel of 20,000.[21] The size of the Polish armed forces thus exceeds the strength of the other countries of the Warsaw Pact, except, of course, the Soviet Union. The duration of service is eighteen months for a conscript to the Army and three years for a recruit in the Air Force, the Navy, or the Special Forces. Courses in "defense preparedness" begin on the secondary-school level and continue through institutions of higher education. Male graduates (and female graduates of medical academies as well) are normally expected to enter the service upon completion of their studies and eventually, after further training, are awarded a reserve commission.

Although the period between the Six-Day War in 1967 and the

disturbances of March 1968 witnessed purges among high-ranking officers, especially of the Air Force—allegedly for expressed professional admiration for their Israeli counterparts—the military are generally perceived as being loyal to the system. By training and by occupation they are wedded to the system, as it were. Being, for the most part, of middle- or lower-class background, indeed sons of the working class and peasantry, they may feel a sense of gratitude to a system which has offered them opportunity for service, as well as education, status, and rank denied to those of their background by preceding systems. Whether in a true crisis-situation the Army of People's Poland will meet the system's expectation and withstand the test is, of course, hard to predict —but the professionals of the Army have a stake in perpetuating the system and the established authority, especially so long as the supreme sacrifice is not demanded of them nor is ever likely to be.

The Search for a Modus Vivendi

If the military tradition has been absorbed and assimilated into the new systemic ethos, if a quasi-parliament has been continued under the old parliament's name, if a bureaucracy has developed with a value system and with a way of doing things similar to the pre-systemic bureaucracy, the position of the church is much more complex and ambiguous. For generations the concepts of "Pole" and of "Catholic" were seen as synonymous, and Poles perceived themselves as the guardians in the Eastern part of the European continent of a Western and a Catholic civilization and culture, surrounded and threatened by hostile, non-Catholic forces. As in the case of others placed by fate and history at frontier outposts, their adherence to the faith was unyielding. Religion and nationhood came together and reinforced each other. Under the banner of the church and under the cross, the Poles expanded their boundaries and brought the pagans of vast Lithuania in the fourteenth century to the Roman fold. United into a commonwealth, the Polish-Lithuanian Union extended from the Baltic to the Black Sea, reaching almost to the gates of Moscow and deep into the lands of Bessarabia. Together the forces of the Union routed the Teutonic Knights at the battles of Grunwald and Tannenberg and were successful in keeping at bay the forces of Ivan the Terrible. What gave the commonwealth its solidity was a common religious faith. Catholicism was a national religion, providing national cohesiveness, and it was precisely this element in Polish culture and society which attracted Rousseau to the Poles.

Nevertheless, while the Orthodox czars of the East consolidated their power and grew stronger and more forceful, and the Protestants of the West and North—once satellites of Polish kings—grew bolder and more expansionist, the commonwealth and the kingdom disintegrated in factional strifes caused by conflicting economic interests and status anxieties. Prolonged periods of statelessness and partition followed, broken up only by periodic flights into romantic resistance and revolt which invariably ended in bloodshed and betrayal. However, even during the darkest moments of Polish history the church maintained itself not only as the continuator of the faith but also as the guardian of traditional national and cultural values, so much so that the defector from the Catholic Church was considered to be a defector from the national community, a traitor to a patriotic cause. Such conditions brought the church hierarchy into politics—a role it gladly accepted—and it placed the church in the position of being the spokesman for the nation, especially in times of troubles. Naturally also, under such circumstances, religion itself came to be perceived as a collectivistic, sociopolitical category rather than a deep-penetrating system of beliefs and morals which would guide individual conduct, even intimate personal behavior. The Pole was thus able to separate his own personal conduct and his attitude towards persons of other nationality and religion from his own loyalty to church and religion, and to see no conflict between the two. The church to him became a political institution; his love was for the pomp and the liturgy; he managed to internalize the catechism rather than the moral principles of the Bible.

This position of the Catholic Church brought the hierarchy into conflict with secular political authorities, since both the hierarchy and the secular authorities competed for the role of national spokesman and for the supreme place on the loyalty scale of the nation. But whereas past secular political authorities sought legitimization in religion and in God—while often struggling with the hierarchy for power—the present formal political authority seeks legitimization in an ideology which is philosophically opposed to the ideational and metaphysical premises of the church and in an array of symbols rooted in a diverse world outlook. The two forces, that represented by the church, on the one hand, and that represented by the party, on the other, seem therefore to be pitted against each other as never before. The problem becomes more complicated from the point of view of the secular political authority, because, unlike the clergy in other East European countries, the Polish clergy remained loyal to the cause of independence during the years of Nazi occupation and cannot be charged, as elsewhere, with betrayal, although the political leadership attempts from time to time to charge the religious leadership with being more loyal to the Vatican than to Warsaw.

The present system tries consciously to establish for itself an image of being secular, divorced from church and religion. Since 1948 questions regarding religious identification have been omitted from the census and from official personal documents (birth certificates, draft books, passports, and so forth); in 1949 a secular oath replaced the religious one in the courts and in 1950 the same thing was done in the armed forces.

In many ways smaller religious denominations which lacked legal status before the establishment of People's Poland enjoy toleration, and their practices are constitutionally guaranteed. The constitution also prohibits the spreading of religious animosities or the propagation of ideas hostile to the state under the guise of religious preaching.

Yet, the Catholic Church remains, as it always has been, a powerful social and political force, and the political authorities tacitly acknowledge the extent of the church's influence. Thus, when the Polish cities were still in ruins in the immediate aftermath of World War II, great energy and resources were expended in rebuilding damaged church structures and in carefully moving whole church buildings if their location interfered with new urban plans. The church can frustrate such administrative decisions as those calling for widening of streets and highways by refusing to relinquish some of its property which is in the way, and the authorities are reluctant to force a showdown. In the villages peasants, including members of National Councils, will donate their labor, scarce material, and hard-earned zlotys in order to erect a new church structure, while the schools—symbols of the secular political system—suffer from disrepair and old age. Faced with official animosity, however, the hierarchy grows more stubborn and conservative, and as a rule the Polish clergy opposes the various liberalizing measures demanded by the clergy elsewhere, including introduction of the vernacular into the liturgy.

However, when faced with the popular revolt against persistent Stalinist patterns and Soviet overlordship and when confronted with the choice of further inflaming rebellious national passions and courting massive Soviet reprisals or, alternately, of reaching some kind of modus vivendi with the more liberal elements of the UPWP, Cardinal Stefan Wyszynski chose the latter route and threw his support behind Wladyslaw Gomulka. What followed that October 1956 could indeed be described as a honeymoon in church-party relations. However, such a honeymoon could not last long since the union was basically one of convenience and made in response to very tangible but momentary external threats by a common enemy. Moreover, many Poles, especially young Poles, flooded to the church, seeing in it a center of opposition and symbol of national resistance, and viewing the institution of religion as having emerged suffering but unblemished from the period of Stalinist repression. The teaching of catechism was introduced on a voluntary basis in the public schools, although the priest teaching it lacked formal faculty status. Crosses and holy pictures appeared on railroad stations and other official buildings. Attendance at catechism and service in church became a manifestation of political defiance, of continuing revolt, adding strength to the political posture of the hierarchy but threatening, at the same time, the position of the party. Children of Communists, atheists, agnostics, or even Jews, who chose not to attend lectures on catechism in the schools were singled out and often made the objects of ridicule by peers. Almost in self-defense, in order to preserve its own increasingly threatened authority, the party and the government grew increasingly conservative, hostile, and quite consciously launched upon a policy of stealing, as it were, the nationalistic and traditional "patriotic" thunder from the church. And by the end of the fifties, religious instruction was eliminated from the public schools, restricting priestly activities to church grounds only.

The celebrations commemorating the Millenium of Polish Christianity and nationhood in 1966 provided an occasion which brought the opposing forces into open confrontation since both the church and the party made equal claims to that thousand-year heritage. In connection with these celebrations, Professor Konstanty Grzybowski wrote: "The Polish church hierarchy assumes that since the Poles are a Catholic nation it has the right to speak on behalf of that nation and to forgive the enemies in its name."[22]

And Gomulka charged at a mass meeting that it is not the party and the political leadership which is "countering the Millenium of baptism with the Millenium of statehood but rather it is the episcopate, and particularly Cardinal Wyszynski, who want to place the Millenium of baptism in opposition to People's Poland."[23]

The charge of "forgiving the enemies" was made when the Polish hierarchy extended, in a spirit of conciliation, an invitation to the German bishops to participate in the Millenium celebrations. The German clergy responded by saying in effect that, while they would be delighted to participate in the event, they could not forget the plight of the Germans expelled from their "ancient homes" in the western territories annexed by Poland after World War II in compensation for the territories lost in the East. However, neither the Polish hierarchy's offer to the Germans to "forgive and forget" nor the German reply could satisfy Poles, whose memories of the wounds brought on by the war and occupation are still fresh and who are in a mood neither to forgive nor to forget. The political authorities were quick to seize upon this invitation and appeal to popular resentments. And many Poles, although faithful to the Catholic Church, indeed resented the exchange of letters between the Polish and the German bishops. However, in the final analysis, this resentment did not quite radically change Polish attitudes towards the two competing authorities, which remained stubbornly at odds. When on April 17, 1966, at an open-air mass held at the Cathedral Square in Poznan, a city of traditional nationalism, Archbishop Antoni Baraniak in the presence of Cardinal Wyszynski and the rest of the Polish espiscopate delivered this prayer: "We plead with you, God, Father of Nations . . . grace with your blessings the temporal authority of Polish society so that it may indeed become the servant of truth and peace, justice and love," it only aggravated further the ire of that authority, since it interpreted the prayer as a refusal to accept "the Republic which is."[24]

Yet, young and old continue to attend church service, and children of party dignitaries are often, without the knowledge of their busy fathers, taken to Sunday school by their faithful mothers, grandmothers, or aunts; holy pictures adorn the homes of officials; and at First Communion time it is almost impossible to make an appointment with the photographer, who is all booked for portraits of youngsters in communion attire. Moreover, the influence and informal pull of the parish priest can often work wonders in getting a child admitted to a certain school, gaining scarce dormitory space for him, or even in obtaining a job for a "good" Catholic who frequently is competing for the position against a member of the UPWP who is without official party endorsement. Connections, pull, or what the Poles call *"protekcja"* means a great deal in that society, status conscious and socially tradition oriented as it is, and any kind of organized or semi-organized support stands the individual in good stead when competing against someone with no sponsorship at all. The church can informally affect decisions in areas where the party is either indifferent or not too committed to a particular decisional outcome. UPWP members frequently complain that within various institutions of the government and within the enterprises and trade unions Catholic "cabals" are "conspiring" to push their "own" for choice positions or privilege and that such activities amount, in effect, to subtle but quite conscious discrimination against party rank-and-file.

Whatever the veracity of these allegations, the Catholic Church remains a visible and organized center of real or perceived opposition. Moreover, the church has the advantage over the party in that it can link itself to a tradition which it continued and symbolized in the national consciousness without interruption, while the party is a relative newcomer to the political culture, still seeking its foothold. Yet, neither can afford to push the other to the brink, and there is evidence of a *renewed modus vivendi.* Such accommodation can come about on the basis of *shared values, and these are national in character and conservative in orientation.* There is further indication that *wherever the church and the party in Poland are forced into prolonged coexistence, it is the latter which is eventually compelled to "bend" and to compromise its rigidity and ideological purity.* But there is also evidence that the more pragmatic "wheelhorses" of the UPWP, especially the middle-level cadres in the big towns and provinces, do not really mind the compromise so long as authority patterns in which they have an interest and stake are maintained. And under the pressure of these middle-level cadres, the top party leadership itself may lessen its ideology-rooted expectations and settle on "socialist patriotism" and "morality" which is socialist in language but quite traditional and Catholic in nature.

The Party: Conflict and Solidarity

The Communists, once persecuted and forced into illegal existence, are presently in power. They are now organized in a mass party, and as such they attract people who themselves are not "socialized" into the normative values of the system, who join not because they share the party's ideological goals and objectives but rather for reasons more prosaic in nature, such as career, economic security, and authority. Having reached the ranks of the UPWP for reasons non-ideological in character, the younger members are less concerned over the maintenance of ideological purity and suffer fewer qualms—if any at all—when the party deviates from its lofty programmatic purposes in the process of everyday government than do the older party veterans, the idealists, whose motives for joining were altruistic in nature and who suffer disappointments in the face of the realities of power. However, from the standpoint of purely organizational interests and the maintenance of the UPWP as an authority symbol, the former are more reliable and trustworthy than the latter. The non-idealists have a stake in advancing the party's power and authority since they advance their own power and authority with it. The UPWP is serving them merely as a vehicle and a convenient form of legitimization. The non-idealists, in effect, are the mainstay of the system, of the status quo. Authority-oriented, they tend to be conservative, prudish, traditionalist, culturally and nationalistically introspective, suspicious of those who would "rock the boat," cast doubts, experiment, question or deviate in politics, in art, sex or whatever. They become the guardians of a conventional morality. They also become the party's bureaucrats and in Poland they are referred to as *"tepaki,"* literally meaning "dullards" but serving as the equivalent to the term "party hack" in American political jargon. In 1964 only thirty-four percent of the party membership belonged to the pre-1948 organizations, the Polish Communist Party and the Polish Socialist Party, prior to merger.

The number of "old-timers" is diminishing, however, time taking its toll. In addition to time, disappointment with reality has also taken its toll among those who joined the movement during the war or earlier, when such act carried more risk than personal benefit. Some of the veterans have left the ranks voluntarily, others have been purged—and among the latter were many Communists of Jewish descent who somehow survived the war and who had attained leadership positions because of their education and skill as well as long service in the party. The prewar Polish Communist Party (liquidated by the Comintern in the thirties on the order of Stalin and then recreated as the Polish Workers' Party during World War II) indeed contained within its ranks a disproportionate number of persons of ethnic minority background. A Jewish worker, for example, blocked from access to industrial employment and condemned to a marginal ghetto existence, or an intellectual of a minority group, particularly Jewish, frustrated in educational opportunities, professional advancement or government employment in prewar Poland, could have become attracted to the Communists—what with their universalistic promise of salvation and solution to all problems—both for reasons rooted in ethnocentric considerations as well as in dialectic reasoning and intellectual commitment to ideals which transcend purely personal and existential motives. Their motives for joining the movement, however, are placed under doubt once the party is in power and needing closer identification with the masses of the ethnically dominant core group, the "true Poles," who were always suspicious of the religiously, ethnically, and culturally "alien." While the prewar Polish Communist Party annually celebrated the "Day of the Three L's"—Lenin, Liebknecht, and Rosa Luxemburg—a nationalistically oriented party bureaucrat, such as Andrzej Werblan would currently criticize the old party tradition and its old leadership as suffering from the heritage of "Luxemburgism." What he would mean would be that Rosa Luxemburg (daughter of the Polish-Jewish middle class, a contemporary of Lenin, often in disagreement with him but one of the leaders of the Polish radical Left and, after migration to Germany, a leader of the German Left; murdered together with Karl Liebknecht by German *Junkers* while imprisoned in 1919) joined the revolution for specifically "Jewish reasons" alone. This would imply that Jews become Communists only because they are Jews and thus for a rationale different from that compelling ethnically pure Poles to join the party, and that by ridding itself of the heritage of "Luxemburgism" the party could come closer to the traditional values, aspirations, and norms of the Polish masses.[25]

Polish-Jewish relations have always represented a complex web of love and hatred, feelings of warmth and suspicion. Postwar Polish literature and films attest to the depth and complexity of this relationship and the deep-seated guilt. The Poles saw "their" Jews slaughtered en masse, and they witnessed the uprising of the Warsaw Ghetto in 1943—an uprising against a common German enemy in the midst of hopeless despair, doomed from the beginning partially due to the indifference of the majority of the racially "pure" populace. Anti-Semitism was thus simply not fashionable in People's Poland for a long time. However, first Khrushchev's rustic anti-Semitic humor, then the much more conscious toleration of anti-Semitic practices in the Soviet Union —partially in response to foreign policy exigencies—and, finally, the break with Israel following the Six-Day War opened a flood of resentments which previously were hidden only skin deep. Ethnically pure Polish bureaucrats felt blocked in their upward mobility by Jews occupying high positions. Whereas in the past even criticism of individual Jews for their personal misconduct or lack of ability had to be couched in careful phrases lest it be interpreted as ideologically and officially frowned-upon anti-Semitism, the barriers were lowered, and accumulated hostilities of whatever kind could now be released under the guise of such terms as "anti-Zionism," and "cultural alienation."

By the end of 1963 the UPWP consisted of 1,491,100 members—that is 7.6 percent of the population over eighteen, the age of eligibility. In addition, there were at the time 2,900 candidate members waiting for admission. In June 1968 the party claimed a membership and candidate membership of 2,000,000—an increase of 506,000 persons in 4½ years. Although there are more females than males in the country, the ratio among full party members is close to five to one in favor of males, a result, no doubt, of the greater activism of the males, the persistence of traditional sociocultural prejudices which assign more passive roles to females, and a higher level of religiosity among women.

By the end of 1963 employees in such branches of the public economic sector as industry, the building trades, transportation and communication, and commerce, constituted fifty-two percent of the UPWP membership. Peasants constituted only a fraction of the membership and, interestingly enough, most of the peasant party members are engaged in private farming (of a total of 167,700 peasant members in 1963, only 6,900 belonged to state farms or collectives). More revealing, however, is a glance at how many within the various branches of the economy do belong to the party. Only 9.4 percent of those in the building trades are party members; only 14.3 percent of those employed in commercial enterprises of the public economic sector; only 16.1 percent of those in transportation and communication. On the other hand, 29.1 percent of those in intelligentsia professions are party members, and most of them teachers, due to higher pressures on that group. However, *the bulk of the UPWP membership, close to two-thirds, are bureaucrats directly engaged in governmental administration, and the ratio of their party membership goes up with the level of their bureaucratic activity and with rank.* It could therefore be said that the UPWP is an *organization of full-time bureaucrats who rule on behalf of the working class and the peasantry, aided in this task by an intelligentsia engaged primarily in the institutions of socialization of the system.*

While most of the basic party cells (64.9 percent) consist of fifteen members or less, only 25 percent of the membership belongs to these, reflecting the weak party foothold on the village and smalltown level as well as in the minor economic enterprises. On the other hand, 33.2 percent of the members belong to basic party cells of one hundred, and 18.5 percent belong to cells numbering four hundred or more members each. Attendance at party meetings is generally low unless, as during special occasions, attendance is compulsory. Large cell membership inhibits discussion and individual participation. Party cells operate within the various enterprises, institutions, and offices, as well as within the various military units. Yet many enterprises lack party cells, in which case a member will be assigned to a cell operating within a neighborhood block or the closest vicinity. In 1964, 13,000 villages lacked a party organization.

Table 7 indicates that the bulk of the membership is between the ages of twenty-five and forty-nine, that is, the ages of greatest economic productivity, competitiveness, and upward mobility. The ratio of young people (between the ages of eighteen and twenty-four) is low. The same table also reveals that the general educational level of the party membership is rather low, contributing to its cultural parochialism, anti-intellectual bias, and conservatism. Many UPWP members, even those of rank, utilize the many opportunities for adult education, but to most of them, it seems, party membership and political activism serve as substitutes for education and skill. That is, their claim to position is more frequently based on political criteria than on merits derived from skills acquired through education and training. The generally low level of education also places extra burdens on the members of intelligentsia professions, particularly teachers, who are assigned extra-organizational duties, more frequently than not of an auxiliary and ex-officio character, and must serve as back-up men to less educated and less skilled party officials of deeper roots within the community or of "desirable"—from an ideological point of view—class background.

TABLE 7

Age and Education of Members and Candidate Members of
United Polish Workers' Party (PZPR), as of December 31, 1963

	Number	Percentage
Age		
18–24	115,000	7.7
25–49	1,061,000	71.0
50 and older	318,000	21.3
Total	1,494,000	100.0
Education		
Elementary, not completed	298,800	20.0
Elementary, completed	776,880	52.0
Secondary	328,680	22.0
Higher	89,640	6.0
Total	1,494,000	100.0

SOURCE: Based on data in *Polska Ludowa: Slownik encyklopedyczny* (Warsaw: Wiedza Powszechna, 1965), pp. 241–46.

However, the party leadership is making special efforts to draw into the ranks of the UPWP and its own bureaucracy younger and better educated elements, especially of working-class and peasant background. They are to constitute the "New Intelligentsia." The most talented among these are sent to the party-maintained School of Social Science, which claims the status of an institution of higher learning. The extent to which such efforts may indeed be successful is indicated by the increase in intelligentsia membership in the party—in 1945 only 9.6 percent of the Polish intelligentsia belonged to the party, whereas by 1963–64 the percentage was 29.1, an increase of 19.5 percent. During the first quarter of 1966 alone, the UPWP accepted close to 46,500 new members of candidate members and 40 percent of these were twenty-five years of age or younger, mainly with a technical or general education.[26]

Life in the party, especially among the full-time functionaries but involving the rank-and-file members as well, is highly competitive and full of friction. In Cracow, for example, many first secretaries of large party cells failed to be reelected to their positions. An analysis indicated that most of the reasons were rooted in "personalized" grievances and animosities (for example, high-handedness, resentment of the membership toward a party secretary attempting to get promoted or obtain an academic title on the strength of his political connections, malfeasance in office, and extensive travel abroad).[27] Most of the frictions, however, are deeper and more ominous in nature, and involve the conflict of diverse vested interests, values, and outlooks on all levels of the party hierarchy.

Khrushchev's denunciation of Stalin has caused irrevocable damage to the very principle of leadership infallibility and to the authority of *the* leader. His own demise, in turn, in 1964 has deprived the entire top leadership echelon, as represented by the Politburo and the Secretariat, of the aura of immunity and has brought the middle cadre levels into a collective position of influence with which the leaders must reckon. As indicated before, the middle-level cadres are less interested in ideological subtleties or intellectual debate over alienation and the like than they are in problems of economic improvement of the standards of living—primarily their own—as well as in the preservation of the existing patterns of authority. As are middle classes in most other political systems, the "middle strata" of party officialdom in Poland is interested in the continuation of the status quo. It shares with the established and self-satisfied middle classes of bourgeois society a mistrust of all those who would question the established order, conventional morality, and the hallowed, traditional way of doing things. In common with the petty bourgeois, the middle-level party bureaucrat feels uncomfortable with intellectuals who, he suspects, may rock the boat, students who "naively" are disturbed over the gap between the normative order and the real world, the "long haired" who pursue unconventional life styles. In common, further, with the petty bourgeoisie, the middle strata of the Communist organizational establishment are nationalistic, chauvinistic, ethnocentric, and easy prey to slogans calling for animosity and hostility against alien targets—targets which change with political exigencies and may at one time be focused on Germans, at another time (openly) on Jews, Chinese, Czechoslovaks, or even Russians. They adhere to Marxism, but in a simple-minded manner, and are knowledgeable of Marxist literature in the same way as devout Catholics are knowledgeable of their catechism. To them Marxism is limited to the streamlined slogans contained in *The Communist Manifesto;* it is not to be found in the works of the young Marx, which the Marxist intellectual finds so disturbing.

This organizational middle class occupies a key position within the system because it contains the workhorses, as it were, not only within the administrative apparatus but also within the public sector of the economy, education, the media, and the armed forces. It feels very much akin to its organizational and socio-economic counterpart within the Soviet Union. However, while the Soviet bureaucrat and apparatchik still carries the scars of Stalinist terror (to which those in position of authority were the most exposed), the Polish bureaucrat's familiarity with that terror is relatively limited inasmuch as, while severe, it did not assume in Poland the dimensions it did in other East European countries, not to speak of the Soviet Union itself.

The middle-level party bureaucracy is more or less cohesive and united on basic values and common interests. To be sure, as already indicated, life is keenly competitive, and individuals are engaged in constant jockeying for position. The keenest competition, however, is at the highest level of leadership, where the authority rewards are also the greatest. The middle-level bureaucracy's power is thus further enhanced by the need of those at the top level to appeal to the middle strata for support in order to increase their own individual bargaining abilities.

Students, restless intellectuals, and members of the intelligentsia aided by broad social groupings, including those dominated by the Catholic Church, were instrumental in bringing Gomulka back to power in 1956 and thus, temporarily at least, were important in weakening the entrenched party bureaucracy. Subsequently, although Gomulka called a halt to the liberalization process, he nevertheless remained the symbol of liberalization and of the liberalization forces, and thus the thrust of General Mieczystaw Moczar, former Minister of the Interior, and his supporters (popularly known as "the partisans" since they draw upon the veterans of the country-based guerrilla organizations of which Moczar was a leader as opposed to those who spent the war years on foreign soil) are aimed against that symbol, the First Secretary of the UPWP. The student riots of March 1968, which came, as indicated, on the heels of the events in the Middle East of June 1967, and the liberalization in Czechoslovakia, strengthened the hand of the "partisans," since the situation called for harsher measures against those who would threaten the system in any manner.

Gomulka was caught in between. On the one hand, he too felt the system to be threatened by the rebelling students and intellectuals but, on the other, he also felt personally threatened by Moczar and his group. He had personal links to the old party ideologues, among whom were many Jewish intellectuals, but he was also fearful of the repercussions should they move too far along "revisionist" lines. Intellectually more akin to the "partisans," he nevertheless felt that he and his supporters would be among their victims in the event of an organizational reshuffle. While ideologically rejecting anti-Semitism—being molded by the old school of Communist internationalism—he had to "string along" with the "anti-Zionist" campaign in order to appease traditional prejudice and the pressures from below, and also because of Comecon solidarity and policy following the war in the Middle East, which called for a strong anti-Zionist and anti-Israeli position. As a result of these conflicting pulls, Gomulka had to give in on many ideological and personnel policy fronts in order to preserve his own position as well as that of his closest associates. In a Politburo and a Secretariat in which Jews once played a substantial role (highly disproportionate, to be sure, to the number of Jews left in the country), Gomulka managed to save only one of his former associates of Jewish descent, his own trusted intellectual, Artur Starewicz (who *did* spend the war years in the USSR, studying and working and for a short period sharing the fate of other Polish Jewish refugees in the USSR—"internment" in a camp in Uzbekistan).

However, what decided Gomulka's continuation in power was not his ability to maneuver between opposing factions but the attitude and the intervention of the post-Khrushchev Soviet leadership which saw him as "their man" in Warsaw, opposed to the *more Stalinist-oriented but also more nationalistically inclined "partisans"* of General Moczar. From one whose return to power the Soviet leadership under Khrushchev opposed bitterly in 1956, Gomulka became—given the available alternatives— the one whom Brezhnev and Kosygin preferred. While Gomulka's loy- alty was tested and proven over the years, that of Moczar remained an unknown and thus risky quantity. Unlike Khrushchev, the Soviet leader- ship in 1970 is not inclined towards experimentation, neither in foreign nor in personnel policy. Their primary interest is the preservation of the existing order and status quo within their hegemony. From the viewpoint of the Moscow hierarchy, while the middle-level Polish bureaucracy led by Moczar was also committed to the status quo, their resort to Polish nationalist symbols sounded rather disturbing. The joint military inter- vention in Czechoslovakia—against a liberal non-Moscow-dominated version of Communism—an invasion in the planning and execution of which Gomulka, along with Walter Ulbricht of the German Democratic Republic and Janos Kadar of Hungary played crucial roles, served further to cement the position of the First Secretary of the United Polish Workers' Party.

In the meantime, members of the middle-level bureaucracy—ethni- cally and nationally "clean"—managed to move into positions from which Jews and assorted "revisionists" were expelled. While Moczar himself experienced a setback in his bid for increased power, the spirit of "Moczarism" has survived and become more deeply entrenched, and, at the same time, the old-line Gomulka leadership has also preserved its authority. To maintain and strengthen itself in its position, the leader- ship adheres to an arsenal of ideologically correct verbal symbols, but it mixes these with symbols rooted in the traditional political culture and traditional values and biases. To appease the various powerful interests, the system's leadership feels a need to operate with both these sets of symbols, stressing one over the other depending upon the occasion and the audience. Significantly, however, the lower one moves down the cadre ladder the more one discerns a deeper commitment to the values of national conservatism and a more pro-forma adherence to the ideology.

The Fifth Congress of the United Polish Workers' Party, which convened in November 1968, formalized the existing composition of the party hierarchy (Politiburo and Secretariat). This hierarchy, while manifesting a great deal of continuity and stability, (inasmuch as it perpetuates itself more or less unaltered) is reflective, however, of the arrangement of authority which is current, and it freezes, as it were, the top leadership contenders on basically their old, previously held positions. Some Gomulka followers were elevated to higher posts (for example, Jozef Tejchma and Stanislaw Kociolek, were moved up a notch in the hierarchy). Some identified with Moczar (most notably Wladyslaw Wicha) were demoted, while others, such as Jan Szydlak, and Stefan Olszowski were promoted. Mieczyslaw Moczar himself failed to gain full membership in the Politburo but was promoted nevertheless to alternate membership status. Of the eighteen persons constituting the top party leadership (that is, full or alternate members of the Politburo and members of the Central Committee Secretariat), eight (44.4 percent) are clearly identified with the Gomulka wing, four (22.2 percent) with the Moczarites. Gomulka can count on the support of people like Jozef Cyrankiewicz, the long-time Prime Minister and the acknowledged "brain" of the leadership as it stands in 1970; Zenon Kliszko, the First Secretary's closest comrade-in-arms; the young Stanislaw Kociolek (born in 1933) in whom many see Gomulka's heir apparent chosen by the leader himself; Ignacy Loga-Sowinski, the trade union leader; Marian Spychalski, the gifted architect turned party activist who attained the highest rank within the Polish armed forces and later became Chairman of the State Council; Jozef Tejchma, who made his way to the United Polish Workers' Party via the peasant movement; and Artur Starewicz, the lone Jewish intellectual left in the exclusive leadership circle. As of 1970, among the Moczar supporters are Ryszard Strzelecki, a former vocational school teacher; Jan Szydlak, whose entire career has been limited to party-held posts, although he joined the party only after it attained power; and Stefan Olszowski, another former teacher. Three of those within the top UPWP leadership (or 16.7 percent) pursue very much an independent role, maneuvering their way among the competing factions while at the same time building up their personal power bases. These are Edward Gierek, the leader of the *wojewodztwo* organization in Katowice, the wealthiest and most urbanized and industrialized region of Poland, a man who is identified with the elite of industrial managers and technologues; Stefan Jedrychowski, a well-known prewar Communist youth leader and economic planner, who has been elevated to the post of Polish Minister of Foreign Affairs; and Boleszaw Jaszczuk, a former teacher and trained electrical engineer with close ties to the Soviet technocratic elite. The factional loyalty of three other Politburo-Secretariat members (Wladyslaw Kruczek, Mieczyslaw Jagielski, and Piotr Jaroszewicz) is unknown, although the likelihood is that they support Gomulka. Only one of the well-identified Moczar supporters, Ryszard Strzelecki, is a full member of the most powerful Political Bureau.

Of greater significance is the fact that only four of the eighteen top leaders (22.2 percent) were charged with "nationalist-revisionist" deviation during the Stalinist period which ended in October 1956 with Gomulka's return to power. These were Kliszko, Loga-Sowinski, and Spychalski, in addition to Gomulka himself, and only three of them, Gomulka, Kliszko, Spychalski, suffered imprisonment and physical torture during that period. Not surprisingly then, these three form the most cohesive and mutually supportive group among the old leadership. The fourth, the trade-union leader Loga-Sowinski, although charged with heresies during the Stalinist-Bierut period and deprived of his direct party posts, was nevertheless delegated to a trade-union leadership position in the provinces and sent to study at the Central Party School, after which he assumed the post of Secretary of the Central Trade Union Council in 1954. The others maintained themselves in high positions throughout the Stalinist-Bierut period. Thus, for example, the prewar Socialist (non-Communist) leader, Jozef Cyrankiewicz, has held the posts of Prime Minister or Vice-Premier alternately since 1947, Stefan Jedrychowski was identified with the central economic planning organs before and after 1956, Wladyslaw Kruczek held similar high provincial party posts since 1951, Strzelecki continued as Minister or Vice-Minister of Transportation since 1949, Mieczyslaw Jagielski alternated between heading the UPWP Central Committee Agricultural Department or the similarly functional government ministry since 1952, and Jaroszewicz served as Vice-Chairman of the Council of Ministers without interruption since 1952. The break from Stalinism did not disrupt the career patterns of Mieczyslaw Moczar, of Jan Szydlak, or of Artur Starewicz, although Gomulka's return to power might have shifted them from one high post to another (in the case of Starewicz, for example, it meant moving from the job of Secretary of the Central Trade Union Council to that of assistant editor of the Central Committee organ, *Trybuna Ludu*). Whatever the "Polish October" meant to the intellectuals and reformers or to the rebelling youth, in terms of authority and power the pattern was one of continuity, despite the facts that a new man assumed top leadership position and a promise of changes to come was in the air.

Similarly, despite the rumblings of the middle-level party bureaucracy in 1968 and its attempt to upset, however slightly, the top leadership structure (Starewicz, for example, was defeated originally as candidate for delegate—one of forty-five from the district—to the 1968 Fifth Congress of the UPWP by the anti-Gomulka forces in Zielona Gora, the area whose organization he was supposed to represent at the Congress), this structure remains substantially unchanged. Yet the leadership had to assure its security by continuing to placate the middle-level cadres' hunger for jobs and economic benefits, and this was partially achieved, as indicated, through the purge of Jews and others and the subsequent creation of job vacancies as well as by the leadership's adoption of a more conservative, nationalistic, and parochial line in matters of culture and the resort to administrative measures more reminiscent of the Stalinist era than of the "reforms" of the Polish October. These measures were necessary, in part, in order to assure the system's middle strata that the existing patterns of authority in which they had a stake would remain undisturbed and protected from various dissident elements. And in this the party functionaries found allies among those within the broader society whose commitment to authority and traditionalism transcends formal and official systemic ideology (that is, the traditional conservatives and the right wing within Polish society). These citizens legitimize their position in terms of their adherence to patriotism—a value they subscribe to regardless of who is in power or in the name of what or on whose behalf such power is exercised.

Basically, despite fluctuations in domestic policy, the political elite which emerged and established itself in power during the period of Stalin and under the leadership of Boleslaw Bierut (Stalin's man in Poland after whom the university at Wroclaw is still named) remains in command. As in other Communist systems, from time to time this elite has to ward off threats to its power—sometimes from liberal intellectuals, sometimes from experts or others. The problem of "Red" vs. "Expert" is not unknown in Poland. In a real confrontation: in a contest in which authority is at stake, "politics" invariably emerges superior to "expertise." Ideally, from the system's point of view, its future and security would be assured when the experts would be politically loyal and the loyal would be technically expert. In the meantime, however, while not all experts are "political" and not all politicians have the needed technical skills, what has emerged and has taken charge of the system is an alliance of the technocratic managerial elite and the party-governmental bureaucracy, especially of middle level.

Gone are the days when ideologues held power and enjoyed the esteem of the party's rank-and-file. Those who occupy power today—those who staff the bureaus, offices, and economic enterprise posts—are not Communist idealists but the *tepaki* referred to earlier in this chapter. Their commitment is to the system as an established authority structure rather than to the particular ideology. The ideology merely serves them as a legitimizing mantle for the authority they jealously guard. The old-line ideologue, the doctrinaire, the purist of socialist or Communist morality is viewed by the technocratic-bureaucratic alliance as a potential threat, a disturbing factor. The fact that so many ideologues are Jews has made the task of dislocating them easier. They, the ideologues and the "purists" of socialist morality, are looked upon as people who have "the mind of Marx and the heart of Cato," the Roman censor. Not that the presence of the ideologues disturbs the conscience of the authority-oriented elite, but they make life uncomfortable and they stir up waves, especially among the young who have been socialized through the schools and youth organizations into the normative values and goals of the system and thus are expecting more from it.

Although Khrushchev was no Lenin, he was one of the few within the post-Stalinist leadership who at least had a physical connection with the revolutionary experience and an emotional affinity for the old visions it conjured. The same cannot be said about Kosygin and Brezhnev. If anything, they symbolize the alliance in the Soviet Union of the party, government, and managerial bureaucracies. Their equivalents are in power in Poland, and, like the Soviet model, those in Poland are nationalistic, conservative, status-quo-oriented, culturally and esthetically narrow, and committed to the system as an authority structure, a structure of power, rather than one of beliefs and values which would set the world on fire. Setting the world on fire is the last thing they want, having found the world as is rather comfortable to live in. Not having themselves deeply internalized a "socialist consciousness," they suspect the sincerity and the loyalty of others and are disturbed over *nonconventional* professions of faith. Perhaps they do not believe that some might have developed a deeply felt socialist consciousness devoid of cynicism. Rather than a "socialist consciousness"—the *internalization of a set of moral values, norms, and beliefs rooted in the ideology and in the particular philosophical world outlook* and giving rise to instinctive "socialist" behavior patterns—they merely expect and seek to extract from the environment the assimilation of a "legal consciousness." The latter is based upon *conformity to the established rules and laws of behavior,* and such conformity is further assured through the application of a whole array of administrative measures, backed up with appropriate sanctions against nonconformers.[28]

As George Bernard Shaw remarked after his visit to Russia in 1931: "When the revolution triumphs, revolution becomes counterrevolution."[29]

4

Bulgaria Under Zhivkov

Marin V. Pundeff

Country Profile: THE PEOPLE'S REPUBLIC OF BULGARIA

Head of State: Georgi Traikov, Chairman of the Presidium of the National Assembly
Premier: Todor Zhivkov, Chairman of the Council of Ministers
First Secretary, Central Committee of the Bulgarian Communist Party: Todor Zhivkov

Party Membership (1966): 611,179 (Candidate membership was abolished in 1966)[2]
Armed Forces (1969): 154,000 (Army: 125,000; Navy: 7,000; Air Force: 22,000)[2]
Population (1968): official estimate: 8,404,000 (Sofia: 950,676)[3]
Area: 110,912 square kilometers (42,729 square miles)
Population Density: 76 per square kilometer (194 per square mile)
Birth Rate (1968): 16.9 per thousand[4]
Death Rate (1968): 8.6 per thousand[4]
Divorce Rate (1968): 1.2 per thousand[5]
Gross Material Product (1968): 21.63 billion leva ($18.49 billion at official rate)[6]
National Income Total (1968): 8.56 billion leva ($7.32 billion at official rate)[6]
National Income by Sectors (1967):[6]
  Industry: 49.0%
  Construction: 9.0%
  Agriculture: 25.0%
  Transportation and Communications: 5.0%
  Trade: 9.0%
  Other: 3.0%
Foreign Trade by Area (1968):[7]
  Socialist Countries (including USSR): 77.6%
  USSR: 54.2%

Foreign Trade by Commodity (1968):[8]	Export	Import
Machinery, capital goods	24.5%	44.4%
Industrial consumer goods	21.7%	6.9%
Raw materials, semi-finished products	24.1%	44.6%
Comestibles	29.7%	4.1%

SOURCES:
1. *Spravochnik na propagandista i agitatora 1967* (Sofia: Nauka i izkustvo, 1968), p. 3.
2. *The Military Balance 1969–1970* (London: The Institute of Strategic Studies, 1969), p. 12.
3. *Statisticheski godishnik na Narodna Republika Bulgariya 1969* (Sofia: Nauka i izkustvo, 1969), pp. 18 and 405.
4. *Ibid.,* p. 21.
5. *Ibid.,* p. 64.
6. *Ibid.,* p. 87.
7. *Ibid.,* pp. 310–311.
8. *Ibid.,* pp. 307–308.

4. Bulgaria Under Zhivkov

Marin V. Pundeff

Within the context of Bulgarian developments, the years since 1962 represent the period when Todor Zhivkov, First Secretary of the Bulgarian Communist Party (BCP) since 1954, completed his victory in the intense intra-party struggles following Stalin's death and, already in effective control of the party, took as the new Prime Minister direct control of the government as well.[1] Although 1970 party historiography extends the Zhivkov period back to the so-called April Plenum of 1956, at which Zhivkov emerged as the spokesman of the new line from Moscow,[2] the first part of the Zhivkov era has a lesser impact on Bulgarian politics than the second part. The developments since 1962 clearly bear his imprint and represent a process with a certain cohesion and unity which has not been dealt with in the literature.

The Leadership

Whatever Zhivkov's other achievements may be, he has proved to be the most durable of Bulgaria's Communist leaders in the postwar era. Georgi Dimitrov, the leader of the party in exile and renowned Secretary-General of the Comintern, was in poor health when he returned to Bulgaria and died in 1949. Vasil Kolarov, also of Comintern fame, was even older than Dimitrov and died a few months after him. Vulko Chervenkov, the third in the line of succession, a brother-in-law of Dimitrov, and a Stalinist lackey for twenty years in the Soviet Union, was a younger man (born in 1900) with a great future when he took over in 1950, but the death of his mentor in 1953 and the emergence of a "New Course" in the USSR made him a man of the past and brought his career to a close in 1956. Zhivkov alone has had an uninterrupted rise since 1944 and a period of rule longer than those of his predecessors.

Zhivkov's rise and durability as a leader naturally evoke the question of why he has succeeded where others have failed and how he has done it. To begin with, in origin, mentality, and appearance (save for expensive suits), Zhivkov is a typical Bulgarian from the provinces. Born on September 7, 1911, in a poor peasant family from Bulgaria's heartland (the village of Pravets, forty-five miles northeast of Sofia), he moved like many other country lads to the capital in search of a better life. By 1929 he had become a printer's apprentice in the State Printing Office and completed his high school education as an external student. The following year he joined the Komsomol (Communist Youth League) of the outlawed Bulgarian Communist Party and soon became its secretary for the State Printing Office. In 1932, at twenty-one years of age, he was admitted into the party and made secretary of its unit in the printing office. The same year he was elected a member of the party's committee for the second urban district of Sofia. Two years later he was its secretary and a member of the party's committee for the entire region of Sofia. By 1934, he had begun a career as a party functionary in the capital of the country.

The next seven years, to 1941, however, were a period in which, if we are to believe the official biography, Zhivkov did nothing worth recording. Where he was and what he did in these years remain open questions. There is no basis for conjecturing that he spent some of them in the Soviet Union or fighting in the Spanish civil war; if he had, the fact would have been stressed, for the biographies of party functionaries as a rule make much of such training and experience. More plausible is the explanation that the intense police repression during this period, the crises in the party, and the contradictions between the line coming from Moscow and the views of local leaders induced inactivity. It is also likely that on occasion he had zigged where Traicho Kostov, then Secretary of the Central Committee and in charge of party affairs in the country, had wished him to zag. Young and inexperienced, he may have been often confused and rejected.[3]

In 1941, the official biography reports him as party secretary for the Iuchbunar district in Sofia, a working-class neighborhood in the capital. As the Stalingrad victory infused new confidence in Communist ranks, the Central Committee of the party undertook to organize existing guerrilla detachments in a unified "People's Liberation Insurgent Army" to operate under a central command and in twelve "Insurgent Operation Zones," each with its own command unit. In early 1943, the command of the First Zone (the Sofia region) dispatched Zhivkov to his native area to organize the guerrilla activity there. His efforts focused on the so-called Chavdar Brigade, which became the principal guerrilla arm of the party leadership in Sofia for sabotage, raids, and intimidation around the capital. Zhivkov, it would appear, shuttled between brigade units and the central command in Sofia, maintaining the necessary liaison. In July 1944, he was named Deputy Commander of the zone and as such had a key role in the seizure of power on September 9, 1944.

In fact, 1970 party historiography allots him the central role in the preparation and execution of the coup. As head of a committee of four, Zhivkov is said to have been entrusted with the coordination of all preparations and activities and to have carried out the operational liaison in the course of the takeover. After the operation in Sofia was completed, he took charge of organizing the so-called people's militia made up of party functionaries, security men arriving from the Soviet Union, and partisans to replace the old police. Under his direction the militia in Sofia became the security arm of the new regime and rounded up for execution and imprisonment thousands of avowed and alleged fascists and enemies of Communism in Bulgaria. The commander of the Soviet troops in Bulgaria, General S. S. Biriuzov, remembered him as the political commissar of the Chavdar brigade who directed the coup in Sofia and, although only thirty-three years old, the focus of "seething activity."[4]

In the ensuing years Zhivkov's rise in the Sofia party machine was steady. In 1945, he was made a candidate member of the Central Committee, and he became a regular member in 1948. In 1948–49, when the hunt of Titoists began, he was in charge of the Central Committee's department for organizational and instructional work. In addition, he ran the party's committee for the city of Sofia (as its secretary) and headed the municipal council. In these positions he was in charge of party cadres and in effect the boss of Sofia, much in the same way as Khrushchev had at one time been the boss of Moscow under Stalin. Chervenkov, who conducted the purge of the party and executed Traicho Kostov and others for Titoism and nationalist leanings, found in Zhivkov a younger man of proven Stalinist record, loyal to Moscow, and eager to please. While the purge decimated the older leadership, Zhivkov became one of Chervenkov's secretaries in the party general secretariat (January 1950), took complete charge of the Sofia city and region, and was even co-opted candidate member of the Politburo which Chervenkov picked. Feeling that he had nothing to fear from the pliant and inconspicuous young *apparatchik* (Zhivkov's abilities as an inspiring leader and speaker are modest), Chervenkov raised him to regular membership in the Politburo in 1951. His rise to the top as one of Chervenkov's protégés marked him in the agonized party as a hench-man of the new leader. After the death of Stalin, when changes were required from Moscow to pacify and revitalize the party, Chervenkov felt it safe to yield to Zhivkov the functions of Secretary-General (or First Secretary, as the post was renamed in imitation of the change in Moscow), while retaining those of Prime Minister.[5]

Events proved Chervenkov's judgment wrong. Just as the separation of functions in the Soviet Union led to the downfall of Malenkov and the emergence of Khrushchev, in Bulgaria it made easier the removal of Chervenkov and the elevation of Zhivkov, his eventual accuser, to the job of Moscow's man in Sofia. The process took several years to complete. Chervenkov's cause was not helped by the intense dislike he and Khrushchev apparently had for each other, but while the struggle for power was still unresolved in Moscow, he remained the leader in Sofia. With Khrushchev's emergence as the victor and his policy of appeasing Tito, however, Chervenkov's fate was sealed. His opponents in the party were encouraged, under the formulas of "bringing the party leadership closer to life," "democratizing political life," and "enforcing socialist legality," to question the abuses and crimes, especially the use of terror within the party, perpetrated in the years of Chervenkov's leadership and to put through some remedial measures such as amnesty for "persons convicted in the so-called trials of Traicho-Kostovites" and Agrarian leaders and review the activities of the Ministry of Internal Affairs. If party historiography is to be believed, this was accomplished "primarily because of the pressure exerted by the healthy forces in the Central Committee" headed by Zhivkov, who "as First Secretary in-creasingly welded them together and sought to overcome the cult of personality methods in work and leadership."[6] The climax came in the wake of the Twentieth Congress in Moscow when it became necessary, because of Chervenkov's adamant opposition to the Khrushchev line, to remove him from power. Yielding the post of Prime Minister to Yugov, however, Chervenkov remained a member of the Politburo of the party and Deputy Prime Minister.

The so-called April Plenum of 1956, at which Zhivkov triumphed over Chervenkov, is now viewed as the opening of a new era in the evolution of the Communist regime. As in the USSR, however, what was opened at first was a Pandora's box of grudges, feuds, and policy conflicts—some dating back to the 1920s, others from the coming to power in 1944—which Dimitrov's prestige and Chervenkov's repressive methods had kept within bounds. They now broke out in general and bitter factionalism. Since neither Chervenkov's removal nor Zhivkov's victory was complete, the two and their factions remained locked in a prolonged struggle. A third faction developed around Yugov, the new Prime Minister, who continued to see in Zhivkov a junior man and a former subordinate without experience in a top government position. (As Minister of Internal Affairs in 1944–48, Yugov had had charge of the militia throughout the country, while Zhivkov had performed subordinate responsibilities for the city and region of Sofia.) Yugov was also the natural spokesman for many party functionaries, high and low, who had been hurt in the Traicho Kostov affair—concocted, as they saw it, in Bulgaria by Chervenkov with the help of men like Zhivkov and finally exposed as one of the crimes of the Stalin era.

The fourth faction to form in the fluid situation was led by Georgi Chankov, a product of the Lenin Comintern Academy who had returned to Bulgaria in 1933. After 1944, Chankov became one of three secretaries of the party (the other two were Kostov and Chervenkov), with responsibility for party cadres, and as such preceded Zhivkov in this area of party work. Chervenkov, who knew Chankov in the Soviet Union, made him Deputy Prime Minister and his right-hand man. Like his former boss and Yugov, Chankov tended to regard Zhivkov as a junior apparatchik who had much less basis than himself for high pretensions. Beyond these four identifiable factions, there were—in the language of the party history—"unstable petty bourgeois elements" whose "rudderless behavior" became a "principal menace to the unity of the Party." In a number of places "revisionism" reared its head.[7] In plainer language, a substantial portion of the membership of the party hoped and demanded that the new era replace Stalinist dogmatism with liberalism and the dictatorship of the proletariat with democracy.

The struggles inside the party in 1956 released, as in Poland and Hungary, many inhibitions and stirred the intellectuals, long oppressed by the paralyzing controls, to demand freedom from party dictates. A "writers' revolt" grew to such proportions that when the upheaval in Hungary turned into a revolution, the warring Bulgarian leaders closed ranks and even assigned Chervenkov to quell the agitation of the intellectuals. Having weathered the storm, however, they resumed the infighting and by July 1957, Zhivkov—increasingly enjoying the support of Khrushchev, who defeated his own opponents the preceding June—scored a new victory. Like Khrushchev, he succeeded in isolating and routing an "anti-party group" led by Chankov. Holding Khrushchev's confidence, Zhivkov became a steady visitor to Moscow and his dependable, if lackluster, supporter at various international meetings and conferences.[8]

Control of the party secretariat provided Zhivkov with opportunities to build steadily his own apparat, while Khrushchev's backing gave him the strength to deal with the rest of his competitors. Opponents ("doubters" as the party press called some of them) were pressed out of the Politburo and other positions of importance and replaced by men generally younger than Zhivkov, loyal to him, and products of Bulgarian conditions. The funnel through which most of them (Stanko Todorov, Boris Velchev, Mitko Grigorov, Pencho Kubadinski, and others) arrived was the party secretariat. In regard to Chervenkov, the opportunity to remove him from the Politburo again came from developments in Moscow. The Twenty-Second Congress of the Soviet Communist Party in October 1961 was the stage of a renewed attack on Stalin and Stalinism by Khrushchev, at which the Chinese delegate demonstratively left the proceedings. Chervenkov, a member of the Bulgarian delegation led by Zhivkov, apparently could not conceal similar feelings at the denigration of his old idol, for as soon as the delegation was back in Sofia he was removed from the Politburo and the government. The last of the factional leaders, Yugov, presented little difficulty. Having none of Chervenkov's appeal as a hard ideologist of classical Stalinism and only a minor following in the party, Yugov was swept out by the Zhivkov machine at the Eighth Congress of the Bulgarian Communist Party in November 1962. With him went a number of other unreconstructed survivors of the Stalin era, while Chervenkov, who had continued to engage in "anti-party activity," was thrown out of the party altogether.[9]

In the years since 1962, Zhivkov has been able to control the changes in the positions of leadership without any apparent difficulty.[10] He survived without injury the fall of Khrushchev in the Soviet Union and has adapted himself well to the new Soviet leadership in general, and to Brezhnev in particular. Within the country, the Ninth Congress of the Bulgarian Communist Party in November 1966 was entirely dominated by Zhivkov and was hailed in party propaganda as a "triumph of the April Plenum line" which had been "victorious in all spheres of our life."[11] The congress slightly revamped the Politburo, consisting of Zhivkov, Todorov (1920–; member of it since November 1961), Velchev (1914–; since November 1962), Grigorov (1920–; since November 1961), Boian Bulgaranov (1896–; since June 1957), Ivan Mikhailov (1897–; since March 1954), Encho Staikov (1901–; since March 1954), Zhivko Zhivkov (1915–; since November 1962; no relation to Todor), and three candidate members, Dimitur Dimov (1903–68; since July 1957), Kubadinski (1918–; since November 1962), and Tano Tsolov (1916–; since November 1962). Two old but adaptable Stalinists, Tsola Dragoicheva (1898–) and Todor Pavlov (1890–), were added to provide, according to Zhivkov, a firmer link between the young and the old in the party. Also added was Ivan Popov (1907–), professor of engineering and Chairman of the State Committee on Science and Technological Progress, in recognition of the rising importance of science and technology.[12] Two old candidate members were raised to full membership (Kubadinski and Tsolov) and six new ones were added (Luchezar Avramov, 1922–; Peko Takov, 1909–; Angel Tsanev, 1912–; Kostadin Giaurov, 1924–; Krustiu Trichkov, 1923–; and Ivan Abadzhiev, 1930–). The only significant demotions were the removal of Grigorov and Staikov, who remained members of the Central Committee. In distribution of functions, Todorov is Zhivkov's understudy and troubleshooter-at-large; Velchev deals with party cadres; Balgaranov, with Army questions; Mikhailov, with social affairs, including the churches; Zhivko Zhivkov, with economic problems; Kubadinski, with transportation and communications; Tsolov, with the Soviet bloc's Council for Mutual Economic Assistance; Dragoicheva, with propaganda; Pavlov, the leading Marxist philosopher and honorary President of the Bulgarian Academy of Sciences, with intellectual affairs; Avramov, with foreign trade and youth questions; Takov, with domestic trade; and Tsanev, with military security. The three youngest members, Giaurov, Trichkov, and Abadzhiev, are respectively secretaries of the party organizations in the Plovdiv, Blagoevgrad, and Vratsa districts.

In the party secretariat, Avramov was elevated to the Politburo and Grigorov and Nacho Papazov (1921–; Secretary since November 1962) were dropped. The secretariat, consisting of Todor Zhivkov, Todorov, Velchev, Bulgaranov, and Ivan Prumov (1921–; Secretary since November 1962, with responsibilities for agriculture), was replenished with Venelin Kotsev (1926–) and three aides, Vladimir Bonev (1917–), Stoian Giurov (1915–), and Stefan Vasilev (1919–). In the Central Committee, the 1966 congress ratified substantial changes that further strengthened Zhivkov's team. Of the 98 members it had in 1962, 5 had died and 11 were dropped. The new Central Committee of 137 was made up of 82 holdovers, 30 raised from candidate to regular member status, and 25 new members.[13] The congress also elected 87 candidate members (66 in 1962) and a Central Auditing Commission of 73. Among the new members of the Central Committee, noteworthy is the inclusion of Kotsev, who has risen steadily in Zhivkov's apparat and comes from the committee's Department for Art and Culture; Angel Balevski and Liubomir Krustanov, present and past presidents of the Bulgarian Academy of Sciences and representatives of the scientific community; Pantelei Zarev, rector of the University of Sofia; Vladimir

Topencharov, a member of Traicho Kostov's team and now Ambassador to France; Georgi Dzhagarov, president of the Writers' Union; and David Elazar, a representative of the Jewish community.

The changes in the central leadership since 1966 have been minor and for the most part a matter of distribution of functions in the machinery of government. Potentially the most significant of them may be the appointment of Roza Koritarova and Georgi Bokov to the secretariat, replacing Giurov, who became Ambassador to the Soviet Union, and Vasilev, who was appointed Minister of Education. Koritarova, like Giurov, came from the chairmanship of the Central Council of Trade Unions while Bokov (1920–) has been editor-in-chief of the party's daily organ *Rabotnichesko Delo* since 1958 and president of the Journalists' Union since 1960; both were made members of the Central Committee in 1962.[14] Zhivko Zhivkov, First Deputy Prime Minister, has become Chairman of the newly-formed Committee on Economic Coordination of the Council of Ministers; Tsolov, Kubadinski, and Avramov, also deputies of Todor Zhivkov as Prime Minister, have been made Chairman of the State Planning Committee, Minister of Construction and Architecture, and Minister of Foreign Trade, respectively; and Elazar has been appointed head of the Institute of Party History, replacing Ruben Avramov who has become Director of the party's new Institute of Social and Ideological Studies.[15]

Beyond the central bodies of the party, there are approximately two thousand key positions throughout the executive and legislative agencies of the government, armed forces, regional administration, mass organizations, professional associations, scientific and educational institutions, information media, and other areas.[16] Through a careful approach to staffing they are interlocked with the party's central bodies so as to serve as "transmission belts" for the Politburo and the Central Committee, which make all policy, and for the secretariat, which supervises the execution of established policy and prepares the ground for new policy through the elaborate apparat of departments of the Central Committee.

Judging from the composition of Bulgarian delegations to meetings in Moscow and elsewhere and the assignment of tasks at home, the core of most trusted men around Zhivkov in 1970 consists of Todorov (whose association with Zhivkov goes back to the four-man committee that organized the coup in 1944[17]), Velchev, Kubadinski, Zhivko Zhivkov, and Kotsev.[18] All are younger than Zhivkov, products of Bulgarian conditions, with substantial records of underground work before 1944 (except Kotsev, who was too young), and associated with Zhivkov in their careers. Like him, they are colorless, lack charisma, striking intelligence, or independent stature, and depend, because of their past records, on Soviet backing for their survival. In the general vacuum of leadership created by the various liquidations since 1944 and amidst such men at the top, Zhivkov seems quite safe from challengers who possess a power base of their own. He is, of course, not safe from changes that might occur in Moscow.

Zhivkov's dependence on Soviet backing to help him hold power and provide security for his regime has been in plain evidence on several occasions. In 1963, in a spy case which led to the execution of the Bulgarian delegate to the United Nations, Ivan-Asen Georgiev, it became known that the Bulgarian diplomat had been hunted down and arrested by Soviet security men. In 1965, an astounding attempt by Communist army officers and civilians in Sofia to overthrow Zhivkov's regime was also uncovered by Soviet intelligence. The plot itself involved a candidate member of the Central Committee, Ivan Todorov-Gorunia, who committed suicide, the commander of the Sofia garrison, General Tsviatko Anev, and eight other Communists, who were tried behind closed doors by the military division of the Supreme Court and sentenced to various terms of imprisonment. While the motives behind this unique attempt within a ruling Communist party to overthrow the leadership by force remain shrouded in secrecy, Zhivkov's explanation has been that it was a scheme of isolated adventurers seeking to give the country a pro-Chinese orientation.[19]

The Government

Doctrinally, Bulgaria continues to be defined by the Communists as a "socialist state with a people's democratic form of government," which in essence is the same as the Soviet form of government.[20] The common denominator in both is "the rule of the working class in alliance with, and at the head of, working people from the cities and the countryside." The rule of the working class or, in classical Marxist terminology, the dictatorship of the proletariat, is effected by the Bulgarian Communist Party. The framework of its alliance with the working intelligentsia and the peasantry, the only two social strata the doctrine recognizes, is the so-called Fatherland Front (FF), which originated during World War II as a coalition of left-of-the-center political forces in Bulgaria (Communists, Agrarians, Socialists, Republicans, and others) and is described in party historiography as the work of Georgi Dimitrov. Following the breakup of the coalition in 1945–47, the Fatherland Front was preserved as a loose umbrella organization useful to the party as a "transmission belt" in internal propaganda. It claims a membership of

3,781,000 (out of a total population of 8,310,000 in 1968)[21] and functions through local FF committees topped by a National Council of the FF (chaired by Boian Bulgaranov). The main force in it, the Bulgarian Communist Party, has a membership of 621,846 (of whom 144,004 are women) constituting 7.4 percent of the total population.[22] The only other political party that survived the breakup of the original coalition is a remnant of the Agrarian Union which has a membership of 120,000 and serves as a minor partner of the BCP in the Fatherland Front and the government and provides some reality to the theory of workers-peasants alliance.

Structurally, the government has remained the same as outlined in the so-called Dimitrov Constitution adopted in 1947. Like the Stalin Constitution of 1936, after which it was patterned, it affirms the principle of popular sovereignty, that is, all power belongs to and is derived from the people. On paper, therefore, the country is a representative democracy: general elections, held every four years with everyone over eighteen entitled to vote, produce "people's representatives" who sit as a legislature (National Assembly) and constitute "the supreme agency of the government." Originally the National Assembly consisted of one representative for each thirty thousand persons of the population, but amendments introduced in 1961 and 1965 as part of Zhivkov's program of "democratization" reduced that figure to twenty-five thousand and then to twenty thousand. As a result, the Assembly elected in February 1966 consists of 416 representatives, of whom 280 are Communists, 99 Agrarians, and 37 unaffiliated prominent personalities. In terms of its work, the Assembly meets twice a year for brief regular sessions lasting less than a week each to approve legislation presented by the Council of Ministers. To carry on its function between sessions, the Assembly elects a standing body (Presidium) of nineteen members whose chairman (Georgi Traikov, 1898–; leader of the Agrarian Union) is the nominal head of state. The Assembly also elects the members of the principal executive agency of government, the Council of Ministers, the judges of the Supreme Court (for five-year terms), and the Chief Prosecutor of the Republic (also for five years).

The administration of the country is headed by the Council of Ministers, which at present consists of a Prime Minister (Todor Zhivkov), a First Deputy (Zhivko Zhivkov), five other deputies (Mikhailov, Tsolov, Kubadinski, Avramov, and Petur Tanchev, an Agrarian), twenty ministers as heads of the various departments, and seven chairmen of state committees for planning, control, science and technology, art and culture, youth and sports, labor and wages, and state security. Local administration is organized in two layers: an intermediate layer of 28 districts (*okruzi*) and a bottom layer of 1,158 communes (*obshtini*) for 174 towns and villages. Among the 28 districts, the city of Sofia (as separate from the region of Sofia) is constituted as one, subdivided in six urban areas (*raioni*). Each of the districts and communes is administered by a people's council elected for three years, the lower layer being subordinated to the higher and both to the Presidium of the National Assembly.[23] Under the principle of democratic centralism, however, the councils are also subordinated to the central executive agencies (headed by the Council of Ministers) and are thus in effect the local extremities of a highly centralized system of administration.[24]

The Judiciary

The judicial system is also a pyramid, at the top of which is the Supreme Court with divisions for civil, criminal, and military cases. Below it are the twenty-eight district courts, whose judges and assessors are elected by the people's councils for five years. The lowest level is constituted by the people's courts elected by the population in their jurisdiction for three years. In addition, there are military courts, whose judges and assessors are elected by the National Assembly (or the Presidium) for five years. The courts are presumed to be independent of the other agencies of government and subordinated only to the law.[25] A special agency in the administration of justice is the network of government prosecutors headed by the Chief Prosecutor of the Republic and appointed by him. The prosecutors are charged with making certain that the laws of the regime ("socialist legality") are observed by the courts, public officials, and private citizens. They are also presumed to be independent of the judicial and executive agencies of the government.[26]

Constitutional provisions and legal presumptions, however, are one thing, realities another. In regard to representative democracy, the Communist doctrine of the party's monopoly of power as well as the de jure proscription and de facto suppression of political dissent since 1944 have eliminated the possibility of genuine choice from the election process. The BCP thus predictably must win all "elections"; in the legislative elections in February, 1966, 99.63 percent of the electorate cast ballots and of that number 99.85 percent approved the candidates (one per electoral district) drawn up by the Fatherland Front. In regard to the independence of the judicial process, the fictional nature of this presumption anywhere party interests are considered to be at stake is well illustrated by the Traicho Kostov case. When the party under Chervenkov required it, the courts found Kostov and many others guilty of assorted charges and sentenced Kostov to die, but when the line changed the BCP exonerated him and in effect nullified the court sentences.[27]

Governmental Reforms

It should nonetheless be noted that, within the limits set by the party's determination to have monopoly of power, it has moved during the Zhivkov years to soften the most offending features of the dictatorship, encourage more discussion and initiative, introduce science as a help-mate of administration, and in general improve the government of the country. The most comprehensive effort in this direction came in July 1968, when a Central Committee plenum, enlarged with representatives of the Agrarian Union, heads of government departments, and others, heard a lengthy report by Zhivkov on "Basic Lines of Further Develop-ment of the System of Management of Our Society" and adopted a series of decisions.[28] The gist of Zhivkov's report was that the experience accumulated from the trial reforms in economic management since 1965 allowed the consolidation of the reforms in the economy and their extension to the sphere of government so as to bring, in doctrinal terms, the political superstructure into conformity with the socio-economic basis. In regard to the government reforms, Zhivkov stressed that they were to be based on the Leninist principle of democratic centralism balanced with "socialist democracy" and on the Marxist-Leninist princi-ple of the unity of the legislative and executive activity. The reforms are to apply to a greater degree the findings of the science of social manage-ment and to bring about a better system of self-government in the various spheres of life. The work of the agencies of government from top to bottom will continue as heretofore, he emphasized, to be directed by the Bulgarian Communist Party.

Specifically, the following reforms in the government of the country were mapped out. The role of the National Assembly, "curtailed and arrogated for many years by the executive agencies," is to be enhanced by involving it above all in the preparation, deliberation, and adoption of legislation. The Assembly also is to be involved to a greater degree in the economic planning function and receive reports by the executive agencies on the implementation of the annual plans. In conformity with the Assembly's new role, the electoral system and the nomination of candidates are to be improved. The greatest and potentially most signifi-cant innovation proposed is the creation of a State Council in lieu of the Assembly's Presidium, also to be elected by the Assembly from among its members. Unlike the Presidium, however, it would have both legisla-tive and executive functions and thus put into effect at the highest level of government the doctrinal principle of the unity of legislative and executive power. As a constantly operating organ of the Assembly, the State Council will supervise the work of the Council of Ministers and all executive agencies and, in another direction, the work of the local people's councils. The State Council will have special agencies for supervision of the people's councils, implementation of the results of science in the processes of government (Institute of Organization of Government), and preparation of legislation (Council on Legislation, at this writing under the Ministry of Justice). Measures are also to be taken to enhance the role of the prosecutors and the Supreme Court in the enforcement of socialist legality.

In the executive area of government, the reforms envisage the subordination of the Council of Ministers to the guidance and direct control of the Assembly and the State Council. Special attention is to be paid to its functions in the area of planning in which it is to act through a new Committee on Economic Coordination within it. Changes are also envisaged for the committees on planning and science and technological progress, the ministries of finance and domestic trade, and other agencies. The proposals include the creation of a Committee on Labor and Social Welfare and a Ministry of Supply and State Reserves. In regard to the local system of government, the people's councils are to have greater independence and initiative in handling the administrative, economic, and socio-cultural problems in their territory. Beyond the structure of the government, the trade unions and the Fatherland Front, which together with the Communist Youth League are the principal conduits of party policy to the masses, are to be refurbished along the lines of reorganization decreed by the Central Committee for the Komsomol in December 1967. In regard to the role of the party, the proposals and the discussions called for a clear demarcation between the functions of the BCP and its organs and those of the government on all levels so as to free the party units from preoccupation with current administrative and economic problems and make them more effective loci of ultimate policy formulation and supervision.

In potential impact on national life, the decisions of this so-called July Plenum may well match the impact of the April Plenum of 1956. The propaganda of the party is certainly endeavoring to establish the parallel. However, how far the reforms will go still remains to be seen. Of greatest interest to watch will be the functioning of the State Council and the shifts in the personnel created by the establishment of the New State Council. If, as is expected, it becomes the principal legislative-executive agency operating on the daily basis and Zhivkov becomes its President and thus the titular as well as actual head of state, conditions will be favorable for a de jure exercise of monolithic political power by him and by the party. If, on the other hand, the powerful role of the Council of Ministers is preserved while Zhivkov becomes President of the State Council, the emergence of a new Prime Minister in charge of the extensive government bureaucracy might lead to a realignment of power at the highest levels of leadership.[29] The full implementation of the reforms is contingent upon the adoption of a new constitution, the drafting of which has already begun, and of a new party program by the Tenth Congress in 1970.[30]

Pending a constitutional reorganization, steps have already been taken to implement certain parts of the July Plenum decisions. The next plenum of the Central Committee, held in November 1968, took up the question of the people's councils and resolved, on the basis of a report by Stanko Todorov and remarks by Zhivkov, to put into effect an extensive program of building up the councils as "agencies of local self-government and socialist democracy."[31] Zhivkov's speech revealed plainly what was on the party's mind. The question went, according to Zhivkov, far beyond the matter of improving the administration to developing socialist democracy in the country. The question of democracy had always been pressing, but of late it had become an especially urgent and even cardinal theoretical, political, and ideological problem. It was the question of democracy that was raised by "the counterrevolutionary and revisionist forces in Czechoslovakia to confuse the Communists and the nonparty people and make easier their assault of the socialist system." Their aim everywhere was to drive a wedge between the people and the party by charging that socialism was incompatible with democracy. "We, the Bulgarian Communists," Zhivkov said, "have never concealed it and have always been proud of the fact that our system is a dictatorship of the proletariat in the form of people's democracy." As Lenin taught, the question was not "democracy for all" but "freedom for whom, for which class." So long as Communist rule encountered opposition, "democracy shall express the will and interests of the ruling class."

In further implementation of the July Plenum decisions, in December 1968, the National Assembly approved the following changes in the structure of the Council of Ministers: a new Committee on Economic Coordination was formed; the ministries of Construction and of Architecture and Public Works were combined; the Ministry of Internal Affairs and the Committee on State Security were also combined; a new Ministry of Labor and Social Welfare was created on the basis of the Committee on Labor and Wages; another new Ministry of Supply and State Reserves was created; the Central Statistical Office was reorgan-

ized as a State Office of Information.[32] The National Assembly has also
begun the practice of receiving and discussing annual reports from the
Chief Prosecutor and the Supreme Court on the state of law enforcement in the country.[33]

Internal Affairs: The Economy

Beyond the decision-making and decision-executing processes, the
ranking concern of the party is the economy of the country. As in
politics, the change in the line in economics is tied in party historiography to the April Plenum of 1956, which found that under Chervenkov
"serious weaknesses and mistakes had occurred in the economic development of the country, the pace of its industrialization was slowed
down, and grave damages were inflicted on agriculture, where the principle of material interest was set aside."[34] The gross errors in planning,
economic difficulties, and stagnation which party policy had brought
about were conveniently blamed on Chervenkov as the scapegoat, and
the party set out to do better. The Seventh Congress of the Bulgarian
Communist Party in 1958 sought to grapple with some of the problems,
but policy continued to be confused by the power struggle, and for a
while the party was even swayed toward schemes of Chinese-style
communes in agriculture and a "great leap forward" in industry. Greater
clarity came as a result of the Twenty-Second Congress of the Soviet
Communist Party in 1961 which adopted Khrushchev's new party program (also adopted by the Bulgarian Communists as their own[35]) and a
twenty-year projection for the USSR and the bloc in Eastern Europe.[36]
The Bulgarian five-year plan (the third, adopted in 1958) was cut short,
declared fulfilled, and replaced by another for 1961–65. The Eighth
Congress of the BCP in 1962, conducted under the sign of the closest
coordination with Soviet plans, further aligned the Bulgarian projections
with those of the USSR.[37]

The fourth plan for 1961–65 presumably registered satisfactory
growth in its main directions. According to official figures, the average
annual rate of growth of the gross national product was 8.6 percent, and
that of the national income 7 percent. Industrial production (2,133
plants in 1965) had risen 174 percent over the 1960 level (11.7 percent
annual rate of growth); agricultural production (98.5 percent collectivized in 920 cooperative farms, or TKZS, and 104 state farms, or DZS in
1965), 117 percent (3.2); transportation of goods, 204 percent (15.3);
capital investment, 152 percent (8.7); retail trade, 142 percent (7.2);
and foreign trade, 197 percent (14.5). The fourth plan presumably also
marked the "definitive consolidation of industry as the dominant branch
of the country's economy."[38] As in the USSR, the 214 machine and

tractor stations servicing the farms were reorganized in 1962 by selling the machinery or most of them to the nearby TKZS.

The (fifth) five-year plan for 1966–70 was intended in the main to "continue the construction of the socialist society" in the country by accelerated rates of growth in all branches of production. National income was to rise by fifty percent over 1965, gross national product by ninety percent, industrial production by more than seventy percent, agricultural production by more than thirty percent, volume of consumer goods by about forty percent, and real income by more than thirty percent.[39]

As in the USSR, the most retarded area in the economy remains collectivized agricultural production. It has consistedly lagged behind the rate of growth of industry and has been unable to keep pace with the demands created by industrialization and urbanization. The contribution of the TKZS and DZS has dropped from 78.2 percent of the total agricultural production in 1960 to 72.5 percent in 1967, while the contribution of the peasants' private plots and other privately run lands has remained steady and significant (20.6 percent in 1960 and 21.3 percent in 1967). Under the new system of economic management, material incentives are provided to raise production, and to increase efficiency the collective farms are steadily consolidated into larger units, but the problem of inadequate agricultural production has not been resolved. Bread queues in the cities have been a recurrent phenomenon, and Bulgaria, a country of agricultural surpluses in the past, has been compelled on occasion, like the Soviet Union, to import grain. A severe spring drought in 1968 added to the difficulties.[40] To give the collectivized peasants some sense of involvement in the making of policy that governs their lives, the regime called in 1967 a congress of the TKZS which adopted a new standard statute for the cooperative farms and established a union of the TKZS.[41] The congress was followed by a congress of the Agrarian Union (the thirty-first since its establishment in 1899).[42]

The regime also has financial difficulties. Liberal use of paper money and necessary wage increases have periodically pushed prices up and created inflation. The regime's response to the problem has included currency manipulation (the latest came in 1962), whereby the old money is exchanged for lesser amounts of new to eliminate excess purchasing power and the pressure for consumer goods. The inflationary trend in 1968 produced insistent rumors that the government was preparing another "currency reform." One novel device adopted in the face of the financial difficulties is the cultivation of tourists and vacationers from the West in order to bring in hard currencies. Since the early 1960s when travel restrictions for Westerners were eased, there has been a spectacular growth of the tourist business. In 1969, the country prepared to accommodate the astounding number of two million foreign visitors.

Science

In looking for helpmates to attain its objectives, the regime has consistently paid a great deal of attention to science in the sense of the Bulgarian term *nauka,* or scientifically developed knowledge in both the natural and social sciences. Its main tool in this regard has been the Bulgarian Academy of Sciences, which dates its beginnings from 1869 and was traditionally oriented to the humanities and social sciences. In the years after 1944 it was purged and restructured under the presidency of Todor Pavlov so as to make it an "academy of the socialist type exemplified by the Academy of Sciences of the USSR" and an instrument for the "building of socialism" in Bulgaria.[43] From a society of primarily humanistic scholars it was made into a government agency with the mission to work in the entire spectrum of the sciences, including technology, and coordinate all research in the country. This ambitious assignment proved beyond its powers, and with the advent of greater realism after the April Plenum of 1956, its mission was trimmed in line with its traditional strengths. The sciences pertaining to agriculture and related pursuits were separated in 1961 into an Academy of Rural Economy, following the pattern in the Soviet Union and other Eastern European countries.[44] The creation of the State Committee on Science and Technological Progress in 1962 placed the function of planning, coordinating, and financing all research in the country in the Committee and made it, in a further division of national scientific labor, responsible for technology, while the Academy of Sciences was confined primarily to the social and natural-mathematical sciences.[45] Within the Academy a number of dogmatic Stalinists were gradually replaced by more flexible scholars on its governing bodies and as heads of institutes, and the new leadership made some serious effort to bring about "a radical change in the style and methods of the direction of scholarly work" and to "liquidate fully the wicked survivals from the past" which had "paralyzed all creative initiative and condemned entire fields and trends of scholarship to stagnation."[46]

Financed liberally in comparison with the past, the scientific establishment of the country has grown impressively and in 1970 consists of more than 250 institutes, laboratories, and other research units staffed by 11,700 scientists and specialists and operating in four jurisdictions: the Academy of Sciences (48 institutes, over 1,200 scientists), the

Academy of Rural Economy (56 institutes, 1,120 scientists), the Ministry of Education (28 institutions of higher learning, more than 5,000 instructors of various ranks), and individual ministries and plants (130 research institutes and laboratories).[47] National scientific and intellectual life, however, continues to be, as before 1944, inordinately concentrated in Sofia; two-thirds of the scientific institutions are located there and of the remaining one-third the majority are experimental farms and stations of the Academy of Rural Economy.

Since the early 1960s, when it was recognized that it was impossible for a small country like Bulgaria to develop to an equal degree all fields of science and in all current directions, a new approach has been taken to improve the international division of labor within the Soviet bloc and derive maximum benefit from Western scientific advances. As a result, Bulgaria has entered into bilateral agreements (mainly through the Academy of Sciences and the Academy of Rural Economy) for scientific cooperation, exchange of scholars and publications, and work on joint projects with the USSR and other Communist countries.[48] With the expansion of the functions of the bloc's Council of Mutual Economic Assistance, since 1962 the country has also been involved in Comecon's multilateral agreements for scientific coordination, specialization, and joint research. The new policy has, furthermore, made possible significant contacts and agreements for exchange of scholars, scientific information, and publications with Western countries.

Progress through science and technology has become one of the by-words of the regime. The party's policy-makers, in line with Marxist doctrine and Soviet practice, never neglected this lever of power and change, but it has been in the past decade that the question was brought into sharp focus. In a comprehensive policy paper issued in 1959 the Central Committee and the Council of Ministers set the general lines for "developing science in Bulgaria, enhancing its role in the building of socialism, and tying it ever closer to life."[49] The paper listed seven areas of weakness and specified measures to overcome them: detachment of science from life in general and the economy in particular, lag of important branches (atomic physics, electronics, automation, and other applied sciences "which are creating a new technological revolution in the world") behind science in the advanced countries, inadequate coordination and squandering of scientific cadres and resources, poor selection and preparation of cadres, inadequate cooperation with scientific institutions in the USSR and the other socialist countries as well as those in the West, shortcomings in the direction of research activities, and poor working conditions in terms of equipment, machines, and physical plant. These and other problems have been the subject of a number of subsequent policy papers, the latest of which, presented by the Chairman of the State Committee on Science and Technological Progress, Professor Ivan Popov, has dealt with measures to accelerate technological progress in the economy.[50] The paper indicated that since 1957 the number of specialists with higher education had risen from 74,613 to 130,088, the greatest increase being in engineers (13,346 to 30,843 in the same decade), and stressed inter alia the need for a unified system of scientific, technical, and economic information to meet speedily the requirements for data on domestic developments and on scientific advances throughout the world.

Education

On the level below, education, like science, is thoroughly geared to the objectives of the regime and shaped by Soviet models and pedagogical practice. In a direct sequence to Khrushchev's reforms in the USSR, in 1959, Zhivkov introduced the so-called polytechnical schools, which were to combine study with work and thus relate education more fully to life.[51] The reform's expanded curriculum raised primary (compulsory) education from seven to eight years (ages seven to fourteen) and general secondary education from eleven to twelve years, with the transition to be completed by 1965, and required teachers for the fifth to twelfth grade to have at least four years of higher education.[52] The congress of the Teachers' Union in 1962 aired some of the difficulties, old and new, that plagued education: polytechnical instruction was handicapped by inadequate facilities and teachers and was conducted in a primitive way; the presence of students in factories and farms impeded production; academic subjects in the humanities as well as science were suffering from the polytechnical orientation of the overburdened curriculum; students were indifferent to their studies and assignments and susceptible to Western influences that were turning many of them into a "nylon intelligentsia"; graduates "displayed a low sense of duty" and a "negative attitude toward physical labor" and whenever possible dodged working in the field.[53]

With Khrushchev's fall in 1964, the polytechnical reforms went into low gear and some aspects were dropped, including the twelfth year in the secondary schools (1965). At the 1966 congress Zhivkov said only that it was necessary to recognize the limits of students' capabilities at the various age levels and that educational change should guard against "undue haste" and should come after "wide experimentation, deeply probing studies, and sober deliberation." Expanding the criticism, the education press pointed out that the reforms had been dogmatic and sectarian (that is, dictated from above and off the beaten path) and that their "basic weakness" was the fact that they were "put through rashly, without prolonged comparative study and experimentation, and largely in imitation . . . of reforms in other countries." Rash reforms, it was argued, "damage the proper education of the young" and "in contrast to material production, their negative results are revealed too late and leave lasting consequences in the preparation of the new generation which are difficult to correct."[54] Since Zhivkov was intimately associated with the imitation of Khrushchev's reforms in Bulgaria, the education press and the last congress of the Teachers' Union in 1967 did not dare to go farther and shed light on the damage done.

As elsewhere throughout the world, the educational establishment of the country has grown vastly in the postwar quarter of a century. During the 1967–68 school year it comprised 5,645 schools of all types with an enrollment of 1,585,898 and a teaching staff of 81,061 (4,916 general schools with 1,212,892 students and 56,330 teachers; 703 vocational and other special schools with 295,517 students and 17,389 teachers; and 26 institutions of higher education with 81,489 students and 6,342 instructors).[55] Bulgarians have traditionally valued education highly and are understandably proud of the ratio of students, especially on the level of higher education, to general population. It may be pointed out, however, that, for example, the University of Sofia, which is still the only full-fledged university in the country, has a high rate of enrollment in correspondence courses which are weaker than the regular programs.[56]

The central objective the regime has undeviatingly pursued in education since 1944 is the creation of a "new, socialist intelligentsia," or an "army of specialists with higher and secondary education" which is, first, loyal to the party and the system and, second, competent and numerous enough to man the jobs of a modern society.[57] The construction of the outlook of loyalty begins in kindergarten and continues throughout the years of schooling in the introduction of the young generation to the national milieu and heritage through the prism of the official ideology and, extramurally, in the indoctrination carried on by the party-sponsored youth organizations.[58] For the purpose the schools utilize all suitable subjects—above all, history, literature, and geography—and pedagogical techniques.[59]

The efforts of the schools and of the Pioneer and Komsomol organizations, however, have not been altogether successful. A national conference held in July 1967 on the problems in character formation was told by Venelin Kotsev on behalf of the BCP that "the principal target of the ideological assault by the West is the young generation and the intelligentsia." The West calculated, he said, that if it could poison the young generation and knock the intelligentsia out of the battle, socialism would be dealt an irreparable blow. The young were offered "in a thousand ways" the American way of life as a model, while the adult intelligentsia was subverted with novelties in ideas and art. The foreign cultural exchange and especially the influx of foreign tourists provided avenues for this subversion and required measures for the "ideological and political steeling of our people and our youth" to assure "the best armor and political immunization against the pressure from the enemy." The pressure from the West, Kotsev noted, had brought on some troubling results: apolitical attitudes, ideological vacillation, consumer attitude to life, snobbism, loafing.[60]

In the face of this threat to its objectives among the young, the party moved into high gear and adopted a set of vigorous countermeasures. Outlined in the "Zhivkov Theses on Youth" and passed by a special plenum of the Central Committee in December 1967, the new approach was based on four lines of action: reorganization of the Komsomol and increased involvement of youth in society's affairs, Marxist-Leninist education and intensification of the struggle against "bourgeois ideology," increased emphasis on patriotic education, and improvement of party work in the Komsomol and the youth.[61] In his theses Zhivkov noted that the Komsomol was a "carbon copy" of the BCP, that it governed rather than inspired the youth, was devoid of content, and existed apart from the real interests and aspirations of youth. With remarkable candor he called the Komsomol flabby, hackneyed, paralyzed in its forms and methods, and cliché-ridden in its thinking. To turn youth onto new directions, he cited a long list of government agencies and public organizations that could help and cited in particular the school, Army, and family for what each could do. For coordination he proposed the establishment of a Committee on Youth attached to the Council of Ministers and headed by the First Secretary of the Komsomol. Within the Komsomol he suggested an elaborate program of organizational "rituals" (a code of behavior reduced to the form of the Ten Commandments, flags and banners, badges, uniforms, marching songs, jamborees, and so forth) to inspire the youth with the necessary emotions. Turning to the overall shape of the nation, he noted the "alarming trend of decline of the birthrate" (from 42 per thousand in 1900 to 15 in 1965) and offered a program to encourage child-bearing (with such enticements as financial incentives, care of illegitimate children, total support of the third child by the state, and reduction of infant mortality) in order to keep the nation from becoming senescent and expand its size "to ten million in the next few years."

To implement its decisions, the BCP urgently summoned in January 1968, a new congress of the Komsomol (the last was held in 1963), which dutifully accepted the new program formulated without the Komsomol's or the youth's participation and once again demonstrated that the Komsomol had no life of its own.[62] In line with the decision to involve the younger generations in affairs run by the old, one of the party's transmission belts, the Writers' Union, voted in February 1968 to add a number of young writers to its membership of 274. Stressing the theme that the conflict of generations was promoted by "bourgeois propaganda" and that "we trust our young people," the party announced a special gesture to co-opt into its ranks a contingent of Komsomol members by the end of 1969.[63] Run by men considerably over thirty, the BCP has shown no signs of yielding any ground of decision-making to those under thirty.

In the discussions on youth Zhivkov and other party spokesmen attached "exceptional importance" to the so-called patriotic education, which is a massive program enlisting the schools, public organizations, media of mass communications, and even the Bulgarian Orthodox Church, to cultivate patriotism, national pride, and national dignity in young and old. Pressed in its current form since 1965 in apparent relation to the Vietnam War and in anticipation that a larger conflict might develop, the campaign of fanning up patriotic sentiment has its beginning in the early 1960s and aims not only at preparing the nation psychologically for such a contingency, but at transforming the elements of latent anti-Soviet nationalism and natural love of country into a controlled emotional force for attainment of greater national unity and the regime's political and economic objectives. One aspect of the campaign with the resulting return to the nation's individuality, traditions, and heritage has been the removal of objectionable names of localities and institutions imposed during the Stalin era. The State Library in Sofia, at first named after Kolarov, was renamed the Cyril and Methodius National Library; after being known as Stalin for some years, Varna resumed its name; Kolarovgrad once again became Shumen; the official gazette and one of the symbols of the Bulgarian state since 1879, *Durzhaven Vestnik,* was restored to its traditional name and appearance after more than a decade of de-nationalized title and format.

Another aspect of the patriotic campaign has been the return to the themes, emphases, and interpretations of traditional Bulgarian historiography. After a decade and a half of barren doctrinaire historiography on the Soviet models of the Stalin era, the historical craft was gradually led to rid itself of the paralysis, sycophancy, careerism, distortions, and dogmas that had pervaded it after 1944[64] and produce not history fitted into preconceived socio-economic schemes, but history filled with national achievements, glory, and heroes. The new circumstances required revision of the two-volume Marxist version of Bulgarian history written in the Stalin era, and even a cursory comparison of it with the new version under the same title[65] reveals the features of the new patriotic historiography. In contrast to the earlier hostile treatment, the medieval khans and tsars of Bulgaria—Asparukh, Krum, Omurtag, Boris, Simeon, Kaloian, Ivan Asen—are extolled in the center of the historical account as the builders of the state and the nation rather than presented as incidental figures produced by socio-economic forces and ruling on behalf of the class of feudal magnates.[66] The new historiography takes obvious pride in the empire-building activities of the Bulgarian medieval kings and in the unique position of Bulgaria under Boris and Simeon as one of the three empires—next to those of the Byzantines and the Carolingians—and one of the three cultural centers of contemporary Europe. It is particularly careful to stress that the Bulgarian empire included Macedonia and that Macedonia has played in the medieval as well as the modern period an essential role in the life of the Bulgarian nation.[67]

Since history provides the best material for inculcation of patriotism, in the discussions of youth party spokesmen called for an even greater effort on the part of those who write and teach history to bring out those elements which feed national pride in the students and to curb the widespread tendency of "nihilism" toward the nation's past achievements. In response to such official exhortation and encouragement, Bulgarian historians, educators, and propagandists began to seize upon all conceivable occasions to extol the nation's traditional heroes and great men and reassert, often against the views of historians in the neighboring countries, the various claims of the old nationalist school of history. An example of this trend was the series of celebrations of the 1,100th anniversary of the death of St. Cyril, including a visit to his grave in Rome by a high-level Bulgarian delegation. At home and in Rome it was asserted, in line with Bulgarian views held since the Middle Ages, that Cyril and Methodius were Bulgarian Slavs, that the language of their translations of religious texts was Old Bulgarian, and that their work made Bulgaria the cradle of the new civilization of the Slavs.[68]

Culture and the Arts

On the broad "front of culture and the arts," as in education, the dominant theme pressed by the BCP in recent years has been patriotism. In the central field of literature, the party has restored to honor for their patriotism many writers of the post-1878 period (Ivan Vazov, Zakhari Stoianov, Pencho Slaveikov, and others) who were previously castigated for "nationalist tendencies." Writers of the current generation who utilize historical and patriotic topics in their works are the object of particular praise. Among them, the party has especially lionized Dimitur Talev, a Macedonian of Bulgarian national consciousness, who made "the national awakening of the Bulgarians in Macedonia" the main theme of his numerous novels.[69] The same kind of attention is accorded to those playwrights, film-makers, stage directors, architects, painters, sculptors, and composers who weave patriotism into their art.

The cultural front has been, however, far from simply patriotic or meek in obeying the wishes of the BCP. The most articulate group, the writers, even during the Stalin era showed signs of resentment of the ideological straightjacket enforced by the party in literature and the arts, but repression was swift and the voices that were heard were few. In the relative thaw on the cultural front after Stalin's death, an increasing number of writers ventured to question and criticize the Leninist-Stalinist tenets of *partiinost* (subordination of literature to the interests of the party), socialist realism, and the requirement of Marxist-Leninist content, and declared that the time of dogmatism and dictation from above had passed.[70] Despite its internal troubles, however, the BCP held firmly to its views and controls and weathered the upheaval in the 1950s. Looking back on the "political vacillation of certain writers," Zhivkov declared in 1960 that the party would accept "free creative discussions" but only on the basis of *partiinost* and socialist realism.[71] The line was reaffirmed at the 1962 and 1966 congresses of the BCP, although it was implicitly recognized that if the "workers on the cultural front" were to be useful to the propaganda of patriotism, a certain relaxation of the controls and "democratization" of the management of cultural life were needed. To this end, the State Committee on Culture and Art, established in its present form in 1963,[72] was to be reorganized by a general "Congress of Bulgarian Culture" (the first of its kind), which the party called in May 1967. A gesture in "socialist democracy," the congress made some minor changes in the committee, renamed it Committee on Art and Culture, and "elected" its chairman (Pavel Matev, a member of the party's Central Committee) and its members.[73] In another gesture of democracy, the regime established special councils for art and culture on the district (*okrug*) and commune (*obshtina*) levels to administer this field in their territory.

Events on the cultural front since the congress have shown that nothing of essence was intended to change. According to the new approach, the writers were allowed to hold in May 1968 a "First Congress of the Union of Bulgarian Writers," but before the congress met the BCP organ recited what the party expected from literature: to instill love of the socialist fatherland; to be permeated by *partiinost;* to inspire the people to strength, faith, optimism, and work; and above all to portray in strictly positive terms the builder of socialism. The editorial admitted that there was some room for criticism but cautioned that bourgeois modernist and decadent influences would be fought, that "manifestations not in harmony with our Communist ideology" would not be tolerated, and that the writers must, as always, be "faithful helpmates of the party."[74] At the congress itself, the union's president (and member of the Central Committee of the BCP) Georgi Dzhagarov assured his fellow writers that the party would not return to the old administrative approach, tutelage, gross meddling, and subjective evaluations of literary works by the political leaders, but also stressed that negativism toward the aims and record of the regime and tendencies of anarchism would not be tolerated.[75] The party's skillful use of the reins, alternately loosening and tightening them, may be responsible for the fact that the Czechoslovak events in 1968 produced no audible echo among the literati of Bulgaria.

The continuing tug-of-war over the question of party controls should not, however, obscure the fact that much creditable work is being accomplished in literature and the arts. Because of the various barriers, little of it receives due notice in the West. A recent work that has received recognition is the novel *Time of Parting,* by Anton Donchev, based on the patriotic theme of the forcible conversion of Bulgarians to Islam by the Turks in the seventeenth century.[76]

Religious and National Minorities

Finally, on the domestic scene one should note the condition of the religious communities. The largest of them, the Bulgarian Orthodox Church, has seen a certain improvement of its position vis-à-vis the state since the election of Patriarch Kiril and the reestablishment of the patriarchate at the end of the Stalin era.[77] A resourceful leader and a systematic student of the history of the church,[78] Kiril has been able to reach a modus vivendi with the regime, which is based on the common ground of "patriotic service to the fatherland" and allows the church to lead a significant life of its own (funded to a considerable degree by a subsidy from the state) in exchange for support of the regime's policies at home and abroad consistent with the interests of the church. The church participates in the Fatherland Front (through Kiril, who is vice president of the National Council), the domestic programs for fostering Bulgarian-Soviet friendship, the preservation and restoration of historical landmarks (many of which are monasteries, churches, and shrines) for the purposes of patriotic education as well as the foreign tourist trade, and the campaign to cultivate patriotism among young and old.

The patriotic campaign in particular has given the church much new latitude to reassert its place in national life. Many of the nation's great men from the ninth century to the nineteenth, who are currently extolled in the fanning up of patriotic sentiment, were also men of the church, and the church press misses no opportunity to point out this fact and to stress the crucial contribution of the church in the creation and preservation of the nation. As Kiril has stressed on occasion, the men of the church, past and present, "are convinced patriots" and "as patriots we are always defending the interests of the Bulgarian people." On the basis of working together "for the good of our country," he has contended, it is possible to cooperate with the atheist government just as within a family believing and non-believing members "love each other because they are tied together by blood."[79] The party press in turn often features articles on monasteries and churches as historic "citadels of Bulgarianism and the Bulgarian spirit."

From the premise of patriotism the church renders assistance to the regime in various areas of foreign policy, which is also useful to the Soviet government and the Russian Orthodox Church. It is an active participant in the World Peace Council, the Christian Peace Conference, and other Soviet-sponsored campaigns "in defense of peace;" it has backed the regime in the condemnation of Israel for the war in 1967 and its consequences; and it generally lends support to the Moscow Patriarchate in interorthodox and interconfessional meetings and relations. In the ecumenical movement and the World Council of Churches, which it joined in 1961, its stance has been skeptical but cooperative. Within itself, the church has been able to maintain with its limited resources a diminished hierarchy of 1,785 parish priests (down from 2,486 in 1938) in twelve dioceses (subdivided into fifty-eight vicariates) headed by metropolitans, vicarial bishops, and other higher clergy.[80] Replacements of deceased prelates and vicars are promptly appointed, and the church is able to educate new cadres for its hierarchy and educational institutions. It has its own bookshop and press which continues to publish a significant number of works. In line with the patriotic campaign, the church has added two patriotic clergymen of the period of the national revival, Father Paisii and Bishop Sofronii of Vratsa, to its saints, has cooperated in bringing to public view Bulgarian religious art from the Middle Ages, and in 1967 was allowed to reoccupy the Rila Monastery, a national shrine and major tourist attraction, as a monastic community. It has taken steps to modernize the translation of the Bible, originally published by the Holy Synod in 1925, and it appointed a special Bulgarian Orthodox Bible Commission in 1961 to produce the new text.[81] In another move of modernization explained with the "ecumenical spirit," it decreed in 1968 the radical change from the Julian to the Gregorian calendar, which made it possible for Bulgarians to begin to celebrate Christmas with the Christians in the West.

The second-largest religious community, the Muslims, comprising some 650,000 Turks, 200,000 Gypsies, and 140,000 converted Bulgarians (Pomaks), have for obvious reasons not fared as well. Holding to Islam as central element of their identity and influenced by Turkish nationalism, since 1944 they have been subjected to various measures meant to overcome their resistance to the aims and policies of the regime and to end their traditional separation from the Bulgarian majority. These measures included, in the Stalin era, the deportation of more than 150,000 Turks to Turkey and, in 1958, the closing of the minority schools in the districts with Turkish population. As a result of the regime's policy, the number of Muslim priests dropped from 3,715 in 1956 (4,417 before the war) to 560 in 1969 and of mosques from 2,300 before the war to 1,300.[82] The openly repressive policy toward the other religious minorities (60,000 Catholics, 16,000 Protestants, 6,000 Jews, and others) in the Stalin era has been relinquished in favor of appealing to their patriotism as native Bulgarians, but the improvement of their position as religious communities has been slight.[83]

In regard to all religions represented in the country, the regime conducts a well-organized campaign of atheist propaganda and displacement of religion from the life of the people. Its main thrust is into the two largest communities, the Orthodox and the Muslim. The basic guidelines of the campaign were formulated by the Politburo of the party in December 1957, in the wake of the Hungarian revolution.[84] Defining the tenets of the Orthodox Church as a "reactionary ideology" opposed to the "dominant ideology in our society," Marxism-Leninism, the document noted that the church had been successful in achieving "closeness and cooperation with the people's democratic state" in a number of areas of domestic and foreign policy and that this fact and the reliance of party workers on "the old atheist traditions in our country and the religious indifference of the greater part of the population" had resulted in an "underestimation of the ideological struggle against reactionary religious views." In these circumstances the church had strengthened its position and even drawn significant number of young people to itself. It was not infrequent, the document noted, that even members of the BCP and activists from the Komsomol "openly or secretly carry out religious rites and thus become propagators of religious superstitions and prejudices." In the period after Stalin's death "clergymen of a reactionary frame of mind became brazen and openly called for insubordination to the laws and the previsions of the constitution," and their actions were encouraged by "disloyal statements of some high church functionaries" in the religious press. As to countermeasures, the document stipulated that all aspects of the atheist propaganda were to be intensified and that secular rituals, holidays, and festivities of "socialist content" were to be developed to deflect the natural tendency of the people to turn to religious traditions at such occasions. Additional general guidelines for the conduct of anti-religious propaganda "without injuring the religious sentiments of the believers" were included in the decisions of the Central Committee plenum of April 1962 concerning the state and tasks of the ideological work of the BCP, followed by others in 1964 specifically for the work among the Turks to combat the manifestations of "religious fanaticism" and "Turkish nationalism and chauvinism."[85]

To place the atheist propaganda on firmer ground of facts and scientific analysis, an elaborate sociological survey of the religious attitudes of 42,664 adults (born before 1944) was conducted in 1962 under the auspices of the Bulgarian Academy of Sciences.[86] From it the Bulgarian experts in atheism have extrapolated that only 32.76 percent of the Bulgarians were religious (compared to approximately 80 percent before 1944), that the Turks remained strongly religious (67.02 percent), and that the number of Orthodox believers was decreasing both in absolute number and relative to the total population, the Muslims and the Catholics were decreasing in proportion to the total population but increasing in proportion to the total number of believers, and the Protestants were increasing both in absolute number and relative to the believers in the country.[87] The party press, however, also notes on occasion that the new rituals lack meaning and inspiration, that the new holidays are crudely politicized and too uniform, and that people still tend to their religious traditions at the great moments in their lives (birth of children, marriage, death) and for the annual cycle of holidays.[88] The evidence is thus by no means clear whether religion is being driven out of or deeper into the human soul.

Conclusions

In conclusion, the review of the internal developments in Bulgaria since the early 1960s leaves several unmistakable impressions. Foremost among them is the fact that Zhivkov has staked, like Dimitrov and Chervenkov before him, everything on a policy of working with the Soviet Union or, more accurately, of complying with every Soviet wish. His part in the bloody establishment of the regime in 1944 and the purges of the opposition in the Fatherland Front as well as the BCP and the resulting isolation from the people at large and even from the party compel him to seek political and physical survival through total subservience to the Soviet leaders, who alone can provide him with the necessary security and prestige. In the tendency of all men, he has rationalized his predicament as something good, not only for himself, but for the BCP and the nation. As he has stated on occasion to visitors: "I am bound to the Soviet Union in life and death; the same is true of our party and our people." [89]

Stemming from this basic predicament is his policy, so far endorsed by the Soviet leaders, of surrounding himself with generally younger men of similar background in the resistance movement, who also have no strength in the BCP or support among the people-at-large and depend for their survival and careers on the goodwill of the Soviet leaders. The result is a group of men at the top who cannot be, collectively or individually, a threat to Zhivkov unless the Soviet leaders wish them to be. Since his age or health is not a problem, he is likely in these circumstances to remain in power for a long time, as long as he is able to satisfy the ruling elites in Moscow. If and when they are no longer satisfied with his performance, Zhivkov's replacement is likely to be picked from the younger men he has raised as his lieutenants in the past ten years or so.

As to Zhivkov's domestic policies, they seem set to continue in the established directions. The constitutional reform, when it comes, will be presented as a decisive step toward the democratization of the institutions and political life of the country and inauguration of more perfect socialism, but the "dictatorship of the proletariat," that is, the monopoly rule of the BCP will continue to operate as thoroughly as it did under Dimitrov and Chervenkov. In the area of the country's development, Zhivkov has sensibly identified with science and technology more than his predecessors did and will no doubt give them the same high priority in the future. Above all, he will continue to cultivate and appeal to the patriotic sentiment in the nation, since it provides a basis on which internal unity can be built and gives him an element of strength in relations with countries he considers antagonistic. In relation to the Soviet Union, he is certain to work with the present formula that "socialist patriotism" is fully compatible with "proletarian internationalism" and that the touchstone of both is loyalty to the USSR.

One of the most important factors helping Zhivkov has been the Soviet Union's troubles with other Communist countries and leaders. As these troubles compel the Soviet leaders to modify their policies in the handling of the satellite states, the beneficiary of the change, without exertion or pain, has been Zhivkov. This was evident in the wake of the Hungarian revolution and is evident in the wake of the Czechoslovak events. To the extent that Zhivkov draws from the USSR's difficulties advantage to benefit his people, he may yet qualify to be rated as one of his nation's statesmen.

5

Walter Ulbricht's
German Democratic Republic

Donald D. Dalgleish

Country Profile: THE GERMAN DEMOCRATIC REPUBLIC

Head of State: Walter Ulbricht, Chairman of the Council of State
Premier: Willi Stoph, Chairman of the Council of Ministers
First Secretary, Central Committee, German Socialist Unity Party: Walter
   Ulbricht

Party Membership (1967): 1,769,912[1]
Armed Forces (1967): 127,000 (Army: 85,000; Navy: 17,000; Air Force:
   25,000)[2]
Population: End of 1968: 17,087,000 (East Berlin: 1,083,913)[3]
Area: 108,174 square kilometers (41,659 square miles)
Population Density: 158 per square kilometer (415 per square mile)
Birth Rate (1968): 14.3 per thousand[4]
Death Rate (1968): 14.3 per thousand[4]
Divorce Rate (1968): 1.7 per thousand[4]
Gross Material Product (1968): 143.07 billion DME ($109.49 billion at
   official rate)[5]
National Income Total (1968): 102.24 billion DME ($46.05 at official
   rate)[6]
National Income by Sectors (1968):[6]
   Industry 59.7%
   Construction 7.8%
   Agriculture 13.4%
   Transportation and Communications 5.1%
   Trade 12.3%
   Other 1.7%
Foreign Trade by Area (1968):[7]
   Socialist Countries (including USSR) 76.1%
   USSR 42.7%
   Non-Socialist countries 23.9%

Foreign Trade by Commodity (1968):[8]

	Export	Import
Machinery, capital goods	55.9%	33.2%
Industrial consumer goods	19.5%	32.6%
Raw materials, semi-finished products	22.6%	33.8%
Other	2.0%	0.4%

SOURCES:

1. U.S. Department of State, Bureau of Intelligence and Research, *World Strength of Communist Party Organizations* (Washington, D.C.: U.S. Government Printing Office, 1969), p. 56.
2. *The Military Balance 1969–1970* (London: The Institute for Strategic Studies, 1969), pp. 12, 13.
3. Staatliche Zentralverwaltung fur Statistik, *Statistisches Jahrbuch der Deutschen Demokratischen Republik 1969* (Berlin: Staatsverlag der Deutschen Demokratischen Republik, 1969), p. 3.
4. *Ibid.,* p. 444.
5. *Ibid.,* p. 17.
6. *Ibid.,* p. 41.
7. *Ibid.,* pp. 296–99.
8. *Ibid.,* p. 300.

5. Walter Ulbricht's German Democratic Republic

Donald D. Dalgleish

On October 7, 1969, the German Democratic Republic (DDR) celebrated its twentieth year of existence. Indeed, the DDR's attainment of two decades of increasingly more prosperous, autonomous, stable, and self-confident community existence, under the same political leader, Walter Ulbricht, is all the more impressive when measured against the political longevity of the Adenauer era in West Germany, the DeGaulle era in France, the Khrushchev era in the Soviet Union, the Ho Chi Minh era in Viet Nam or, by no means conclusively, the "interrupted" era of Gomulka in Poland.[1] Ulbricht's 1948–49 survival of the intra-bloc reverberations of the Tito-Cominform break and the Berlin blockade, his 1953 survival of Stalin's death and the subsequent phases of de-Stalinization, not to mention the Berlin Uprising, his emergence through the smoke and dust of the satellite system's interlocked upheavals of 1956 in Poland and Hungary, his audacious and risky erection of the Berlin Wall in 1961, his deft political triumph over the involuntary retirement of Nikita Krushchev in 1964, and his jaunty, loyalist, and self-righteous participation in the Socialist motherland's successful commonwealth punitive expedition in 1968 against Dubcek's runaway Czechoslovakia —constitute merely the highlights of a unique record of personal political accomplishment. In short, no other leader in the entire post-World War II history of Soviet-dominated Eastern Europe has managed so long to retain at least the form, if not the substance, of real personal direction and political power than Walter Ulbricht.

Among the secrets of his exemplary success may be found the tendency of friend and foe alike to underestimate him, his Prussian-bucolic (*Bauernschlau*) wariness of his own official "genius," his nearly sixth

[123]

sense for anticipating changes in Soviet policy, his corresponding ability to attune himself to the latest ideological emphasis, and his precise awareness of the outer limits of permissible national freedom circumscribed by Warsaw-Pact foreign policy and the presence of twenty Soviet army divisions.[2] These talents, combined with his relatively good physical health and a heavy share of good luck, greatly explain how the First Secretary of the Socialist Unity Party (SED) has survived fifty-seven years of professional political activity.

How monumental an East German creation these personal skills have accomplished with a quarter century of political opportunity depends upon the stability of its governmental, party, economic, and military organizations and upon the smoothness with which the SED will handle the inevitable succession crises. Naturally, since he was born on June 30, 1893, the question of Ulbricht's heir is already a topic of increasing speculation in all informed quarters. Death, abdication, or a "fade-out" are equal possibilities for bringing about a succession crisis. The swiftness with which political agreement upon a new leader develops among all interested factions, as facilitated or impaired by the DDR's institutional structure, will determine how legitimate to all social domestic forces the new selection is, how strong his initial endorsement and even future prospects are, and how systemic tensions are converted in the general process into permanent antagonisms.

The New Principles of Government

As Stalin was considered author of the 1936 Constitution in the USSR, Ulbricht is considered the chief architect of the 1968 Socialist Constitution in the DDR. The new constitution serves in a variety of ways as a historic pronouncement on the prevailing constitutional "order of things."

First, it retains the indispensable features, provisions, and institutions of the otherwise outdated Constitution of 1949. The form of the state is republican, of course. The form of government is parliamentary, in the sense that a nominally omnipotent assembly, free from any system of checks or balances, is the representative body from which all legislative, executive, and judicial powers apparently originate. The pretense of a multiple-party state has also been preserved, thereby providing unanimity of the assembly parties in accordance with the bloc technique of mandatory coalition government. Finally, as before, not only are mass organizations represented in the assembly along with parties, but no party can exist as a political force outside of the assembly nor as a source of loyal opposition within it.[4]

Second, the 1968 Constitution confirms the various revisions of the old constitution effected by amendment, disuse, convention, or expediency. Noteworthy of citation here is its reaffirmation of the unitary and unicameral characteristics of East German Government, first developed by the amendments of 1955 and 1958, with which the upper chamber (*Landerkammer*) was simultaneously eliminated as an organ for the representation of historically meaningful state polities (*Lander*) and stripped of its qualified power of legislative veto over the proposals of the lower chamber (*Volkskammer*). The 1960 amendment, adopted after the death of thrice-elected (1949, 1953, and 1957) President Wilhelm Pieck, replaced the presidency with the Council of State (*Staatsrat*).[5] Each of these alterations constituted deliberate steps in retreat from the illusion which the original constitution of 1949 was expected to convey internally, within Germany, and abroad—namely, rather than moving ahead towards the adoption of a Stalinist constitutional order, East Germany had reverted to the bourgeois, democratic, and republican order of the 1919 Weimar system.[6] The 1968 Constitution, however, openly proclaimed itself to be proletarian, democratically centralist, monistically instituted, and historically unique. The April decision of the SED's Seventh Congress to provide the DDR the following year with a new constitutional basis, hence, was a revolutionary rejection both of the earlier pre-Nazi Western democratic and the post-World War II antifascist and reformist phases of German political development.[7]

Thirdly, the new constitution asserts and summarizes the theoretically valid and new foundations of state, government, and society, requiring for this purpose 108 articles divided into five parts. They cover respectively, the foundations of the socialist social and state order, the role of citizens and organizations in socialist society, the structure and system of state management, the nature and administration of socialist legality, and a miscellaneous composite of concluding provisions.[8]

Among the many theoretical propositions incorporated into the theoretical underpinnings of the 1968 constitutional system is the proposition that neither the DDR nor the Soviet Union bear any responsibility for the division of Germany.[9] Elsewhere, whereas allegedly all political power in the DDR is exercised by the working people, it is nevertheless provided that the working people in town and country are jointly implementing socialism under the leadership of the working class and its Marxist-Leninist party.[10]

Whereas the DDR is constitutionally obliged never to undertake a war of conquest or employ its armed forces against the freedom of another people,[11] this theoretical obligation was obviously violated in the very same year of the constitution's adoption by the DDR's military participation on August 21 in the Warsaw-Pact intervention against the Czechoslovakian national-reformist government under Dubcek.

The constitution also commits itself unreservedly to reciprocal inter-action, joint promotion, and shared progress as normative expectations about the pattern of dynamics to be developed between the state and society, on the one hand, and the individual and the collective organiza-tion, on the other.[12] The theme of an economically rational, socially non-exploitive, centrally managed, and nationally planned economy, is especially highlighted in the 1968 document.[13] Besides pursuing a for-eign policy serving peace, socialism, international friendship, and secu-rity, because of the present improbability of German reunification on the basis of democracy and socialism, no other external association is possi-ble for the DDR than one of all-round cooperation and friendship with the Soviet Union and the Soviet bloc states on the basis of socialist internationalism.[14]

The legitimacy of the new constitution depends upon the fact that it was revised on the basis of popular discussion, confirmed by the People's Chamber on March 26, 1968, and voted on by the people on April 6, 1968, before being put into effect on April 12, 1968.[15] The new constitu-tion's legitimacy derives from its affirmation of the independence, law-fulness and popularity of the DDR as a separate German state, imbued with a high spirit of socialist patriotism and defended as his socialist homeland by every citizen.[16]

Why a new constitution? It can be argued that a new constitution was necessary because the intervening two decades of domestic and interna-tional change had rendered the old one irrelevant and obsolete. Socialist constitutions, within certain practical limitations, of course, basically do not concern themselves with the proper ordering and engineering of power by way of the specification of institutional competence or the application of such power checks as periodicity, staggering, balance, compartmentalization, or limitation. No particular value is attached to blessing a society with the security, stability, and service of an ongoing constitutional system capable of self-correction and preservation. In-stead, upon exhaustion of a constitutionally designated program, the old phase must be historically terminated, thus necessitating the sacrifice of its constitutional order as well—just as a reptile's irresistible growth naturally compels it to shed its skin at the moment of its maximum restraint.

In the new constitution there is a disproportionate weight, when measured against the West German Basic Law, given to socio-economic, as compared with legal and political, features in the areas of labor, culture, education, sickness, youth, vocation, recreation, sport, and old age. As in the old, so in the new constitution, social security substantially displaces individual freedom. Since the leading role of the worker's party no longer can be directed against another element of the society, the SED identifies itself in the forthcoming phase of socialist development as a "party of the whole people" (*Volkspartei*). Consequently, there is nowhere even a hint at the future prospect for the East German citizenry of obtaining from the SED a choice of two or more socio-economic models after which it might alternately choose to fashion itself. Furthermore, the constitution no less firmly is opposed to any such proto-political group activity as could assume the form of what is called in West Germany an "extra-parliamentary" force, alternative, or opposition. The expanded and real meaning of Article 3 is that "the alliance of all forces of the people finds its organized expression in the National Front of Democratic Germany."

A final observation concerns the constitution's tone, style, and craftsmanship, which are not always separately distinguishable characteristics in the new document. The tone is assertive, promotional, declaratory, verbose, and ambiguous; the style is lengthy, complex, programmatic, and partisan; the craftsmanship is unpolished, uneven, dated, and provincial. However, as the symbol by which the antifascist, democratic revaluation was terminated and with which the socialist revolutionary phase was commenced, its apologists retain the privilege of final judgment, to confirm the validity of the final observation:

> The Socialist Constitution, which came into force on 8 April 1968, is a firm basis for completing the construction of socialism in the German Democratic Republic. It proves that the forces of democracy and socialism have triumphed in the GDR once and for all, that the working people of all strata are determined, under the leadership of the working class and its party, to advance jointly on the road of historical progress and to protect the achievements they attained in hard work against the enemies of socialism. The socialist system of society has a firm basis in the German Democratic Republic.[17]

Popular Sovereignty and the People's Chamber

The sovereignty of the working people, which is implemented on the basis of democratic centralism, formally must be regarded, under the 1968 Constitution, as the fundamental principle underlying the structure and system of state management. The institution through which working people's popular sovereignty is actually asserted is the People's Chamber (*Volkskammer*), the supreme organ of state power in the German Democratic Republic and the body which allegedly decides in its plenary sessions the basic questions of state policy. Just as nobody can limit the powers of the British Queen-in-Parliament, so no one apparently can limit the rights of the People's Chamber in its role as the sole constitutional and legislative organ in the DDR. Furthermore, in at least superficial conformity with the classical parliamentary tradition's concept of a fusion of executive and legislative power, the People's Chamber, by its activities, implements the principle of the unity of decision and enforcement.[18]

Because of the 1952 abolition of the five states of Saxony, Brandenburg, Saxony-Anhalt, Mecklenburg, and Thuringia as independent legal entities and the de jure confirmation of this decision by the abolition of the upper chamber (*Landerkammer*) on December 8, 1958, quite expectedly the new constitution establishes the legislature as a unicameral body for a unitary system of government. Also, given the DDR's territorial compactness of about 41,700 square miles (108,174 square kilometers, or the size of Tennessee),[19] the smallness of its population (17,100,000 persons),[20] and its almost ideal ethnic homogeneity,[21] another arrangement along federal lines would have been an unnecessary recollection of an embarrassing pre-Nazi tradition, on the one hand, and incompatible with the economic objective of central state planning and the political commitment to democratic centralism, on the other.[22]

The People's Chamber is the institutional stock or trunk from which emanate several legislative, judicial, and executive offshoots. Among these extensions are, as executive-type bodies, the Council of Ministers (*Ministerrat*), its inner Presidium (*Prasidium*), and the National Defense Council (*Nationale Verteidigungsrat*); as judicial arms, the Highest Court (*Oberstes Gericht*) and the Procurator General (*Generalstaatsanwalt*); and, as legislative-type derivations, the Council of State (*Staatsrat*), Presidium, Council of Elders (*Altestenrat*), Fractions (*Fraktionen*), Committees (*Ausschusse*), and miscellaneous agencies. The People's Chamber elects at least the primary functionary to all of these institutions and usually all of their ordinary members, as well as exposes them to recall if necessary. Policy control reinforces constitutional and electoral control, inasmuch as the People's Chamber also lays down the principles to be adhered to by the Council of State, the Council of Ministers, the National Defense Council, the Supreme Court, and the Procurator General.[23]

Besides generating anew its own, its executive, and its judicial instruments every four years and besides approving or rejecting state treaties and other international agreements, determining a state of defense, and deciding to hold national plebescites, the new constitution contains no specifically enumerated and inclusive list of legislative powers. In form, therefore, the range of the legislative process appears to be practically unlimited, both as to subject matter and as to the source of its introduction.[24]

The deputies are expected to maintain close contact with their electors and to heed their proposals, suggestions, and criticisms and to ensure conscientious attention to them. Presumably, if a deputy does not maintain regular consultation hours and discussions and duly report to his electors on his activities on their behalf, besides fulfilling the previous set of obligations, he may be recalled. Deputies have the right to participate in the sessions of local popular representative bodies in an advisory capacity, to put questions to the Council of Ministers and each of its members, and the right to immunity. Deprivations of the right of immunity, in the form of limitations on their personal liberty, house searches, confiscation, or prosecution, can only be effected by the agreement of the People's Chamber. Every deputy enjoys the privilege of protection against compulsory disclosure concerning persons who have confided facts to them in the course of their duties as deputies, or to whom they have confided facts in the course of their duties as deputies and about these facts themselves. Finally, deputies may be exposed to no professional or other personal disadvantage as a result of their activities as deputies, and, insofar as this is necessary for the fulfillment of their duties as deputies, they are to be released from their ordinary occupation and to continue to receive their salaries or wages.[25]

The latter provision suggests several novel features and attitudes: (1) a conflict of interest between one's duties as deputy and one's attachment to his employing enterprise is presumably impossible or doesn't make any difference; (2) long careers as deputies are generally so infrequent as not to justify termination of employment for a mere four-year term; (3) the deputy's salary is so modest that prolonged service as a deputy is economically impossible; (4) the performance of his governmental duties requires so little time and energy over a four-year period that a deputy should really regard service as a legislator more as an amateur than a professional engagement.

The People's Chamber must be convened no later than thirty days after elections to it have been held, being convened by the Council of State. Unless two-thirds of the deputies so decide, all sessions are public. Except for constitutional amendments, which require a two-thirds vote of the Chamber's total elected membership, all measures are passed by a simple majority vote, with a quorum consisting of any number over half of the total membership. Except if two-thirds of the elected deputies decide otherwise, the People's Chamber cannot be dissolved before the expiration of its electoral term. In the ordinary event, new elections must be held no later than sixty days after the expiration of the electoral term or, in the exceptional event of its own dissolution, no later than forty-five days thereafter. All laws emanating from the Chamber must be promulgated within one month after their passage, and normally they come into force on the fourteenth day after promulgation. Lastly, the Chamber has the right to summon appropriate ministers or outside experts in order to possess itself of expert information.[26]

The Committee System

Whereas the Chamber's Rules of Order of July 14, 1967, only list thirteen legislative committees, as of March 1969 there were actually sixteen. The committee system discloses a rather conventional breakdown along functional lines and a similarly typical variation in respective total committee size, ranging from the nine-member Rules Committee to the forty-member Committee for Industry, Building, and Commerce, while the Inter-Parliamentary Group's membership is both unknown and necessarily variable. The SED ruling party holds ten out of sixteen chairmanships, thirteen out of thirty-one deputy posts, and nine out of fifteen recorder or secretariat positions. The Committee for the Budget and Finances, the Committee for Health Affairs, and the Mandate Review Committee are the only cases in which the SED does not hold either the chairman's or deputy chairman's post, and in all three of those instances the recorder belongs to the SED. In some cases, like Youth, Culture, Trade, and Industry, both the chairmanship and first deputy chairmanship are in the hands of the SED. The ruling party's control is, therefore, obviously assured.

Confusion and curiosity must surround certain other aspects of the committee system, in the absence of more extensive information, such as what other criteria besides party membership influence chairmanship assignments, what role expertise plays in members' assignments, what the variations are in committee work loads, what research and reference aids are available to the legislative process, and what have been the various levels of legislative activity from one chamber to another since 1949.

The Presidium of the People's Chamber

Responsible to the People's Chamber for its activities and serving as the Chamber's in-session guiding hand is the Presidium of the People's Chamber. This nine-man body is composed of a President (until his death on February 22, 1969, Professor Johannes Dieckmann, an LDP (Liberal Democratic Party) deputy, who had been Chamber President since 1950 and who was succeeded as Deputy President by Hermann

Matern, an SED deputy from Berlin), and seven ordinary Presidium members: Otto Gotsche, an SED deputy also from Berlin; Hermann Kalb, member of the Christian Democratic Union's (CDU) own presidium and chief editor of its party organ, *Neue Zeit;* Friedrich Ebert, an SED deputy from Berlin; Ernst Goldenbaum, DBD (Democratic Farmer's Party) chairman and deputy from Berlin; Margarete Muller, FDGB (Free German Labor Union) deputy from Kotelov; Wolfgang Rosser, NDP (National Democratic Party) deputy from Berlin; and, lastly, Wilhelmine Schirmer-Proscher, DFD (German Women's Association) deputy from Berlin.[28]

A closer scrutiny of the Presidium's nine members, in fact, reveals that three of them represent the SED outright (Matern, Gotsche, and Ebert), while the other six represent the SED indirectly through formal membership in some auxiliary organization.

The Council of Elders and the Council of State

The Chamber's Council of Elders (*Altestenrat*), composed of the entire Presidium and either the Chairman or the Deputy Chairman of each and every parliamentary fraction, serves as the organizational nexus through which the Presidium transmits its directive impulses beyond the nine fractional terminals into the Chamber's assembly membership per se.[29] Beyond its consultative, coordinating, and transmitting functions, the Elders' Council's full range of duties otherwise remains rather vague.

The People's Chamber, at its first session following a new election, is obliged to elect for a parallel four-year term a Council of State (*Staatsrat*), responsible to its parent organization for its activities, and operating as its steering and executive organ between Chamber sessions and between the cessation of an old Chamber and its successor's post-electoral convocation. The composition of the Council of State is as follows:[36]

Walter Ulbricht, Chairman	SED
Deputy Chairmen:	
Willi Stoph	SED
Johannes Dieckmann	LDP; deceased
Gerald Goetting	CDU
Heinrich Homann	NDP
Manfred Gerlach	LDP
Hans Rietz	DBD
Otto Gotsche, Secretary	SED

Members-at-large:

Erich Correns	DKB (German Cultural League); President of the National Front
Friedrich Ebert	SED
Erich Grutzner	SED; since 1959 Chairman of the Leipzig District Council
Brunhilde Hanke	SED; since 1961 Potsdam Ober-burgermeister
Lieselotte Herforth	SED/FDGB; Rector of Dresden's Technical University
Friedrich Kind	CDU; First Chairman of the Pots-dam District Executive Committee
Else Merke	DBD; Deputy Chairman of the DFD's Executive Committee
Gunter Mittag	SED: member of the Politburo; Secretary of the Committee for Industry, Building, and Commerce
Anni Neumann	FDGB/SED; member of the Committee for National Defense
Karl Rieke	SED; member of the SFD's Central Committee and Agricultural Council
Hans Rodenburg	SED; Deputy Chairman of the Committee for Culture
Maria Schneider	FDGB/SED; member of the Parent's Advisory Council
Horst Schumann	SED; member of SED's Central Committee, the National Council of the National Front, and the Committee of Anti-Fascist Resistance Fighters
Hans-Heinrich Simon	NDP; member of the Halle District Executive Committee
Klaus Sorgenicht	SED; Director of the SED Central Committee's Department of State-and-Judicial Matters; member of the Committee for Constitutional and Judicial Affairs
Paul Strauss	SED; member of the SED's Central Committee and the Presidium of the FDGB's Executive Committee

It is thus unmistakenly evident that the SED has truly penetrated the entire governmental apparatus. The principle of the "interlocking directorate" has clearly been incorporated into the Council of State at its highest and most sophisticated level of symbiotic effectiveness.

Walter Ulbricht, in his role as Chairman of the Council of State, directs its work of fulfilling all of the fundamental tasks resulting from the laws and decisions of the People's Chamber (Articles 69 and 66).[31] One such task is the right to decide fundamental issues of national defense and security and to organize national defense with the help of the National Defense Council, which body is responsible for its activities to both the People's Chamber and the Council of State and whose membership the Council of State must appoint (Article 73).[32] Wholly unclarified here are such questions as what problems, issues, and matters are to be constitutionally regarded as fundamental matters of national defense and security, how the State Council is responsible to the People's Chamber for the actions it takes in this province, how many persons, selected on the basis of what qualifications, shall constitute the National Defense Council (*Nationale Verteidigungsrat*), and how the Defense Council specifically can endure the insecurity of having both the State Council and the Chamber as its undifferentiated set of constitutional masters.

Another key power is the State Council's responsibility, on behalf of the People's Chamber, to erect a continuous control over the constitutionality and legality of the activities of the Supreme Court and the Procurator General (Article 74).[33]

Finally, the State Council has the power to issue decrees and decisions dealing with the basic tasks arising from the laws and decisions of the People's Chamber, provided that they are submitted to the People's Chamber for confirmation (Article 71).[34]

Several questions arise in connection with these constitutional provisions: (1) what is the meaning of a "basic task" arising from the Chamber's actions; (2) who resolves disagreements of interpretation arising on this score between the Council and the Chamber; (3) when must the Council submit to the Chamber its decrees and decisions, and how; (4) what vote, a simple majority vote or a qualified vote, is necessary to confirm or reject a Council decree; and (5) how are Council-Chamber confrontations resolved if a decree is rejected, and what legal consequences ensue from a rejection during the period the Council presumed the decree was in force. The ultimate answer to these questions, of course, is that the SED's smooth control of the flow of power throughout the governmental apparatus prevents such constitutional possibilities from ever becoming concrete problems.

The National Defense Council

The National Defense Council, composed of persons appointed by the Council of State and simultaneously responsible to it and the People's Chamber in a wholly unclear manner, apparently is a fourteen-man body, with a chairman, secretary, and twelve members.[35] Inasmuch as the constitution already assigns to the Council of State primary responsibility for making fundamental decisions in the national defense and security areas, the National Defense Council appears a superfluous organ, the more so since nowhere are its functional competence, membership, or qualifications set forth. Its true composition, in fact, is partly a matter of conjecture.

The Council's Chairman is Walter Ulbricht (SED); its Secretary, Erich Honecker (SED); and Paul Frohlich (SED); Heinz Kessler (SED); and Willi Stoph (SED) are four of its required twelve members. Speculation suggests that Heinz Hoffman (SED), Erich Mielke (SED), and Friedrich Dickel (SED) are among the other eight unknown members on the basis of their ranks and positions. Hoffman is a General of the Army and Minister for National Defense, Mielke is a Minister for State Security and a General-Colonel, and Dickel is Minister of the Interior, Chief of German People's Police and a General-Colonel. For their part, Willi Stoph is a member in his capacity of Chairman of the Council of Ministers, Scheibe as a General-Lieutenant in his role as Chief of the Air Force and Air Defense, Kessler as a General-Colonel because he is chief of the National People's Army's (NVA) General Staff, and Frohlich as the Chairman of the Chamber's Defense Committee.[36]

The most conspicuous and perhaps most vital characteristic exhibited by the National Defense Council is its imposition of civilian authority over military expertise. Chairmanship of the Defense Council goes to Walter Ulbricht in his capacities as Chairman of the Council of State, First Secretary of the SED's Central Committee, and as a member of the party's Politburo. The secretaryship goes to Erich Honecker because he is also a member of the Politburo, the Central Committee's Secretary for Security Questions, and Chief of the Politburo's Commission for National Security. Neither holds a military position of command or staff importance in any branch of the DDR's armed forces; neither man has ever directly wielded such authority at any point in the postwar development of East Germany. Paul Frohlich's career is similar in this regard. He has split his attention between party service as First Secretary of the Leipzig SED apparatus since 1952, full member of the Politburo since

1963, and member of the Chamber's Committee for National Defense since 1960. However, the remainder of the known membership of the Defense Council either now enjoys military rank and fulfills a professional responsibility (Kessler, Scheibe, Hoffman, Mielke, and Dickel) or was approximately so qualified in the past (Stoph, Minister of the Interior, 1952–55, and Minister of National Defense, 1956–60).[37]

Whereas the Defense Council is a creation of the Council of State, on which organization appeared a modest representation of non-SED party members, such as Heinrich Homann of the NPD, the Defense Council is composed exclusively of SED party members. This characteristic of the National Defense Council assumes a special significance when it is observed that every Council member is also a member of the SED's Central Committee (Scheibe is a candidate member, however), that four members also enjoy membership on the SED's Politburo (Ulbricht, Honecker, Frohlich, and Stoph), and that two members further epitomize SED party control in their capacity as Central Committee Secretaries (Ulbricht and Honecker).[38] Hence, the National Defense Council is the point of organizational intersection of legislative, executive, military, ministeriat, security, and party controls.

A final characteristic of the National Defense Council is the revelation of an inconspicuous psychological, historical, and, perhaps, personal association affecting Ulbricht, Hoffman, Mielke, and Dickel—all of them served directly or in an associated capacity with the International Brigade during the Spanish civil war of 1936–39. This common experience not only would have been acquired in areas of concern like those in the fields of military affairs, secret police, and national defense with which the Council is now constitutionally concerned, but it would also have accustomed all four men to the acceptance of Soviet secret police, military and psychological controls of the type that were first imposed upon the Soviet Zone's early military formations and which have been largely retained over the DDR through the Warsaw-Pact structure.

The Council of Ministers

The essence of the form of government, according to Karl Loewenstein, is the legislative-executive relationship—whether in coordination or in subordination.[39] The legislative-executive relationship established by the DDR's 1968 Constitution confirms the earlier observation, made with reference to the 1949 Constitution, that the SED controls the East German state by an assembly system of government rather than through a classical model of parliamentary government. For, "in the place of coordination and cooperation . . . (between executive and legislative institutions) . . . there exists by a curious inversion characteristic of assembly government, a strictly hierarchical system of subordination. . . . No simpler, less complex, and more direct technique for the exercise of political power ever has been put on paper."[40]

The formal subordination of the executive to the legislative institution of power results from the constitutional responsibility (Article 80, 1) of the State Council's Chairman (Walter Ulbricht) to propose to the People's Chamber for its confirmation the head of government, the Chairman (Willi Stoph) of the Council of Ministers (*Ministerrat*). He, in turn, is charged by the People's Chamber with the formation of the body of his intended executive branch, whereupon the Chamber elects the executive composite for a four-year term of office (Article 80, 2).[41]

The following aspects of the process whereby the formation of the executive power is accomplished are unclear, however. (1) What considerations, qualifications, and constitutional criteria should guide and control the selection by the Chairman of the State Council of a possible Chairman of the Council of Ministers? (2) Does he act in this capacity under previously adopted instructions issued to him by the Chamber, or does he operate without instructions during this phase, while the Chamber satisfies itself with the power to refuse the nominee of his unfettered search? (3) Are there no political qualifications attached to the position of Chairman of the Council of Ministers, that is, may he come from any party? If not, what partisan electoral considerations will limit the Chamber's choice as to party and as to individual function and rank for the nominated Chairman within the particular ' party constitutionally favored? Is the proposed Chairman of the Council of Ministers only conditionally so designated by the People's Chamber while he is engaged in the formation of his intended Council of Ministers, until he and his cabinet are jointly confirmed at the subsequent stage of the Chamber's approval, or does he remain the formally preferred Chairman, at liberty to make a second attempt, should the Chamber reject his slate of proposed ministers? (4) Must the Chamber approve the entire slate or does it have a power of selective and progressive approval? (5) The Council of Ministers is composed of the Chairman, Vice-Chairman, and the Ministers. Who is constitutionally empowered to determine the number and respective functions of the Vice-Chairmen and the Ministers—the Council Chairman, the Chairman of the Council of State, and/or the Chamber? (6) If each Minister is responsible for the particular field assigned to him, if all members of the Council of Ministers are collectively accountable for its activities, and if the Council is elected for a fixed term of four years, by what institutional techniques and continuous processes, such as the power of legislative investigation, votes of non-confidence,[42] and assembly questioning, is the Council of Ministers ever kept accountable, alert, responsible, and sensitive to the Chamber's desires and instructions?

The total failure of the 1968 Constitution to resolve any of the above ambiguities, indisputably standing at the heart of any classical effort to establish a sound parliamentary process, demonstrates the persistence of the assembly tradition in East Germany between 1949 and 1968, the procedural and substantive continuity with which all forms of East German government are infused because of the sublimated influence of SED power throughout, and the degree to which assembly government rejects traditional parliamentary requirements, such as the political responsibility of executive power to the assembly, the advisory recommendation by the head of government to the head of state to dissolve Parliament, and the supremacy of Parliament as a whole over its two constituent parts of mutually unpreferred government (Council of Ministers) and assembly (People's Chamber).[43] Therefore, in view of the power of the Council of State, through the personality of Ulbricht as SED party chief, to recommend and to assure the Chamber's appointment of the head of government and his cabinet and in view of its capacity to issue legally forceful decrees and decisions of a quasi-executive character, three conclusions are inescapable: (1) the SED, not Parliament as the fusion of the People's Chamber and the Council of Ministers, is the focus of power in the East German political system; (2) the Council of State, not the Council of Ministers or its Presidium as the inner cabinet, is the real source of true executive power; (3) executive power, in order of diminishing natural virility, really embraces the Council of State, with the National Defense Council as a specialized adjunct; the Presidium of the Council of Ministers, including its Chairman particularly; the Council of Ministers, including its Chairman particularly; the Council of Ministers per se; and a host of miscellaneous quasi-executive line or staff agencies.

The juncture at which executive and legislative powers are fused, in other words, is not in the Council of Ministers but in the nexus of relationships buckling together the Council of State and the ministerial Presidium. For the State Council is more executive and less legislative, and the ministerial Presidium is more executive and the Council of Ministers more administrative than formal constitutional appearances initially suggest. Walter Ulbricht's self-arrogation of the position of Chairman of the Council of State, in preference to the equally available post of Chairman of the Presidium and Council of Ministers, confirms simultaneously where real executive power has been relocated and how peculiar a rendition of parliamentary government assembly government becomes under socialist experimentation in the field of constitutional engineering.[44]

The Presidium, or "inner cabinet" of the Council of Ministers, consists of the Chairman (Willi Stoph, SED), a First Deputy (Alfred Neumann, SED), ten Deputies (Alexander Abusch, SED; Kurt Fichtner, SED; Manfred Flegel, NDP; Wolfgang Rauchfuss, SED; Gerhard Schurer, SED; Max Sefrin, CDU; Werner Titel, DBD; Gerhard Weiss, SED; Herbert Weiz, SED; and Kurt Wunsche, LDP), and three Ministers (Georg Ewald, SED; Siegfried Bohm, SED; Walter Halbritter, SED).[45] The Chairman, First Deputy Chairman, and seven of ten Deputies to the Chairman do not simultaneously administer specific ministries but are unencumbered with responsibilities for specific departments, in order to perform more effectively as general supervisory administrators. Schurer as Chairman of the State Planning Commission, Sefrin as Minister for Health, and Wunsche as Minister of Justice are the three exceptions to the general rule prevailing among the order of the Chairman's Deputies. Halbritter as Director of the Office of Prices, Bohm as Minister of Finance, and Ewald as Chairman of the Council for Agricultural Production and Foodstuff comprise the group of ordinary members of the Presidium without deputy status. The Chairman, First Deputy Chairman, Deputy Chairmen without Portfolio, Deputy Chairmen with Portfolio, and ordinary ministers, therefore, constitute an implicit functional stratification within the Presidium.

Eleven out of fifteen of the Presidium's members enjoy SED membership, while one each is a representative of the NDP, CDU, DBD and LDP, respectively. Further evidence of the SED's overwhelming political mastery of the Presidium consists of the fact that both the Chairman and First Deputy Chairman are simultaneously members of the SED's Secretariat, Politburo, and Central Committee—not to mention that two others (Ewald and Halbritter) are simultaneously candidate members of the Politburo and full members of the Central Committee, or that an additional seven presidial members (Abusch, Rauchfuss, Schurer, Weiz, Ewald, Bohm, and Halbritter) are full members and one deputy (Weiss) is a candidate member of the Central Committee. How the power principle of the interlocking directorate is applied is evident from the following illustration.

The thirty-nine member Council of Ministers, next regarded as the general cabinet, consists of the fifteen-man "inner cabinet" and an "outer cabinet" of another twenty-four ordinary ministers, all but one of whom (Rudolf Schulze, CDU) further contribute to the Council's general SED imbalance of thirty-four out of thirty-nine cabinet-level positions.[46] Hence, an overall view of the Council of Ministers reveals thirty-four out of thirty-nine are SED-party members, twenty-four of thirty-four SED members are full members of the SED Central Committee, and five are Central Committee candidate members.[47] The absence from the "outer cabinet" of SED cadre elite from either the Politburo or the Secretariat confirms again the earlier observation that the party's supreme policy-makers regard the juncture of the Council of State and the ministerial Presidium as the main socket into which its directive current should be plugged.

Each ministry is organized according to a very consistent pattern. In the case of the Ministry of the Interior, as a random illustration, General-Colonel Friedrich is the department's chief administrative officer and Chief of the People's Police, General-Lieutenant Herbert Grunstein is State-Secretary and First Deputy of the Minister, General-Lieutenant Willi Seifert is Deputy of the Minister and Chief of Staff, followed by General-Major Heinz Huth and General-Major Gerd Uhlig as ordinary Deputies of the Minister. The ministry for Chemical Industry consists of Gunter Wyschofsky as Minister, Karl-Heinz Schafer as State-Secretary and First Deputy of the Minister, and, as Deputies, Hans Adler, Horst Grufe, and Gerhard Mobius. Besides the ministers in these two cases, of course, both State-Secretaries and every Deputy Minister belongs to the SED. The distribution of SED party membership for all twenty-five regular ministries and the Minister for the Direction and Control of District and County Councils, at the level below the full minister himself, are 115 SED party members, 2 CDU members, 1 LDP member, and 1 NDP member.[48] In short, nearly ninety-seven percent of the administrative posts at the ministerial level is in the hands of the SED.

The linchpin by which the party-state, legislative-executive, and intra-executive specializations are bound together under a coherent, ubiquitous, and objective censorial policy, is the Committee of the Workers-and-Peasants Inspection. Its Chairman (Heinz Matthes), First Deputy Chairman (Werner Greiner-Petter), and seven Deputy Chairmen (Herbert Ebert, Fred Goldmann, Kurt Hoffmann, Gunter Lewinsohn, Harry Schwermer, Heinz Stiebritz, and Gunter Vogel) are responsible, as members of a powerful state central control agency, for the faithful execution of the decisions of the SED's Central Committee, the laws of the People's Chamber, the decrees of the Council of State, and the decisions of the Council of Ministers.[4] Whereas, heretofore the control technique of interlocking has been exposed by analysis in its personnel and policy dimensions, here it reveals itself in an overt and deliberate *institutional* form. Naturally, all of its membership is SED, with its minister-ranked chairman belonging to the Central Committee.[50]

In the final analysis, therefore, it seems that the powers assigned to the whole range of East German governmental activity are vaguely defined, if at all, even in those exceptional cases where certain powers, like defense policy, are assigned to a particular agency. In many cases no clear lines of constitutional responsibility between different agencies are established. In some cases, like the National Defense Council, overlappings or double lines exist. Furthermore, except for the requirement of the People's Chamber that a two-thirds vote is required to alter by amendment the supremacy of the new constitution itself (Article 63), no constitutional definition is ever provided for the difference between laws passed by the People's Chamber and decrees and decisions issued by the Council of State (Article 71), or between the latter and regulations and decisions which the Council of Ministers may issue. Jurisdictional confusion, institutional irresponsibility, and the omission of a hierarchy of laws are combined with a dependent judiciary responsible to the People's Chamber and, between its sessions, to the Council of State (Article 93). The Council of State exercises continuous control not only over the constitutionality and legality of the whole judicial system's activities (Article 74) but over the activities of the Council of Ministers and other state organs as well (Article 89).[51]

The functional and dynamic symbiosis effected by the SED's permeation of the governmental process with its peculiar personnel, policies, and tight organization, however, explains not only why this system does not exhibit the conventional disorders associated with such an apparent constitutional misconstruction, but it also conclusively confirms assembly government as a separate species of government rather than a mere perversion of parliamentary government. It should be obvious that the Socialist Unity Party's political control progressively intensifies as the legislative function arches up into the executive—with the keystone of the span being constituted of the fusion of the State Council and ministerial Presidium—and arches down into the administrative functions.

The same remarkable strength engendered by the SED's irresistible integrative and directive guidance, of course, is equally a measure of the system's vulnerability to paralysis and collapse should the party's own decisiveness and unity degenerate into ideological skepticism, factional schisms, or policy bewilderment. Another, but by no means last, strength-weakness unity characteristic of the East German governmental system is the complexity, range, and refinement of its executive-administrative establishment, epitomized in the organizational breakdown of the Council of Ministers. Through this establishment the party-state ubiquitously manifests to the populace its presence, activity, concern, mastery, prestige, and monopoly. Yet, these strengths in an overdeveloped form mean bureaucratic inertia, indifference, duplication, inefficiency, conservatism, and expense, with the attendant dangers of popular frustration, alienation, withdrawal, and passive or active resistance. The SED's duty, in the interests of its own survival, therefore, is to avoid the extremes of innovation, reform, and reaction. The 1969 celebration of the DDR's twentieth anniversary attests in this regard to the professional competence of both Walter Ulbricht and the SED.

The Role of the Party

The Seventh Party Congress, held April 17–22, 1967, established the organizational form and composition of the leading organs of the Socialist Unity Party current in 1970 (except insofar as subsequent deaths, reassignments, and less obvious alterations and trends have produced changes). In accordance with the party statute adopted at the Sixth Party Congress, in January of 1963, around two thousand delegates assembled for the 1967 event. They unanimously endorsed the slate of nominees proposed by the party's elite to compose the new Central Committee.[52]

The Central Committee (ZK) elected by the Seventh Party Congress consisted of 131 delegates (4 had died as of March 1969) and 50 candidates.[53] Once electorally liberated from the womb of the party congress, the ZK becomes the rootstock from which all other policy agencies are generated. The previous permanent party agencies facilitate each phase by which the ZK is elected by the party congress and by which the Politburo, Secretariat, and Control Commission (ZPKK), in turn, are derived from the Central Committee.

The scheme by which a body formally totaling 181 persons is enabled to formulate meaningful policy decisions is specialization, which breaks up the organization into thirty-five sections and eight commissions.[54] Such an organizationally detailed division of labor reveals the totality of the Central Committee's range of policy interests in nearly every aspect of national, economic, and social life. It also reveals, in certain regards, a high degree of correspondence with the breakdowns of the People's Chamber committee system and the Council of Ministers. Hence, internally, topically, and laterally, the Central Committee is able to blend party policy and governmental execution into an indissoluble force of societal transformation. Hardly anyone can ignore the significance to their awakened understanding of the principle of interlocking functional combinations evidenced by Ulbricht's chairmanship of the Commission for Long-range Planning for the SED. It enables him personally to link the Central Committee proper, the Politburo, the Council of Ministers, the Council of State, and the party Secretariat. The inclusion within the Central Committee's overall organization of several components dealing exclusively with party affairs (for example, cadre, party organs, and party finances), further facilitates the immediate transmission of his wishes.

Whereas, until recently the Central Committee functioned almost exclusively as an acclamatory and representative device, it has lately also begun to function increasingly in the serious and expert discussion and preparation of fundamental party-state decisions. The increase in the Central Committee's functional capacities results partly from the reassignment by the Politburo and Secretariat to the ZK of certain of their separate and joint responsibilities and partly from the progressive acquisition of new capacities as a consequence of its changing composition. Table 1 discloses this dynamic alteration in terms of emerging patterns of functional assignment and educational background as they affect members and candidates. Hence, for the 1963 Central Committee, the overall picture reveals that 32 (26 percent) of 121 full members and 35 (58 percent) of 60 candidate members were graduates of any of three kinds of higher institutions, while, for the 1967 ZK, 70 (53 percent) out of 131 full members and 38 (76 percent) out of 50 candidate members had attained the quivalent experience four years later.

The increase in the 1967 ZK partly explains the relatively greater importance now attached to the party and state apparatuses as compared to the 1963 pattern, although this effect has also resulted from a modest relative decline in the significance of the mass organizations and a minor diminution of the economic sector's importance. Between the two relatively preferred functional sectors a further pattern is evident in the greater expansion of full membership created in the state section (plus nine members) as compared to the party sector (plus five members). Whereas the academic and polytechnical training rose significantly in every single category, both for members and candidates, of particular significance for the party's future development is the considerably greater improvement among the candidates compared with the full members and the phenomenal improvement in the economic specialty. The overall elevation of the ZK's educational training has resulted from both a limited number of reelected members and candidates who completed programs by 1967 and from the disproportionately qualified new full and candidate members (eleven out of thirteen full members and nineteen out of twenty-five candidate members complying with the new educational emphasis).[55] Finally, from the viewpoint of the SED's future capacity to be stabilized and led by its superior organs, the overall

TABLE 1

Educational Background of SED Central Committee Members

| Area of Service | Full Members | | | Candidates | | |
| | Total | Graduates of universities, technical schools, advanced party schools | | Total | Graduates of universities, technical schools, advanced party schools | |
		No.	%		No.	%
Party Apparatus						
1963	49	13	26	13	6	46
1967	54	15	54	29	10	67
State Apparatus						
1963	30	12	27	8	6	50
1967	39	13	46	18	9	69
Economic Direction						
1963	15	14	20	3	10	70
1967	14	9	78	11	8	89
Mass Organization						
1963	11	6	27	3	3	50
1967	8	5	50	4	5	100
Education, Culture, Science, and Free Professions						
1963	10	13	50	5	10	77
1967	11	8	73	8	6	75
Base Occupations						
1963	4	2		—	—	
1967	5	—		—	—	
Miscellaneous						
1963	2	—		—	—	
1967	—	—		—	—	

NOTE: This table is a combination and chronological adaptation of tables 3 and 4 appearing in *Die SED* by Eckart Fortsch with Rudiger Mann (Stuttgart: W. Kohlhammer Verlag, 1969).

improvement within the Central Committee considerably exceeds the rate in the party's lower levels.

The largest single group is the hardcore of the party's cadre, sixty-nine all told. Included in the hardcore are all ten members of the ZK's Secretariat, all sixteen first district secretaries (including the province of Wismut), thirteen ordinary district secretaries, and fifteen divisional-level leaders of major Central Committee functional specializations. The remaining members of the party component consist of county-level first secretaries (three), secretaries of major SED-enterprises (three), one chairman of the Central Party Control Commission, and one District Party Control Commission, besides limited representation from such party organizations as the ZK's Institute for Social Science, the Party Graduate School, the Institute for Marxism-Leninism, and the Institute for Public Opinion Research (total of seven).[56]

It is also interesting to note that, of a total of fifty-two ZK members and candidates from the state apparatus, no less than twenty-five are members of the Council of Ministers. Another distinctive ZK component consists of eight directors of specific People's Cooperative Enterprises (VEB) and four general directors of the Association of People's Cooperative Enterprises (VVB). A fourth cohesive group meriting attention is that comprised of the six heads of the various mass organizations and at least another seven high-level lieutenants, including in the former rank Herbert Warnke (Free German Trade Union/FDGB), Gunter Jahn (Free German Youth/FDJ), Max Burghardt (German Cultural League/DKB), Ilse Thiele (Democratic Women's League/DFD), Manfred Ewald (German Gymnastics and Sport League/DTSB), and Kurt Thieme (Association for German-Soviet Friendship/GDSF).[57] While it is difficult to determine exactly how many, there are also a number of inconspicuous subgroupings in the ZK covering several other auxiliary functions. For example, there are the scientific, the fine arts, and the professional groups, not to mention the social scientists (thirteen), the teachers (seven), the economists (twenty-one), the lawyer-jurists (eight), or the agricultural specialists (seventeen).[58]

The 1970 Central Committee is relatively younger than the 1963 Committee, with an average age of approximately fifty-one years for the full and forty-two years for the candidate members.[59] Because of its functional specialization, educational qualifications and youth, and because its composition reflects the interlocking of party, state, economy, culture, education, mass organizations, and security and military affairs, the Central Committee, therefore, is exceptionally well equipped to integrate, coordinate, comprehend, and direct the whole complex of East German national existence.

Elevation to the Central Committee (as well as from it to the Secretariat, the Control Commission, and the Politburo), really takes place through co-optation from below, ratified in a mere formal elective act by the party congress, in accordance with the party's implicit standards of selectivity. The truly positive standards of promotion nonetheless remain unclear in most regards, except as the previous analysis reveals a preference for specialization, youth, education, and diversity, although the party elite naturally attempts to exclude the opportunistic, unreliable, incompetent, and eccentric.

However, beyond these limited insights, little is externally manifest about the process by which the ZK deliberates, decides, and resolves upon courses of action in situations and conditions of stress, danger, normalcy, or confusion. The real test of its maturity will be how quickly, smoothly, and wisely it contributes to the solution of the succession problem upon Walter Ulbricht's withdrawal, retirement, or death as First Secretary.

The Supreme Directorate

The supreme directorate of the Socialist Unity Party is comprised of the joint and partly overlapping memberships of the ZK's ten-man Secretariat and twenty-one-man Politburo, producing a total elite of twenty-two policy and executive leaders. All but one (Werner Lamberz) of the ten Secretaries are simultaneously members of the Politburo, with two of the nine (Hermann Axen and Werner Jarowinsky) serving the latter agency as candidate and the other seven (Gerhard Gruneberg, Kurt Hager, Erich Honecker, Gunter Mittag, Albert Norden, Walter Ulbricht, and Paul Verner) as full members.[60] The nine doubly employed party personalities constitute the SED's "old and inner" elite, from whose ranks Ulbricht's successor probably will come.

Reliable knowledge of the respective competences exercised by the Secretariat and the Politburo is very limited. The 1963 party statute also fails to clarify the functional distinctions beyond the point of providing vague descriptions. Decisions of the broadest possible political impact in the areas of domestic, foreign, economic, cultural, and security policy seem to be formulated in the Politburo, while the Secretariat transmits them through the appropriate party channels for execution by the state apparatus. The Secretariat also routinely attends to such typical intra-party work as cadre and organizational matters. The Politburo membership assembles around a U-shaped table, with Ulbricht sitting at its head, for collective action at least once a week, when each participant addresses himself to such problems as fall within the area of his particular speciality. The members enjoy the services of a small bureau which prepares the Politburo's agenda, position-papers, and other documents.[61]

The supreme elite has endured little social or personnel change since 1963, in contrast to the pattern observed for the Central Committee. The 1963 Politburo contained five members (Erich Apel, Karl-Heinz Bartsch, Werner Jarowinsky, Gunter Mittag, and Margarete Muller) with university-level training in economics who were actively employed in appropriate party assignments. Apel, at the time of the negotiations over the Russo-German trade agreement in 1965, committed suicide, and Bartsch was removed from his post upon disclosure of an SS-career during the Nazi period. In September of 1966, Mittag advanced to full member, while Halbritter and Kleiber replaced the depleted ranks of the

candidate members, thereby maintaining the presence of five academe-
cians. Using the six Politburo candidates as a standard, the current trend
in changing the Politburo's composition would be toward increasing youth and academic preparation.[62] For candidates, the ages range
from thirty-eight years of age (Kleiber and Muller) to fifty-three years
of age (Axen), while for full members it stretches from forty-three years
of age for Mittag to Ebert at seventy-five and Ulbricht and Matern, both
at seventy-six.

Closer analysis of the supreme elite's composition reveals four groupings: (1) a political core, composed of Frohlich, Hager, Honecker,
Matern, Neumann, Norden, Sindermann, Stoph, Ulbricht, Verner, and
Axen; (2) representatives of functional provinces, including such state-
economic specialists as Halbritter, Jarowinsky, and Kleiber, and such
state-party types as Ewald and Gruneberg; (3) historical and evolutionary symbols, such as Ebert and Muckenberger, personifying the political
misfortunes of the worker's movement during the Nazi days, with Muller
simultaneously epitomizing woman's new role in socialist democracy and
the academic mastery of agronomy; and (4) a mixed grouping of people
like Warnke, who, in terms of age, career, and political bearing, belongs
to the first and third groups and, in terms of his FDGB chairmanship, to
the second, or Mittag, whose youth, academic and practical background
in economics, previous FDGB career, and ideological orthodoxy, clas-
sify him less conveniently in any of the other four categories than
separately, as a utility man.[63]

The strength of the supreme elite lies not only in its relatively high
stability of membership and range of practical skills but also in its
educability. Both Walter Ulbricht, personally, and the political core,
especially, have managed to rationalize effectively a firm politico-ideological commitment with the need to lead the modernization, industrialization, technicalization, and vitalization of their overall system—without
ever losing complete control or suffering truly major disasters during the
last decade. Not only have the old elites recognized the necessity of
controlling new elites by manipulating the diversity of their respective
interests and, thus, reserving for themselves the final articulation of
cultural, economic, social, and political goals, but they have admitted no
pure technocrat to their ranks until after he has convincingly demonstrated an acceptable political aptitude. Finally, among additional reasons in explanation of the supreme elite's stability and effectiveness,
citation still remains to be made of a complex of other equally relevant
factors: the sharper wits, sensitivity, and timing developed in the challenging circumstances of Germany's division; the DDR's role as socialism's most exposed European bastion; the system's unmistakable suc-

cesses (particularly economic); the system's record of resolving its intra-party disputes in a basically bloodless style; Soviet military presence; the tactical sophistication of the old guard itself; and the canny ability and good luck of Walter Ulbricht himself.[64]

To be sure, if the supreme elite has been relatively stable and if the alterations in the Central Committee have been somewhat more progressive, as well as obscure, it is nevertheless also true that the overall quality of the intermediate and base levels of the SED apparatus has impressively advanced educationally, energetically, and practically. In 1963, for example, for the party-at-large, about thirty-three percent of all political members had obtained a university-level or polytechnic-level degree, with the specific distributions in this regard being seventy-five percent for the Central Committee, fifty percent for the district-level apparatus, and twenty-five percent for the county-level cadre.[65]

However, it should never be forgotten that these qualitative changes have been at all times initiated, accelerated, and controlled by the supreme elite. In short, the increase of the elite's professionalization, through acquired and co-opted skill specialities, has not occurred at the price of increasing depoliticization of the ruling process.

Conversely, the beneficiaries of a policy of deliberate professional emphasis, conditioned by the milieu of the system embracing them, naturally tend to accept both the political goals and the presence and prestige of the supreme elite. Those at the lower levels of the system who have not yet managed to develop a broader perspective than that entailed by their functional assignment are too deeply immersed in organizational routine and pressures to judge the system critically.

Hence, even if the supreme elite has increasingly failed to transmit its revolutionary tradition, mentality, and romance to the younger generations of cadre, a break has occurred only in the sense that the older virtues have been less rejected out of hand than transposed into a number of newer and more relevant commitments. They are preferences for devotion, involvement, utility, expediency, efficiency, and ruthlessness. The supreme elite attempts, for its part, to minimize, discipline, and channel these inferior, unworthy, and escapist inclinations by the employment of ideological, institutional, and organizational techniques of systemic integration. Increased rather than diminished frustration on both sides more and more will be the future prospect.[66]

The Primary and Secondary Party Levels

Below the elitist levels are to be found the organizational support levels of the district, county, and city and basic hierarchical strata, resting finally upon the SED's membership as the largest party in

Germany—with 1,769,912 members and candidates in December of 1966. This total membership constituted 10.4 percent of the DDR's total population of 17,080,000 at that time and 15.6 percent of its electorate, figured at 11,340,000. At the time of the creation of the SED through the merger of the SPD (German Social Democratic Party, 53 percent) and KPD (Communist Party of Germany, 47 percent), the total membership was 1,298,415 in April of 1946, rising to its all-time high of about 2,000,000 in June of 1948, before dropping to an interim low of 1,221,300 in June of 1951. Thereafter, the SED expanded at a modest but steady rate to its present levels.[67]

The last general purge of the party occurred between December and January of 1960–1961, when an "exchange of party documents" initiated the present phase of intra-party stability. The party's overall composition reveals a disproportionate under-representation of youth, women, and collective farmers, despite the party's repeated efforts to alter these profile blemishes. Between 1946 and 1948, the SED regarded itself at the membership level as an open mass-party, followed by the 1949–54 period of representing itself as an elitist party with a mass character, up to the contemporary phase. In 1970 it displays itself as a people's-and-state-party, with elitist pretensions, skeletal hierarchy, and a mass character.[68]

Structure is first introduced among the SED's nearly two million members by some 52,800 primary organizations located in places of work, villages, city residential areas, and educational institutions. The party leadership of primary organizations, chosen secretly for usually a term of one year by the respective membership, ranges between a single secretary to one secretary and fifteen to twenty executive members, with five to six being the probable average. About 98.3 percent of the secretaries at this level serve without compensation. Considerable stability prevails here inasmuch as 66,179 out of 66,295 primary party secretaries were reelected in the 1967/1968 party elections, in comparison with the fact that about 33 percent of the executive membership is rotated.[69]

The second level consists of 252 county-level party organizations, of which 215 are territorially defined, including the six city organizations of Leipzig, Halle, Dresden, Karl-Marx-Stadt, Erfurt, and Magdeburg. The remaining thirty-seven units are established in people's cooperative enterprises, universities, polytechnic schools, and the like. At a delegates' conference held every two years, a minimum executive organization is chosen, consisting of a secretary, deputy secretary, county council chairman, county planning commission chairman, county agricultural council chairman, county FDGB chairman, and county FDJ (Free German

Youth) chairman, with as many as another fifty-three executive members possible. The latter have to have been party members for at least two years, while secretaries have to have three years of membership behind them. Besides performing such typical services as intra-party organizational, personnel, ideological, and supervisory work, county-level organization is also expected to conduct weekly convocations of primary organizations' secretaries; group them functionally, as appropriate; conduct party instruction and seminars for them; serve as administrative contacts with upper-echelon party organizations; generally set an exemplary style and record for them to emulate; and report about the state of party morale and other problems in the fields of culture, economy, cadre, agitation, and policy and propaganda.[70]

If the primary level is the "non-commissioned" functional rank and the county-level the "company-grade" rank, then the district-level (*Berzirk*) is the "field-grade" category in the SED's organization hierarchy. It embraces fourteen actual districts (Rostock, Erfurt, Schwerin, Neubrandenburg, Potsdam, Frankfurt/Oder, Cottbus, Halle, Magdeburg, Gera, Suhl, Dresden, Leipzig, and Karl-Marx-Stadt) and East Berlin as the national capital, with Wismut administered under a special classification.[71] Roughly typical of the organization of these fifteen areas is Leipzig, fitted out with a first secretary (Paul Frohlich), deputy secretary, and four ordinary chairmen for economics; agriculture; agitation/propaganda; and science, education and culture, respectively. Also included are the various chairmen of the district council, district economic council, district planning commission, district agricultural commission, and FDGB district executive committee, as well as the first secretary of the FDJ district leadership and first secretary of the SED city leadership of Leipzig itself.[72]

Techniques of Integration, Control, and Systemic Management

Several principles of party organization, conduct, and life derive from the central dogma, axiom, and ideal of the SED as a party of a new type attempting to personify the Leninist virtues of political unity, ideological purity, and organizational resolution. These principles are: Democratic centralism, self-criticism, party discipline, collective leadership, competitive peaceful coexistence, and anti-factionalism.[73]

Besides the principles of integration of party, state, and mass organizations, the joint collaboration of government and party, and the de facto constitutional character of party decisions emanating from the level of the party's supreme elite, there are a limited number of unaccounted techniques of systemic control and management. There is, for example, the technique of penetrating, orchestrating, and implicating relatively distinctive social, age, sex, political, and religious inclinations in state-party processes through their representation in the various mass organizations, a multi-party system, and in the National Front.[74] A second example is the recent invention of a variety of SED-sponsored processes by which social conflicts, frustrations, and dissatisfactions can be positively harnessed and/or dissipated through public discussions of specified topics and selected problems, by centrally sponsored campaigns and recruitment drives, and by arbitration and conflict commissions. Another control technique is the system of agitation, mass propaganda and multi-faceted education, directed especially at the DDR's youth, with which the SED attempts to develop a deeply committed socialist German citizen, proud of the system's accomplishments and his contributions to them. A final example of control techniques and policy involves the party elite's deep commitment to the development particularly of those scientific areas like cybernetics, organizational theory, and sociology, in which theoretical contributions to the practical art of societal control are likely to be forthcoming. At worst, mere infrequent reference by the SED to the presence of Soviet troops in the DDR suffices to remind the entire population of an overwhelming background control condition.[75]

The SED's self-image comprehends both the nexus of coexisting characteristics and the cumulative effects of the party's historical evolution in the post-World War II era. The necessity of the party to acquire expert knowledge in a variety of spheres, the post-1961 relative recession of popular opposition to the SED's rule of the Soviet Occupation Zone of Germany, the irresistible decentralization of bureaucratic authority, and an attitude of increasing self-confidence comprise one set of factors influencing the party's recent development. Ulbricht's 1963 declaration that class antagonisms no longer exist in the DDR, the dispassionate necessities of economic rationality and efficiency, and the increasingly greater importance of science and technology over ideology constitute a second set of influential forces shaping the party's character. The political and personal diminution in the contemporary importance and relevance of revolutionary élan, the impersonalization of leadership style, and the proclamation that the party's hard-core now must confine itself to the solution of essential problems and, therefore, must delegate less vital executive and administrative responsibilities and powers, represent a third set of compelling influences changing the party. The combined impact of all of these factors of change, growth, and development has been to force the party to reassess its role in East German society.

Since the summer of 1968, therefore, the SED has found itself under compulsion to work continuously at the task of revising its own "job definition."[76]

The ingredients for a new definition will be derived from the party's past experiences, its current perspectives, its operational performance, and its future projections. The party's traditional inheritance of self-conceptions is rich, diverse, and conflicting. Morally and representatively, the party regards itself as a "people's party," especially since the decade of the sixties ushered in the era of the victory of socialist relations of production, collectivization, labor stability, and industrial success. Numerically speaking, the SED is just as easily portrayed as a "mass party," particularly as a result of recent easing in the standards of admission, although, from an intra-party structural and personnel point of view, it obviously is a "cadre" or "elite party." Throughout 1968–69, however, the SED has increasingly depicted itself as a "worker's party." Yet, in accordance with its general political function, the SED must also regard itself as a "state-and-economic-party." In a national sense the SED can view itself as a "patriotic missionary party," indefinitely condemned by diverse historical circumstances to playing the role of a morally qualified but practically impotent "keeper" of its bigger but degenerate Bonn "brother." Finally, in the light of the 1968 Czechoslovakian illustration of how not to develop a model of democratic socialism within the socialist community of states, the SED now can even manage to display itself as the epitome of a true "reformist party."[77]

The problem for the SED in 1970, however, seems to be less a difficulty of traditional poverty in elements of self-perception than one of a fruitless search for a theory with which to blend all these various forms of self-perception into a qualitatively new and superior synthesis. The one-time self-proclaimed "party of a new type" has apparently resumed a pilgrimage in search of its own lost novelty.

The Economic Miracle

With a population of 17,087,236 persons in 1968, the DDR ranks unexpectedly high in industrial output and attainment. Among Communist countries, in this field the DDR is second only to the Soviet Union; among European countries, sixth; and tenth among the nations of the world.[78]

This standing is all the more impressive when measured against the starting point of 1945 and against the monumental range and depth of objective adversity subsequently prevailing, even as late as 1960–63. This adversity included: (1) extensive dismantlement of plants and equipment by Soviet occupation authorities, estimated to have been between five and ten billion Reichsmarks; (2) exorbitant reparations payments made to the Soviets, which exceeded twenty-five percent of the DDR's total industrial production for the first eight years; (3) high Soviet occupation costs, which cost the DDR five hundred million (Ost) Marks annually, not to mention less direct forms of occupation expenses; (4) continuous Soviet economic exploitation in other forms, estimated to have exceeded sixty-three billion Marks between 1945 and 1960; (5) inadequate international integration, including isolation from this German area's natural trading partners; (6) extensive labor losses to West Germany, which amounted to over three million persons, some in very highly skilled areas, between 1949 and 1961; (7) faulty planning and investment policies, especially preferences for excessive autarky and centralization; and (8) a serious lack of hard currency, necessary as reserves and to cover the current imbalances in foreign trade.[79]

An especially severe problem in 1970 centers upon the population factor, especially so far as it contributes to a labor shortage. First, the age structure of the population is becoming progressively unfavorable, because of a static birthrate (a 0.00 ratio of live births to deaths in 1968), too many old people (23 percent receive full or partial pensions, with 3,287,104 men and women over sixty-five years of age in 1968), too few young people (3,920,780 children under fifteen years of age in 1968), too many employed women (47.4 percent of the total employed labor force in 1968), too few men in the middle-age group (seven age groups are seriously deficient in those categories that would have seen World War II military service), and too many young men allocated to police and military duty (214,000 men total, to the army, navy, air force, border troops, and security forces, not to mention 350,000 armed workers comprised in a part-time militia force). Second, this distribution means that the DDR's labor force, which so far has stagnated at around 7,711,800 workers, will begin to decline in 1970 and not increase until 1980 or thereabouts. Third, with the female percentage of the work force already so high (about 13 to 15 percent higher than in West Germany), a policy of overcoming this maldistribution of the age factor by increasing the rate of female employment will only compound and prolong the structural difficulty in the form of an even greater reduction in the birthrate. Fourth, the relative improvement in the DDR's level of prosperity in the 1960s has had the ironic but typical effect of confining married couple's family plans to a desire for one child only. Finally, the continued housing shortage also continues to affect the rate of family formation, as well as the importation of foreign labor. The SED will be exceedingly confined in the possibilities of remedial action in this sphere.[80]

Even the briefest of surveys of recent structural changes effected in the DDR's economy cannot neglect the increase in the percentage of Gross Social Product (GSP) contributed by nationalized enterprises, measured over the period 1950–68:[81] As Table 2 demonstrates, private ownership clung to a considerable sphere of economic activity in several sectors, even as late as 1950, with the resistance to nationalization strongest in construction and agriculture.[82] Steady erosion occurred over the next ten years in every other sector but agriculture, which was extensively subdued by the sudden introduction in 1960 of forced collectivization.[83] The result of the last twenty years of emphasis upon industrialization, the collectivization of the farms, the reduction of the number of farms, the resort to greater mechanization, the application of

TABLE 2

Economic Contributions of DDR Nationalized Enterprises

Year	Total GSP	Industry	Construc-tion	Agricul-ture	Transporta-tion and Com-munications	Trade	Remaining Sectors
1950	61.8%	70.7%	31.6%	12.6%	83.6%	62.1%	—
1955	73.3	78.9	56.0	25.0	87.7	83.8	—
1960	84.4	84.5	78.0	80.1	92.6	86.6	—
1966	86.8	85.4	83.7	91.3	94.9	88.8	93.6%
1967	86.8	85.2	86.0	91.6	95.5	88.4	93.7
1968	85.1	82.6	79.3	94.1	94.0	86.5	94.5

more fertilizer, and the absorption in the cities of surplus farm labor is that the agricultural section generates only ten percent of East Germany's total product compared to twenty percent in the prewar period, while industry's contribution has increased by at least forty percent, and retail trade and commerce have proportionately declined.[84] Whereas prior to 1955 East Germany's planned economy paralleled Soviet emphasis upon heavy machinery, locomotives, shipbuilding, railway cars, and iron-and-steel production, the post-1955 trend has been towards chemicals, electronics, optics, precision tools, light machinery (of which the DDR is the fourth largest exporter), and major consumer products.[85]

The New Economic System (NOS)

Analytical specification of the process by which the DDR attained prewar industrial production by 1950, doubled that level by 1956, and doubled the previous record by 1966,[86] not to mention subsequent progress, is of less direct interest here than an analysis of the economic planning process by which these results were obtained. The New Economic System (NOS) was heavily indebted for its general tone and rationale to the formula for economic reform and progress created by Professor Y. G. Liberman of the Kharkov Academy of Engineering and Economics, published in *Pravda* on September 21, 1962.[87] Walter Ulbricht incorporated much of Liberman's thesis in his address to the Sixth Congress of the SED in January of the following year. The statute promulgating the "Guidelines for the New Economic System of Planning and Directing the Political Economy" was issued on July 11, 1963.[88] It was the fifth effort to realize a long-term economic plan—being preceded by the First Five-Year Plan (1951–55), the Second Five-Year Plan (projected for 1956–60, but which started late and was scrapped in 1958), the First Seven-Year Plan (1959–65, which was abandoned in 1961), and the Second Seven-Year Plan (1964–70, which was transposed into a Four-Year Plan before its abandonment). All of these plans broke up because of the incalculable speed of technological change and because of such weaknesses in central planned economy as the separation of planning and its execution into distinctive organizations. As long as this approach to planning was employed, the economy suffered from an overconcentration of decision-making in the hands of central authorities, an unpredictable pattern of overproduction in some areas and intense shortage in others, and a lack of correspondence between production and market conditions and requirements.[89]

The NOS, announced in 1963, therefore, was to redress such past systemic limitations and weaknesses as a lack of initiative at all levels and the worker's sense of alienation from the means of production—weaknesses which had caused the DDR to lag behind the West in certain strategically important industrial sectors. As correctives to these problems, the new system sought to effect the following reforms: (1) the confinement of central planning authority to the formulation of long-range goals, (2) the devolution of responsibility upon the factory and enterprise managers themselves, (3) the reform of the industrial price system along with the gradual elimination of state subsidies, (4) the revaluation of capital equipment and inventories to provide for a more realistic basis of estimating production costs, (5) the employment of a comprehensive cost-accounting system to replace the previous production volume techniques, and (6) the preference of quality over quantitative standards. The whole objective of the NOS was not to junk central planning but to make it more effective by institutionalizing a greater and more rewarding degree of autonomous management at the plant level.[90]

The first step in the realization of the New Economic System was the administrative reorganization of the SED in accordance with production emphases and specialization (*Productionsprinzip*). This process was completed by the summer of 1963, as well as the corollary process of converting and expanding the old institution of the Associations of Nationalized (*Volkseigene*) Enterprises (VVB) into some eighty new socialist concerns (VEB). The second step was a price reform executed progressively in three stages. The first stage effected new price structures for most basic and raw-materials industries, for the most important branches of transportation, and for the chemical industry, all of which were undertaken after April 1, 1964. The second stage commenced January 1, 1965, and encompassed the unreformed price structures of the remaining basic and raw-materials industries and related means of production. The third phase of the industrial price reform began on January 1, 1966, and intended to complete by the end of the year the reform of the price structures in the remaining industrial branches of machine tools, finished chemical products, textiles, clothing, leather goods, services, and various elements of the construction industry. Whereas the first two phases rolled to success with little difficulty, the third phase was more difficult to integrate into the cumulative pattern of the previous reforms.[91]

New depreciation tables were introduced, allowing for considerably accelerated rates of write-off, ranging from 20 percent to 26 percent, depending upon the industrial sector. The latter reform, in combination with the others, now permitted the creation of a production reserve capital fund, managed under the motto of "everything in one pot—everything from one pot," from which the major industrial branches (the various so-called VVB's) drew their respective general allotments for subsequent discretionary allocation to their subordinate enterprises (VEB's), in accordance with the latter's specific needs for capital improvement, inventory accumulation, current operations, and the like. Whereas this scheme obviously permitted considerable flexibility, adaptations, and variations, all VVB's and VEB's nonetheless were expected to conform to the framework of the basic plan.[92]

After the fall of Khrushchev in October of 1964, Walter Ulbricht reviewed the advisability of continuing the NOS, in the light of the theoretical and practical difficulties which developed in the First Seven-Year Plan. Hence, at the Eleventh Central Committee Plenum of December 15–18, 1965, the NOS was modified to the extent of requiring the VVB's and VEB's to submit to the Central Planning Commission several alternative plans of their production expectations for 1966 and 1967, so that only the most rational and defensible plan would be certified by state authority. At the same time, because the NOS require-

ment of organizing the SED itself along the lines of production specialization had threatened to split the party into an agricultural and an
industrial wing, increase the difficulties entailed in the assignment of
jurisdiction at the district level especially, and compel party secretaries
to become involved in matters better left to economic specialists, the
whole organization of the NOS was radically altered to restore party
organizational unity.[93]

Compounding the above problems and dangers was the additional
disruption to the administration of the modified version of the NOS plan
entailed in the fulfillment of the hard and compulsory terms of the
Soviet-DDR long-term (1966–70) trade agreement, signed December 3,
1965. Analogous effects of a lesser sort were produced by over ten other
trade agreements concluded at the turn of the year with West European,
East European, and several underdeveloped countries. The severe terms
of the Soviet-DDR trade agreement, coupled with the necessity of
completely reformulating the recently formulated provisional version of
the Second Seven-Year Plan, apparently induced such an attitude of
hopelessness in the mind of the Chairman of the State Planning Commission, Dr. Erich Apel, that he committed suicide early the same day
the agreement was actually signed. In short, Apel's suicide, as the act of
a major architect of the whole NOS scheme, was not only a protest
against current Soviet trade demands and a reflection of professional
futility about the future prospects of true planning. It should have
alerted even Western observers to the fact, Ulbricht's verbal gymnastics
notwithstanding, that the NOS had been almost completely abandoned
in practice.[94]

The Eleventh Central Committee Plenum decision of December 1965
to undertake the transition to the so-called "second stage" in the development of the NOS (which was actually a return to centralism from
limited autonomy), was the first step in the SED's retreat from the NOS.
The commitment of the Seventh Congress of the SED on April 17–22,
1967, to the formation of the "Economic System of Socialism" and the
State Council decree of April 1968, under which further steps toward
the construction of the Economic System of Socialism were announced,
were the next two steps. The October 1968 meeting of the SED ZK, at
which the preeminence of the party as the only helmsman of the
socialistic ship of state was reaffirmed, and the notions of a "third way"
(à la Dubcek's Czechoslovakia) and the "convergence of capitalism and
socialism" were rejected, was the final move in the SED's carefully
paced retreat from NOS.[95] The noteworthy feature of this retreat, of
course, is that through it Ulbricht managed the complete volta face in
policy necessary to move into the Brezhnev era without conspicuously

faltering. In the process he also no less deftly managed to avoid a headlong rush down a military, political, and economic cul-de-sac of the sort into which the Czechoslovak Communist Party was rushing at exactly the same time.[96] Once again, Ulbricht's sense of political timing and policy commitment can only be admired.

Therefore, the record simply meant that the party had suspiciously, opportunistically, and half-heartedly experimented with economic reform, always under conditions of excessive political restraints, only to abandon indefinitely any basic and genuine program of domestic political consolidation and economic rationalization. Before the end of 1968, in fact, both party and government figures were making the same kinds of criticism of the DDR's political economy as had been previously heard in the 1950s, before the erection of the Berlin wall: (1) planning materials required by central authorities are too voluminous, preoccupy too many enterprise personnel, distract them from vital work, and create an excuse for central authorities to involve themselves improperly in local matters; (2) the planning process is too repetitious, unending, arbitrary, and self-cancelling; (3) scientific principles of socialist industrial organization are still being insufficiently employed throughout; (4) long-range is separated from annual planning in too many plants, while annual plans are too frequently mere compilations of sectional plans; (5) annual planning is still so inflexible that it frustrates timely responses to changed market conditions; and (6) planning and accounting continue to suffer from inadequate correlation.[97]

So evidenced, the SED would seem to have abandoned a centrally planned economy for a modified system of industrial autonomy, only to arrive back at the starting point of a rationalized, updated, and reformed Stalinist-like system. How to plan socialistically still remains for the SED an unsolved "socialist" problem in the twentieth year of the DDR.

Future Economic Prospects

In addition to the above-mentioned shortcomings in the DDR's economic system, there are other—more serious—problems plaguing the economy. One such problem is the inadequate rate of reinvestment, for which the statistical record shown on Table 3 is available.[98] Clearly, by whatever standard, the DDR's economy is relatively undernourished with reinvestment in comparison with West Germany, ignoring the additional but incalculable *qualitative* differences between the two economies experiencing equal inputs of reinvestment.[99] Reinvestment as a share of the total gross social product would show for 1965 a rate of 19 percent for East and 28 percent for West Germany (FRG). Within this pattern there existed a further refined difference, however, since the

TABLE 3

	Investments in Billions of Marks		Per Capita Investments in Marks	
Year	East Germany	West Germany	East Germany	West Germany
1956	8.2	49.3	465	933
1960	13.8	79.2	802	1419
1961	14.0	86.6	818	1527
1962	14.4	93.7	842	1655
1963	14.7	97.4	855	1679
1964	16.1	113.9	947	1944
1965	17.6	125.7	1035	2119
1966	18.9	123.5	1105	2065

TABLE 4

Combined DDR Import-Export Trade

Country Traded With	Percent of Total Trade 1966	1967
Comecon Countries (Soviet bloc)	68	69
Soviet Union	41	42
Other Comecon partners	27	27
OECD Countries (excluding West Germany, Portugal and Spain)	10	10
Remaining world (excluding West Germany)	12	12
Inter-German Trade	10	10

NOTE: OECD refers to the Organization for Economic Cooperation and Development.

DDR allotted approximately one-half of its total reinvestment to the industrial sector as compared to the FRG's allotment of only one-fourth, thereby favorably closing the gap between East and West German industrial reinvestment as a percentage of the total social product to 7.8 percent for East and 6.1 percent for West Germany, respectively.[100] Measured in terms of production, quality, and distribution, therefore, the West German record is a more sustained and healthy one.

A final corollary economic problem to be considered here is the politically cramping pattern into which the DDR's foreign trade has developed, illustrated well enough on Table 4 by the profiles it exhibited for 1966 and 1967.[101] The DDR's trade with the Soviet Union is more than four times the volume of its trade with West Germany, its trade with fellow bloc powers almost three times the interzonal trade, and total intra-bloc trade is nearly seven times the volume with the BRD. In fact, the DDR's trade with Czechoslovakia alone is as important (ten percent) as her trade with the Bonn regime, not to mention the nearly identical trade relationships existing with the Organization for Economic

Cooperation and Development countries and the non-OECD areas of the outside world.[102]

The unavoidable conclusions are that the DDR is further away from equating and surpassing the FRG in per capita production in 1970 than it was in 1960 and that, despite the DDR's unmistakable relative progress over the last decade, it has been unable to use rare opportunities like the West German 1966–67 economic crisis to reduce the relative differences in East-West development. Furthermore, rationalization, mass production, and mechanization are only in their infant stages in East Germany, not to mention the steady deterioration of the East German transportation system.

Despite a stable, rather than a growing, population, an acute housing problem exists. Whereas in the post-World War II period the FRG has built almost eleven million living units, the DDR has only one million. Concomitantly, the West German space per unit has increased from fifty-six square meters in 1955 to almost eighty square meters in 1970, but the DDR's has declined in per unit space from sixty-six to not quite fifty square meters. Although the DDR today is the second largest power in the Soviet bloc and the tenth largest industrial power in the world, trailing only fifteen percent behind West Germany in per capita production, the question is whether East Germany can maintain this record if judged by such criteria as the costs of product manufacture, the speed of manufacture, the price of product delivery, the quality of the product, and the pace of an industrial system's technological research and development. Thus far the truly miraculous feature of the East German *Wirtschaftswunder* is that it has been able to manifest itself in spite of the system.[103] The decade of the seventies, however, for all of the above reasons, looks much dimmer for the DDR, internally and comparatively.

The Role of the Military

With a total population slightly over seventeen million people, based upon eighteen months military service for the National People's Army (NVA) and twenty-four months for the Navy and Air Force, the DDR enjoys the national security provided by 137,000 regular forces. In addition to these combined regular forces, there are available 54,000 border troops under separate command, 23,000 internal security troops, and an armed workers' militia (*Betriebskampfgruppen*) of 350,000 men.[104]

Despite its relatively low ranking in size compared to other socialist armies, the military power of East Germany has received preferential treatment in terms of armament and equipment, especially so far as its armored units are concerned. Their high level of technical efficiency and combat readiness places them in the first line of East European armies, thereby indicating the relatively high combat value attached to them by the Soviet Union and the Soviet Union's confidence in their political reliability. The NVA's participation in the Warsaw Pact sponsorship of Czechoslovakia's chastizing can only confirm this judgment.[105]

However, measured by certain provisions of the Warsaw Pact Treaty of May 14, 1955, especially under the provisions of Article 4, a certain degree of intra-pact discrimination against the DDR is manifest. In the case of an armed attack upon any Warsaw Pact power except East Germany, the form and extent of each power's response is expected to be full and automatic, while the form and extent of the military assistance to be provided by the DDR will be collectively decided, that is, as the Soviet Union sees fit. In the event of an attack upon the DDR, each Pact power decides at its own discretion how much force, in what composition, and at what time protection against aggression will be made available to East Germany. The Soviet-DDR Military Assistance Pact of June 12, 1964, did not alter these policies. Finally, whereas the DDR must place all of its armed forces, including her border police, under the joint command of the Warsaw Pact Headquarters in Moscow, all other powers are only obliged to place a part of their forces under joint command as the situation may require in cases falling short of all-out war.[106]

The fact that the DDR, except for certain ships, replacement parts, equipment, and light infantry weapons, is completely dependent upon the Soviet Union, Czechoslovakia, Poland, and Hungary to supply her with tanks, aircraft, artillery, and heavy weapons, further corroborates this second-rate status.[107] Besides these various external restraints, of course, there exists a whole constellation of internal controls, beginning with Walter Ulbricht as Chairman of the National Defense Council, Erich Honecker as Chairman of the Politburo Commission for National Security, General-Major Walter Borning as Director of the Central Committee Section for Security Questions, Army-General Heinz Hoffmann as Minister for National Defense, and Paul Frohlich as Chairman of the People's Chamber for National Defense.[108]

This close liaison between the Politburo, the Central Committee, and the Ministry of National Defense is further bolstered by five other internal controls: (1) the principle of civilian control over the military and the principle of military hierarchy and command authority, a self-explanatory institutional control; (2) the Chief Political Administration, which is the highest *politorgan* located in the armed forces, infusing all branches of service with a vast organization penetrating horizontally and vertically throughout all units, down to companies and batteries; (3) the Ministry of State Security (SSD), which similarly infuses the armed forces with an overlapping system of watchful surveillance, to which even the Chief Political Administration is not immune; (4) the SED's own hierarchy of party organizations within the armed services, to which belong ninety-seven percent of the officers, eighty percent of the professional noncommissioned officers, thirty-five percent of the conscripted NCO's and ten percent of the ordinary enlisted men; and (5) the mass youth organizations (FDJ) within the services, to which belong about eighty percent of the soldiers under twenty-six years of age.[109] Such a system of institutional multiplicity, overlapping, mutual reinforcement, interpenetration, and indoctrination practically eliminate the possibility of a Bonaparte coming to power or an elite formation staging a successful coup d'etat.

* * *

When the enthusiasm generated by the twentieth anniversary celebration of October 7, 1969, has dissipated, the ruling elite will once again be faced with certain unsolved problems, foremost among them, how, when, and by whom will Walter Ulbricht's successor be determined.

It is conceivable that Ulbricht will succeed in designating an interregnum under Hermann Matern, whose advanced age and limited power base would make him briefly acceptable to everybody else because he is not, by the same token, a serious threat to anyone. A second solution might be a teutonic rendition of the Brezhnev-Kosygin duumvirate, with Willi Stoph as head of government playing the role of the less "equal" partner and Erich Honecker as head of the party playing the role of the more "equal" partner, thereby welding together, respectively, the man of the homeless middle and the representative of the SED's orthodox militants.[110] The possibility of this solution, given the DDR's natural compulsion to adopt the Soviet Union's latest political line at any one time, however, depends upon whether or not the Soviet example of a duumvirate is itself still fashionable at the time the succession issue actually appears, not to mention the related political difficulty of its acceptability to other members of the supreme elite. A third solution might occur in the form of a selection of Paul Verner, Horst Sindermann, or Hermann Axen, singly or in some combination, especially if either or both of the first two solutions develops into an impasse. The final possibility is, of course, Comrad X! Except possibly in the latter case, no matter how the crisis of ultimate leadership is resolved, the resulting leadership will probably intensify the war against the SED reformist element. The party reformist element, the so-called young elite, in anticipation of exactly such a reaction on the part of the supreme elite, will be occupied with their search for Comrade X, behind whom they will hope to head off Stoph, Honecker, Verner, Axen, or Sindermann.[111]

The solution to the succession problem, in turn, will greatly affect the issue of economic development in the DDR. Any of the following combinations could evolve: (1) totalitarian-centralistic; (2) authoritarian-centralistic; (3) authoritarian-decentralized; or (4) pluralistic-decentralized.[112] Which combination of political and economic forms will be eventually introduced in the DDR will depend on the extent to which the various models will become an issue in the succession crisis, on the domestic and international situation with which the party will be faced politically and economically at the time of the struggle for power, and finally on the interventionist mood of the Soviet Union.

The status of Berlin, the Oder-Neisse line, interzonal trade, consumer goods, technological lag, the level of growth rate, international recognition, German reunification, West German recognition, unequal trading relations with the USSR, and Bonn military power are a few of the other major problems, besides the succession crisis, still awaiting solution by the leader who will ultimately replace Ulbricht.

6

Czechoslovakia —
A Case Study of
Social and Political Development

Jan F. Triska

Country Profile: THE CZECHOSLOVAK SOCIALIST REPUBLIC

Head of State: Ludvik Svoboda, President of the Republic
Premier: Lubomir Strougal, Chairman of the Council of Ministers
First Secretary, Central Committee, Czechoslovak Communist Party:
Gustav Husak

Party Membership (1966): 1,698,002 (1,638,695 full members: 59,307
candidate members)[1]
Armed Forces (1969): 230,000 (Army: 175,000; Air Force: 55,000)[2]
Population: End of 1968: 14,388,603 (Prague: 1,102,134)[3]
Area: 127,869 square kilometers (49,370 square miles)
Population Density: 112 per square kilometer, 290 per square mile
Birth Rate (1968): 15.1 per thousand[4]
Death Rate (1968): 10.7 per thousand[4]
Divorce Rate (1968): 1.5 per thousand[4]
Gross Material Product (1968): 601.3 billion koruny in 1967 prices ($83.5
billion at official rate)[5]
National Income Total 1968): 250.6 billion koruny in 1967 prices ($34.8
billion at official rate)[6]
National Income by Sectors (1967):[6]
Industry: 61.0%
Construction: 11.3%
Agriculture: 10.5%
Transportation and Communications: 4.4%
Trade: 8.9%
Other: 3.9%
Foreign Trade by Area (1968):[7]
Socialist Countries (including USSR): 71.5%
USSR: 33.6%
Non-Socialist countries: 28.5%

Foreign Trade by Commodity (1967):[8]	Export	Import
Machinery, capital goods	48.6%	30.6%
Industrial consumer goods	18.3%	5.5%
Raw Materials, semi-finished products	28.6%	47.5%
Comestibles	4.4%	16.4%
Other	0.1%	– – –

SOURCES:
1. U.S. Department of State, Bureau of Intelligence and Research, *World
   Strength of Communist Party Organizations* (Washington, D.C.: U.S. Government Printing Office, 1969), p. 53.
2. *The Military Balance 1969–1970* (London: The Institute for Strategic
   Studies, 1969), p. 12.
3. See *Statisticke prehledy,* no. 4 (1969), p. 99 and *Demografie,* no. 2 (1969),
   p. 182.
4. *Demografie,* no. 3 (1969), p. 272.
5. Statni statisticky urad, *Statisticka rocenka CSSR 1968* (Prague: Statni-
   nakladatelstvi technicke literatury, 1969), p. 153.
6. *Ibid.,* p. 154.
7. *Statisticke prehledy,* no. 4 (1969), p. 114.
8. *Statisticka rocenka CSSR 1968,* pp. 419–20.

6. Czechoslovakia —
A Case Study of
Social and Political Development

Jan F. Triska

Czechoslovakia is a small country about the size of New York state. It appeared on the map in 1918 by an act of the victorious allies as one of the successor states to the Austro-Hungarian empire. H. G. Wells called Czechoslovakia "the only positive outcome of World War I." And, indeed, Czechoslovakia became an outpost of democracy in the heart of Europe between the two world wars. In 1938, twenty years after it was founded, it was deserted at Munich by its allies France and England; and Czechoslovakia became a victim of Nazi German aggressiveness. It lost Sudetenland in September 1938, and six months later, in March 1939, it was occupied and divided by Hitler. Ten years later, in February 1948, Czechoslovakia, placed in the sphere of Soviet influence by an act of the Western allies, underwent another transformation: with Soviet blessing the Communists in Czechoslovakia took over the country in a coup d'etat. But twenty years later, in 1968, Czechoslovakia emerged almost overnight and unexpectedly on the threshold of a modern social democracy—only to be occupied again, this time by the Warsaw-Pact forces.

Thus, of the cataclysmic events in the recent history of Czechoslovakia—in 1918, 1938, 1948, and 1968—only one was a truly homegrown, entirely homemade political and social change brought about by the

NOTE: This study is based on extensive in-depth interviews in Czechoslovakia and Poland, East Germany, Hungary, Yugoslavia, Rumania, and Bulgaria during the academic year 1966–67; in Czechoslovakia in the late summer of 1968; and again in Czechoslovakia, Hungary, and Yugoslavia in the summer of 1969. I am grateful to the Ford Foundation and the American Philosophical Society for the support which made my field research possible.

people themselves. How was this latter change possible? How did it happen?

Different stages of economic development in East European Communist party-states call for different economic organizations; those which fit one developmental stage manifestly do not fit another. The failure of the Stalinist mobilization system, which may have been suitable for an earlier developmental stage of forced industrialization but not for a more complex advanced stage, has created irresistible pressures for changes in the basic patterns of production, distribution, consumption, and control. Changes in these economic patterns have significant social consequences. The nascent economic organizations tend to produce social structures different from those produced by preceding economic organizations. The new social structures, once established, tend to press for corresponding changes in the structure of authority. In other words, the more functional requisites change, the greater the push for change in political decision-making. In Eastern Europe, in addition, the ruling party elites perceive the economic organization as the independent variable which conditions and determines the sociopolitical structure. Thus, not only do the functional requisites of the advanced industrialized polity call for appropriate translation into the output structures, into political authority—they are expected to do so. Party elites in Eastern Europe are thus not only bound to respond politically to the increasing economic complexity of their respective systems, but, given their own basic mission as modernizers and socializers into modernity, they know they must do so. Unfortunately, the East European elites are not masters in their own houses. The structural domestic changes have foreign policy implications. The intervening variable here is the perception and evaluation of the changes by the Soviet elite as to the effect on their own interests. The Soviet intervention in Czechoslovakia in August 1968 illustrates the point.

Economic Changes

The first question posed by the popular East European conundrum, "Are 'socialist countries' poor because they are socialist, or are they socialist because they are poor?" is not difficult to answer. The historical evidence is sufficiently enlightening: the "socialist countries" became "socialist" by association with the USSR. The demands of the Soviet leadership upon its associates, however, were not limited to heavy economic assistance. In addition to the rapid transformation of his new allies' respective political organizations, Stalin insisted on the complete conversion of their respective economic and social structures as a function of their membership in the alliance. Consequently, the first experiences of members of the new international association, even those less economically developed than the USSR, were traumatic spirals of rapidly increasing deprivation. To socialize the new members into the Soviet international system, Stalin put them on the common system denominator of economic underdevelopment by assigning them exceedingly heavy system tasks; to do so more effectively, he forced them indiscriminately to adopt the Soviet political and socio-economic model. (It goes without saying that by entering the Soviet international system, the new members abdicated all options of assistance emanating from membership in or association with the rival Marshall Plan system, which catapulted their fellow Europeans in the West to a new level of prosperity.)

"Socialist countries" are thus poor because they are socialist. The equalization has been thorough and has lasted long. But are they socialist because they are poor? The majority of the East European countries had been capitalist, and a few even relatively wealthy, either before the war or before they experienced the Soviet embrace. Czechoslovakia was a relatively modern advanced industrial state with a high living standard within a market economy before World War II. The only developed capitalist nation that ever entered the Soviet alliance system without direct Soviet military interference, Czechoslovakia became economically bankrupt fifteen short years after its abrupt transition to "socialism." By 1963, the country's economic growth, a healthy eight percent before Czechoslovakia joined the Soviet system, had come to a complete standstill—in fact, it had begun to decline. The stagnating antagonism between the superimposed centrally planned methods of managing the economy for the sake of the alliance system, on the one hand, and the demands of a complex modern industrialized society, on the other, could not be reconciled over time even by the most determined Stalinist leadership in Czechoslovakia: neglected and undercapitalized agriculture, costly but moribund plants employing excessive manpower, a price system with no rational relation to economic reality, and the growing menace of severe inflation could not be argued away.

The spectacular failure of the socialist economy in Czechoslovakia, admitted by the government in 1965, proved again that the Stalin model of socio-economic development with its sustained emphasis on heavy industry to the neglect of everything else, may have been an important original contribution to the theory of socio-economic development of backward countries, but that it was not suited for more advanced societies. Backward nations, with their meagerly skilled minute proletariat and primitive, inefficient mass peasantry, might do well to sacrifice their societal well-being for development of heavy industry with which to build their roads to modernization and a higher standard of living. In this first basic round, the masses do not need to be satisfied; they must be socialized into their difficult roles by persuasion if possible, by coercion if necessary. The fundamental economic transformation of the society demands universal hardship and sacrifice.

In this way Russia was indeed transformed and developed into a modern world power. Unfortunately, Stalin was convinced to the day he died—his 1952 *Economic Problems of Socialism* proves it—that the same socio-economic principles and command strategy he employed in the Soviet Union were applicable to *all* societies. Failing to differentiate among social conditions brought about by different stages of economic development, he lumped all societies together. He failed to realize that the socio-economic strategy he used in his own backward country would paralyze and grind to a halt the advanced, industrial, complex economies of more developed nations.

Stalin went a long way without satisfying the masses of the USSR; but he socialized them, by hook or crook, into their primary economic roles and in fact did accomplish the first developmental round. Khrushchev, and Brezhnev and Kosygin after him, have been coping with the incomparably more demanding and complex second round ever since. "Profit motives," "incentives," higher and more stratified salaries, a wider selection of quality consumer goods, shorter working hours, travel abroad, installment buying, and more family cars—these are the widely shared demands of modern citizens of the USSR. No exhortation to accept deprivation for some glorious but distant future can replace them—and mass coercion, in forms such as the infamous but economically useful labor camps of the retarded past, would plummet the complex Soviet economy into the dark ages of the thirties. A modern skilled labor force is as important to the national economy as the costly, sophisticated machines it works with; not to satisfy materially the labor force is not to socialize it into its proper role relevant to an advanced, demanding economy; not to motivate it; to employ it marginally; to waste it.

At first the Communist economists and bureaucrats in the East European countries either failed or did not want to understand that economic advancement and modernization conditions social expectations, and that these expectations and demands may be ignored in the new conditions only to the peril of the sustained growth rate of the advancing economy.

The Czechoslovak economists explained the need for economic change in this way: work has failed to become the primary need of people under socialism simply because most of it—unparadoxically—is not of creative character. The motivation to work, and to work hard and well day after day and month after month behind a machine or in the fields, manifestly lies in the satisfaction of not only human moral need but also human material interest. In slavishly following the Stalin model despite different economic conditions, the Czechoslovak Communist elite tended to overestimate moral incentives and to underestimate material interests as motivating forces. They forced the constituents to be poor in the hopes that thereby their individual economic organizations would become rich. Unfortunately, in the second, more complex round of the economic development process, it no longer works that way.

With the serious economic slowdowns and breakdowns in Eastern Europe, the Communist economists and bureaucrats discovered this hidden, dark side of the Stalin socio-economic model. After the Yugoslavs, with their decentralized planning, workers' councils, and decollectivized agriculture, came the Poles—and the citizens of the USSR with their Liberman plan of profits and incentives for plants, teams, and individuals. Soon almost all East European elites had elaborated new economic "patterns," "models," or "blueprints," which in most cases are already being gingerly put into effect.[2]

Essentially, the Czechoslovak New Economic Model professed the need to free the economy from exaggerated centralization (which was termed a form of management), administrative rigidity, and the inflexibility of artificial price-fixing. The new model stipulated that market prices must oscillate around new, realistic trade prices for services and commodities—including consumer goods, so as to solve the discrepancy between use-value and value, between supply and demand. For this reason, the character and role of money had to change, the new economic blueprint had to be postulated, not as Proudhon's "working money," but as a chief measuring stick for assessing particular work forms as "socially necessary," purchasable work. But the principal target was the human motivation under socialism—the professed need to motivate people to work more and better. It was conceded and emphasized that "the sectarian [Stalinist] viewpoint," which expected citizens to accept present deprivation for the material satisfaction of future generations, was no longer correct. An advanced economy does indeed depend on motivating individuals by stratified higher real wages, with which they can purchase a higher standard of living.

The Czechoslovak economists would thus be the first to admit that "socialist countries have been poor because they have been socialist"; they had hoped to change all that and to bring their "socialism" to rest on a common denominator with their particular economic stage of development. In the process they had hoped to prove false the second alternative of the conundrum—to show that socialism can be both an effective solution to poverty and an appealing answer to the needs of economically advanced nations.

With the reluctant blessings of the increasingly desperate party elites, the Czechoslovak economists were thus prescribing what they felt they must to bail their economy out of the sinking ship of harsh Soviet-system production demands far beyond their capacities. The old Soviet model had failed in Czechoslovakia in less than twenty years; no new Soviet system model was forthcoming, and no relevant allied assistance was available either. In the depths of a serious and widespread crisis, the party leadership was thus helping itself by emphasizing for the first time the needs, demands, and aspirations of its own country. This is not to say that thereby the Czechoslovaks were opting out of the Soviet system as the Yugoslavs did, or as the Poles and Hungarians tried to do; they were, in fact, attempting to balance the costly Soviet-system membership requirements with the staggering needs at home. It is to say that, because of the scope and intensity of their planned economic reforms, their new economic structures were bound to affect deeply Czechoslovak socio-political organizations.

The economic restratification in Czechoslovakia meant not only the end of production of over three-fourths of the total world spectrum of types of heavy machinery, a Soviet-system task far beyond this small country's capacity, but also a change in Czechoslovakia's assigned role of heavy industrial supplier and modernizer of others in the Soviet system. At home those who added significantly to the gross national product would have more money with which to buy more and better goods and services—a process inevitably leading to formulation of socially differentiated pluralistic groups, almost in classical Durkheimian terms[2]—a powder box of differing interests in a society where excessive egalitarianism and social nonantagonism was celebrated as the basis of complete political homogeneity.[3]

Others in Eastern Europe facing similar problems and solving them in ways similar to Czechoslovakia were likewise affected. Here the supranational division of labor, the specialization and rationalization of productive functions, and the role assignment of system members in terms of system means and goals began to be seriously threatened because the members' interest in the system's maintenance, development, and growth tended to diminish. With their new economic models, the system members were expected to concentrate on domestic problems and to search for foreign partners less on the basis of political prescription than of economic utility and advantage.

However, the Czechoslovak New Economic Model as put into force on January 1, 1967, was a half-hearted compromise, which little resembled the original far-reaching reform proposed by the economic planners. The party elite, despite its mildly positive attitude toward the new model and its nationwide implementation, continued to view the economic reform with great suspicion. Antonin Novotny, in his speech to the Party Central Committee Plenum in March 1967 put it this way: "As long as economic measures are not in harmony with our political aims and our political program, these measures cannot be accepted by us, no matter how effective they may be."

But the public admission by the party elite of the dramatic failure of the socialist economy of Czechoslovakia and its at least partial acceptance of the economic reform, accompanied by a nationwide public debate, brought about an almost universal awareness on the part of the population that the party was, indeed, wrong in at least some of its decisions on crucial matters of state and society. This recognition, and an awakening of expectations that, this being the case, other national reforms should and perhaps would follow, gripped the nation. The traditional Communist decision-making mode of behavior was now officially admitted to be inadequate. The potential politically relevant citizens, suddenly aware of the new, broadening limits, were ready to move from submission to bargaining. The rapid and large role proliferation and group and class formation perceived as possible, and indeed as feasible, under the umbrella of the New Economic Model, made definite and growing societal aspirations and demands almost legitimate. The statistical evidence from public opinion polls and surveys affirmed the general national dissatisfaction and made it public property. The hesitant beginning of economic restratification in Czechoslovakia was thus universally expected to lead to broad social restratification.

Social Changes

Economic decentralization, resources determination and allocation extending to the local level, and disequalization of the labor force thus brought about emergence and proliferation of social and economic groups.

Disequalization of the labor force is de-massing the masses: in the command economy the masses may be socialized into their primary developmental roles of personal sacrifice for the sake of rapid modernization by mass coercion; Stalin showed the basic indispensability of mass coercion as a raw means for attaining his goals. Later, however, in the more rapidly industrializing economic stage of development, the return of mass coercion became overwhelmingly dysfunctional to advanced economic processes and to attaining more advanced and sophisticated goals. Diffusion of choices, competition, upward social mobility of the able, labor shortage, differentiated roles, and social stratification have tended to transform the masses, the original instruments of the socio-economic process, increasingly into stratified validators of this process. The masses have tended to cluster into groups and classes. They simply could not be forced to perform their tasks any longer; they had to be at least minimally satisfied if they were to continue to perform them. An awareness that a higher standard of living may be achieved by the industrious, an "awakening to potentialities," as Hadley Cantril puts it —brought about by the recognition that one's reward should be dependent on one's contribution and the realization of the massive inequality of living standards between the few leaders and the many led—has been the first step. The contrasting model swiftly awakened the masses to the potentialities of a better life.[4]

In the advanced round of the economic endeavor, overall satisfaction —rather than overall coercion—tends to condition the output. Only by allocation and distribution of enough resources on a differentiated-according-to-performance basis can the leadership acquire enough resources to reach its goals. Satisfaction, however, does not simply mean greater abundance of material resources. It means a greater share in *all* societal values—so much greater as to make the instruments of the process into validators—in order to increase the responsiveness of the constituents to the leadership goals in new circumstances. The economic transformation makes the former social structure obsolete and unworkable.

Was greater responsiveness of the governors to the governed too much to expect? The example of Yugoslavia, where these things had happened, served as an indicator of things to come in Czechoslovakia. Lacking the Yugoslav freedom of maneuver due to its early political dissociation from the Soviet Union, Czechoslovakia, like the other party-states in Eastern Europe, labored longer in increasingly inefficient organizations, in which the decreasingly modernizing party elites enjoyed rapidly evaporating popular support. However catholic their views of the Soviet system and however critical they might be of the Yugoslav experiment, the East European party elites could hardly help observing that despite the social and political dangers inherent in it, the Yugoslav formula had in only comparatively rare instances been unable to cope with the challenges that had arisen. At the same time, they had seen the Ulbricht example in East Germany—a Stalinist sociopolitical organization with increasing economic affluence—where the social and political consequences of advanced modernization had been carefully checked and cut at the bud.[5] Is this not in itself proof enough of what can be done economically without sacrificing the former social and political structures in the process?

The Czechoslovak party elite would have naturally preferred to have its cake and eat it too, as long as possible. It was still in firm control. How much could it lose so long as it remained vigilant? Its adaptability and capacity to respond to increasing pressures had been fairly adequate in the past. Could it not be expected to continue to maintain its absolute control in the future?

The empirical evidence showed that it could not. The reason for the change taking place in Czechoslovakia was that in the sixties the old Stalin mobilization model turned into a kiss of death for the professed socialist modernizers and their authority. Rapid, horizontal, across-the-board industrialization differs from the previous peaked development process in that it introduces the law of universal, mutual interdependence into the economic system; particular efficiency and productivity depend on the efficiency and productivity of the economic organization as a whole. This concept was the common basis of the New Economic Model. Its adoption called for conscious, extensive formation and proliferation of new roles in the Czechoslovak society—and a large complex of new adaptive or modified roles fit this concept.

The problem for the directors was not so much integrating and controlling the new role relations, both vertical and horizontal, though even these tasks were hard enough, but coping with the social consequences of the rapid and large role proliferation and group and class formation. The groups had definite and growing aspirations, expectations, and demands, which increasingly tended to be perceived as legitimate. They could not be handled easily or at all by the existing social structures. And here is where the Czechoslovak party elite was most vulnerable: the social consequences of the functional requisites of rapid industrialization *ultimately* called for modification and change in the structure of authority and decision-making. Fortunately, this alteration did not require a formal act—but in the long run it had to be effective enough to cope with the problem.

Out of the initial and partial economic reforms and the expectations of a better life which they aroused, there emerged various competing social and institutional groups, within as well as without the party. They appealed to different segments of the party elite for action, and to them the elite ultimately appealed for support. These groups may be broadly and briefly identified as follows:

1. *The economic reformers.* The initiators of the change were the academic economists, relatively young, energetic, and increasingly aggressive risk-takers, whose articulate, strictly professional diagnosis of the economic maladies, combined with the actuality of the dramatically and dangerously ailing economies, forced the harassed party elite to

consider seriously their critical proposals. The party elite had little choice at this point; the relief of having something new to which to turn their attention must have been considerable in itself.

The staffs of the new chief planners have grown in direct proportion to the desirability of the new economic alternatives. They were housed in Czech and Slovak Economic (and Planning) Institutes and were closely associated with the respective Academies of Sciences. Hand-picked men with high and modern professional skills, they were scientific planners, large-management engineers and specialists, econometrists, mathematicians, and computer analysts, selected almost exclusively on the basis of their advanced expertise and talent. The result was a large proportion in these institutes of non-party people (although party members were usually in administrative positions) indifferent or at least insensitive to purely party needs and independent of party pulls in their professional careers and upward mobility. Their ideas counted, not their party membership, and they knew it.

2. *The professional social scientists.* The respective institutes, engaged in planning and allocating the resources called for by the New Economic Model, demanded increasingly more information and intelligence previously unavailable and/or untapped. *At home* this need created additional opportunities not only, as in the past, for technical personnel (statisticians, administrative experts, agronomists) and managers, but also for such experts as social economists, sociologists, psychologists, social psychologists, and social statisticians. (Here the organizational pattern was the same as in the economic institutes: the various information specialists had their own institutes, associated with the National Academy of Sciences, and the administration was more often than not in the hands of party members. But again, what counted was ideas and talent, not party membership.) *Abroad,* the new technocrats desperately needed literature and contacts. Since they were pragmatic, rational, professional, and scientific, and since the great advances in their respective fields of knowledge were made in the West, particularly in the United States, "while they [themselves] slept," they knew they now must learn fast—all of them, party members or not—from the West.

In this broadening circle, data, information, and intelligence, and the ways and means of gathering, storing, processing, and interpreting them, were at a premium. Having acknowledged the great need for new data as the raw basis for social engineering within the frame of reference of the New Economic Model, the ruling elite permitted the social technocrats to insist on more data, on a flow of information previously impossible or illegal, and even to concentrate on data often only marginally functional to the New Model. The result was greater accessibility and availability of information, not only about population mobility and migration, manpower (the time-budget type sponsored by UNESCO),[6] census, and such, but also about people's demands, preferences, and aspirations; the hesitant beginnings of resource allocation according to real societal needs; and the slow ascendancy, within as well as outside the party, of men who were empirically oriented, scientific and professional, proud of their modern skills, and contemptuous of the old-fashioned "know-nothing" party hacks.

While the party elite's own functions of social engineering were no longer perceived as relevant to societal needs, social scientists, with their opinion and preference surveys and empirical political and social studies, were being elevated to a new status, perceived as more appropriate to the new demands. The social scientists' undisturbed and supported existence within new information structures allowed them to expand and extend their roles. They became an important group because of their unique position of access to data and information otherwise unattainable, in a state where efficiency was the basis of authority. And they were barometers of change in a society which only lately had they been permitted to investigate.

3. *The creative intellectuals,* and, in particular, *the creative writers.* Before the 1948 Communist coup d'etat, the Czechoslovak intellectual elite tended to be left of the center. During the first decade of rule by the Communist Party of Czechoslovakia (CPC), when popular participation in politics sharply subsided, the intellectuals, now mostly in the party, on the whole supported the regime. Recruitment of cadres to staff the new ruling party came principally from this group. But in the second decade of CPC rule a widening gap appeared between the party elite and the intellectuals. The party elite proved unable to put down effectively the rapidly growing sharp criticism of the regime by the intellectuals— and it failed to mobilize the support of the masses against the intellectual elite. This is why the June 1967 Fourth Congress of the Writers Union, a climactic affair, should be viewed as a major catalyst of future political development. Here the irate members of the Congress for the first time attacked the party leadership publicly and collectively. Said Ludvik Vaculik, a novelist, author of the famous "Two Thousand Words": "Instead of a resilient cultural community, we have an easily dominated, amorphous human mass whom it is a sheer joy to rule—even for a foreigner."[7] And the Congress demanded changes in existing policies and practices. The party leadership responded by suppression.

4. *The students.* In November 1967 university students in a Prague hostel staged a march through Prague for simple economic reasons;

there had been no light or heat in their hostel for months. The police intervened in force. Many students were arrested and beaten, but the police brutality was so widely criticized that the CPC agreed to investigate the incident. The result was an unprecedented admission of public mistakes. The date was December 14, 1967.

5. *The Slovaks.* The second largest national group in Czechoslovakia, the Slovaks have always occupied an ambiguous position. During the Stalinist period the political, social, and cultural freedoms of the Slovaks, formulated in the 1945 Kosice program, had been gradually curbed by the Czech party leaders. An interesting dichotomy, in fact, existed: while political and social freedoms were rapidly diminishing in Slovakia, the economic build-up of the underdeveloped country was making relative progress. The key to solving the nationality problem was considered to be the Stalinist formula of economic equalization between the two dominant subcultures, the Czechs and the Slovaks. Since 1963, Slovak intellectuals had criticized more and more openly the centrist policies of the CPC. They pointed out that economic growth which is not founded in the subcultural social and political life but which rests on the quicksand of political coercion, is both lopsided and artificial. By 1967, the Slovaks had become most restive.

The social and cultural groups described above were joined by others demanding substructural autonomy: mass associations such as *trade unions* and *youth organizations;* people working in mass communications media such as the *press, radio, TV,* and *film;* formerly suppressed and powerless *political parties,* members of the National Front, both Czech and Slovak. Brand-new organizations, such as the so-called *Club of Engaged Non-Party People,* citizens who wanted to participate actively in the political process; the *K231,* a club of victims of the Stalinist terror of the fifties, dedicated to the rehabilitation of former political prisoners; and the *Society for Human Rights,* emerged in the spring of 1968, as did formerly suppressed organizations like the *Boy Scouts* and the national athletic association, *SOKOL.*

Such were the major social and institutional groups which appeared or reappeared to represent and defend the new pluralistic social interests. The resistance to social change, on the other hand, resided not so much in the CPC leadership as a group, who had earlier realized that since the party had ceased to be the instrumentality of advancement and economic progress, they had to find some substitute, but in the CPC subleadership, the nonprofessional, noncareer, revolutionary universalists, the "wise men" of the past, the agitators, the revolutionary heroes, the party organizers, the experts in ideology. These entrenched CPC bureaucrats knew well the danger they faced; they knew that this was a question of their own—and their party's—survival. They realized that their own existence—as opposed to the new technocratic, intellectual, societal wave—was bound to push the CPC leadership increasingly into positions as referees, brokers, and mediators. For the subleaders it was not enough merely to survive in the new conditions; that would ultimately mean victory for the functional upstarts. They had to win.

This was an important group. The stability of the CPC depended on the quality of this middle stratum. Any intellectual or moral deficiencies in this group, Gaetano Mosca pointed out, "represent a graver danger to the political structure, and one that is harder to repair, than the presence of similar deficiencies in . . . the state machine."[8] With the increasingly apparent lack of suitability and the growing inability of the CPC leadership to tackle the difficult tasks the party faced, this entrenched substratum became a great danger to the party's maintenance of effective control over the polity. Without this group's support, meaningful innovations were impossible; but with this group firmly within the CPC, no meaningful innovations could take place.

As a group, the CPC subleaders tended to be insensitive to demands from below and relatively slow and bureaucratic in their response to orders from above. Remnants of the Stalinist model, they had learned well the danger of initiative, speed, responsiveness, and unorthodoxy. But they were also skilled politicians, sensitive to major changes which might spell their doom; should the New Model succeed to a degree perceived as significant and should these people view the social change as truly fundamental, they would be quick to reevaluate and recalculate their attitudes.[9] (This they began to do in fact in the spring of 1968.) They may not have been wise, but they were smart; the learning process they underwent to reach and to maintain their precarious positions in the party was rather impressive. They were far from ready to give in prematurely, but neither could they be expected to fight to the bitter end.[10] Thus, of the three alternative solutions to the conflict—withdrawal, compromise, and integration of interests, the first was unrealistic and the third unattainable in this generation. Compromise—modification of the extreme alternatives and reduction or even renunciation of hostility—implied a degree of acceptability of divergent interests, a partial shift in value-ordering, and a supply of new, not entirely unsatisfactory, workable conditions for both parties, the old guard as well as the new wave. When the CPC subleadership indeed registered as real the shock of the perceived need to change, a frantic search for substantive compromise on their part took place.

This bureaucratic resistance group in the CPC had many important allies in the state bureaucracy, in the trade unions, and in other agencies. In plants and enterprises, the great majority of managers were party members, many of whom had been promoted from the state bureaucratic apparatus—ministries, commissions, and other leading agencies —and whose education and skill were entirely inadequate for their managerial responsibilities. Under the old system these individuals survived handsomely; they had everything decided from above, and they simply executed orders. But under the new conditions the realm of decision-making on this level suddenly increased—and with it the risks that go with the job. And this Kafkaesque grand alliance of middle-stratum bureaucrats, suspicious of and cool to all experiment and change, played it up to the workers: Had they as yet received substantive benefits from the new model? Had they not in fact been asked to work harder, had they not been subjected to dislocation, and had they not even been threatened by unemployment in plants and enterprises which were being closed down as wasteful? Taught by experience and past promises, the workers were indeed at first skeptical about innovations. They had been misled by the authorities too often to take the promises of the New Economic Model at face value. Higher wages would persuade them; but these were coming too slowly to make an impact.[11]

And this was the position, approximately, in which Czechoslovakia found itself in late 1967. On the one hand, important possibilities and opportunities were opening up for Czechoslovak society through the new and growing functional wave, the new instrumentality of the party toward rapid industrialization and thus legitimization of the party's authority under new conditions: the professional-technical-social scientific experts, specialists with modern education, functional skills, and advanced technical training—bright, aggressive, young people with imagination, insight, and initiative. These young technocrats were joined by the subcultural groups such as the Slovaks; the creative intelligentsia such as the writers; people in mass communications; the students; and the social and institutional groups already described, in and out of the party, all determined to gain and maintain substructural social autonomy for themselves as well as for others.

On the other hand, the brakes were provided by the still influential, militant armchair Communists and Marxist manipulators high in the hierarchical structure of CPC authority, who claimed moral superiority for their side—and who had key alliances not only within the Czechoslovak economic and political structures, but also within the Soviet and other socialist countries' elite organizations.

Political Changes

The principal function and responsibility of the party elite at this stage was to integrate the economic and social changes into the Czechoslovak political system. The question was, first, what kind of political response was called for, and, second, what kind of response the elite was willing to supply.[12]

A convenient clue to the first question may perhaps be found in the behavior of nonruling Communist parties—Communist parties which have not succeeded in capturing control of government within their respective states. For our purpose it is possible to distinguish between nonruling Communist parties operating in backward nations and those active in economically advanced countries. In *developing nations* nonruling Communist parties tend to be *revolutionary*. Here they follow the traditional Leninist concept of dynamic revolutionary forces in societies which are not yet integrated and often not politicized. The nonruling Communist parties perform here, in addition to their Communist-system objectives, the function of socializers toward modernity. They feed the aspirations and ambitions of those frustrated by the inability of the developing society to use their skills. The resulting high want/get ratio brings into the Communist party all those who wish to mobilize and transform their society rapidly into modernity. In *developed nations,* on the other hand, where there is no legitimate function for a revolutionary, deviant Bolshevik party, Communist parties either persist and go underground, or they give in, conform, and become *electoral parties:* the former alternative tends to mean failure, and the latter, success. The electoral parties compete for votes with other national parties, and the competition forces them to reduce greatly their differences from other parties, both structurally and functionally.[13]

The French (PCF) and especially the Italian (PCI) Communist parties are good examples of this latter type of nonruling Communist party. These two largest Communist parties in the world today (the Italian Community Party also has the highest percentage of the adult population among all nonruling Communist parties) are, in membership, leadership, organization, and programs, constitutional, compromise, alliance parties which have cast away their revolutionary, conspiratorial, Bolshevik spirit and strategy with economically advancing conditions in their countries. For these two parties, conspiracy and sabotage are things of the past, and orderly vote-seeking and proper parliamentary activities their present game. They owe their success to

their essential compatibility with the socio-economic standards and political conditions in their respective countries. (For the Italian Communist Party this description is correct for the North, where its leadership
resides, not for the South, which is the party's appendage, not its heart.)
These are socialist parties which have traded revolutionary programs
and activities, which no longer appeal to the satiated members and
voters, for middle-class respectability, parliamentary bargaining, and
piecemeal social progress. In 1962, for example, Palmiro Togliatti seriously asked the PCI whether the classical class struggle made sense in
the economically developed West European countries.[14] And in 1964
Giorgio Amendola, a leading member of the PCI's *direzione,* admitted
that in Western Europe ". . . the Communist solution has not, up to
now, revealed itself to be valid to reach the goal of achieving a socialist
transformation of society. . . . A political organization that does not
reach its objectives in fifty years, with at least three generations of
militants, must search out the reasons for this failure, and know how to
transform itself." He called for a new party of the working class which
would be "neither Communist nor Social Democratic."[15]

The lesson here and the clue to the first question is that economic
development, that is, affluent and relatively stable economic structure, is
a crucial negative catalyst of nonruling Communist party politics. But, of
course, it is not the only catalyst: the origin and historical experiences of
the party; socialist traditions and the competition of socialist parties; the
imaginativeness, professionalism, flexibility, and competence of the
party leadership, especially in times of stress; and the degree of dependence on other Communist parties are catalytic variables as well. They
make some parties in the developed countries adapt better than others.
By answering the central question of how to change the political formula, some—like the Communist parties of Canada and the U.S.—
chose to resist and suffered the consequences; others went along, reinterpreted their stand, and adapted to the existing political structure. Should
the leadership of the PCI or the PCF wish for any reason to transform
their party functions back to the revolutionary model, for example, this
switch would result in complete breakdown, chaos, and anarchy in their
respective party organizations, from the lowest "sections" (formerly
"cells") to the leadership organs. Having successfully transformed their
parties' structures to serve the new political functions, the leaders have
become prisoners of their own respective Golems. To compete better for
votes, they have emulated their rival political parties. In the process they
have traded their own uniqueness for the commonness of routine electoral parties. The cause was economic advancement, and the need was
the survival of the parties under changed sociopolitical conditions. Yet,

because of their indisputable success, these parties did influence other Communist parties, even the Bolshevik ones, on issues such as the thesis of structural conversion, recognition of a whole variety of possible socialist systems, and a common stand on China. Still, if these parties go the Social Democratic road all the way, as well they might, they will gradually sever their tenuous links with the Communist movement.

The dilemma which the CPC elite faced at this juncture was similarly severe: on the one hand, the Stalinist prescription had proved too simplistic for the Czechoslovak stage of modernization. The party's direction and control of the faster, more demanding, and more complex next stage of economic development had proved inadequate. But as advancement and modernization were professedly the most significant objectives of the party, the failure to achieve these objectives in a sustained, fairly rapid manner would have been prejudicial to the party's authority, depriving it of much` of its legitimacy. If, in modernizing societies, the measure of all things is modernization, yet the party ceases to be the instrument of modernization, then, what right has it to govern?

On the other hand, drastic economic innovations at this point meant problems. The New Economic Model was virginally pure, untested in a "socialist setting"; it may have been theoretically well founded, with a whole national school of economic thought behind it, but it represented national, *not* Communist-system innovation; compared with the original Soviet model it was revisionist; and it was complex. Its even partial adoption meant automatic growth of confusing complexity in human affairs and relations, which the CPC had to integrate and control. In other words, the increase in economically and technologically important functional roles which this blueprint called for brought about general role proliferation and differentiation which in turn had significant social consequences within which the CPC had to act, and which it had to integrate and shuffle into new organizational structures. This was by no means a small undertaking for a party bred on command economies, coercion, absence of political opposition and public opinion, historical determinism, and simplicity.

Inevitably the Czechoslovak party elite tended to be increasingly permissive toward economic experimentation and innovation, however original (revisionist) and nationalistic (nonsystemic), as long as it was effective. Novotny did not agree, at least not rapidly and fully enough, and had to go. Dubcek had hoped to be able to cope with the reform's social and political consequences, however dangerous to the party's monopoly of direction and control, so long as the reform provided renewed legitimacy of the party's authority. Other alternatives were significantly limited: to avoid the subsequent dangers Novotny may have tried to slow down or even (temporarily) to halt further application of the new economic blueprint by increased manipulation of the old mobilization symbols—heroism, coercion, abstinence; but then the CPC would have had to resupply the revolutionary conditions and emergency environment in order to make its demands for sacrifice credible, and to accept the low economic yield, retardation, and inefficiency which would have resulted. Also, Novotny may have in the meantime pressed the coalition organizer, the USSR, for more immediate assistance and help, supposedly to offset the nationalistic tendencies of the new economic proposals. Judging from past experience, such assistance would have hardly satisfied the actual needs, in kind as well as in degree, for a relevant time period.

The answer to the first question, then, namely, what kind of political response was objectively called for by the higher level of economic development of Czechoslovak polity, is not too difficult. Supported by considerable literature on comparative politics, both theoretical and empirical, the general proposition that modernization tends to determine the nature of political authority has been extensively and well argued.[16] The new economic structures in Czechoslovakia, perceived as the independent variable upon which the social and political structures depend, dictated the changes even more forcefully. (This stance corresponds with the hypothesis, generated and tested by Dennis C. Pirages at Stanford, that the higher the level of modernization in the one-party states, the greater the responsiveness of the elites to their constituents.[17]

The CPC leaders, of course, did perceive the dangerous relationship between economic reforms and the need to overhaul the outmoded political structure long before the spring of 1968. The post-mobilization economic reorganization would be bogged down, they realized, without appropriate political changes. They were experienced politicians, sensitive to the political threat which tinkering with economic structures implies. This is why they were so eclectic in their approach to the reform, at least initially selecting those features representing the least political cost. Unfortunately, the politically acceptable economic changes tended to be the least effective economically.

Given this situation, what kind of political response was the party elite ready to supply? Like all ruling political parties, the Communist Party of Czechoslovakia had one goal above all others: to stay in office. It may have permitted experimentation, innovation, and social change so long as it perceived the situation crucial to its own staying in office. The nascent class structure, social factionalism, and pluralism not only rapidly increased the party's role as broker of multiple competing political interests at lower levels—a role the CPC leaders had learned to play effectively only on top decisional levels in the past[18]—but also created a demand for their supplying a mechanism for resolution of a growing number of conflicts. Under cumulative stress the party elite faced the problem of trading the broad functions of social engineers and mobilizers for some narrower functions. Structurally, the elite had to absorb the shock of transition—a transition for which it was almost totally unprepared.

In attempting to absorb and colonize the multiplying leaders and subleaders of the mushrooming social groups and classes on the one hand, and the non-party social engineers and professionals on the other hand, the party elite realized that it must provide incentives, rewards, and party careers that would be preferable to the new opportunities opening up on the outside. This was becoming increasingly difficult. Why should the young, often alienated and deviant; the talented; the articulate; the creative; and the skilled enter or remain in the party and accept the heavy demands of the CPC on their energy, time, and resources? And even having entered, why should they remain if more attractive new opportunities on the outside came to their attention? Furthermore, the CPC, because of its changing functions and structures, would have less to offer its members, while at the same time making greater demands on them than in the past.

It was up to the party elite to supply the reasons why. The strength and soundness of the political system, and thus the party's own strength, would ultimately depend on the scope of support and the level of institutionalization it would provide through the procedures and organizations it would devise. These, in turn, would have to be adaptable, autonomous, complex, and coherent enough to cope with the difficult tasks ahead. As already shown, past political organizations and procedures were inadequate for the purpose.

To put it another way, and using Samuel P. Huntington's model,[19] it becomes even clearer that the Czechoslovak economic changes had outrun the political structures to such a degree of political instability that a search for stable political institutions became imperative if the system was not to decay rapidly. Problems centered around the following. (1) The CPC found it difficult to adapt to environmental changes. Created to perform one set of functions, it found it hard to switch to a new set. In existence for a relatively short time as a ruling party, with few intergenerational changes of the elite, it had had little experience in coping with the young Turks. (2) Neither did it have experience—or mechanism—for coping with the impact of emerging social forces. It lacked tools with which to moderate among the several social groups whose interests it wanted to articulate and aggregate and whom it wished to socialize politically. (3) Its organizational complexity, built for its mobilization functions, was not relevant to its new, demanding role of a political screening and guiding mechanism. (4) And in its search for coherence through consensus instead of coercion, the party elite was hard put to cope with overt alienation and dissent without instrumentalities created for the purpose.

The dangers looming ahead were the progressive decline of the CPC as a distinctive channel of recruitment; greater fluidity in party membership, accompanied by increasing lack of internal cohesion; and the gradually more problematic task of selecting and maintaining quality top party leadership. Having reluctantly agreed to replace its heavy-handed and compromised mobilization system of the past, and under rising pressure of demands, aspirations, and expectations of the citizens, the party elite faced the problem of accepting some autolimitation of its authority. To maintain political control and monopoly of political interest and articulation, aggregation, and communication as organizationally distinct and autonomous organs was becoming ever more difficult. The party's social functions and corresponding structures tended to shrink.[20] Depoliticization of social life was forcing the party to attempt a search for new motivational structures and broader consensus among the emerging consent groups. This was hard, but under the circumstances acceptable.

What options then were available to the Czechoslovak party elite in its search for a political model of socialism which would correspond to the real needs of modern socialist society? How could it maintain and increase the scope of its popular support? How should it build appropriate political organizations and procedures which would institutionalize conflicts and contradictions brought about by the postmobilization socio-economic developments without destroying its own existence?

The leaders of the increasingly vociferous social and institutional groups had many demands. Cumulatively, these demands were of such a nature that they could not be simply handled by the existing political structures. What were these major demands? Legal abolition of censorship and freedom of the press; the rehabilitation of all victims of the past terror; and a federal system which would guarantee the Slovaks political equality with the Czechs. In addition, the several groups now pressed for legal freedom of assembly, freedom of religion, more active and independent foreign policy (but clearly within the frame of the existing regional arrangements, namely, the Council for Mutual Economic Assistance, the Warsaw Pact, and the close ties with socialist neighbors and the Soviet Union); and they asked for freedom to participate in national political life and freedom of elections. The groups and classes did not ask for more decision-making power for more people, but insisted that more people with ideas and information be given both a forum for presenting their ideas and access to those making the political decisions.[21] They thus collectively demanded things which could not be accommodated within the existing political organization. Cumulatively, they forced upon the party elite the need to rethink the basic political question: what is the role of the party in the present stage of socio-economic development in Czechoslovakia? The party conservatives, understandably, wished to return, with minor concessions, to the past of absolute party control. The party liberals, on the other hand, went so far indeed as to ask for the establishment of "friendly socialist opposition parties," namely, genuine political opposition parties within the frame of reference of Socialist Democracy. The in-betweens, the centrists, demanded that the party democratize its own structures, permit expression of minority views, introduce internal differentiation, and engage in a public dialogue within the party community and thus prove that it deserves to survive as a single ruling monopoly party.

These demands came not from non- or anti-Communists but from thoughtful CPC members who originally rebelled against men less capable than themselves in positions of leadership. This phenomenon had been on the upswing with, on the one hand, the party's attempt in self-defense to absorb the skilled and the articulate, and on the other, these individuals' realization that the CPC was the only proper forum for criticism. To an ever greater extent, these demanding CPC members came into collision with various compromises and asked that a larger area of decision-making be extended from the elite to the party itself. Moreover, these critics pointed out, adapting to social development outside the CPC required absorption into the political process of social forces producing social conflicts, and they argued that the consequence of this absorption—breakdown of the unanimity model in public policy-making—was something the party elite would have to live with, not hide from. In short, under the new social conditions the party elite had permitted to develop, they would have to free themselves from the classical prerogatives of absolute monopolies of all power.[22] With the decreasing need of the party elite to function as constantly and forcibly in the task of mobilizing central agencies to sustain pressures upon elements in their societies, the CPC could relax more. Having accomplished the basic transformation from the mobilization stage, which gave a certain credibility to its moral claim to leadership, the future, though uncertain, looked more secure than the past. Besides, the transition process was expected to be relatively long, and the elite should be able to test every new step carefully.

The gradual process from hierarchical to polyarchic and even bargaining party system indicated a trend from complete domination of politics to basic political guidance, formulation of principles, moral leadership, and ideological education. All this would have taken time. But this would have permitted the party elite to control the process, to direct it, and to ensure that the fundamentals would be perceived as untouchable (that is, that the socialist order, under CPC guidance, would be lifted from any dialogue and left alone as given), and that there would be no open challenge to the ideological or moral authority of the party. It also would have given the party elite the opportunity to funnel socio-economic forces into the state apparatus.

The chief emphasis and responsibility for administration of daily routine might then go to the state, the organs of government, the state officials. This would make the state organs the chief regulators of economic, social, and political life. The old-fashioned, inflexible, top-heavy state administration, influenced, modernized, and transformed through the new blood of energetic socio-economic forces, which would generate a flexible plurality of affiliations and local power centers, would assist a pluralistically disposed socialist structure to take root. A genuine dialogue, safely within the frame of reference of socialist order, would take place—something that popular demands stressed the most. Within this framework even real elections for state and governmental offices could take place, as in Yugoslavia. But there would be genuine discussion with broad citizen participation, thus establishing a basic effective instrumentality for citizens' political education. After all, "The vanguard cannot be more narrow-minded, timid, more intolerant, and more incapable of winning particular ideological clashes and controversies than the people whose vanguard it is supposed to be."[23]

This would have required separation of party and state—a delicate problem for the CPC. And it would have assumed that pluralism in Czechoslovakia would not become merely a matter of institutionalization from above, but would involve social groups having impact on the political system and proceeding at a rate at least as rapid as the process of institutionalization. This process may be perceived as successful when the distance between the two rates at least remains constant.

The second alternative, more discrete and perhaps less realistic, would have been for the ruling elite to permit establishment of one or several friendly opposition parties. This would have amounted to more than allowing expressions of minority views, democratization of party structures, internal party differentiation, and dialogue within a limited party community; for the party elite, it would have meant giving up its monopoly position, accepting some sharing in decision-making, and maintaining a voluntary, sustained, legitimate check on all its own activities. The scope might be limited by the stipulation that this be a party or parties operating within the socialist order. Yet it is difficult to see the ruling elite opting for this alternative. True, "it has never been postulated in the socialist classics that only a single party can exist in a socialist country."[24] But there is a difference between autolimitation of authority and the granting of permission to a rival party or parties to set up shop for the single purpose of sustained criticism of the ruling party. This is a far-reaching structural difference for which the Czechoslovak party elite was not yet ready.

Faced with the proliferation of social groups and classes and their bold demands for, first, substructural autonomy and, subsequently, political innovations, the aging Czechoslovak party leadership of Antonin Novotny displayed visible signs of wear and tear. The gravest challenges to the Novotny regime came from the young Turks—the functional intelligentsia with its widely shared hunger for staunch pragmatism and its proclaimed vested interest in effective economic, social, and political change; from the creative intellectuals, demanding freedoms compatible with their cultural attainments and goals; from the Slovaks, with their long-suppressed hopes for autonomy, federalism, and equality; from the youth; and from the other interest and social groups. Not to respond meant economic disaster. To respond in a relevant manner may have meant "to adjust gracefully to the desirability of its own gradual withering away,"[25] a fate no party could be expected to contemplate serenely.

Given these alternatives—and had Novotny been wise—what was perhaps most likely to happen was a kind of increasingly asymmetrical muddling through—asymmetrical in the sense that in the transitional mix, the mobilization aspects of the party rule would have decreased and gradually disappeared as the compromise aspects increased and were accepted. Attainment of the party's principal goal, sustained economic progress and rapid modernization, would have been the function of the rate and direction of this gradual process—the evidence of the party's adaptability to new social conditions. But Novotny could not even begin to cope with political debates and demands such as these. This is when his usefulness ended—when he failed to realize that he could not shove these demands under the rug of simple and simplistic political coercion as he had in the past. Novotny certainly was not the man for all seasons.

Rightly perceived as legitimate by Dubcek, the new political aspirations could indeed no longer be dealt with by and within existing political structures. Changes in political organizations to accommodate these interests could not but affect political authority in Czechoslovakia. Public discussion of issues such as the extent of responsiveness of the governors to the governed, access to and share in the political process, the function of bureaucracy, the nationality and minority problem, and the substance and channels of economic and political foreign policy all signaled the breakdown of the unanimity model of the past. They also signaled the beginning of a new political era, an era of the creative development of a socialism which would be capable of accommodating democracy. The Dubcek regime, then, though at times hesitantly and in spurts at other times, was on its way to offering the kind of political response which, at a minimum, was in fact objectively called for.

Foreign Reaction to Domestic Changes

This crucial deliberation on the essentials of the new national political life in Czechoslovakia took place in the spring and summer of 1968. It led to the Soviet intervention and occupation in August. This Soviet action raises a fundamental question: what was the significance of the evaluation abroad of what happened at home?

The degree of dependence on the original system organizer, the USSR, is crucial in Eastern Europe. Historically, the greatest parametric restraint on the domestic satisfaction variable in Eastern Europe, though it varies in degree from state to state, has been the satisfaction variable *abroad,* the satisfaction of the founder and organizer of the one-party-state system, the USSR.[26] But the case of Czechoslovakia has taught us that the East European party elites must be viewed as having two major validators: the USSR, as organizer and coalition leader abroad, and the constituents at home. In the command stage of economic development, the chances of the party elites staying in office may be calculated simply by the ratio of domestic goal attainment to the satisfaction variable of the USSR. As long as the East European parties faithfully follow Soviet wishes in their respective countries, all is well. In the advanced stage, however, with changes in the economic, social, and political structures, the chances of the party elites staying in office must be calculated increasingly by the ratio of domestic goal attainment to the satisfaction variable of the stratified constituents. The wishes, aspirations, and demands of the citizens now become much more important than before. But as the amount and kind of satisfaction the respective elites can bestow at any time remain essentially constant (though, of course, both change over time), the relationship between the two validators, the citizens and the Soviet Union, as to the satisfaction variable is essentially inverse: the more satisfaction for the citizens, the less for the USSR. By making substantial concessions to Czechoslovak social groups, the Czechoslovak party elite was viewed as having decreased its tribute to the USSR. The political consequences of the new social complexity in Czechoslovakia were perceived by at least some of the Soviet decision-makers as a dangerous reduction in the degree of Czechoslovak solidarity with the USSR. The result was the Soviet intervention.

This proposition may be illustrated by reference to the issue of nationalism and national identity. As James Billington points out, "a separate [national] identity and [a separate national] development is a [necessary] prerequisite to full and dignified participation" in any political system, national or international.[27] Billington compares this search for separate national identity and tendency to turn back to national tradition in Eastern Europe with a similar search and tendency among the advocates of Black Power in the United States today. The Czechs and Slovaks indeed have a shared feeling that they have been treated as "semicolonial, faintly inferior, and—worst of all—historically irrelevant second-class" citizens.

In political attitude-formation, development and maintenance of national identity is of vital importance. Social psychologists like Erikson and Doob demonstrated this in their studies of the psychology of identity.[28] Political scientists such as Pye and Verba built on this work in their studies of political development.[29] They all agree that when national identity is in question, a frantic search for restored identity begins. The psychology of identity certainly provides "a clue to the tenacity of national attachment."

Deutsch, Russett, and others confirm this finding.[30] They point out that successful international systems have stopped short of total integration and have accommodated autonomous national units. In other words, the integrative capacity of international systems is limited by the autonomy of, as well as the kind of, national identity within the national units. If these units are in flux, the international system is bound to be unstable.[31]

A stable Eastern Europe depends on the existence of stable separate national identities. The Soviet intervention in Czechoslovakia was a move to preserve integration in Eastern Europe, but it had the opposite effect. It destabilized both Czechoslovakia and probably Eastern Europe as well. East European integration is being preserved at the expense of perpetuating and deepening the fundamental identity crisis in the area. If the Soviet Union wished to create a stable, supra-national community in Eastern Europe, then its invasion of Czechoslovakia was a terrible mistake. If it wished merely to preserve and strengthen its own protective wall on its western border, namely to place Soviet tanks as close to Germany as possible, then the occupation of Czechoslovakia was the most clumsy way to do it. In either case, the Soviet perception of the Czechoslovak net gain in the spring of 1968 as becoming a Soviet net loss was based on a short-term calculation. Long-term stability and settlement in Eastern Europe suffered great harm.

But the Soviet Union is not free from external constraints either. As the organizer it is also the captive of its alliance system; the legitimation-socialization process works both ways. The possibility of being charged with condoning revisionism and with alienation from socialism, not only by the Chinese but also by their less critical allies, such as Ulbricht and Gomulka, undoubtedly helps the Soviet leaders to toe the line. Their freedom of maneuver is limited by their socialist allies, the external validators of their legitimacy. The external pressure upon the Soviet leaders to cope with the Czechoslovak situation must have played a significant role in the Soviet decision to intervene.

Moreover, the demands for social and political change in Eastern Europe are not really understood in the Soviet Union. Although the East European countries differ a great deal among themselves, collectively they differ even more from the Soviet Union: their party bureaucracies are less firmly established and are less autonomous and less pressure-resistant than the strong Soviet party bureaucracy; memories of multi-party rule in the not-too-distant past are still alive; traditions of at least a certain amount of political freedom have not been forgotten; the longing to rejoin the West is considerable; the consummatory values of the West are widely admired; the relative improvement over the past two to three decades, considerable in the USSR, is almost nonexistent here when compared with pre- or post-World War II conditions; religious ties, though limited, have survived; we also should not forget that while the Soviet technocratic elite, created and supported by the party, is dependent on and even proud of its affiliation with the CPSU, the East European technocrats and professionals, alienated from, economically suppressed by, and socially and politically discriminated against by their parties, feel differently, whether in the party or not; and while changes in the USSR (de-Stalinization, economic reforms, new harshness against writers) tend to influence its East European neighbors, changes in East Europe do not tend to influence the USSR, at least not so much.[32] As a consequence, the demands for change—and the elites' potential political responsiveness—are considerably greater in the small East European countries than in the Soviet Union.

The changes in economic, social, and decisional structures in Czechoslovakia—actual, nascent, planned, and anticipated—made for less solidarity with the USSR in both Czechoslovakia and Eastern Europe. Maintenance of the East European alliance became more costly for the organizer, the USSR, and maintenance of party rule in Czechoslovakia became more costly for the party elite. The Soviet intervention brought both costs down in that it created preconditions for return to the status quo ante.

7

Decompression in Hungary — Phase Two

Bennett Kovrig

Country Profile: THE HUNGARIAN PEOPLE'S REPUBLIC

Head of State: Pal Losonczy, President of the Presidential Council
Premier: Jeno Fock, President of the Council of Ministers
First Secretary, Central Committee, Hungarian Socialist Workers' Party:
Janos Kadar

Party Membership (1968): 600,000[1]
Armed Forces (1969): 97,000 (Army: 90,000; Air Force: 7,000)[2]
Population: End of 1968: 10,275,000 (Budapest: 2,000,000)[3]
Area: 93,000 square kilometers (35,919 square miles)
Population Density: 111 per square kilometer (285 per square mile)
Birth Rate (1968): 14.8 per thousand[3]
Death Rate (1968): 11.2 per thousand[3]
Divorce Rate (1968): 2.7 per thousand[3]
National Income Total (1968): 221.24 billion forints ($18.85 billion at
official rate)[4]
National Income by Sectors (1968):[5]
Industry: 40.6%
Construction: 11.9%
Agriculture: 22.8%
Transportation and Communications: 4.6%
Trade: 19.3%
Other: 0.8%
Foreign Trade by Area (1968):[6]
Socialist Countries (including USSR): 70.2%
USSR: 37.0%
Non-Socialist countries: 29.8%

Foreign Trade by Commodity (1968):[7]	Export	Import
Machinery, capital goods	28.7%	27.6%
Industrial consumer goods	24.4%	7.6%
Raw materials, semi-finished products	25.7%	54.0%
Comestibles	21.2%	10.8%

SOURCES:

1. U.S. Department of State, Bureau of Intelligence and Research, *World Strength of Communist Party Organizations,* (Washington, D.C.: U.S. Government Printing Office, 1969), p. 57.
2. *The Military Balance 1969–1970* (London: The Institute for Strategic Studies, 1969), p. 13.
3. Kozponti Statisztikai Hivatal, *Statisztikai Evkonyv 1968* (Budapest: Statisztikai Kiado Vallalat, 1969), p. 38.
4. *Ibid.,* p. 64.
5. *Ibid.,* p. 64.
6. *Ibid.,* pp. 256–59.
7. Kozponti Statisztikai Hivatal, *Statisztikai Havi Kozlemenyek,* no. 10 (1969), p. 49.

7. Decompression in Hungary — Phase Two

Bennett Kovrig

If proverbs enhance the obvious, then the aspirations of most Hungarians and their country's fate in the postwar world are aptly depicted by two mutually antagonistic maxims. At the Yalta Conference, Winston Churchill admonished Stalin: "The eagle should permit the small birds to sing and care not wherefore they sang."[1] The definitive Soviet reply, voiced by a certain General Grebennik, came in the aftermath of the 1956 revolution: "Soviet troops will leave the territory of Hungary only when crayfish whistle and fishes sing."[2] In the interval, Hungary's political system underwent several major convulsions, all of them due to more or less overt foreign intervention. The ostensibly democratic, but rather authoritarian prewar system symbolized by the head of state, Admiral Nicholas Horthy, was replaced in October 1944 by a quisling administration that derived its authority from the German occupying forces. This regime gave way in 1945 to a pluralistic interregnum, with the Communists gaining only 16.9 percent of the popular vote in the first general election. The pattern whereby the Communists under Matyas Rakosi eventually came to power despite massive popular opposition— by means of his blatantly unconstitutional "salami tactics"—was repeated throughout Eastern Europe. The omnipotence and assistance of the Soviet High Command proved to be the decisive factor, and by the middle of 1948 the democratic facade had vanished, leaving the Hungarian Workers' (Communist) Party in absolute control.

The Rakosi Era

As Stalin's foremost admirer and imitator, Rakosi imposed on Hungary an iron rule that even his Communist successors condemned for its brutality and economic mismanagement.[3] In addition to persecuting anti-Communists and "class enemies," Rakosi had by 1952 purged some two hundred thousand members of his own party. The execution of his onetime Minister of the Interior, Laszlo Rajk, offered a sacrifice to Moscow's anti-Tito campaign; the imprisonment and torture of others, including the present party head, Janos Kadar, served to eliminate the risks of intra-party opposition. Concurrently, ideological indoctrination and cultural Russification were pursued with procrustean single-mindedness, while the economy was restructured according to the Stalinist-autarkic model in order to turn resource-poor Hungary into a "country of iron and steel." The first two policies only exacerbated the cleavage between the party and the masses and strengthened a nationalistic dislike for the USSR that had its historical roots in the Russian contribution to the crushing of the Hungarians' anti-Habsburg revolution of 1848 and in the short-lived Communist dictatorship of Bela Kun in 1919. As for the economic reforms, they proved to be by-and-large retrogressive and ill-suited to Hungarian conditions; between 1949 and 1952 the real income of workers fell by eighteen percent.[4]

A conjuncture of events in 1953 led to the first phase of decompression in the Hungarian system. Rakosi's program of intensive socialization had predictably alienated any mass support that he may have had, but even in party circles and among the official intelligentsia there arose doubts regarding the viability of his ideological preconceptions. Stalin's death provided the catalyst. With the shift to collective leadership in the Kremlin, Rakosi found himself out of tune with the ultimate source of his power, and in June he was forced to relinquish the premiership to Imre Nagy, all the while remaining as party boss.[5] Nagy had been responsible for the 1945 land reform, later nullified by Rakosi's unpopular collectivization campaign, and he came back to power determined to correct a situation that he subsequently characterized in the following terms:

The "left-wing" deviationists, primarily Rakosi and Gero, in the years 1949 to 1953 brought the socialist reorganization of agriculture to a dead end, bankrupted agricultural production, destroyed the worker-peasant alliance, undermined the power of the People's Democracy, trampled upon the rule of law, debased the people's living standards, established a rift between the masses and the Party and government—in other words swept the country towards catastrophe.[6]

Forced to share his power with Rakosi, Nagy nevertheless succeeded in halting the collectivization drive (bringing about an exodus from the collective farms) and in reducing the disproportionate concentration of investments in the heavy industrial sector of the economy. He released most of the purged Communists and contemplated decentralizing economic administration and strengthening the organs of state as distinct from party.

Nagy's "New Course" proved to be short-lived, but its aftereffects were incalculable. By January 1955, the winds had changed once again in the Kremlin with Malenkov's impending disgrace, and Nagy lost his office amidst charges of right-wing opportunist deviation. Rakosi, however, found the task of restoring the status quo ante hampered by the legacy of the New Course: the increasing "revisionism" of the hitherto sycophantic intelligentsia and an erosion of support among party members as well as a new wave of popular opposition encouraged by the apparent rift within the ruling circles. In addition, the emerging Khrushchevian orthodoxy proved to be incompatible with his ingrained Stalinist dogmatism, and Khrushchev's anti-Stalin speech at the Twentieth Party Congress in February 1956 finally sealed the fate of the Hungarian leader. Concurrently, and despite Nagy's expulsion from the party, the intellectual establishment voiced its opposition to Rakosi more and more openly, notably through the Petofi Circle, while Nagy himself wrote a dissertation that attempted to justify the New Course, called for the party's moral and political regeneration, and indirectly accused the Soviet Union of inflicting humiliating slavery upon the Hungarians.[7]

The forces unleashed by the modest political decompression in 1953–54 gathered such momentum that the eleventh-hour replacement of Rakosi by his scarcely less dogmatic lieutenant Erno Gero failed as a palliative, and a student demonstration of sympathy for the Poles on the evening of October 23 marked the beginning of open revolt. The thirteen days of revolution have been subjected to scholarly scrutiny as have few other Hungarian historical events.[8] In the first phase, Nagy was returned as figurehead premier, but under the pressure of the revolutionaries his regime acquired the outlines of a multi-party system. Following rather than leading the uprising, he found himself insisting on the evacuation of Soviet forces and ultimately announced Hungary's withdrawal from the Warsaw Pact and appealed to the United Nations for recognition and protection of his country's neutrality. Overcoming its apparent earlier hesitation, the Soviet leadership launched a military counteroffensive in the night of November 4 and effectively reintegrated Hungary into the Communist system.

The revolution offered a brief glimpse into the genuine political aspirations of the Hungarians. These amounted, in the words of the populist scholar Istvan Bibo, to a "third road" between Communism and capitalism, embodying a pluralistic political system, a mixed economy, a neutral international stance, and a constitutional rule that ensured personal and religious freedom.[9] Instead, the regime that was implanted by

Soviet force and headed by Janos Kadar failed to reach any compromise with the revolutionary groups and workers' councils, and was indeed for a time faced with the humiliation of a general strike. Yet the ambivalence of Kadar and most of his associates in the Politburo of the reformed Hungarian Socialist Workers' Party was evident in their definition of the main causes of the "counter-revolution": (a) the mistakes of the previous sectarian and dogmatic leadership; (b) revisionists in the Party; (c) hostile elements in the country; (d) the insidious efforts of world imperialism.[10] Admittedly, they refused to acknowledge that the revolution had been an intensely patriotic outburst against both Soviet hegemony and Communist totalitarianism, and they attempted to propagate the myth that the genuine working classes had stood by in impotence while reactionary elements drove the Nagy regime to disaster; but, with a few exceptions such as Rakosi's old ideologist, Istvan Revai, the Kadar group assiduously avoided any identification with the pre-revolutionary leadership and practices.[11]

The initial actions of the new regime appeared to diverge only marginally from the Stalinist pattern. Thousands of anti-Communists were once again executed, imprisoned, or exiled, the gulf between the overwhelming majority of the people and a government that derived its authority from the presence of Soviet troops being much too great to allow Kadar to make a credible appeal for popular support. Nevertheless, Kadar was Khrushchev's man and basically in sympathy with the latter's attempt to cautiously relax and liberalize the system that Stalin had created. By the early 1960s there were indications that, while the Hungarian people had lost the war, they had nevertheless won a few small skirmishes, which in view of the growing Western acquiescence in Soviet rule over Eastern Europe was no mean achievement. The remainder of this study will examine the most salient changes that have come about in recent years, changes that add up to a second and more controlled experiment in decompression.

Reappraisals of Economic Theory

The period of intensive socialization under Rakosi had seen the rise of an omnipotent bureaucracy charged with the direction of the highly centralized planning system. Economic priorities, such as the rapid development of heavy industry, were determined by ideological preconceptions rather than by a realistic appraisal of markets or by the optimum utilization of the factors of production. Implementation of the plans proceeded by means of directives that bore little questioning on the part of management or labor. Furthermore, the requirements for political reliability at both ministry and managerial levels produced a class of administrators whose competence was extremely low; according to statistics published in 1958, up to half of the directors in the economic ministries had not even completed their secondary education.[12] The industrial labor force manifested its disillusionment by its support of the revolution, although it must be noted that the workers did not favor a return to an unqualified capitalistic system. Rural discontent with the collective system became even more evident at the end of the revolution, by which time some seventy percent of the arable land had been returned to private cultivation.

The economic problems facing the Kadar regime were manifold. One, a twenty percent decline of the gross national product, was a direct consequence of the revolution. A more secular phenomenon was the diversification of the economy following the partial abandonment of Rakosi's emphasis on heavy industry; for if the centralized planning system had had difficulty in coping with such a relatively simple developmental program, it faced a far greater challenge in administering the diversified economy that was. more suited to Hungarian conditions. Hungary's partners in the Comecon granted her credits totaling $295.75 million, but, while this assisted economic recovery, it did not go a long way toward resolving the more fundamental structural problems. As a first step, the new regime appointed in 1957 several committees of economic experts to advise on possible reforms; their collective report denounced the autarkic tendencies of the Rakosi era and recommended looser and more long-range central control.[13] The plan, argued the noted economist Jozsef Bognar, must be viewed as a dialogue rather than as an order. The economists also advised against a wholesale reimposition of the collective system of agriculture.

The campaign against revisionism in the aftermath of the revolution ruled out official sanction for the reforms recommended by the experts. Instead, the pre-revolutionary structures were reactivated with minor modifications, while in agriculture an even bigger step was taken backwards; following the CPSU's Twenty-first Congress in 1959, in the course of which revisionism was once again excoriated, Kadar overruled the advice of economists and of some of his colleagues and ordered that collectivization be resumed. Through a combination of threats and incentives the peasantry was reintegrated into the collective farms, which by 1967 accounted for 80.4 percent of all arable land (the socialist sector, including the state farms as well as the collectives, encompassed 97.1 percent), but agricultural production suffered accordingly.[14] Increased investments in farm machinery and various incentive systems of payment in kind failed to rally the peasantry, and by the end of the second Five-Year-Plan period in 1965 production had risen by ten percent only, instead of the projected target of twenty percent. At the same time, the tiny household plots allotted to cooperative members had produced a disproportionately large part of the total meat, poultry, egg, milk, and fruit output of Hungary. This clear predilection of the Hungarian peasant for private farming was acknowledged in a resolution of the Central Committee praising the contribution of household plots,[15] but the government took no immediate measures to extend the farmers' independence; compulsory deliveries and the incompetence of local party officials as well as the lure of a higher urban standard of living occasioned a drop of twenty-two percent in the agricultural labor force between 1960 and 1967.[16]

Stagnation in the agricultural sector was not compensated for by any spectacular growth in industrial production. The drive for higher productivity was accompanied by tight labor discipline and a relatively slow rise in real wages, although a few tentative reforms were introduced: investments were now concentrated in the more labor-intensive areas of medium and light industry such as telecommunications, the managerial ranks were for the first time opened to non-party experts, and an interest charge of five percent on the value of the fixed and working capital of the enterprises was introduced. All these palliatives notwithstanding, there remained the key stumbling block of a central planning and price-setting authority, which, in the absence of any market mechanism, could seldom harmonize production and domestic and foreign demand. The stress on quantitative quotas worked at the expense of quality, and with four to five percent of the annual production being unmarketable, stockpiling reached alarming proportions. By the last year of the plan the situation was critical, for, while the actual forty-seven percent rise in industrial production over the entire period of the plan came close to the original projection, the rate of growth had declined drastically. As one Western analyst observed, "It became clear that the centralized planning system was simply unable to cope with the problems involved in the transition from a predominantly investment-oriented economy, with demand determined by the central planners themselves, to a period when effective consumer demand was beginning to assert itself."[17]

In order to forestall economic collapse, and encouraged possibly by the momentary popularity of Liberman's theories in the Soviet Union, the Kadar regime dusted off the eight-year-old report of the experts and produced its own economic revisionist in the person of Politburo member Rezso Nyers. The substance of the proposals, differing little from the recommendations of such prominent Hungarian economists as Bognar, Varga, and Vajda, involved a wide-ranging decentralization of planning, price-setting, and investments.[18] Only very large-scale projects were to be financed directly from the state budget, with enterprises and collectives assuming a major responsibility for modernization and marketing; the cumbersome price bureaucracy was to be pared down through the establishment of a three-tiered pricing system comprising fixed-price, maximum-price, and free-price scales for different groups of products. Finally, the actual plan was to be more limited and flexible in its guidelines. After protracted debate, the Central Committee recommended in May 1966 that this "New Economic Mechanism" (NEM) be made operational effective January 1, 1968.[19]

While the reform could not be construed as even a partial return to free enterprise (in fact, as a result of official policy, the contribution of the private sector to the national income declined from 9.2 percent in 1960 to 2.7 percent in 1967), in its conception the NEM represented a radical departure from the economic systems prevailing in the Communist bloc, all the more so because apart from its structural aspects it implied a diminution in the influence of the party at the enterprise level. The similar Czechoslovak experiment in 1968, fathered by Ota Sik, did not go as far as the NEM on the question of pricing, and it was aborted by a spiral of political demands and ultimate invasion; in Hungary, as will be noted later, the concurrent political reforms proved to be exceedingly modest.

The short experience with the NEM precludes any definitive appraisal of the system in 1970. According to official statistics, the national income rose by five percent in 1968 (as opposed to one percent in 1965), and this despite a minimal increase in agricultural production due largely to inclement weather; industrial production and exports both grew by five percent, leading to a more favorable balance of trade.[20] However, these increases are partly accounted for by the natural expansion of the labor force and therefore do not indicate a significant improvement in productivity. The most intriguing aspect of the NEM lies in its diffusion of economic decision-making and in the resulting new patterns of state-management-labor relations.[21] A key aspect is the transference of major responsibilities for planning, investment, and marketing to the enterprise managers, whose greater control over profits should at least in theory lead to improvements in productivity by providing an incentive for technological modernization. This decentralization remains qualified, however, by the continued—if less direct—supervision of state organs and by the absence of independent sources of credit.

In addition, the NEM has only emphasized the dearth of managerial expertise; whereas in the past incompetent party appointees administered the enterprises according to minutely specific ministerial directives, the somewhat freer market conditions have turned qualified economic consultants into a scarce commodity. Conflict between enterprise policy and the regime's perception of social utility is another possible complicating factor; one party expert noted apprehensively the possibility of speculation by enterprise managers in a free pricing system.[22] It remains to be seen whether the new mechanism will be more responsive within the domestic market and whether it can reduce the wide gap in productivity between Hungarian and Western industries. The persisting imbalances between supply and demand result partly from the production of unsaleable goods that must be stockpiled and partly from the inefficient marketing (or allocation to valuable export markets) of other goods, notably certain foodstuffs, in which endemic shortages have led to widespread consumer dissatisfaction.

Up to this writing, the main beneficiaries of the NEM have been the enterprise managers. Thanks to the one-man management principle, the directors enjoy far greater freedom of action than in the past, a situation that affects not only state-management relations but also management-labor relations. Under the new system, the residue of profits after taxes and reinvestment is distributed according to a differentiated scale, with managers, "experts," and workers receiving up to eighty, fifty, and fifteen percent respectively of their normal salaries. Since on the average such "premiums" amounted to twenty-eight days' wages in 1968, they significantly increased the basic disparity in incomes, giving rise to widespread discontent among the workers. That it seems willing to alienate the very class upon which, at least in ideological terms, its power rests is a mark of the regime's new stress on boosting productivity through incentives. Observed the daily of the Patriotic People's Front, "the trend of change cannot be toward egalitarianism, as is being suggested by many persons right now."[23]

Despite the slogan of "enterprise democracy," it appears that the workers must bear the brunt of the drive for higher productivity, because the modernization of plants is retarded by a shortage of funds for both capital investments and research and development. The statutory mobility of the workers has not been curtailed, and the government has enacted a new Labor Code which grants—at least on paper—additional powers to the unions. The need for this was made clear by the Secretary-General of the National Trade Union Council, Sandor Gaspar:

The new management system allows factories much greater independence— they can draw up their own plans, with due account to local potential and resources, and determine the funds necessary to implement the plans. This means that basic union organizations must enjoy wider jurisdiction, which, moreover, has to be precisely defined to avoid overlapping.[24]

Since hitherto trade unions (and, indeed, managers) in Hungary had served in effect as extensions of the state apparatus, having an only illusory independence, their newly acquired rights represent a radical alteration of the ideological concept of an indivisible public interest; according to the new orthodoxy, "there can be a certain divergence of interests, certain contradictions which the unions make it their job to disclose and resolve."[25] Briefly, the new Labor Code grants unions the right of advice and veto over working conditions, and of advice regarding plant operation and the appointment and dismissal of managers. Unresolved management-labor disputes are to be settled by "higher bodies," presumably the relevant ministry, although Gaspar claims that if necessary the unions can submit differences between state and trade union bodies "to the judgment of the public." The effectiveness of the veto power as a substitute for the right to strike remains to be demonstrated conclusively. In July 1968, two locals of mailmen and transport workers effectively challenged decrees of their parent ministries, establishing a precedent of sorts, but there is evidence of official pressures to limit the use of the veto and to prevent it from developing into a political weapon.[26]

The NEM has brought about changes in the agricultural sector as well, again in the direction of greater autonomy and better incentives as a means of increasing productivity. Although the basic structure of collective farming remains unaltered, the reforms aim to transfer ownership of the land to the collectives themselves, to extend the three-tiered price system to agricultural products and allow the collectives greater freedom in marketing their produce, to enlarge the highly productive household plots and supply more light machinery, and generally to bring agricultural wages more into line with those prevailing in other sectors of the economy. Since agricultural products account for over one-fifth of Hungary's exports, the ultimate effect of these reforms will be critical; it remains to be seen whether the morale of the long-disaffected peasantry will be much improved.

The immediate goal of the Kadar regime in the conception and implementation of the NEM was neither to increase the standard of living nor to satisfy consumer demands but rather to improve Hungary's trading position. With forty percent of the national product being exported, the economy is highly sensitive to fluctuations in foreign demand, and its competitiveness (except perhaps in agricultural products) is weak even in the relatively protected Comecon market, which has since the early 1950s accounted for two-thirds of Hungary's trade. Urging that the domestic economy should ultimately approximate world market norms, Bognar outlined in 1967 a new mechanism for intra-Comecon trade that would: a) render more efficient the international division of labor by means of new price and value relations, b) accelerate technological development by raising quality requirements and by stimulating the industries of the various countries, c) provide wider scope for the industrial enterprises of the various countries to compete for market, d) promote the conclusion of direct agreements between the enterprises by decentralizing spheres of competence, and e) encourage the conclusion of multilateral agreements and cooperation in the sphere of the third market by introducing convertible currencies.[27]

Trade relations within the Comecon have been long plagued by the lack of convertibility and of a multilateral payments system, and the originally intended "socialist division of labor" never came about, largely as a result of Rumania's adamant opposition. Instead, bilateral trade agreements have prevailed, together with a few joint ventures such as the Hungarian-Polish Haldex Company for the processing of coal slack. Apart from the obvious political constraints, Hungary's dependence on the Comecon market is accentuated by economic factors, notably her lack of most raw materials (the major exception being bauxite) and of sources of energy. A more competitive position, both within the Comecon and in Western markets, depends upon improvements in productivity, research and development, and marketing techniques. With regard to the latter, the NEM now permits most enterprises to bypass the hitherto monopolistic and grossly inefficient state trading agencies, and it is conceivably due to this and various incentives (such as "foreign currency multipliers") that Hungary's trading position improved in 1968. Meanwhile, the recent negotiation of a fifteen-million-Eurodollar loan to develop a Hungarian aluminum-processing industry indicates the increasingly pragmatic approach that the regime is taking in the drive for economic modernization.[28]

Ideology and the Party in Evolution

Indeed, a cautious pragmatism has characterized most of the Kadar regime's policies since the early 1960s. In official parlance, this orientation is known as centrism or "the struggle on two fronts"—defined by Zoltan Komocsin, Kadar's close associate and ambassador-at-large, as "a safeguard against repetition both of the old sectarian-dogmatic mistakes and of Right-wing revisionist deviations."[29] For the first five years after the revolution, the shock waves of that event within both Hungary and the entire Communist system gave primacy to the battle against the heresy of "national Communism"; but the underlying tendency in the

Khrushchevian approach, to which Kadar subscribed wholeheartedly, was to improve (at least in appearance) the responsiveness of the party to popular demands.

Of course, on certain basic tenets there could be no compromise. One was the position of the Soviet Union as unquestioned ideological fountainhead and protector of the "socialist" system in Hungary. Largely thanks to the presence of an eighty-thousand-strong Soviet garrison, the regime now claims that it "did demolish this nationalistic, anti-Soviet 'national unity,' which never included the major force of socialist revolution."[30] As we will see later, nationalism remains the strongest integrative and anti-Communist force in Hungary, and the regime has been engaged in a protracted and seemingly hopeless struggle to turn it to its own advantage. There periodic exhortative attempts to identify patriotism with the building of a socialist society, but Komocsin himself concedes that the party "cannot compete with the class enemy in nationalism"; however, he adds optimistically that if the Communists "openly and unambiguously uphold their principles, then, sooner or later, their efforts will be met with success."[31]

The monopolistic position of the party will suffer no alteration or criticism, and intra-party debate is still circumscribed by the principle of democratic centralism, but in recent years the dominant "centrist" Kadar faction has been experimenting with a secularization of administrative functions that serves not only to veil the party's rule but also to infuse a much-needed expertise into certain areas of government and management. This evolution became pronounced mainly after the Twenty-second Congress of the CPSU in 1961, when the dangers of sectarianism (that is, Stalinism) received renewed emphasis, and was not noticeably affected by Khrushchev's subsequent demise. Kadar's famous slogan, "those who are not against us are with us," came to symbolize the regime's new set of priorities: these placed economic modernization and internal stability ahead of any early conversion of the masses to ideological orthodoxy, and subsumed a moderation of the arbitrariness and terror tactics that had characterized both the Rakosi era and the post-revolutionary period. The more humane standards of "socialist legality" led to the return from exile of a number of discredited Stalinists such as Gero, and to the release of the majority of anti-Communist political internees.

Within the party, the new pragmatism did not prevail without some opposition from conservative cadres as well as from those revisionists who felt that de-Stalinization was progressing too slowly. In 1962, three of Kadar's more dogmatic colleagues—Dogei, Kiss, and Marosan—were quietly removed from office; opposition from those middle-level members of the apparat who felt threatened by the admission of non-party experts to positions of responsibility was kept under control, partly by the diplomatic expedient of urging this "new class" to exhibit correct ideological consciousness. At the same time, Kadar made an attempt to rejuvenate and raise the level of expertise of the Politburo with the inclusion of Rezso Nyers and of Miklos Ajtai, an engineer turned economic planner.

Changes in the social structure of the population at large, a perhaps inevitable concomitant of economic modernization, have accentuated the isolation of the Communist establishment from the mainstream of Hungarian life. Socially, the party was never very representative, since it drew most of its adherents from the urban and rural proletariat; such is the background of all but two of the chieftains in the 1970 Politburo. In addition, the predominance of apparat members among delegates to party congresses indicates a pattern of careerism which, taken in conjunction with the rise of a new stratum of non-party managers and professionals, contributes to the party's remoteness.[32] The later emphasis on the recruitment of middle-class technocrats into the party may improve the latter's representativeness, but only at the price of making the concept of a "worker-peasant alliance" even less meaningful than before.

These new patterns of social differentiation and stratification strike at the heart of the basic Communist tenet of a classless society, and within party circles attempts to reconcile ideology and reality have proliferated. For instance, one finds in the party's ideological monthly the explanation that the "differences between us and capitalist societies lies not in that their structure is hierarchical and ours is not, but rather in the qualitative differences that characterize their class-based society."[33] The role of official iconoclast has been assumed by Andras Hegedus, Rakosi's Premier in 1955 and 1956, who subsequently returned from exile in the Soviet Union to begin a second career as head of the newly formed Sociological Research Group of the Hungarian Academy of Sciences. Advocating an updating of Marxism through the findings of modern sociology, Hegedus spoke up in defense of those Communist and extra-party elements which pressed for major reforms:

[As] the inevitable expression of the controversies in the social structure of European socialist states, a commitment toward the road of social progress develops which is aimed against the apologetics of the existing institutions. This—on the basis of a Marxist orientation of values—demands the realistic analysis of existing conditions, in order to select on this basis the most suitable alternatives of development. Among other things, it was the appearance of this force which made possible the critical analysis of the so-called strongly centralized "planned" economy and the working out of a new economic model.[34]

Socialist society, in his view, remains differentiated both in structure and in interests, and consequently the party can best function as an ultimate but rather remote supervisor. Other, more orthodox members of the establishment have attacked this type of revisionism as being inconsistent with the party's essential task of gaining the allegiance of all social groupings.[35] The official view that has evolved is a pragmatic compromise: the people can be converted in the long run not by compulsion, but rather by its absence. Komocsin succinctly outlined the scope and limitations of this new tolerance:

> There has never been, nor is there likely to be for a long time to come a Communist Party that could on a class basis attract to its side every citizen of a country without exception. But the Party and its leadership should always be able to attract—chiefly through conviction—the majority of the working people. And the main method of winning the working people for socialism is action that accords with their interests and aspirations. Of course, we should debate with our political enemies, too. But in a country committed to the building of socialism we cannot, in our view, renounce the use of the instruments of power in relation to those who actively oppose socialism and the socialist system.[36]

He emphasized further that concepts of abstract democracy, sovereignty, and humanism are subordinate to the class approach and to "internationalism," for only the latter two can lead to an understanding of sociopolitical life.

Nevertheless, there is a growing and increasingly outspoken awareness, particularly among social scientists, that conflicting group interests are inherent in social life and consequently should not be ignored, and that the planning and governing institutions should adapt to this reality rather than vice versa. Kadar himself acknowledged this when, in November 1967, he told the Central Committee that the dichotomic view of the society and the individual had to be expanded to include the collective interests of certain socio-economic units.[37] But whereas economic decentralization was dictated by dire necessity and brought with it relatively few risks, the recognition of pluralistic tendencies was potentially more explosive and has found only limited practical application. The regime's greater tolerance, or rather its confidence in its own stability, has been manifested in a degree of decompression. Reforms in the educational field have mitigated earlier discrimination against the offspring of "class enemies" and other unreliable elements.

Freedom of speech has also benefited from Kadar's pragmatism, to the extent that the Hungarians' inbred but long-muted love of political debate can now find an outlet at the individual level, and even such official experiments as the NEM can be held up to ridicule in the odd cabaret. Rakosi's notorious secret police, the AVH (State Security Authority), has been disbanded and replaced by a slightly less oppressive and omnipresent branch of the Ministry of Interior. The literary establishment is free to criticize the excesses of the Rakosi era as long as it abstains from drawing parallels with existing conditions. Even so, the party issues frequent warnings against bourgeois tendencies, and in 1968 Kadar pointedly advised the Writers' Association that creative freedom does not obviate their duty to defend working-class interests.[38] In a country where writers have traditionally functioned as channels of political protest—most recently during the period of decompression preceding the revolution—creative freedom and ideological orthodoxy coexist today in a tenuous state of symbiosis.

At the institutional level, the regime's determination to strengthen its legitimacy through wider popular participation in the political process has been tempered by a caution that found ample justification in the disastrous conclusion of the Dubcek experiment. One reform, approved by the party's Ninth Congress in November 1966, introduced a hypothetical element of choice in parliamentary elections; candidates still required the sanction of the Patriotic People's Front, and at the general elections of 1967 all nine "opposition" candidates were defeated.[39] A somewhat more meaningful attempt has been made to enlarge the functions of the state (as distinct from party) organs; in particular, the National Assembly, which hitherto could consent but seldom oppose or advise, has received official encouragement in its representative function. Kadar's chief lieutenant, Bela Biszku, observed just before the elections that the government's constitutional obligations toward Parliament required greater practical application, and consequently the question period and parliamentary committees did undergo a modest revival.[40] A full-fledged political opposition remains, of course, totally inconceivable.

The mass organizations, established originally as unidirectional agents of mobilization and indoctrination, also reflect the slightly more pluralistic ethos of Kadar's Hungary. Both the Patriotic People's Front and the Communist Youth League (KISZ) have in recent years provided forums for minor grievances, and, as noted earlier, the trade unions' role has been enhanced by the new Labor Code. Their spokesmen, however, are careful to emphasize their subordination to the party:

The leading role of the Party does not in any way infringe on the basic principle that the trade unions are self-acting organizations with their own constitution and an elected leadership to supervise their day to day activities.

The unions consider it their honourable duty to help the Communist Party. We frankly speak of our association with the Party as the only politically sound solution.[41]

Thus mass organizations and interest groups are recognized as valid interlocutors and aggregators of opinion only to the extent of their narrow technical competence; yet the dynamics of political participation are such that disputes over trivia may well lead to a contestation of fundamentals, as proved to be the case in the first phase of decompression, or indeed in Czechoslovakia in 1968. And therein lies Kadar's dilemma, for as a newspaper editorial declared, "Our political mechanism has been and will remain the dictatorship of the proletariat."[42]

Social Change: Youth and Values

The myth of a socialist society suffered a shattering repudiation in the 1956 revolution; workers, intellectuals, young people almost unanimously rose up not only against Soviet rule and economic deprivation but also in protest against the spiritual barrenness and unresponsiveness of the totalitarian political system. Following the invasion, some two hundred thousand fled the country. Those who remained presented the new regime with a monumental challenge: to legitimize Communist rule without destroying the structural preconditions for its maintenance.

The tacit recognition that a classless or undifferentiated society is little more than an eschatological concept was one notable manifestation of Kadar's realism. The orthodox view of a monolithic "worker-peasant alliance" prevailed until the early 1960s, but thereafter official sanction for sociological research prompted numerous studies of the emerging patterns of stratification.[43] While the size of the ruling party elite— around three percent of the total population—has remained relatively constant, a new middle stratum has radically altered the atomized and diffuse social structure of the Rakosi period. Composed of professionals, managers, and intellectuals, this predominantly technocratic middle class accounts by rough estimate for fifteen percent of the population, and it has presented the regime with the predictable problems of vested interest and internal recruitment.[44] Lacking political power and offering the party a loyalty that is at best opportunistic, the new class embodies values that are essentially non-ideological and individualistic. Attempts to rationalize this phenomenon by pointing to the working-class origins of up to half of the new class have foundered on the shoals of its progressive consolidation; year by year the proportion of working-class students in institutes of higher education has declined (to 39.2 percent of applicants in 1969), and official observers have noted with dismay the poorer performance of this latter group.[45] The development of an autonomous and privileged middle class with its own secular value system is placing the regime in the difficult position of abandoning the principle of ideological purity for the sake of economic expediency.

The significance of these new patterns of social stratification is enhanced by the system's failure to imprint the "socialist consciousness" requisite for its legitimacy, for in the absence of such consciousness the regime's authority remains largely circumstantial. Growing links with the West, dictated by a pressing need for hard currency, have only strengthened popular scepticism.[46] The failure of indoctrination in the Hungarian context does not signify a wholesale rejection of all aspects of socialism, for over a period of twenty years the population has become attached to the more tangible benefits of a welfare state. It does mean a resistance to one-party rule and to dogmatic collectivism that neither Rakosi nor Kadar have managed to eradicate; as one ideologist conceded a few years ago, the replacement of old-fashioned individualism by a new collective social spirit remains an unfulfilled goal.[47]

Instead, the social ethos has been characterized by collective and inter-generational alienation, by obsessive materialism and a partial breakdown of traditional morality, as well as by a deeply rooted patriotism and a habitual pattern of religious practice. At the time of the Communist takeover, two-thirds of the population belonged to the Roman Catholic Church, with most of the remainder being distributed among the various Protestant persuasions, and, despite a persecution that was most pronounced in the Rakosi era, the churches retain a certain influence. Although the regime frowns upon religious education and practice, frequently incarcerates outspoken priests and monks, and is adamantly opposed to the reinstatement of Cardinal Mindszenty (living in the asylum of the American embassy since 1956), it has settled on a modus vivendi, particularly with the Catholic Church. Eight Catholic high schools survive, and in January 1969 an agreement was reached with the Vatican over the appointment of a number of new bishops. Earlier, a conference on the sociology of religion had concluded that the tenacity of religious faith made necessary the cooperation of believers in the building of a socialist society.[48]

Patriotism, and its more pronounced manifestation, nationalism, continue to be the most powerful integrative forces in Hungary. Under Hapsburg as well as Soviet hegemony, the Hungarians have manifested a national consciousness that sparked open rebellion as well as passive resistance. With the setback to national self-determination inflicted by the USSR in 1956, the patriotic impulse reverted to its passive state, but anti-Soviet sentiment remains impervious to the regime's concerted efforts at presenting the Soviet Union as a benevolent protector. An additional source of nationalistic feeling lies in the contentious issue of Hungarian minorities, which dates back to the dismemberment of the Austro-Hungarian empire in 1919. These minorities, including over half-million Magyars in Slovakia and in northeastern Yugoslavia, and over 1½ million Transylvanians in Rumania, gave rise to a powerful irredentist movement in the interwar period, and while irredentism has waned, popular empathy, particularly for the oppressed Transylvanians, remains in evidence. The ideological commitment to "internationalism" and to fraternal relations within the socialist community having ruled out any response on the part of the regime and its mass media, this tenacious aspect of nationalism is seldom articulated.

For all their persistence, religious faith and patriotism have been overshadowed by more existential values that arise out of the vicissitudes of everyday life in Hungary. Twenty years of harsh economic circumstances have created an understandable materialistic hunger for consumer goods; although the standard of living is exceeded within the Communist bloc only by East Germany and, at least until recently, by Czechoslovakia, the symbols of a mass-consumption society—refrigerators, automobiles, and the like—are still scarce and highly coveted commodities. On the other hand, cultural manifestations of all sorts proliferate and are easily accessible; for instance, in 1967 more than forty-seven *million* copies of books were printed in Hungary.

The decline in moral values can be related to rapid industrialization and social restratification, an endemic housing shortage, and economic insecurity; in recent years, Hungary's divorce and abortion rates have been among the highest in the world, and petty theft of "social property" has become rampant. The absence of looting and other anti-social behavior (if one excepts reprisals against the hated secret police) during the revolution testified, however, to the nation's capacity for moral regeneration in moments of crisis.

Alienation and a rejection of ideology have, among other social and psychological phenomena, drawn the attention of Hungarian writers. Peter Veres, a member of the prewar populist movement, has been notably candid in his appraisal of the mental state of those who work within the socialist system without having the comfort of ideological conviction or the means to participate in the decision-making process.[49] Other intellectuals, including the president of the Writers' Union, Jozsef Darvas, have renewed the tradition of the populist "village explorers" with their revealing accounts of abysmal living conditions in certain rural areas. Such criticism on the part of the literary intelligentsia, though reminiscent of its behavior in the first phase of decompression, is articulated within the correct ideological context and is therefore tolerated by the regime.

Apart from such surrogates, and despite the greater responsiveness inherent in Kadar's pragmatic approach, the absence of adequate channels for political participation and the maintenance of an ideological superstructure that is demonstrably irrelevant and unproductive have occasioned a rather apolitical apathy; the underlying resentment is reinforced by suspicions of Soviet economic exploitation and by a blatant abuse of privilege on the part of a select few apparatchiks. The constant threat of Soviet intervention has also contributed to a consciousness of collective impotence which incidentally bolsters the system's stability, for in spite of its shortcomings the Kadar regime is recognized to be more humane than any Soviet-imposed alternative.

In the period of intensive socialization, the Communists had placed their hopes on the young as being the core of a future, genuinely socialist polity. Dashed by the experience of the revolution, these hopes were revived under Kadar, but once again, and this time on its own evidence, the regime is confronted with youthful disillusionment. One study, by a Marxist primary-school teacher, testified not only to widespread anti-Soviet sentiments among her students, but also to a marked preference for the great figures of Hungarian history over the much-touted if often apocryphal heroes of the "workers' movement."[50] Another local survey among older adolescents and youths disclosed that over half adhered to a traditional value system, one third also admitted to religious faith, and only fourteen percent appeared to espouse Marxist values.[51] A further survey, carried out by the Communist Youth League among its membership, found that eighty-three percent of the respondents considered patriotism to be a desirable value.[52]

The phenomenon of youthful rebellion, which has attracted so much attention in the West these past few years, is also apparent in Eastern Europe, where the greater dearth of outlets promises to make it less vocal but more explosive. This prospect is discussed at length by a Marxist writer in the literary and political weekly *Elet es Irodalom*.[53] Focusing on the over two-million-strong "KISZ generation," Veszpremi notes that as yet they have not turned against society nor exhibited the rejection and anarchic behavior of their Western contemporaries, but they are nevertheless profoundly frustrated by a socialist order which has been "unsuccessful in resolving the problem of productively channeling the energies of the young," and are reluctant to be transformed into obedient factors of production. Since it did not need one in its early application, Marxism lacks a youth theory, and the author of the article deplores the fact that the original revolutionaries turn into a retarding force at the very moment when the young are becoming impatient with prevailing inconsistencies and faults and beginning to concentrate on the possibilities for change rather than on evidence of past progress. In defense of the young, Veszpremi argues that they are the product of a socialist upbringing, that regardless of Western influences they are concerned about Hungarian problems, and that it is futile to maintain—as the leadership evidently does—that there are no "social contradictions." Warning that the younger generation almost seems to threaten to sweep away those whose ideas do not keep pace, he concludes, "I am convinced that the historical task of our society is to create a political, moral and economic 'arena' within which man can live out his life without losing his individuality. The one thing man cannot bear is to be excluded from the battlefield."

The problem of integrating the young must not be the least among the regime's dilemmas. Youth's cult of Western fads, including anti-social behavior and a disrespect for parental authority, is but the surface manifestation of a more deeply rooted sense of futility and of dismay at their future prospects, and Kadar's pragmatism has yet to offer a credible answer to their implicit demands for participation and self-realization.

The Perilous Path to Humane Socialism

While in recent years the Hungarian regime has become more liberal than any of its counterparts in the Soviet sphere of influence, its external orientation has remained closely attuned to the fluctuations of Soviet foreign policy. Kadar consistently sided with Moscow in the Sino-Soviet schism, avoiding any identification with Rumania's economic nationalism and reluctance to censure the Maoists, and never deviated from the Kremlin's stand on Vietnam and other East-West issues. Although the government has strenuously denied it, reports from Radio Tirana indicate that a detachment of Hungarian troops was dispatched to the Manchurian border. The regime did take one initiative in the mid-1960s with a proposal for Danubian regional cooperation that would include Austria and Yugoslavia,[54] but apart from a few bilateral agreements (notably with Austria on the exchange of electric power) the proposals seem to have lost any actuality, and Kadar has taken up Moscow's cue in advocating a major conference on European security.

Conceivably, this loyalty to Moscow was the price paid for internal liberalization. If so, Kadar's behavior during the Czechoslovakian crisis may bring about a marked deceleration in the process of decompression. Meeting Dubcek on at least three occasions prior to the invasion, Kadar acted as a concerned intermediary who realized that the Czechoslovak experiment's failure—inevitable unless the pace of political liberalization could be checked—was bound to have repercussions throughout the bloc, and particularly in relatively progressive Hungary. Official Hungarian sources deplored the criticism of the political trial and execution of Imre Nagy voiced in a Czechoslovak periodical, but it is clear that up to the ultimate application of the Brezhnev doctrine of limited sovereignty, sympathy for Dubcek's reforms was not limited to the mass public. Although Hungarian troops joined in the Warsaw Pact's police action, local speculation to the effect that Kadar had been reluctant to sanction this participation and had been brought to heel by unambiguous Soviet threats may be well founded. He disappeared from public view for over two months, and thereafter he combined apologetics for the invasion ("unavoidable and necessary because of the danger of counterrevolution") with reassurances that the economic reforms would continue.[55]

There are signs, however, that the regime's stated commitment to the development of "socialist humanism and democracy" may have been momentarily suspended. After criticizing the invasion, Hegedus was removed from his post, and the Central Committee offered directives for sociological research which dismissed pluralism as an irrelevant concept and stressed instead the task of defending the ideological unity and purity of Marxism-Leninism;[56] evidently empirical research methods had produced results that were unpalatable to the party. The popular reaction in Czechoslovakia to the relaxation of political controls, and the dogmatic and draconian response of the Soviet leadership must have served as a warning to Kadar that any constructive acknowledgment of the pluralistic and participatory pressures in Hungarian society would not only release cumulative demands and potentially sweeping forces but also invite swift retribution from abroad.

On the other hand, Kadar can have little confidence in the maintenance of his regime without Soviet support. When early in 1958 a partial repatriation of the Soviet occupation forces took place, officials felt the need to issue a stern warning:

There are—here at home as well as abroad—counter-revolutionary elements who nurse high hopes in connection with the withdrawal of Soviet troops. These believe that the time has come again when their reactionary dreams shall come true. We wish to state that they are mistaken in hoping for a weakening of the democratic regime. . . . Our faithful allies, the remaining Soviet units, will stand at our side in the future also.[57]

Since that time, Kadar has made tangible gains in popularity, but one of his colleagues has testified again to the presence of oppositional elements: "The main conclusions drawn by the class enemy from the 1956 defeat was that haste must be avoided in favour of a stage-by-stage operation."[58] The limiting factor in Kadar's quest for popular support remains his set of non-negotiable, fundamental premises regarding the monopoly of party control and the elitist structure of that organization. Dilution of either premise, while undoubtedly desired by a majority of his reluctant constituents, carries with it impossible risks for not only the regime but also for the people themselves. Thus there prevails in Hungary a dichotomous and almost surrealistic political culture marked by a ubiquitous ideological superstructure whose sincere supporters account for less than one-tenth of the population.

The new mechanism may well bring about a slight amelioration of economic conditions, and there are no indications at this writing that the regime is under Soviet pressure to curtail it; on the contrary, official spokesmen continue to urge the introduction of currency convertibility as a means of improving the flexibility of trade relations and of facilitating the more decentralized commercial operations of individual enterprises. In the social and political spheres, however, the prospects for further relaxation are dim. While specialized interest groups such as the trade unions are likely to exert a growing influence on matters within their frames of reference, it is improbable that any extension of their political role will materialize. The reactivated National Assembly may gradually come closer to fulfilling its constitutional advisory and investigative functions, but any reforms in the direction of pluralistic representation and genuine participation in the decision-making process would create a competing power center that no ideologically orthodox party could sanction.

Thus the ancient political question, who governs the governors, finds no answer within the confines of Hungary. Although it is at moments when decompression reaches a plateau that popular frustration becomes most pronounced, the likelihood of effective radical change, whether peaceful or through violence, remains as remote in Hungary as in the rest of Eastern Europe. To recall the proverbs cited earlier, the small birds still scarcely sing; the crayfish are still mute.

8

Yugoslavia —
The Process of Democratization

George Klein

Country Profile: THE SOCIALIST FEDERAL REPUBLIC
OF YUGOSLAVIA

Head of State: Josip Broz Tito, President of the Republic
Premier: Mitja Ribicic, President of the Federal Executive Council
President, League of Communists of Yugoslavia: Josip Broz Tito

Party Membership (1967): 1,013,500[1]
Armed Forces (1969): 218,000 (Army: 180,000; Navy: 18,000; Air Force:
20,000)[2]
Population (1968): 20,154,000 (Belgrade: 697,000)[3]
Area: 255,804 square kilometers (98,766 square miles)
Population Density: 79 per square kilometer (205 per square mile)
Birth Rate (1968): 18.9 per thousand[3]
Death Rate (1968): 8.6 per thousand[3]
Divorce Rate (1968): 1.0 per thousand[3]
Gross Material Product (1968): 108 billion new dinars ($8.3 billion at
official rate)[4]
National Income Total (1968): 101.8 billion new dinars[5]
National Income by Sectors (1968):[5]
　Industry: 34.0%
　Construction: 8.9%
　Agriculture: 22.7%
　Transportation and Communications: 7.6%
　Trade: 19.1%
　Other: 7.7%
Foreign Trade by Area (1968):[6]
　Socialist countries (including USSR): 30.4%
　USSR: 12.9%
　Non-Socialist countries: 69.6%

Foreign Trade by Commodity (1968):[7]	Export	Import
Machinery, capital goods	28.4%	40.7%
Industrial consumer goods	19.3%	13.3%
Raw materials, semi-finished products	36.9%	41.0%
Comestibles	15.3%	4.9%
Other	0.1%	0.1%

SOURCES:
1. U.S. Department of State, Bureau of Intelligence and Research, *World Strength of Communist Party Membership* (Washington, D.C.: U.S. Government Printing Office, 1969), p. 64.
2. *The Military Balance 1969–1970* (London: The Institute of Strategic Studies, 1969), pp. 31–32.
3. *Statisticki godisnjak Jugoslavije 1969* (Belgrade: Savezni zavod za statistiku, 1969), p. 82.
4. *Yugoslav Survey,* vol. 10, no. 4 (November 1969), p. 44.
5. *Ibid.,* p. 43.
6. *Statisticki godisnjak Jugoslavije 1969,* p. 214.
7. *Ibid.,* p. 213.

8. Yugoslavia —
The Process of Democratization

George Klein

The years from 1950 to 1970 represent two decades of peaceful development in Yugoslavia. These were the first two peaceful decades of this century for that country. During these years Yugoslavia underwent a great transformation from a classical underdeveloped, agriculturally based society to the ranks of states which have more than fifty percent of their population employed in industry and non-agricultural pursuits. The cities of Yugoslavia underwent particularly impressive growth in view of the devastations of World War II.[1] Nationality, for the first time in memory, was not a cause for conflict and slaughter. Few economists would dispute that northern Yugoslavia, comprising parts of Croatia, Slovenia, and Serbia, enjoys a living standard which is close to that of Western Europe. As a matter of fact, prosperous urban centers can be found in all parts of the country.

The Yugoslav political system is increasingly institutionalized, and few who know Ljubljana would distinguish its way of life sharply from that which prevails in parts of Western Europe. The symbolism associated in the public mind with Communism or totalitarian rule is missing. Pluralism asserts itself at all levels of Yugoslav society, and it is very difficult to fix with precision where the true power centers lie or where key decisions are made because of widespread public participation in the political process.

Since its break with the Cominform in 1948, Yugoslavia has occupied a unique place in the family of nations. The Yugoslav example has been anathema to the leaders of the Soviet bloc, although, paradoxically, it has been the avant garde of almost all the changes within the Soviet bloc itself. Such Soviet bloc innovations as the workers' councils, the decentralization of economic planning, and the opening of the Communist countries to tourism all have followed the Yugoslav example. The terminology employed by the Soviet bloc and Yugoslavia have differed, but there can be little doubt that the Yugoslav example has been a powerful stimulant to change even in the Soviet Union itself.

Yugoslavia, also, provided the West with a new model for relations with a Communist state. When the United States started actively backing Yugoslavia, albeit at times reluctantly, few would have suspected that this Balkan country would be regarded a cornerstone in safeguarding the stability of the area. The Yugoslav example has proved that not every Communist state is by definition aggressive toward its non-Communist neighbors nor desirous of subverting the established social order in all parts of the world.

The precipitous nature of Yugoslav economic development brought with it great differences in the level of living achieved by various regions. The economic development did not come cheaply; there are few Yugoslavs who would deny the high social cost of the economic gains. Only a victorious revolution could have used as much compulsion or been able to draw on the great resource of youthful enthusiasm for self-sacrifice.

If one were to delineate the most pertinent changes during the last few years, these issues would stand out as milestones in the development of Yugoslavia: (1) the decline of the command economy and statism and the general demythification of the role of the League of Communists, (2) the freeing of the mass media from direct censorship, (3) restraint in the use of force in the exaction of political conformity, (4) the institutionalization of the politics of the several nationalities and the frank recognition that surface unity achieved by compulsion is undesirable, (5) a more benevolent style of life stimulated by a growing prosperity, and (6) the revitalization of the League of Communists of Yugoslavia (the League) based on popular decisions and external pressures.

Every one of these categories could be modified by many qualifications. They stand, nevertheless, in testimony to the positive achievements of the last five years. The subsequent pages will be devoted to a more critical examination of the complexities of Yugoslavia's contemporary situation. The most vexing problems stem from the ethnic complexity of Yugoslavia. The ethnic divisions affect politics, economics, cultural pride, and religion; in fact, this problem is at the heart of most internal questions which have to be resolved by the federal government.

National Problems

Yugoslavia is still a society trying to balance unity with federalism and political liberty with restriction, under conditions of internal and external stress experienced by few other societies in the world. Internal divisions are constantly exploited by her neighbors, large and small, for their own political purposes. Albanians agitate among the Albanians in the Kosmet, the Bulgarians agitate in Macedonia, depending on the tone of Soviet policy toward Yugoslavia.

The very multi-ethnic composition of the country constitutes a standing problem to its stability. There were, according to 1961 statistics, about 7,806,000 Serbs, 4,294,000 Croats, 1,589,000 Slovenes, 1,046,000 Macedonians, 514,000 Montenegrins, and about 2,392,000 Moslems, Hungarians, and Shiptars. Religious cleavages fall along national lines; the Slovenes and Croats follow Roman Catholicism, while the Serbs, Montenegrins, and Macedonians belong to the Orthodox Church. The Moslems represent a separate community, which is difficult to identify as an ethnic group because of their mixed ethnic origins. The situation is complicated by the great disparities in income between the various republics of Yugoslavia. The Republic of Slovenia enjoys a per capita income which is on the level of her neighbors to the north, while in some southern portions of Yugoslavia per capita annual income remains under $300.

The leaders of the most developed republics demand more decentralization. The policy of decentralization enables them to retain the gains within their republics. The greater efficiency of capital in their areas can be clearly demonstrated.[2] They resist all efforts by the South to reinstitute a strong centralized regime which would rely on economic planning because it is easy to see that they would be the losers in a centrally directed effort at redistributing investment and income. The peoples from the poorer areas in general stand for a tighter, more centralistic regime because they hope to gain economically from any government which would redistribute the rewards in Yugoslavia on a planned basis. The "dogmatists," "bureaucrats," and all "centralists"[3] usually originate in those portions of Yugoslavia, and they probably reflect accurately the sentiments of the communities they represent. Their representatives frequently question the benefits of socialism in a society which tolerates five times the per capita income in Slovenia as compared with the Kosmet. It is these fundamental divisions in conception and outlook based on differing levels of economic development which form the basis of almost every political issue in contemporary Yugoslavia. Decentralization and self-management, as implemented since the 1950s, has formally triumphed in Yugoslavia, but it has only underlined the existing disparities. Every political problem, external and internal, touches on the sensitive exposed nerve between the forces of decentralization and democratization and those which would return Yugoslavia to an "etatist" model.[4]

The burden of multi-ethnicity enters into every realm of life. If there are film studios in Serbia and Slovenia, then the Macedonians and Albanians demand parity. Literary productions and the mass media can exist in some national areas only with federal subsidy, since each caters to a limited audience. If parity is demanded in cultural production, it is no less demanded in steel or cigarette manufacturing. This has led to the proliferation of small enterprises which have no chance to raise their production to a high enough level to be competitive either domestically or internationally.

Decentralization and the insistence that each enterprise be permitted to exist purely on its ability to make a profit was designed to cope with these problems. The elements in the society which feel themselves most threatened by competition oppose these reforms by every political means at their disposal. Because of these profound divisions and because the League of Communists of Yugoslavia is organized along regional lines and reflects regional sentiments, the state has suffered recurring crises which involve national feelings.

Between 1950 and 1965, Yugoslavia gradually implemented a system of economic self-management which worked with varying degrees of efficiency in industrial plants throughout the country. The Yugoslav conceptions were enshrined in the Fundamental Law of 1953 and the Constitution of 1963. By 1964–65, the Yugoslav economy was beginning to experience increasing difficulties with the balance of payments and with inflation. The growth rate stagnated, and the country was preoccupied with acrid debate on the remedies which could be applied in order to halt economic deterioration. The country was split, essentially, into the forces which were frequently labeled "centralist," 'bureaucratic," "dogmatic," or "etatist," on the one hand, and the liberal forces for change on the other. The liberals generally came from the more advanced areas; while their greatest strength lay in Slovenia and Croatia, the Serbian intellectuals and others from Serbia formed also a very strong component in their ranks. The forces hoping to see an imposition of more central controls had their center of gravity in the less-developed regions of Yugoslavia. The balance of forces, both in and out of the party, was certainly heavily weighted in favor of the "liberals" or experimenters who wanted to end all aspects of central production planning, stop subsidy to losing enterprises, end price controls, and put the entire economy on the basis of "market socialism," which in Western terms meant on a competitive basis.

The Rankovic Case

The dismissal of Alexander Rankovic, Vice President of Yugoslavia and heir apparent to Tito, marked the end of an era in Yugoslavia.[5] The ramifications of the Rankovic ouster extended to all areas of Yugoslav life. It had some earmarks of a nationality conflict insofar as Rankovic found his greatest support from among the Serbs and Montenegrins from the more backward areas of both republics. Rankovic, in his role as chieftain of the secret police, maintained a measure of control over all aspects of Yugoslav domestic life through the Ministry of Interior, in which the secret police were included. The ouster of Rankovic also involved a crisis of foreign policy because the faction he represented had great popularity in the Soviet Union and among the more rigid governments of East Europe. Rankovic's agents and supporters had heavily infiltrated the Secretariat of Foreign Affairs. The Rankovic case arose out of clashes over the economic policy Yugoslavia should follow after the crisis of 1965, and out of Rankovic's unabashed effort to seize control of the party, perhaps even before Tito retired. His dismissal led to a new situation in Yugoslavia.

The forces led by Rankovic did little to conceal their distaste for the contemplated economic reforms, causing Tito to speak out against the sabotage of reforms by highly placed leaders.[6] The Rankovic case represented not only a succession crisis but also had some aspects of a generation conflict. The Rankovic forces represented the older, less-educated leadership from all republics, which held its position on the basis of contributions to the National Liberation Struggle during World War II. The fall of Rankovic initiated a distinct new phase in the evolution in the Yugoslav government. The dismissal of Rankovic's partisans altered the alignment of forces on which the entire system rested.

The most important aspect of the downfall of Rankovic was the decline of the institutionalized threat system in the form of the secret police. Its ranks were reduced by almost one-half and many of their previous misdeeds were now widely publicized.

The ouster of Rankovic set the ship of state on a new course and placed the forces of liberalization and democratization in clear ascendancy. The Rankovic forces were too deeply discredited to launch a plausible counterattack on the now-triumphant democratizing coalition.

For the time being, at least, the centralistic forces were demoralized and disoriented, and the threat of a centralist coup led by Rankovic and a Serbian-Montenegrin coalition faded into the realm of the impossible.

The liberals were now free to give market socialism its day. With the abolition of the threat system, public debate developed rapidly, and with it came a discussion of subjects which had been carefully avoided on the Yugoslav political scene in the previous years. The removal of tension left the way open for venomous discussions of the nationality problem. Rankovic became initially the scapegoat after the disclosures of secret police brutality among the Albanians in Kosmet.

The discussion ranged over the amount of permissible freedom and democracy in Yugoslavia to the share of investment which each republic should receive. The pattern which emerged out of it most clearly was that power was indeed diffused and that a pluralization of the entire society was at hand. The fall of Rankovic underscored the power of local and republican bodies. Moreover, the reforming branch of the League was committed to an expanding democratization. A self-reinforcing situation developed. The leadership had to adopt those reforms which were popular, and to which the anti-Rankovic forces were committed. The lower administration of government and League eagerly grasped the power offered them through increased decentralization, and power once abandoned is not easily reclaimed by the central leadership. So, on one hand, the League leadership was in the forefront of the liberalizing action, but in the process it also forfeited much authority.

Some Results of Decreased Authority

The fall of Rankovic unleashed long-dormant forces in the society. The main brunt of the discussion took place within the League itself. The tight dictatorship of other East European countries never prevailed in Yugoslavia. Her special international position and the multiplicity of nationalities always demanded a greater capacity for ideological and political compromise. This is the reason why Milovan Djilas could survive his profound differences with the leadership and his challenge to the ideological underpinnings of state ideology. This is also the reason why lesser lights could further all sorts of unorthodox views and receive only mild reprimands in official journals or face minor consequences.[7] With the dismissal of Rankovic it became clear that only the grossest of deviations would face formal consequences from the state organs. The Yugoslav community of Marxist intellectuals had been in turmoil even before Rankovic was dismissed. In effect, the intellectuals tended to oppose any form of imposed Marxism as official state doctrine. Many of the philosophers who published their views in the journal *Praxis* believed that Marxism could give substance to a socialist state only as a philosophy subject to critique and test like any set of ideas which contends for recognition in the intellectual community. They believed that the elevation of Marxism to state ideology was closely related to most negative aspects of the socialist system, namely, totalitarianism. With the dismissal of Rankovic, *Praxis* resumed publication, after an eight-month suspension.

There was an obvious and substantial split on this issue between the party intellectuals and the party politicians. Their differences frequently burst into the press in controversies in which both parties to the dispute utilized the segment of the press they controlled.[8] These polemics disoriented the rank-and-file membership of the party, which had little intellectual equipment to cope with the questions of Marx as an economist or humanist philosopher.

Other Symptoms of Democratization

There is actually no formal press pre-censorship in Yugoslavia as there is in the other Communist states. The decisions on publication are left to the discretion of editors for the most part. These tend to be members of the party establishment who support the system within which they define their careers. Many of them are intellectuals with libertarian tendencies, and, as a result, they are willing to print controversial materials, particularly if they increase circulation.

The Mihailo Mihajlov case arose when an obscure instructor at the Zadar faculty of the University of Zagreb published a highly critical account of a summer's stay in the Soviet Union. Mihajlov's accusations against the Soviets were bound to stir their resentment, since he charged that death camps and genocide actually originated in the Soviet Union rather than in Germany. The articles were published in a Belgrade periodical, *Delo,* and led to a long round of litigation during which Mihajlov became an international political factor, although not necessarily a domestic one. Essentially, Mihajlov flung a challenge to the government to abide by Article 39 of the Yugoslav Constitution, which guaranteed freedom of expression through the mass media.[9] Mihajlov deliberately set out to test this provision with the announced purpose of founding an opposition journal completely outside the official ideological framework.

The government picked up the cudgel by first imposing a suspended sentence; then in April of 1967 it neatly sidestepped the constitutional issues by trying Mihajlov for spreading slanderous and malicious propaganda. The effect of the Mihajlov case was to delineate the permissible limits of tolerance to political dissent. The case was significant because it highlighted the pressures from foreign sources to which Yugoslavia is exposed at all times. Non-action against Mihajlov had infuriated the Soviet leadership at a time when the Yugoslav government was attempting to improve relations with the Soviet Union. The eventual sentencing of Mihajlov meant bad press in the West.

The Serbo-Croatian linguistic dispute, which stirred less interest than the Mihajlov case in the West but was of much greater importance domestically, erupted on March 15, 1967. The Croatian Writer's Association backed by seventeen other cultural and scientific organizations published a manifesto in the Zagreb paper, *Telegram,* demanding that Croatian be recognized as an official and separate language by constitutional amendment. The complaint was that all official communications took place in the Serbian variant of the Serbo-Croatian language, even though documents were always printed in both the Latin and Cyrillic alphabets. Despite the Central Committee's warning against any Serbian reaction, forty-five Serbian writers demanded in the Belgrade publication *Borba* that the 650,000 Serbs residing in Croatia be taught the Cyrillic alphabet.[10] To an outside observer, much of the furor assumed comical overtones as the Central Committee, Tito, and all institutions of government were drawn into the dispute, demanding the imposition of party discipline and severe punishments.

The strong response of the party might seem disproportionate, but the issue touched raw nerves remaining from past ethnic-group conflict; it brought to memory the internecine slaughter of World War II. Prior to the March Manifesto in 1967 it was not decent to mention in print the wounds of the civil war, and the past was spoken of in hushed tones. The scandal was created by the stature of the intellectuals who lent their names to this document. Miroslav Krleza, a writer of European note, joined the signers and left the party rather than recant, despite his membership in the Croatian Central Committee.

In the post–World War II period national grievances were expressed most frequently in terms of rivalry in competition for scarce economic resources. The dispute between the Serbs and the Croats was bound to lead to secondary effects among the Albanians and Macedonians, who were in grave danger of involvements across the frontiers of the country. As a matter of fact, the Albanian minority demanded the creation of an Albanian republic on a legal par with other republics of Yugoslavia in the fall of 1968. This republic was to be formed of areas which comprise southern Serbia, the autonomous area of Kossovo-Metohija, which is included in the Serbian Republic, and from parts of Macedonia. This struck the immediate ire of the Serbs, who reacted violently against the demonstrations which accompanied the political demands.[11]

The nationality question was a Pandora's box which no Yugoslav government could permit to be opened with impunity in view of the tragic past. It defined the limits of Yugoslav permissiveness in the field of political expression because it was a key to the survival of the state. The question of the Albanians confronted the Yugoslav leadership with difficulties because of the ethnic prejudice among the majority of Serbs toward the Albanian minority, which is non-Slav, alien in religion, and suffers from the highest illiteracy rate and lowest income in Yugoslavia. In a state which claims to grant the equality of nationalities, the true status of the Albanians was a challenge both to the official version of the relationship of nationalities in Yugoslavia and to the government's ability to bring about significant economic changes in an area of stark underdevelopment. The realities of the situation were that the Serbs who resided in Kosmet and formed close to twenty-five percent of the population dominated the political situation with the aid of the secret police. This was possible because even the liberals had scant sympathy for Albanian national claims to greater autonomy and because the Albanian minority could be linked with international subversion emanating from Albania proper. That is why the demonstrators who participated in the widespread rioting in that area received much harsher sentences in comparison with punishment meted out to rioters in other parts of the country.

The Student Protest

The greatest internal crisis which the government faced in the post–World War II era was the student protest which erupted in Belgrade on June 3, 1968. It is difficult to pinpoint the precise origin of student unrest in Yugoslavia, much as it is difficult to explain similar phenomena in the West. This was a generation which grew up under the regime and tended to accept the basic premises on which it rested. The leadership of the students consisted of many disparate elements. The bulk of the students merely pointed at the wide gap between the official version of reality and reality itself. They compared the great gap between incomes of the working class and those of the intellectuals. It was an uprising aimed at the privileges of the government establishment. The students were confronting the establishment with the demand that myth and reality be brought into line. The demands made were frequently contradictory. The students wanted enforced egalitarianism and at the same time greater freedom of expression. They refused to raise the question of their own material status or that of the faculty: they claimed to be the conscience of the nation.

The faculty, who largely sympathized with many aims of the students, was divided as to course of action. Some believed that the students should have taken their grievances through the established party machinery; these critics, who were largely backed by the party and governmental organs, interpreted the student strike as a challenge to the existence of the system itself. Yugoslav liberals labeled them as "the bureaucracy." The students confronted the official establishment with the choice of using force or acceding to their demands. The position that various individuals held during this critical period is still the great dividing line in Serbian politics. The students demanded more participation in all aspects of university policy-making, but they also threatened to involve the dissatisfied portions of the working class in their struggle. Ultimately, the government was faced with deciding whether or not to use force. The use of force held the danger of permanently alienating that portion of the young Yugoslav population in which the regime had invested most heavily.

The liberal forces favored a soft approach to the student disorders. The forces of conservatism saw the eruption as a chance to recoup earlier losses and to demonstrate that only a tough approach to socialism could succeed, that anything else was bound to lead to a restoration of bourgeois capitalism and anarchy. While the students were occupying the school buildings and holding continuous meetings with the faculty, the leading elements of both the Serbian and federal governments were in continuous session, arguing about the crisis. Belgrade and the school buildings were ringed by both the armed forces and the militia. On June 9, 1968, Marshal Tito threw his weight behind the student demands.[12] He accepted personal responsibility for the failings of the system and promised to rectify them. The Belgrade City Commission, which had initially used the militia to stop the demonstrators, was castigated from high above.

The effect was to further silence the conservative forces within the society. The victory of the students meant that a new generation which was better educated and more cosmopolitan than the previous one would be now included in the decision-making process. These events terminated the remaining influence that the conservatives held. The rapidly developing situation in Czechoslovakia sidelined the student strike in the press and in the minds of the people. The Czechoslovak Crisis only reinforced the government in the policy set by Tito's decision to support the students.

The Evolution of a System

The internal crises described in the previous pages profoundly affected the very roots of the organization of government. In the first phase of reform after the removal of Rankovic, the principal preoccupation of the government was the diffusion of power among individuals and institutions so that a threat of a coup by a group within the party could not develop again. The principal aim was to institutionalize access to positions of power. This carried with it the danger that the leadership of the old partisans at the top would be no longer able to co-opt their replacements. Increasing institutionalization, in effect, meant a greater reliance on intra-party democracy, and it would call for making executive bodies in the government subordinate to the legislative branch rather than to the top bodies in the hierarchy of executive organs.

The Seventh Congress of the League of Communists in Yugoslavia of April 1958 made a coherent statement of Yugoslav ideology insofar as it reiterated self-management as the core of the Yugoslav system.[13] But it left other ideological issues unresolved; it still stressed the primacy of the League in Yugoslav political life and emphasized the need for party discipline. It also placed a great emphasis on practice as a guide to policy in contrast to the Soviet emphasis on classic Marxist-Leninist ideology. There the matter rested until the Rankovic case.

After the dismissal of Rankovic, both the League and the government were reorganized. One concern was the upgrading of Parliament (*Skupstina*) so that it could play an increased role; the other approach was a major reshaping of institutions which make up the apex of the League. At the Fifth Plenum, in October of 1966, the Central Committee approved a program to strengthen its functions. The Executive Committee of the League was reduced from nineteen to eleven members, and was charged with the day-to-day execution of League policy. At the same time, a new institution was created; it was a thirty-five member Presidium headed by Tito. The task of this body was to make policy when the Central Committee was not in session.

The Central Committee was reorganized as well. Attached to it were five permanent standing committees, which included League officials who were nonmembers of the Central Committee, but represented either professional or ethnic groupings. This broadened the scope of consultation within the Central Committee and brought in younger people who had not been close to the centers of power.

The net effect of the changes was to open the top leadership of the League to new men with a substantially different background from that of the tight circle which had run Yugoslavia since the days of World War II. If Tito wanted to make permanent the changes decreed by the Fifth Plenum, he had to wrest the control of the Secretariat for Internal Affairs from the Rankovic partisans. Secret police forces were cut by one-half and the leadership purged of Rankovic men.[14] Tito also had to assert his authority over the foreign service establishment, which was shot through with Rankovic agents. To achieve this end, the League Committee of Foreign Affairs was disbanded altogether.

The new Executive Committee was composed of "new men," except for its Secretary, Mijalko Todorovich, and its members were barred from holding top government posts. The base of the old guard was in the Presidium, which included most of the old partisan members who were dropped from the previous Executive Committee. Their partisan status did not necessarily make them Rankovic supporters; such old partisans as Vladimir Bakaric, Veljko Vlahovic, and Edvard Kardelj were all firmly within the liberal camp. The new members of the Executive Committee had to pledge to carry out the policies of the Central Committee. It was understood that those who disagreed with any policy would be permitted to resign without being expelled from the League.

This was a great departure from the norms set by the traditions of democratic centralism, which always demanded obedience to every resolution of the Central Committee and other governing organs of the League. It was merely a prelude to the Ninth Congress of the League, which extended the member's option to differ from policies even after adoption.

Paralleling the efforts to increase intra-League democracy was the move to strengthen the position of popularly elected legislative bodies. The very individuals who now entered the establishment to replace the Rankovic group demanded further democratization along these lines. The popular Koca Popovic replaced Rankovic as Vice President. Along with the move to strengthen the Federal Assembly, the Socialist Alliance was reorganized during its Sixth Congress in June 1966.[15] The emphasis was on equality of League and non-League members. The principal mission of the Socialist Alliance was to prepare for the elections of April 1967. The Congress also elected more non-Communists to the governing bodies of the Socialist Alliance. Proof of the growing role of parliamentary institutions came in December 1966 when the entire government of the Slovenian Republic resigned because a major bill failed to clear the Republican Assembly. There had been rejections of government bills in Yugoslavia before, but this was, perhaps, the first time that a government in a Communist state interpreted the rejection of a major bill as a vote of no confidence. The bill dealt with workers' contributions to health insurance and, in effect, bore some marks of a Slovenian revolt against federal power to set the amount of contributions to federal insurance funds. For three weeks the Republic of Slovenia was without a government until the Republic Assembly dropped its objections to the legislation. The Slovene Premier, Janko Smole, stated on the occasion,

"It is not only a question of social security but of the whole attitude towards economic reform. The country cannot afford to go on living as it is. . . . This is not a personal issue. We wish to force the issue on public attention."[16] Kardelj added, "It is becoming more and more and more obvious from parliamentary rostrums that controversial and contradictory opinions are emerging. . . . Unless we accept the fact that people can resign when they disagree we might as well retain Stalinist methods."[17]

Government and Party Reforms After the Czechoslovak Crisis

The June student riots, coupled with the Czechoslovak Crisis, brought the leaders of the Yugoslav League of Communists to the realization that there were serious structural weaknesses in the country. One of these was based on the reality that self-government was effectively introduced on the lower levels of societal structure through the media of the workers' councils and enterprises and through free election of the communes, but that the top structure remained fairly monolithic and stationary. The second reality was that Serbs and Montenegrins held a disproportionately high number of top positions. And, thirdly, no personality had emerged who could even remotely assume Tito's mantle. Lastly, the nationality problem had grown in gravity, and in the absence of traditional forms of compulsion, a more viable system would have to be found to transform Yugoslavia into a state based on a community of interest. These problems led to the constitutional reforms of December 1968 and to the Ninth Congress of the League of Communists, March 11 to 15, 1969.

All the reforms were essentially based on strengthening the concept of a self-governing society based on a voluntary union of nationalities. As discussed below, the powers of the workers to participate in the determination of policy was further extended. The intention was to reconstitute the federal and the party organs on the basis of national representation. These reforms were deemed necessary because of an acute sense of danger stemming from the outbursts of nationalism in Croatia and elsewhere. Even more traumatic was the Soviet invasion of Czechoslovakia and the theory of limited sovereignty by which the Soviet leaders proclaimed their right to intervene in the internal affairs of any socialist country where socialism was directly threatened. These currents led the League in the direction of accommodation of the liberal elements. There was a concerted effort to draw a greater number of participants into the political processes, regardless of their party membership. There was certainly a consciousness that in a time of emergency the ship of state had to rest on all nationalities to preserve the cohesion of the state. The need for this was underlined by Bulgarian agitation of the Macedonian question.[18]

The institutional alterations provided for by the constitutional amendments of December 1968 addressed themselves to these problems. Under the Constitution of 1963 Yugoslavia possessed a unique legislative branch, which was perhaps one of the most complex in the world. The Yugoslav *Skupstina* until December of 1968 was essentially composed of six chambers: one was the Federal Chamber, which was the equivalent of the lower house in Western legislative practice; it was the only chamber which had half of its deputies elected directly by the people. All the other chambers were elected indirectly. They consisted of the Chamber of Nationalities, the Economic Chamber, the Organizational and Political Chamber, the Chamber of Education and Culture, and the Chamber of Health and Social Welfare. All legislation had to secure approval in both the Federal Chamber and the chamber most relevant to the area of the bill.

The Eighth Amendment to the Constitution of 1963 radically changed the constellation of these legislative bodies. The Chamber of Nationalities, which replaced the Federal Chamber, was in effect constituted into a lower house. Each republic sends twenty delegates to the Chamber of Nationalities; both autonomous provinces, Vojvodina and Kosmet, send ten each. This most important chamber is indirectly elected by the republican or provincial assemblies, each of which send their delegation. The only chamber elected directly is the Social-Political (Chamber of the Communes), with one deputy elected from an electoral district, divided on the basis of population. Each of these chambers, including the Economic Chamber, the Educational-Cultural Chamber, and the Health-Social Welfare Chamber, elect 120 members.

In effect, every Yugoslav citizen votes several times. Each votes for deputies to the Social-Political Chamber, but at his place of work he also votes for delegates to the Economic Chamber. If he is a physician, he votes for the Chamber of Social Welfare and Health, and if he is a teacher or a part of the cultural-educational establishment, he votes for delegates to the Chamber of Education and Culture. The amendments to the constitution provide that each legislative proposal shall pass through the Chamber of Nationalities, plus the chamber appropriate to the subject matter of the bill.

The parliamentary reorganization recognizes the paramount position of ethnic problems in the Yugoslav polity. It also ends Serbian dominance in legislative political bodies and in those executive organs which are an expression of the legislature. All members of the Federal Executive Council are now members of the Skupstina and are directly responsible to it as a body. In April 1967 the Federal Executive Council was reduced and made directly responsible to the Federal Assembly. The Tenth Amendment provided that the President, Vice President, and other officials of the Federal Assembly would be elected from the ranks of members of all chambers of the Assembly, pointing up the past practice of electing nonmembers of the chambers to important positions. All these moves were in line with the desire to strengthen the role of parliamentary institutions.

The Ninth Congress of the League of Communists

The Ninth Congress of the League of Communists moved party institutions more in line with governmental institutions by a thorough reorganization of the machinery of the League. The Ninth Congress was held March 11 to 15, 1969, in Belgrade in an atmosphere of some domestic and international tension. It followed the bitterness stirred by the June student unrest and the August occupation of Czechoslovakia. The Congress acted on several fronts: it addressed itself to problems of foreign policy, redrafted the party statutes, and revised the ideology.

The most important of these actions was the redrafting of the statutes. The League signaled its new course by holding the Congress only after the republican parties had held their respective congresses. During previous congresses, the order of events was exactly reversed; namely, the League Congress set the line for the subsequent republican parties to follow. In this Congress, the effort was made to strengthen the grass roots by holding the republican and province congresses first. The drafts of the resolutions were submitted to public criticism for some time before the Ninth Congress took place.

Perhaps the most significant change which emerged from the Congress was the provision that League members who are elected to the top executive posts of the League cannot hold high positions in the government simultaneously. This is a sharp departure from the practices of other Communist countries, where the whole system is based on party members performing a dual role in the party apparatus and in the government. Moreover, there is a limit of two terms on any executive body within the League, as in the government. All positions within these bodies are at least theoretically elected; the practice of co-optation which is ratified by election would be difficult to discern.

The structural changes affected the organization of the central bodies of the League, which had been changed, as discussed previously, in the fall of 1966 after the demise of Rankovic. The eleven-member executive committee, which had been, in effect, the Yugoslav Politburo, was replaced by a new fifteen-member body called the Executive Bureau.

The Executive Bureau is drawn on the principle of nationality; it is composed of two leaders from each of the republics and one from each of the two autonomous provinces. In 1970 Tito is the presiding officer of the Bureau.

The Presidium was expanded in size from thirty-five to fifty-two members; it, too, is based on the principle of nationality. Each republic is allotted six seats, the provinces three, and the party organization of the Army is also allotted three seats on the Presidium.[19] The Presidents of the six republics are also included in the Presidium. Members of the Executive Bureau are simultaneously members of the Presidium.

The key principle enshrined by the Ninth Congress was the frank recognition that nationality problems persist in Yugoslavia and that therefore it is necessary to end the subterranean recrimination as to who is an imperialist or great Serbian chauvinist, particularly since outside forces have been exploiting some of the inequities for their own purpose.[20] For this reason each delegate now is a representative of the area in which his mandate originated.

There was frank recognition that the Tito era cannot continue indefinitely, and the leader himself set the tone by bringing the problem into the open. In his opening speech to the Congress, March 11, 1969, Tito stated: "The League of Communists needs continuity. Some of us are already rather old and continuity must be assured in the top ranking leadership for the experiences of the old to be transferred to the young."[21]

The Executive Bureau was designed to be a young body; the average age is forty-eight years, excluding Tito. Its composition is mainly liberal. The Presidium is substantially more representative of the true alignment of forces within the League; it includes the older generation symbolized by such individuals as Petar Stambolich, former Prime Minister of Serbia, and Milenitje Popovich, former Secretary of the Socialist Alliance. Some of its members, such as Vladimir Bakarich, were pursuaded to abandon their republican home base for the federal party structure for the first time. *The London Times* characterized the Presidium as a War Cabinet because of the effort to combine the disparate ethnic and ideological elements within the League into a cohesive body which would be capable of withstanding both foreign and domestic pressures.[22]

The Ninth Congress made important changes in the realm of ideology. The underpinning of most Communist systems outside Yugoslavia is the reliance on party discipline and democratic centralism. In the Soviet practice this has meant that more and more power has tended to migrate to the top of a pyramidal structure, which ultimately culminates in one man. Challenge to the policies handed from above has been termed as deviation, and any individual in a deviationist position is in danger of facing the threat options which both government and party control. The mildest of these range from reprimand to expulsion, but death and imprisonment have been also frequently meted out. In Yugoslavia, particularly since Rankovic's ouster, the use of force has been ruled out, and the League has had to place great emphasis on compromise and acquire a substantial tolerance for conflict in an area where the natural divisions of country produce a great diversity of conflicting interests.

The Ninth Congress for the first time abolished the heart of the system based on democratic centralism, at least as interpreted in the Soviet Union and the other socialist countries, that once a decision is made there can be no more opposition and that every party member has to support the decision even if he disagrees with its content. The 1969 statute permits party members the freedom of conscience just as much as the Eighth Party Congress in 1964 permitted them the right to criticize high party officials. The member who disagrees with a decision still cannot work against it, at least officially, but he has the option to resign without fear of reprisal from the party or from the body which made the offending decision.[23] In other words, he can retain his opposing opinion.

Greater ideological autonomy has been permitted to the republican parties as well. There is, in effect, a tacit recognition that the needs of the republican parties differ. One of the discussions of the draft statute of the League expresses this in these terms: "The republican leagues of communists . . . have been established at different times and under different conditions. They are acting under specific social conditions. . . . Their definite physiognomy will only be obtained on the basis of a coordination of this document with the republican statutes. . . ."[24]

At this writing the consequences of these innovations are not yet in sight. Once League members are permitted to retain opposition views it is only a short step to the organization of those who share them. Such alignment has no doubt existed informally in the League for a long time. With the official enshrinement of dissent, it could easily lead to the organization of an opposition on other than a factional basis. Factions possess the potentiality of becoming political parties.

The clear aim of the new statute is to permit the greatest freedom of debate within the League consistent with the preservation of an essentially one-party system designed to serve a very heterogeneous community. Only history will tell whether or not this can be achieved.

Self-Management and Economics

The underpinning of the sociopolitical structure of Yugoslavia is the system of self-management. In Yugoslavia self-governmental units such as the Communes and Workers' Councils received unprecedented grants of power in terms of both Western and Soviet-type political systems. The communes, unlike units of local government in the Soviet bloc countries, have autonomous sources of revenue which render them independent. Moreover, they have substantial share in the decision-making power over local investments so that they constitute a genuine power base within the community.

The Workers' Councils have been operating in various forms since the 1950s. Their power has been steadily augmented since their institution. The years 1965 and 1966 represent a true alteration of their status in Yugoslavia. There have been various approaches to "market socialism" in Yugoslavia ever since the early 1960s, but the years 1965–66 represent a true break with the past. These years spelled the end of central planning and central direction in Yugoslavia. In 1965, the country was faced with a major inflation and an extremely unfavorable balance of payments. In addition, the economy was unable to attract further grants from foreign governments and international lending agencies because it was felt that Yugoslavia did not fulfill the obligations on which previous loans were predicated. These were a retreat from multiple exchange rates linked with a realistic devaluation of the dinar. In summer 1965, Yugoslavia devalued the dinar from 750 per U.S. dollar to 1,250 per U.S. dollar. In addition, the "old dinar" was reduced on a one-hundred-to-one basis.

The reforms were also accompanied by a domestic policy of ending all subsidies to various economic enterprises. This meant that the profits of one enterprise could no longer be used to defray the losses of another. The losing enterprises were largely located in the less-developed areas of Yugoslavia, and this policy caused unusual hardship and unemployment in those areas. These were the economic reforms which Rankovic and his group were trying to obstruct in the interests of retaining the advantages of socialism for the poor areas.

The performance of Workers' Councils has always been admittedly mixed. The councils in the prosperous areas where high rates of literacy prevail tended to take a significant hand in the economic decision-making process. Also, the managements tended to be more efficient and democratic in these areas. The Workers' Councils in the less-developed areas, on the other hand, exhibited managerial dominance with some manifestations of participation.

It is the Yugoslav experience that the enterprises which show the greatest trend toward managerial dominance are the same ones which are in greatest need of subsidy. After 1966, it was made very clear to the employees of an enterprise that the profitability of their enterprise would largely depend on the wisdom of the choices adopted by its Workers'

Council, that there would be no more subsidies, and that an enterprise that could not carry its own weight would be permitted to fail.[25]

The new responsibility of the Workers' Councils has led to a lively politicking on the enterprise level. The object of enterprise politics is the redistribution of profits into wages or new investment, the reorganization of the enterprise on the internal or external level, or the election of a new manager. There are many conflicts between different groups. For example, the skilled workers tend to favor high investment rates in the enterprise because they associate these with its increased competitiveness and greater returns in the future. On the other hand, the unskilled workers fear that greater investment in equipment will displace the need for their services, and that is indeed a danger in a society with some unemployment which affects particularly the unskilled levels. The older workers, who seek to maximize their income for pension purposes, tend to join this group.

The position of the management depends on its background. The generation of managers who came to their positions through work which was essentially unrelated to the positions they hold, namely, through the services to the League or the Partisan Movement, generally tend to favor the position of the unskilled and older workers, because more complex methods of operation are not only a threat to the worker element but to their position as well. Younger, technically educated, managerial personnel tend to coalesce with the skilled workers who are upwardly mobile, both in terms of the expectations of their future income and in terms of future education. The old workers tend to ally with the untrained managers, because both tend to view change as a threat to their economic interests. The unskilled manager will frequently resort to demagogic politics by stimulating apprehension in this already-insecure element in the labor force. The result is that many of the factories with this type of management find it difficult to prosper in a system which has made profitability the central test of survival. When this analysis is applied on a national scale, the conclusion can be easily drawn that workers' self-management best serves those who are already well-off and least serves those in the underdeveloped regions. It can be juxtaposed that nobody is helped by the erection of non-economic enterprises in any part of Yugoslavia. The cost of these has to be born by the entire society, and with the decentralization of political and economic decision-making, the best developed regions are not willing to bear the cost.

The situation as it existed before 1965 resulted from a system which still operated with a substantial measure of administrative fiat. It was a system in which many commodities still received the benefit of price support. It was also a system which depended on multiple exchange rates. The penalties for the misuse of capital were low, due to the minimal interest rates set by the planning agencies; investment policies were still ordered by government organs. Due to the controlled prices of basic raw materials and artificial exchange rates, it was almost impossible to make a realistic assessment of the true cost of the investments to be undertaken. In some areas the controlled prices could make an uneconomic investment look like a real bargain or vice versa. In 1965, when the economic reforms were introduced and the test of profitability was applied in almost all enterprises, the result was temporary inflation and unemployment. The unemployment struck the hardest in the areas where the enterprises lived on subsidy—in the least developed areas of Yugoslavia. Of the two hundred thousand registered unemployed about fifty thousand were located in Macedonia. It is no wonder that the centralistic forces resented this policy and had little patience with the arguments that the reforms be given a chance. This is the conflict which led to the struggle between Rankovic and the reforming forces supported by Tito. Tito used the strongest possible terms to denounce these elements, such as ". . . we have taken resources from those who have achieved accumulation and given them to those who operated unprofitably. This practice is now being abandoned."[26]

Veljko Vlahovic, one of the leaders of the liberal faction of the League, stated: "Toward those who impede the reforms but occupy responsible posts, it is necessary to be stricter. . . . [They] must be replaced by men who will resolutely fight for . . . the aims that have been set."[27]

Since the dismissal of Rankovic, the reforms have progressed in a relatively unobstructed fashion. No doubt the initial dislocations caused greater unhappiness and insecurity in Yugoslavia, including in the industrial North. Yugoslavia is in the fortunate position of having a fairly stable foreign exchange income from emigrant remittances and tourism as a stable feature of her balance of payments. Yet, Yugoslavia, as any industrializing country, faces a chronic balance-of-payments problem. The reforms of 1965 were aimed at improving the balance of payments by stimulating exports and inhibiting imports. In 1965 the Federal People's Republic of Yugoslavia experienced the first positive balance of payments in the twenty years of its existence.

The years 1967 and 1968 did not sustain a positive balance of payments. Nevertheless, there was a substantial growth of the economy as a whole. Yugoslavia achieved significant gains in productivity. Yet inflationary pressures tended to persist, and so did an imbalance in payments. The enterprises which were benefited the most by the new economic model were those in the North. There were many reasons for this, apart from the greater technical competence with which they were managed. Under the 1965 reforms they could retain a larger share of their own profits; therefore they had more available for investment and wage increases. As a result, the gap between the have and have-not areas of Yugoslavia tended to widen. At the Ninth Congress the realities were recognized with this statement:

The differences between the developed and underdeveloped parts of Yugoslavia offer a picture of the world in miniature. Widening the gap between the developed and underdeveloped would slow down the progress of the entire community, including its developed part. Coordination of interests in line with self-management provides a new framewok for solving these contradictions, for creating better conditions for the advancement of the underdeveloped.[28]

The New Role of Trade Unions

The trade unions embrace the entire Yugoslav work force in industrial enterprises. The Workers' Councils include just a portion of the labor force in the larger enterprises. The party is represented in varying strength in all enterprise self-management bodies, but the most universal organization is without doubt the trade union (*Sindikat*). From 1958–67, the President of the Council of the Sindikat was Svetozar Vukmanovic-Tempo, a long-time member of the League Executive Committee. This demonstrates the high priority which the party assigned to work with the Sindikat. In the 1950s and 1960s the trade unions did not differ radically from those in the other socialist countries. The dominant theory was that no reason existed for the workers to strike; under a socialist or self-management system they would be merely striking against themselves. This was the doctrine which had been long current in all Communist bloc countries. The trade unions themselves were viewed as another type of organization directed to some extent to the purpose of implementing the League's policies through exhortation, training programs, and welfare policies. The Sindikats were also active in representing the workers in grievance procedures.

Since the Rankovic ouster, the Sindikats have assumed a new role, insofar as strikes in Yugoslav enterprises have become a tolerated aspect of Yugoslav life. In 1958, a major strike took place at the Trbovlje coal mine in Slovenia. Between 1958 and 1966 Yugoslavia experienced approximately 1,365 strikes.[29] In August 1967 there were no less than 10 major strikes affecting many of Yugoslavia's major production centers.[30] Since the Sindikats neither lead nor control the strikes, there has been increasing discussion that the Sindikats would function more smoothly if there were an official recognition of their autonomy from the political structure.[31] This would give the Workers' Council and the management an organized force to bargain with. The trend in this direction might be established even without the League's blessing. There have been some spontaneous moves in that direction such as at the T.A.M. Factory in Maribor, where the local trade union president declared that "it is far better that the trade union be the organizer rather than an observer."[32] The Sixth Congress of the Sindikats in June 1968 took a very independent line in criticizing the entire League establishment.

Foreign Policy

Yugoslavia has faced at least two major foreign crises since 1965. One resulted from the Six-Day War between Israel and the United Arab Republic; the other and far greater crisis was produced by the Soviet occupation of Czechoslovakia. Yugoslav foreign policy has to be seen in the context of the decline of the leading principles on which it is based.

Yugoslav foreign policy had been committed to nonalignment ever since the mid-1950s. Yugoslavia was the only European power to subscribe to it. In the era of the 1950s, when the boundaries of the blocs were well defined, the leadership found this policy an answer to many problems, such as Yugoslavia's fundamental inability to align with either of the two major groupings led by the U.S. and USSR. In the 1950s, Yugoslav leadership could not find allies due to the general bipolarization which accompanied the "cold war"; the country had to look to nonalignment to break out of the isolation imposed by her special situation. During the period of the late 1950s and early 1960s, Tito, Nehru, Nasser, and Sukarno were the outstanding personalities of the nonaligned world. Belgrade was the scene of a conference of twenty-five nonaligned states in 1961, a high point in the force of nonalignment.

Nehru and Sukarno have since disappeared from the political scene through death and enforced retirement, respectively. Nobody was in a position to replace the loss of Nehru in the ranks of the nonaligned, due both to his personal prestige and to the size of the country he represented. Nasser's Egypt suffers from a preoccupation with Middle-East problems; Egypt's unsuccessful adventures in Yemen and the Six-Day War against Israel prevented Nasser from participating in an effective role in the leadership of the nonaligned states. The general deterioration of all blocs contributed to the blurring of ideological lines as bipolarity became a thing of the past. Under the circumstances it became difficult to have a cohesive group of nonalignment, since France was no longer aligned with the Anglo-Saxon powers, and the Soviet Union was no longer an ally of China. This situation has lead Yugoslavia in the direction of an enforced reexamination of the basic tenets on which its foreign policy has rested.

It has been generally admitted that the Yugoslav support of Egypt was not popular domestically and that the controversy reached the highest policy-making bodies in Yugoslavia. As one highly placed Yugoslav stated to me: "This is the first time that the Yugoslav government and its public have split on a foreign policy issue." There are many reasons for this: the Yugoslav public is resistant to the idea of aiding Egypt; another reason is that military prowess evokes great admiration in Yugoslavia, and Egypt lacks this. While Yugoslavia enjoys correct and good relations with many parts of the world and particularly with the West since the Soviet invasion of Czechoslovakia, it would be difficult to state that Yugoslavia still fits into the nonaligned grouping, despite its efforts to revitalize the cause of the nonaligned by proposing another conference. The Yugoslav foreign policy of backing Egypt against Israel, and particularly its synchronization with Soviet foreign policy toward the Middle East, have been controversial.

The brightest hope for Yugoslav foreign policy was an accelerated liberalization of the other East European countries. This would have enlarged Yugoslavia's sphere of influence in the immediate geographic sphere. It would have removed the threat of agitation of various Yugoslav minorities from across the border, and, finally, it would have offered the Yugoslavs a substantial opportunity for meaningful cooperation with the surrounding states. In view of this, the agreements between the Yugoslavs and the Czechoslovaks in August 1968 were far-reaching. These agreements consisted of: (1) establishment of a banking consortium, (2) joint investment in developing countries, (3) Czechoslovak investments in tourist facilities located in Yugoslavia, (4) importation of Yugoslav unskilled labor to Czechoslovakia for training purposes, and (5) elimination of all trade barriers.

The Czechoslovak liberalization movement offered the Yugoslavs the best opportunity to break out of the ambivalence which permeated Yugoslav relations with the other socialist states of East Europe. This was the reason why the Yugoslavs were so courageous in backing the Czechoslovak liberalization to the moment of the Soviet invasion on August 18, 1968, and beyond.

The Soviet position of intervening in any country where socialism was threatened was a weapon which could be easily turned, not only against Czechoslovakia, but against Yugoslavia, Rumania, and Albania as well. Throughout the Czechoslovak Crisis there was obviously close consultation between Rumania and Yugoslavia, and even Albania made some approaches to Yugoslavia in order to achieve the maximum mutual protection. Yugoslavia's mobilization was a clear answer to the Soviet intervention, which was based on a theory of "limited sovereignty" of all socialist states in case they questioned the role of the ruling Communist parties according to Soviet interpretations.

While the Soviet invasion of Czechoslovakia shattered great hopes in Yugoslavia, it also had domestic effects which were not entirely negative. The conservative forces within the party at least temporarily lost wind and voice. The dissatisfaction of the League with the performance of the Yugoslav armed forces during the Czechoslovak Crisis led to a major reorganization of the Army in April of 1969. The Assistant Supreme Commander, General Ivan Gosnjak, was dismissed along with twelve other top-ranking generals, including the Chief of Staff, General Rade Hamovic. The reason most frequently given for their dismissal was that they made inadequate preparation for the defense of Yugoslavia in the event of an attack from her eastern neighbors. They were supposedly incapable of believing that an attack on Yugoslavia could emanate from other socialist countries. A more plausible reason is that the League wanted to strike a better balance in the top command of the Yugoslav Army: nine of the dismissed generals were Serbs.

It was clear that if there was a threat to Yugoslav security it did not emanate from the West. On the contrary, the West again looked like a potential ally and trading partner. Poland and Bulgaria were particularly vociferous in attacking Yugoslav foreign policy. Bulgaria, even previous to this, had openly agitated for Macedonian nationalism by inflammatory broadcasts. The old Balkan rivalries were revived by the split positions of the East European countries on the Soviet invasion. One of the aftermaths of the Soviet action was that the League of Communists of Yugoslavia was opened to young people, who flocked to its banners in the moment of national emergency.[33] The disturbances of June 1968 were forgotten, and the people of Yugoslavia manifested national unity in the face of a perceived threat.

* * *

Any Yugoslav government faces most complex domestic and international situations. There is always genuine potentiality that the country might disintegrate in fratricidal war, and there is always the ever-present threat of neighbors who show hostility on a great range of problems. Under the circumstances, the Yugoslav achievement of economic growth combined with a substantial measure of personal liberty compares favorably with most other states in that stage of development. Yugoslavia, as a state, needs time to grow into true nationhood. The years following the demise of Rankovic have demonstrated a great willingness on the part of the Yugoslav leaders to face the issues of a multi-national state and not to hide behind a false facade of enforced monolithism as practiced in many socialist states and developing countries. Yugoslavia is not a democracy, if a competitive multi-party system is indispensable for that definition. It is questionable that the peoples of Yugoslavia would benefit from a repetition of the regime that prevailed during the interwar period. Self-management and a substantial measure of local autonomy are perhaps the best methods by which the country can evolve into a modern state.

9

Albania in the Sixties

Nicholas C. Pano

Country Profile: THE PEOPLE'S REPUBLIC OF ALBANIA

Head of State: Haxhi Lleshi, President of the Presidium of the People's Assembly

Premier: Mehmet Shehu, Chairman of the Council of Ministers

First Secretary, Central Committee, Albanian Party of Labor: Enver Hoxha

Party Membership (1966): 66,327 (63,013 full members; 3,314 candidate members)[1]

Armed Forces (1969): 38,000 (Army: 30,000; Navy: 3,000; Air Force: 5,000)[2]

Population: Mid-1967 official estimate: 1,964,730 (Tirana: 169,000)[3]

Area: 28,748 square kilometers (11,100 square miles)

Population Density: 68 per square kilometer (177 per square mile)

Birth Rate (1967): 35.3 per thousand[4]

Death Rate (1967): 8.4 per thousand[4]

Divorce Rate (1967): 0.7 per thousand[4]

Gross Material Product (1965): 4.29 billion new leks ($858 million at official rate)[5]

Foreign Trade by Area (1964):[6]
  Socialist Countries (including CPR) 93.3%
  Chinese People's Republic 54.2%
  Non-Socialist countries 6.7%

Foreign Trade by Commodity (1964):[7]

	Export	Import
Machinery, capital goods	—	49.6%
Industrial consumer goods	54.7%	23.3%
Raw materials, semi-finished products	17.3%	15.7%
Comestibles	23.1%	4.2%
Other consumer goods	5.2%	5.2%

SOURCES:

1. U.S. Department of State, Bureau of Intelligence and Research, *World Strength of Communist Party Organizations* (U.S. Government Printing Office, 1969), p. 51.
2. *The Military Balance 1969–1970* (London: The Institute for Strategic Studies, 1969), p. 28.
3. *Vjetari Statistikor i RPSH 1967–1968* (Tirana: Mihal Duri, 1968), pp. 27–29.
4. *Ibid.,* p. 33.
5. *Vjetari Statistikor i RPSH 1966* (Tirana: Mihal Duri, 1966), p. 113.
6. *Vjetari Statistikor i RPSH 1965* (Tirana: Mihal Duri, 1965), p. 314.
7. *Ibid.,* p. 317.

9. Albania in the Sixties

Nicholas C. Pano

November 1969 marked the twenty-fifth anniversary of the Communist seizure of power in Albania. The Communist triumph in Albania was unique in comparison with the other East European party-states by virtue of the fact that it was accomplished without direct Soviet military assistance. In the Albanian case, however, Yugoslavia had played an important role in organizing the Communists both militarily and politically during World War II. At the conclusion of the war, Yugoslav influence was predominant in Albania, and Moscow had apparently delegated to Belgrade the major responsibility for guiding the Albanians in their construction of a socialist society. Indeed, from the autumn of 1944 until the late spring of 1948, Albania was for all practical purposes a Yugoslav satellite.[1]

Under the tutelage of the Yugoslavs, the Albanian Communists consolidated their power position during 1944–46. During this time, the new Albanian rulers destroyed or neutralized the prewar political, social, intellectual, and economic elites; inaugurated legal and economic reforms; and made preparations for the convocation of a constituent assembly to legitimatize the new political order. Running under the banner of the Democratic Front, a slate of candidates comprised almost exclusively of Communists and their sympathizers polled 93 percent of the ballots cast in the December 1945 elections for delegates to the Constituent Assembly. The Assembly began its deliberations on January 10, 1946, when it proclaimed the official birth of the People's Republic of Albania (PRA) and concluded its work in mid-March with the promulgation of the new constitution.

Not surprisingly, the new Albanian constitution was a virtual duplicate of its Yugoslav counterpart, which had been adopted on January 31, 1946. There were, however, several areas in which the Albanian constitution differed from its Yugoslav model. First, the Albanians did not adopt the federal political structure of Yugoslavia. In addition, there was no mention made in the Albanian document of the political supremacy of the Communist party, the state monopoly in domestic trade, or the socialization of agriculture. These latter omissions probably reflect the fact that Albania was still in the first stage of its "socialist" revolution in 1946.

In July 1950, some two years after the Soviet-Yugoslav break, the Albanians, now freed from the control of Belgrade, drew up a new constitution.[2] This revised document was apparently designed to bring the Albanian political system into closer conformity with that of the other East European party-states and to take into account the progress of the socialist revolution in Albania. The Constitution of 1950, as amended periodically, was still in effect in 1970, serving as the legal basis of the Albanian political system.

According to the Constitution of 1950, "the People's Republic of Albania is a state of workers and laboring peasants" which exercises its authority through the popularly elected People's Councils on the local level and the People's Assembly on the national level.[3] It also states, however, that the Albanian Party of Labor (Communist) is "the vanguard organization of the working class and of all the working masses in their endeavors to build the bases of socialism and the leading nucleus of all organizations of the working masses, both social as well as of the states."[4] Thus, like the constitutions at the other party-states in Eastern Europe, the Albanian Constitution of 1950 sanctions the political monopoly of the Communist party—in this case the Albanian Party of Labor (APL).

In content, the Albanian Constitution is similar to those of the East European party-states. It contains the usual clauses defining the rights of the individual in a socialist society, discussing the nature of the socialist economic system, and describing the political structure and organization of the state.

According to the constitution, the People's Assembly is "the highest organ of state power" in Albania.[5] As in the other Communist states, however, the People's Assembly meets only briefly twice each year to ratify the policies of the government and to elect a fifteen-member Presidium, which exercises legislative authority between sessions of the People's Assembly. The Presidium also convenes the Assembly, renders opinions concerning the constitutionality of laws, ratifies international agreements, appoints and recalls diplomatic envoys and military leaders, and grants decorations and titles of honor as well as pardons.[6] Although in theory responsible to the Assembly, the Presidium is in fact the chief legislative agency in the Albanian political system.

The Council of Ministers is, under the constitution, the supreme executive and administrative authority of the nation.[7] Its directives are executed by the ministries and agencies that comprise the executive branch of the government. While the Council of Ministers is appointed by the People's Assembly and legally responsible to that body, it is in reality the instrument by which the policies of the Albanian Party of Labor are transmitted to the various components of the Albanian political system.

The local governmental organs consist of the People's Councils at the village, regional, city, and district levels.[8] These popularly elected bodies have jurisdiction over administrative, economic, and cultural matters within their respective geographic areas. Their activities are closely supervised by the local party organizations.

The People's Assembly elects the justices of the Albanian Supreme Court for terms of four years.[9] The district People's Councils choose the district court judges for three-year terms, while the people's court judges are elected by their constituents for three-year terms. Rounding out the legal establishment is the Office of the Procurator General. This agency oversees the implementation of laws by the ministries, other administrative bodies, civil servants, and citizens. It also appoints public prosecutors and initiates criminal proceedings against lawbreakers.

As in the other Communist party-states, the government is subordinate to the party. The 1950 Constitution, as previously noted, recognizes the primacy of the APL in the political life of the nation. Since party leaders hold the key civil and military positions in Albania, the party line prevails in all areas of Albanian life. Indeed, the first quarter century of Communist control in Albania has been characterized by the steady growth of party influence in every sphere of activity.

An examination of the policies of the APL from 1944 through the 1960s reveals a remarkable consistency. Since their advent to power, the Communists have sought to achieve three objectives: to preserve and consolidate their grip on Albania, to maintain the independence and territorial integrity of Albania, and to modernize Albania in accordance with the Leninist-Stalinist Soviet model.

To realize the first of their goals, the Communists established a Stalinist-type dictatorship and persisted in this type of regime in its most extreme form even after its condemnation by Moscow. The Stalinist system with its narrow, nonresponsive party and state elite as well as its coercive political compliance structure has apparently suited the needs of the Albanian leaders and their socio-economic system. Fearful that any modification of this regime might undermine both their power position and the foundations of the Communist system in Albania, the tightly knit leadership of the APL, headed by Enver Hoxha, made only a token effort to initiate a program of reforms during the post-Stalinist "thaw." But Tirana did not stop here. By 1960 the Albanians, disturbed by the liberalizing trends in the USSR and several of the East European party-states, argued that the abandonment of Stalinism constituted a betrayal of the ideals of "Marxism-Leninism" and an espousal of the concepts of "revisionism." In particular, the Albanian leaders resented Moscow's attempt to make the anti-Stalinist line binding on all Communist parties following the Twentieth Congress of the CPSU in 1956 and the Soviet resort to political and economic pressure against Albania during 1960. The Soviets, however, were unsuccessful in their efforts to topple the Hoxha-Shehu regime or to force it to modify its policies.

Albania's Communist rulers have also enjoyed a large measure of success in achieving their second objective—the preservation of their country's national independence and territorial integrity. They have been able to accomplish this by obtaining foreign assistance and capitalizing on the splits that have arisen within the Communist camp. In 1948, the Albanians took advantage of the Soviet-Yugoslav break to free themselves from the domination of Belgrade and what appeared to be certain absorption into Yugoslavia. The Soviet-Yugoslav rapprochement during the mid-1950s, coupled with the Soviet advocacy of de-Stalinization, apparently revived the anxiety of the Albanian leaders on the issue.[10] On this occasion, Tirana was able to profit from the developing Sino-Soviet rift. By late 1961 the USSR had severed both state and party ties with Albania. A Peking-Tirana axis now emerged within the Communist camp. China's material and diplomatic support enabled the Albanians to continue to defy the dictates of the Kremlin and to preserve their independence during the decade of the sixties.

Although the People's Republic of Albania has enjoyed somewhat less success in attaining its third long-range goal—the modernization of the nation in line with the Soviet experience—it has not abandoned this objective. As in the case of its predecessors, the Fourth Five-Year Plan stresses the development of the industrial sector of the economy. While they have been careful to marshal appropriate ideological arguments to justify their stand,[11] Albanian leaders appear to have sought to develop the country's economy in such a manner as to make Albania virtually self-sufficient and thus largely immune to foreign economic pressure. Albania's persistence in this policy since the late 1940s further strained

Tirana's relations with Yugoslavia and the USSR, both of which regarded the PRA's aspirations as uneconomical and above all harmful to their own interests.

During its first twenty-five years under Communism, Albania has sought to place its own goals above those of the world Communist system. The emergence of polycentric tendencies within world Communism and the intensification of the Sino-Soviet rift have enabled the Albanians to realize their objectives to a great degree. While profiting from this situation, they have repeatedly condemned Communist pluralism and its corollary, national Communism. Instead, they loudly proclaim their loyalty to the doctrines of "Marxism-Leninism," a brand of neo-Stalinism which Tirana (along with Peking) has sought to elevate to the status of a new Communist orthodoxy.

Domestic Trends, 1964–69

The major domestic problems confronting the Albanian leadership following the break with the USSR were, first, to prevent an economic collapse and, second, to eliminate all traces of opposition to the regime and its policies.

Tirana hoped to offset the loss of Soviet and East European economic and technical assistance for the period of the Third Five-Year Plan (1961–65) with a Chinese credit of $125 million which had been pledged in April 1961.[12] China, however, was not able to match the level of the Soviet and East European aid until 1964. Consequently, the Albanians were unable to realize the targets established for the major sectors of the economy during the first three years of the plan.[13] The Moscow-Tirana break thus did have a negative impact on the Albanian economy during the early 1960s.

At the same time, Hoxha and Shehu, after silencing the pro-Soviet elements in the APL, seem to have made an effort to rally the masses around the leadership by developing the line that their quarrel with the Kremlin represented the most recent chapter in Albania's struggle for national survival. To enhance their popularity with their subjects, the Albanian rulers appear to have eased somewhat their controls over the people and the party and state bureaucracies. By mid-1964, however, they experienced a change of heart and gradually began to reimpose their iron-handed domination of all aspects of Albanian life. What disturbed the APL hierarchy most was the gradual breakdown of worker discipline both in the cities and rural areas, the increasing arrogance and independence of party and state bureaucrats, the growing popular discontent over the high prices and limited supplies of consumer goods, and the obvious apathy of the rank and file toward the socialist revolution.

These problems were carefully examined at the July 1964 Plenum of the Central Committee of the APL. The major speakers at this meeting, Enver Hoxha and Ramiz Alia (a leading party theoretician), urged that immediate steps be taken to eliminate all anti-Marxist tendencies within the country. They further demanded that appropriate measures be instituted to improve on-the-job discipline as well as workers' attitudes toward manual labor and state property. Finally, they advocated the launching of a new campaign to stamp out the remaining "bourgeois" and "revisionist" influences in Albania.[14] Before these policies could be implemented on a large scale, Nikita Khrushchev was ousted from his posts as First Secretary of the CPSU and Prime Minister of the USSR on October 14.

The downfall of Khrushchev seems to have raised some hopes in Tirana that the new Soviet rulers, Brezhnev and Kosygin, would be more sympathetic to the doctrines of Stalinism and more conciliatory toward Tirana than their predecessor had been. When these expectations proved illusory, the Albanians resumed their anti-Soviet propaganda campaign and redoubled their efforts to eradicate all remaining "un-Marxist" attitudes and practices in their own country.

It is now clear that there was genuine cause for concern on the part of the Albanian leaders. By early 1965 there were unmistakable signs of popular dissatisfaction with the Hoxha-Shehu regime. Much of this discontent stemmed from the shortcomings of the Albanian economy. Workers and peasants who had been hard hit by the inflation that plagued Albania during the early 1960s openly complained about their high work norms and inadequate wages. There was also some grumbling about the shoddy quality of Albanian-produced goods and the failure of the industrial enterprises to take consumer preferences into account in their planning.[15]

The murmurings against the government were not confined to the masses. During 1964 and 1965 there was apparently a small group of military officers who made no secret of their lack of enthusiasm for the pro-Chinese policies of the leadership.[16] At the same time, there were signs of a breakdown of discipline within some local units of the APL. By the spring of 1965 the Albanian press was accusing regional and district party organs of engaging in the "improper use of criticism," developing a "mania to examine too many problems," and discussing "matters outside their competence." It was also noted that some local party meetings had become forums for conducting personal quarrels.[17]

The Albanian leaders were also becoming increasingly concerned about the attitudes of the nation's intellectuals and youth. Several Albanian writers, for example, were accused of having been influenced by "revisionist thinking" from abroad and "the literature of the lost genera-tion." A segment of the country's youth was described as having been infected with "bourgeois ideology" and as lacking in "class and revolu-tionary warfare experience." Furthermore, it was noted that some young people—especially students—had come to regard themselves as a privi-leged class and had displayed a complete lack of appreciation for the hardships endured by those who had lived through the first stages of the Communist takeover.[18]

During the second half of 1965, the Albanian authorities moved on two fronts to stem the discontent within the nation. First, the govern-ment sought to create the impression that it was taking appropriate action to remedy the economic grievances of the people. Throughout the summer and fall of 1965, the press exhorted the economic planners and managers to make every effort to improve the quality and variety of consumer goods. It was suggested that this objective might be achieved by easing the bureaucratic restraints on individual enterprises and by granting the worker a greater voice in decision-making at the plant level.[19] In August the regime sought to gloss over the impact of the inflationary trend of the 1960s by initiating a currency reform. Accord-ing to the terms of the reform, the value of the lek was increased tenfold (the official lek-dollar exchange rate now became five leks = one dol-lar), and all prices and wages were refigured at the new rate.[20] Neither of these measures, which were primarily propaganda gestures rather than genuine attempts to deal with the economic problems confronting the nation, did much to soothe the restive masses. The disastrous 1965 drought-plagued harvest aggravated the dissatisfaction of the people.

It was also at this time that the APL leadership felt constrained to move against the intelligentsia, whose indifference to the regime had reached alarming proportions. This concern was reflected in the deliber-ations of the Fifteenth Plenum of the Central Committee of the APL on October 24–25, 1965. Ramiz Alia, the party's authority and spokesman on ideological issues, delivered the keynote address. In his remarks Alia warned that Albania was doomed to follow the same "revisionist course" as had the USSR and the East European party-states unless immediate action was taken to curb the "un-Marxist" tendencies in the arts, literature, and education.[21] The tone and nature of Alia's address indi-cate the gravity with which Albania's leaders viewed the breakdown of "ideological purity" within the country.

By late 1965, the Albanian ruling elite was obviously worried by the growing unrest and disaffection of the people. To reverse this tide they instituted at the beginning of 1966 what has come to be called officially the Albanian Ideological and Cultural Revolution. In retrospect, it appears that the major objectives of the revolution have been: (1) to strengthen the grip of Hoxha and Shehu on the party and state apparatuses; (2) to enhance the role of the party in all spheres of Albanian life; (3) to divert attention from the economic failure of the regime during the Third Five-Year Plan and to inspire the people to make an heroic effort to ensure the success of the Fourth Five-Year Plan (1966–70); (4) to combat the alienation and indifference of the masses toward the regime and the goals of the socialist revolution and to rekindle a new revolutionary fervor—especially among the youth; (5) to mobilize popular support for the party's campaign to eliminate "bourgeois" and "revisionist" attitudes and practices in Albania; (6) to show solidarity with the Chinese, who by the end of 1965 had initiated the first phase of the Proletarian Cultural Revolution.

The revolution began in early February 1966 with the announcement that a dozen party and state leaders, including five members of the Politburo, had assumed new duties—primarily in the regional party organizations.[22] Politburo members Rita Marko, Manush Myftiu, and Gogo Nushi were placed in charge of party activities in the Durres, Tirana, and Berat areas respectively. The fourth Politburo member, Haki Toska, was assigned to "special duties" in the office of Prime Minister Shehu while Pilo Peristeri, an alternate Politburo member, became director of the "Enver" Machine Works in Tirana. Since these new assignments did not result in the diminution of the authority or prestige of those involved, they appear to have been designed to strengthen the control of the leadership over local party organs as well as the ministries and selected economic enterprises. This move probably also represented the first step toward reducing the concentration of bureaucrats in Tirana and decentralizing routine party and state operations.

At the same time the Albanian press began to carry accounts of white-collar workers requesting reassignment to manual labor—especially in some of the more remote regions of the country.[23] This marked the onset of the "back to the masses movement," one of the most important aspects of the revolution. The "back to the masses movement" stemmed from the desire of the Albanian leadership to reduce the ranks of the swollen bureaucracy and to alleviate the labor shortage plaguing the country. By the mid-1960s there was a genuine fear among the Albanian rulers that the bureaucracy, which as in other East European nations had become a privileged class, posed a threat to the party and the construction of a socialist society.

In addition to seeking to weaken the position of the bureaucrats, the APL began to intensify its attacks on the intellectuals, who were depicted as having allowed themselves to become alienated from the masses and being mainly concerned with preserving their own interests and place in society rather than with serving the people. To become more sensitive to and appreciative of the role of the masses in the building of socialism in Albania, some intellectuals began to "volunteer" to work in production on farms and in factories for varying lengths of time.

By the end of February 1966, the "back to the masses movement" was in high gear. There were now reports of physicians and other professionals "voluntarily" engaging in manual labor for short periods. The Army at this time also became involved when troops were dispatched to the countryside to engage in farming and reclamation work.[24] It soon became clear, however, that the "back to the masses movement" was merely a prelude to the next stage of the Ideological and Cultural Revolution.

On March 6, 1966, the Central Committee of the APL published the text of an "open letter" to the Albanian people.[25] The purpose of this document was to explain and justify the Ideological and Cultural Revolution to the masses. As defined by the party, one of the major aims of the revolution was to revitalize the revolutionary consciousness of the people—especially the generation which had grown up during the post–World War II era. In its "open letter" the APL maintained that

the successful construction of a socialist society requires every communist, every laborer to work and think as a revolutionary every day, every hour, in every job he does and in every funtion in which he is engaged. He must always regard himself as the servant of the people, wedded to the peasant and soldier in life and death, always ready in the name of the people, the fatherland, the revolution, and communism to sacrifice even his life. . . . This [outlook] . . . is especially important in those of the new generation to whom the baton of the revolution will be passed tomorrow.[26]

Secondly, the revolution according to the APL was designed to combat "revisionist" trends in Albania. On this point the "open letter" observed:

The bureaucratism that arose in the USSR was of great help to the Khrushchevian revisionists in their seizure of power. The creation of a privileged stratum of party and state bureaucrats, economic managers, artists, scientists, and cultural figures who were receiving top level salaries and enjoying a higher standard of living than the working classes served as a secure social base from which revisionist outlooks blossomed. These elements became the staunch supporters of the revisionist groups which sought to gain power and to restore capitalism step by step. The exposure of these manifestations, the roots of revisionism, served as a great lesson for the APL. All trends of this type must be eliminated so that Albania will not repeat the experiences of the Soviet Union. . . .[27]

Having outlined the factors that had prompted it to inaugurate the Ideological and Cultural Revolution, the APL Central Committee in its "open letter" announced the additional steps it proposed be taken to safeguard the purity of Marxism-Leninism in Albania. Specifically, the Albanian leadership called for a drastic reduction in the size of the bureaucracy and the assignment of excess bureaucrats to productive work, the reassignment of certain bureaucrats from central administrative offices in Tirana to local and regional units of their respective agencies, a decrease of bureaucratic red tape and paper work, the lowering of the salaries of highly paid workers and officials, the granting of a greater voice in economic planning to factory managers and workers, and the encouragement of popular criticism of government officials. The day after the publication of the "open letter," the APL announced that military ranks had been abolished and that political commissars had been reintroduced in the Albanian armed forces.[28] Both these measures were designed to enhance the authority of the party over the military establishment and to ensure that this mainstay of the regime would lend its support to the revolution. In keeping with the general line of the revolutionary movement, the government in mid-March 1966 announced that the number of ministries had been reduced from nineteen to thirteen.[29] To involve the "new generation" more fully in the revolution, the party and youth organizations began to issue appeals urging the nation's young people to "volunteer" for service on farms and construction projects.

By early 1966 the broad goals of the Albanian Ideological and Cultural Revolution had been defined and the first phase of its program instituted. But the APL stressed that it "regarded the measures it took during [the first part of] 1966 for its own further revolutionization and that of the nation merely as the initial step in a broad revolutionary process that would continue to intensify and progress."[30] That this was no idle boast was demonstrated not only by developments occurring during the second half of 1966, but also by those taking place during the remainder of the decade of the sixties.

The revolution became one of the major themes of the election campaign for the People's Assembly in July 1966. Hoxha and Shehu in their major speeches let it be known in no uncertain terms that they would brook no interference in their drive to revolutionize all elements of Albanian life.[31] In his speech on July 5, Shehu stated that "this revolutionary process cannot be carried out without a struggle, without class warfare. . . ." He warned potential opponents that the "hostile elements (both within the party and the nation) will be exposed, isolated, and defeated." As expected, in what was interpreted as a popular endorsement of the revolution,[32] the candidates of the pro-Communist Democratic Front won a smashing victory in the July 10 elections. According to the official count, only 43 of the 978,157 voters who went to the polls refused to mark their ballots for the Democratic Front candidates.[33]

Throughout the summer a steady barrage of criticism was directed at those elements whose attitudes and activities were considered dangerous to the revolution. Among those singled out for censure was author Dimitri Zhuvani, whose novel, *The Tunnel,* was roundly condemned for pointing out the stupidity and callousness of the construction engineers and foremen of the Bistritsa power dam project. What especially rankled the APL leadership was Zhuvani's questioning of the high price in terms of human sacrifice and suffering that the Albanian people had to pay for economic progress under Communism.[34] The stand of the Albanian authorities on this matter left no doubt that they did not intend to permit the popular criticism which they had invited to get out of hand.

The APL also took to task those party members who balked at the new assignments given them in connection with the "back to the masses movement." The party spokesmen emphatically rejected the contention of the recalcitrants that they had made sufficient sacrifices for the building of socialism and were now entitled to enjoy the fruits of their labors in the relative comfort of their urban offices. Furthermore, there is evidence that some prominent party members sought to use their positions to obtain privileged treatment for their children who were engaged in "voluntary" labor projects.[35] By ruthlessly exposing the various manifestations of opposition to the revolution and by taking appropriate corrective action where necessary, the APL hoped to silence the dissenters within its ranks.

Besides waging a struggle against the opponents of the revolution, the regime sought to promote the movement in more positive ways. When the membership of the new Albanian government was announced in mid-September 1966, it was revealed that the Ministry of Justice had been abolished on the grounds that the task of creating a new socialist legal system had been completed.[36] This gesture may have been intended to foster the impression that the control of the central authorities over the judicial system would be eased. In early September 1966, the APL proclaimed a moderate agricultural reform program which, among other things, raised the state procurement prices for bread grains, abolished compulsory bread grain and meat deliveries on those collective farms which had brought new lands under cultivation since 1963, and reduced the taxes of low-income farmers from the mountainous regions of the country.[37] By the eve of the Fifth Congress of the APL, the Albanian rulers were making a feverish effort to enlist the support of the masses for the Ideological and Cultural Revolution.[38]

The Fifth Congress of the APL had been scheduled to convene during the first week of November 1966—the twenty-fifth anniversary of the establishment of the party. During its deliberations (November 1–8), the Congress served as a forum for the Albanian leaders both to recite the ills that plagued the nation and party and to whip up support for the revolution as the most effective remedy for these maladies.[39]

In his remarks to the Congress, APL Secretary Enver Hoxha decried the "negative phenomena" that had arisen in Albanian life.[40] Unless these were eliminated, he warned, Albania would follow the USSR down the "road of revisionism." Hoxha was especially critical of "certain" intellectuals, bureaucrats, party members, and young people who had developed "bourgeois illusions" and a "desire to lead a soft life" and had divorced themselves from the masses and their problems. To combat these attitudes, Hoxha called upon his countrymen to become enthusiastic partisans of the Ideological and Cultural Revolution.

Hoxha also reviewed the major achievements of the revolution during 1966. He noted that fifteen thousand former bureaucrats were now employed in productive work; the wage differential between laborers and white-collar workers and specialists was being reduced; ranks had been eliminated in the military services; and large numbers of young people, soldiers, and government and party officials were engaged in volunteer labor in the country. There were, however, other areas of Albanian life which needed to be "revolutionized." The gulf between the cities and the rural areas had to be closed; Albanian culture and education had to be reshaped to reflect the ideals of the revolution, and the concept of democratic centralism had to be firmly established as a guiding principle of the APL and the government.

The APL Secretary also called for a revitalization of the party. To improve the quality of party recruits, he recommended that all applicants for membership be required to spend two to three years at the candidate stage before being considered for full admission to the APL. Henceforth, all candidates would be subjected to rigorous ideological training and required to perform manual labor or accept assignment in the countryside. Furthermore, party members were warned to toe the line established by the ruling elite and not to expect any special favors. In summary, Hoxha called on his colleagues in the APL to become models of discipline and dedication for the rest of the population. No longer was party membership (at least for the rank and file) to be regarded as the key to a privileged position in Albanian society.

Hoxha's underlying theme that the Albanians must learn to think, live, and act as revolutionaries was also reflected in Mehmet Shehu's address to the Congress.[41] The Albanian Prime Minister, however, devoted the major portion of his speech to a discussion of the nation's economic problems. Conceding that the Third Five-Year Plan (1961–65) had not fully realized its objectives, Shehu attributed the difficulties which had arisen during the plan period to the "imperialist-revisionist blockade" imposed on Albania after the Moscow-Tirana break.

According to the statistics presented by the Albanian Prime Minister to the Congress, industrial production in 1965 was thirty-nine percent greater than in 1960—an increase somewhat less that the planned rise of fifty-two percent. Agricultural output had risen only thirty-six percent above the 1960 level instead of the projected seventy-two percent. Albania's national income in 1965 was thirty-two percent greater than in 1960, but substantially below the fifty-six percent predicted in the plan directives. While acknowledging, at least in part, the shortcomings in the performance of the economy between 1961–65, Shehu boasted that no one had starved to death, inflation had been contained, 430 construction projects had been completed, and the health of the Albanian people had improved. He also proudly observed that with the conclusion of the Third Five-Year Plan Albania had made the transition from an agrarian-industrial state to an industrial-agrarian state. Yet this boasting on the part of the Albanian Prime Minister could not conceal the fact that the Moscow-Tirana rupture had a negative impact on Albania's plans for economic development during the 1960s. Indeed, Albania's economic problems had helped to trigger the unrest which had inspired the Ideological and Cultural Revolution.

Despite the difficulties they had encountered during 1961–65, the Albanian leaders were determined to press forward with their ambitious development program. According to the directives of the Fourth Five-Year Plan (1966–70) announced by Shehu, industrial production would increase at an average rate of 8.7 percent and by 1970 would be 50–54 percent greater than in 1965. As usual, the highest priority was assigned to heavy industry, which during the plan period was expected to expand twice as fast as light industry. Much emphasis was placed on increasing the production of the chemical, machine tool, metals, and ceramic industries. The regime also continued to stress the exploitation of Albania's natural resources.

Undaunted by the sorry performance of agriculture during 1961–65, the APL once again set ambitious targets for this crucial sector of the economy. The Fourth Five-Year Plan called for agricultural output to increase at an average annual rate of 11.5 percent with 1970 production 71–76 percent greater than that of 1965. It also urged the full socialization of Albanian agriculture by 1970 and asked that every effort be made to ensure that Albania would be self-sufficient in food by that date. Shehu observed that the resolution of the agricultural problem was the most pressing task of the Fourth Five-Year Plan. To help realize this objective the regime raised agricultural investment by 68 percent over that of the previous plan.

In his speech to the Congress, the Prime Minister profusely thanked the Chinese for the aid they had given Albania in the past and for that which they had promised for 1966–70. At the same time, however, he warned his countrymen that they must strive to become less dependent on foreign assistance. Shehu's remarks were apparently intended both to convince Peking that the Albanians would make every effort to become more self-reliant and to appeal to the national pride of the people. The Albanian government leader also stressed the problems posed by the "capitalist and revisionist blockade" of Albania, and he called for new sacrifices and greater vigilance on the part of the masses as they continued to build socialism "with pick axe in one hand and rifle in the other."

There were no major changes in party leadership at the Fifth Congress. Reflecting an addition of 12,667 party members from 1961 to 1966, the size of the APL Central Committee was increased from 82 to 97. Deputy Prime Minister Abdyl Kellezi, also Chairman of the Chinese-Albanian Friendship Committee, was made an alternate member of the Politburo. Politburo members Rita Marko and Haki Toska were dropped from the secretatiat of the Central Committee and replaced by Xhafer Spahiu.[42] This latter move seems to have been intended to streamline the operations of the secretariat. The three Central Committee Secretaries Ramiz Alia, Hysni Kapo, and Xhafer Spahiu were now responsible for ideological matters, internal organization and relations with foreign parties, and economic problems, respectively. An examination of the composition of the Central Committee elected by the Fifth Congress reveals that only one sitting member was dropped completely from that body by action of the Congress. Indeed, the proceedings of the Congress provided overwhelming evidence that the APL leadership was solidly entrenched and unified.

But while the leadership of the APL may have been stable, there were unmistakable signs of ferment in the ranks. As noted previously, Hoxha had requested and received permission to tighten the procedures governing admission to the party. Between 1961–66, the leadership also had striven to increase worker and peasant representation in the APL. On the eve of the Fifth Congress the composition of the APL was thirty-three percent laborers, twenty-six percent collectivized peasants, thirty-seven percent white-collar workers, and four percent others. It is also interesting to note that sixty-eight percent of the party members lived in the cities, while only thirty-two percent of Albania's population was urban.[43] One of the main objectives of the Albanian leadership during the period of the Fourth Five-Year Plan remained to transform the party membership so that it would be more reflective of the nation's social structure. At the same time, however, the APL hierarchy was determined to raise the quality of those admitted into its ranks[44]—especially as the Ideological and Cultural Revolution continued to unfold.

Following the conclusion of the Fifth Congress, the focus of the revolution shifted to the countryside. By December 1966, the APL instituted a vigorous campaign designed to uproot "backward" customs and practices, reduce the size of private plots on collective farms, and collectivize the farmland still in private hands. Inspired in part by the Chinese Red Guards and in part by a desire to whip up revolutionary enthusiasm among the young, the party made extensive use of the services of "volunteer" youthful agitators in this drive.[45]

Unlike their Chinese model, the Albanian version of the Red Guards was not permitted to establish an independent organization, but instead worked under the close supervision of local party units. The stand of the APL on this issue indicates that the Albanian rulers had no desire to institutionalize any potential source of opposition. It also serves to underline the basic difference between the Albanian Ideological and Cultural Revolution and the Chinese Proletarian Cultural Revolution. The former was, of course, a unified effort on the part of the APL hierarchy to rekindle revolutionary fervor among the masses and to reassert the authority of the party in all sectors of Albanian life, while the latter was essentially a stratagem to mask a power struggle within the ranks of the Chinese Communist Party.

As the Ideological and Cultural Revolution approached its first anniversary, there were indications that it was meeting with resistance among various segments of the Albanian people—especially those residing in the rural areas.[46] It was at this point that Hoxha decided to make a new appeal to the people. On February 6, 1967, the Albanian party leader delivered an address entitled "The Further Revolutionization of the Party and the Regime"[47] to a gathering of party cadres from the Tirana district. This speech, which inaugurated the 1967 electoral campaign for local and regional party offices, ushered in a new phase of the revolution.

On this occasion Hoxha could not hide his disappointment over the fact that the revolution had not succeeded in arousing the hoped-for enthusiasm among the party faithful. Indeed, he placed the blame for the shortcomings of the revolution on the "lethargy," "complacency," and "smugness" that prevailed in many local party units. The APL Secretary urged his fellow Communists to take their responsibilities as party members more seriously. Among other things, he demanded that each party group devote greater time and care to the study of directives emanating from Tirana, take the necessary steps to improve discipline, and expel those members who failed to live up to the ideals of the party. Furthermore, Hoxha called on his comrades to improve their contacts with the masses and to pay careful attention to the needs and criticisms of the people. On this point he observed:

How can a Marxist-Leninist party fear the masses—their voice and their criticism? Any group which fears these cannot be called a Marxist-Leninist party. But it is never the party which is afraid, but rather some individuals— some party members, state functionaries, and bureaucrats. These are the ones who fear the masses. They are the ones who hide under the authority of the party or state to stifle the voice of the masses. These people must be crushed. They must be dealt with in a revolutionary fashion by the party and masses acting together.[48]

Having again stressed his determination to deal sternly with the opponents of the revolution, the Albanian leader renewed his assault on bureaucratism. He implied that the size of the bureaucracy would continue to be reduced until it was comprised exclusively of highly indoctrinated, disciplined, and motivated individuals. Hoxha also reemphasized the obligation of the bureaucrats to volunteer for manual labor and to accept any assignment given them by the regime. Again he urged the people to publicly air their grievances regarding the activities of the bureaucrats.

During the course of his remarks, Hoxha indicated the need to expand the scope of the revolution. He maintained that the "revolutionization" movement could not succeed unless a broad frontal attack was launched without delay on all remaining bourgeois attitudes and practices in Albanian life. Specifically, he called for the emancipation of Albanian women, elimination of religious influences within the country, eradication of the vestiges of capitalism in agriculture, suppression of all manifestations of individualism among the people, and reduction of the gulf between the rural and urban as well as the mountain and lowland areas of the nation.

Hoxha's February 6, 1967, speech was the signal for the intensification of revolutionary activity in Albania. In the weeks immediately following his address, the Albanian press published numerous articles and letters denouncing the activities of several dozen middle-and low-rank party and state functionaries. A few of the accused responded by making abject public self-criticisms, while the government and party announced the dismissal of some of the more flagrant offenders.[49] At the same time, with the blessings of Hoxha, wall newspapers (*fleterrufete*), similar to those that had appeared during the Chinese Cultural Revolution, became an important weapon in the revolutionary arsenal. Largely the work of students and youth, the wall newspapers ruthlessly exposed the "reactionary and anti-revolutionary" practices and attitudes that existed in neighborhoods, schools, and factories or among selected individuals.[50] A third development during this period was the inauguration of a dialogue between Enver Hoxha and the masses in the Albanian press. Throughout 1967, representative groups of Albanians and individuals from virtually every walk of life wrote "open letters" to the APL First Secretary expressing their solidarity with the revolution and pledging their active support to ensure the success of the movement. In his replies, Hoxha warmly applauded the efforts of the people to construct a socialist society and assured them that their sacrifices would result in a better life for themselves and future generations.[51]

Thus, by the spring of 1967, the regime was at last making progress in its drive to enlist public backing for the revolution. Buoyed by this development, the government during the first quarter of 1967 moved to collectivize the farmland (located mostly in the mountains) that remained outside the socialist sector.[52] The APL now also stressed in its propaganda the line that the continued development of the nation's economy hinged on the success of the revolution.

To underline this contention, the Central Committee of the APL and the Council of Ministers of the APR, citing the economic gains made during the revolution, issued on April 30, 1967, a joint decree which provided for a wage reduction for highly paid personnel (those earning over $240 per month); the elimination of direct taxes for laborers earning $136 or less monthly; and a price reduction for consumer goods and tools in the rural areas, interest-free agricultural credits, and the acceleration of the program of rural electrification. In addition, this document called for a reduction in the size of private plots on collective farms by fifty to sixty percent and recommended that all white-collar workers work directly in production for thirty days each year.[53]

The April 30 edict represented an intensification of the revolution. The salary decreases of the highly paid workers, the direct tax exemptions granted the laborers, the recommendations concerning manual labor for white-collar personnel, and the economic concessions given the peasants represented an attempt on the part of the Albanian authorities to lessen economic and social inequalities within the country and to lay the foundations for the establishment of a classless society. While making a gesture to improve the lot of the peasants, the regime, with the completion of collectivization, also sought to weaken one of the last remnants of capitalism in the countryside—the private plots.

The April 30 decree had also taken note of the progress made in the drive to emancipate the women of the nation. Although the APL had issued several calls for action in this area during 1966, it was not until the spring of 1967 that this aspect of the revolution received a high priority. The women's emancipation campaign moved into high gear following the Second Plenum of the APL Central Committee (June 15–16, 1967). Hoxha and Ramiz Alia in their reports to the Central Committee outlined the major features of the movement to "revolutionize" the status of Albanian women.[54] First, they demanded that appropriate steps be taken to guarantee the equality of women in all phases of Albanian life and that all existing customs and practices that degraded the position of females be eliminated. Second, they urged that more women be drawn into production, educated to their potential, and granted more responsibility in the government and party.

There appear to have been two major motives for the women's emancipation campaign. First, by bringing the women of the country into the mainstream of Albanian life and persuading them to abandon their conservatism, the regime hoped to eliminate one of the last significant "bourgeois" influences in the nation. Second, in the face of the labor shortage which prevailed in the country, the state was anxious to add as many women as possible to the labor force.[55]

In keeping with the theme of Hoxha's February 6 speech, the scope of the Ideological and Cultural Revolution continued to expand throughout 1967. By the beginning of the summer an intensive anti-religious campaign was underway in all parts of the country—especially in the rural areas.[56] In the initial phase of this drive, the major emphasis was placed on discouraging attendance at religious services, encouraging clergymen to give up their ministries, and closing houses of worship. It was announced in September that 2,169 churches, mosques, and other religious institutions had been destroyed, closed, or converted into cultural centers. Albania was now proclaimed "the first atheist state in the world."[57] This claim, however, seems to have been made prematurely.

Speaking at the Fourth Congress of the Democratic Front in mid-September 1967, Hoxha observed that the eradication of religious institutions did not mark the end of the struggle against religion. The anti-religious crusade, he warned, would continue until all religious "influences," "attitudes," and "views" had been eliminated.[58] To further weaken the role of religion in Albanian life, the government in November rescinded the charters under which the major religious groups in the country had functioned since the 1950s.[59]

Meanwhile, a new chapter in the revolution was revealed during the Third Plenum of the Central Committee in mid-October 1967. Although the Plenum was concerned primarily with the development of the engineering industry and the "technological revolution" in Albania, Hoxha sought to establish the necessary guidelines to ensure that the nation's economic progress would not conflict with the ideals of the "revolutionization" movement.[60] Citing the "unprecedented economic, political, and ideological anarchy" which had accompanied the Yugoslav technical revolution, the Albanian party leader outlined his plans to shield his homeland from this fate. Among other things, he advocated an intensive program of "ideo-political" training for the new Albanian technical elite. Ideally this program would produce an Albanian technocrat who possessed a definite collectivist mentality and a strong sense of community with the workers. In this manner the Albanians hoped to prevent the rise of an independent class of technocrats who would seek to challenge the primacy of the party in the economic sphere.

In retrospect, it appears that 1967 was the decisive year in the history of the Albanian Ideological and Cultural Revolution. The APL leadership had not only broadened the scope of the revolution, but had also succeeded in mobilizing a substantial amount of popular sentiment to back it. In addition to utilizing the services of the youth to generate support for its program, the regime also enlisted the aid of the nation's leading mass organizations. During 1967, four of these groups—the United Trade Unions of Albania (April 24–26), the Union of Albanian Working Youth (June 26–29), the Democratic Front (September 14–16), and the Union of Albanian Women (October 25–28)—each held their congresses at which they endorsed the revolution.

But despite the efforts of the Albanian authorities, there were still pockets of resistance to the revolution scattered throughout the country. Some of the most troublesome opposition came from the ranks of the intellectuals. Owing to the discord within this group, the Congress of the Albanian Union of Writers and Artists scheduled for November 1967 was postponed.[61] As 1967 drew to a close, the APL, mindful of the growing intellectual ferment in the USSR and Eastern Europe, turned its attention to the task of devising a formula to ensure the ideological orthodoxy of the intelligentsia.

On March 7, 1968, Hoxha presented the regime's response to this challenge in his speech "The Further Revolutionization of Our Schools."[62] The Hoxha address, which marked another important milestone in the Ideological and Cultural Revolution, outlined the leadership's long-range program for inculcating doctrinal purity among the country's youth. Justifying his proposals on the ground that Albania's economic and social progress had made reforms in the education system mandatory, the APL First Secretary demanded that additional agricultural and polytechnical institutes be established; greater emphasis be given to the study of the natural sciences; all textbooks be examined and, where necessary, rewritten to reflect "the principles of dialectical materialism and Marxist-Leninist analysis"; new courses in Marxist-Leninist philosophy, "focusing on the Albanian experience in the building of socialism," be formulated; and some form of "practical work" experience be introduced at the primary-school level. Furthermore, Hoxha called for more discussion in the schools of the political and economic problems confronting the nation.

In his March 7 statement, the APL leader made it clear that he expected the schools to play a more effective role in creating the new socialist man and the new socialist society in Albania. Thus, while the school system would continue to train the skilled personnel required by the country's developing economy, it would now be charged with the task of upgrading its ideological and propaganda programs. A heavy responsibility in these areas would fall on the teachers, who were expected to become model revolutionaries for their pupils. By means of constant indoctrination and required manual labor, the Albanian authorities hoped to insulate the youth of the nation—the future workers and intellectuals—from the "pernicious revisionist influences" emanating from the USSR and Eastern Europe. The Central Committee of the APL underscored the importance it attached to the "revolutionization" of the school system by appointing a special national commission, chaired by Prime Minister Shehu, to supervise and implement this segment of the Ideological and Cultural Revolution.[63]

What appears to have been the last major policy pronouncement of the revolution was made by Hoxha on April 9, 1968.[64] In his speech "The Control of the Working Class," the Albanian leader outlined his plan to transform the industrial proletariat into a new revolutionary elite second only in importance to the party. On this point Hoxha observed: "We are a country governed by the dictatorship of the proletariat, led by the Albanian Party of Labor. This means that the working class led by its party takes the lead in the construction of socialism in alliance with the working peasantry." To fulfill its assigned role, the laboring class was urged to take a greater interest in its work, as well as in social and cultural activities, to ensure that party directives and state laws were obeyed. Specifically, the working class was urged to serve as a check on the technocrats, maintain discipline and morale within its own ranks, and share in administration and planning on the plant or enterprise level in accordance with the principles of "democratic centralism."

At the same time, Hoxha called for the inauguration of a massive campaign to raise the ideological level of the laboring class. Indeed, he urged the unions to concentrate their efforts on improving the political consciousness of the workers. In addition to its desire to use the workers as a counterpoise to the technocrats, the leadership was undoubtedly concerned by the fact that sixty-five percent of the industrial laborers had joined the work force during the 1960s. Since many of these had been recruited from the rural areas of the country and still maintained close ties with their native villages, they tended to be conservative in outlook, socially aloof, and somewhat resentful of factory discipline. The "revolutionization" movement was thus intended to implant a socialist outlook in this group, improve its efficiency in production, and strengthen its loyalty to the regime.

By late 1968 the intellectuals were the only significant element within Albania who had not formally subscribed to the doctrines of the revolution. Throughout 1968 the press relentlessly exposed the shortcomings of the nation's intelligentsia. Among the sins of this class were its reluctance to divest itself of "bourgeois," "petit-bourgeois," and "revisionist" views; its failure to deal with the basic problems of Albanian life in a "meaningful fashion"; its lack of sufficient ideo-political training; and its remoteness from the masses.[65] The APL in late December 1968 confessed its failure in this area by admitting that "actions and movements aimed at revolutionizing the workers in the arts are still not very effective since they are not continuous. . . . These shortcomings have resulted mainly because of the inadequate efforts made by the basic party organizations."[66]

At this juncture the APL leadership apparently gave top-level priority to the task of bringing the intellectuals into line. After several postponements, the Congress of the Albanian Union of Writers and Artists was convened in late April 1969. In his keynote address to the convention,[67] Ramiz Alia condemned the "revisionist" trends in Soviet culture and warned that the regime would permit no deviations "from Marxist-Leninist positions in politics and the arts" in Albania. During the course of his remarks, the APL theoretician made it clear that the party expected the intellectuals to become enthusiastic supporters of and participants in the revolution.

Dhimiter S. Shuteriqi, chairman of the Union, responded by presenting a program designed to bring Albanian art and literature "into the front line of the struggle to develop further the Ideological and Cultural Revolution."[68] The veteran Albanian writer called upon the nation's intellectuals in their work to "safeguard and develop the spirit of communist partymindedness"; "reflect socialist topicality more widely and thoroughly by stressing such themes as the emancipation of women, the struggle against religious practices and backward customs, and the progress of Albania under communism"; "develop innovative, non-bourgeois forms" of expression; and identify themselves more closely with the masses. Thus, by the spring of 1969 the revolutionary line in literature and the arts was firmly established.

While the influence of the Ideological and Cultural Revolution had spread to virtually every sector of Albanian life during the late 1960s, the ultimate success of the movement hinged largely on the ability of the local organs of the APL to translate party directives into reality. By the late summer of 1968, as the Albanian press continued to publish a steady stream of articles cataloging the failures of the revolutionization movement,[69] it was obvious that many local party units had failed to fulfill their responsibilities in this area. Taking this situation into account, the Sixth Plenum of the Central Committee, which met on September 27–28, 1968, ordered a reshuffling of local and regional party cadres in the hope of revitalizing the operations of the APL at the grass-roots level.[70] The party took the necessary steps to ensure that the majority of the newly elected local secretaries were chosen from the ranks of the workers. In this manner the APL leadership sought to strike another blow against bureaucratism, reinforce its ties with the masses, infuse new blood and revolutionary enthusiasm into many of its moribund organs, and reassert its authority over several of its dissident units. Although this reform of the party organization has initially produced a certain amount of confusion at the local level, its long-range impact remains to be seen.

As the 1960s drew to a close, the Ideological and Cultural Revolution continued to dominate the domestic scene in Albania. While in 1970 the revolution has yet to run its course, it is nevertheless possible to make a preliminary assessment of the impact of this movement between 1966–69.

First, it is clear that the grip of Hoxha and Shehu on the party and state apparatuses has been strengthened. The Fifth Congress of the APL and subsequent Central Committee plenums have provided convincing evidence of the solidarity of the Albanian ruling elite and the primacy of Hoxha and Shehu. The leadership's position has been enhanced by the pruning of the bureaucracy and the personnel changes that have been made in the low- and middle-level party units.

Second, the influence of the party in almost every sector of Albanian life has increased. The reintroduction of political commissars in the military services, the "revolutionization" movement in education, the worker control movement, and the imposition of more stringent regulations on the intellectuals all indicate the directions in which the party has moved to augment its commanding position in Albanian life.

Third, the Albanian economy has shown a new vitality during the period of the Fourth Five-Year Plan (1966–70). It appears that, in addition to increased Chinese aid, the reduction in the size of the bureaucracy, the women's emancipation drive, and the "voluntary" labor movement as well as other aspects of the revolution have played a positive role in this development. Between 1966–68, Albanian industrial production exceeded plan projections.[71] Although agricultural output has lagged behind its assigned targets, it seems likely that, barring a natural calamity, production in this sector will establish new records during the 1966–70 Five-Year Plan.[72]

Fourth, while the revolution has not succeeded in overcoming the hostility of a large segment of the pre–World War II generation of Albanians to the regime, it has apparently enjoyed much success in arousing a revolutionary fervor among the young.[73] Since 1966, over one hundred thousand young people each year have "volunteered" to work on construction projects and collective farms during vacations. Thousands of others, under the supervision of the party, have served as agitators in the campaign to uproot "bourgeois" and "revisionist" attitudes and practices. The "revolutionization" movement in the schools should serve to strengthen further the loyalty of Albanian youth to the "Marxist-Leninist" doctrines of the ruling elite.

Finally, the common revolutionary experience of Peking and Tirana during the late 1960s has tended to reinforce Sino-Albanian solidarity. Both the Chinese and Albanian revolutions were in part inspired by the desire of the leadership to curb the rise of a new class of intellectuals and technocrats who, like their counterparts in the Soviet Union and Eastern Europe, would lead the party and state down the "roads of revisionism and counterrevolution." There were, however, several important differences between the Chinese and Albanian movements.[74] The Albanian Ideological and Cultural Revolution was not designed to mask an intra-party power struggle, it did not seek to elevate Hoxha to the status of a major Communist theoretician, it was not characterized by armed clashes or violent purges, and it did not result in the disruption of the nation's economy.

International Trends, 1964–69

The Soviet-Albanian diplomatic and ideological break in December 1961 stemmed mainly from Tirana's espousal of the Chinese line in the growing dispute between Moscow and Peking. The Soviet-Albanian rupture was followed in mid-1962 by the de facto expulsion of Albania from the Warsaw Treaty Organization (WTO) and the Council for Mutual Economic Assistance (Comecon).[75] While the Eastern European party-states, most likely at the behest of Moscow, did not sever their diplomatic or economic ties with the PRA, they did express their displeasure by recalling their ambassadors and conducting their relations with Tirana at the chargé d'affaires level. The Albanian Party of Labor was not, however, invited to send a representative to the congresses of the Bulgarian, Hungarian, Czechoslovak, and East German Communist parties which met between November 1962 and January 1963. At each of these meetings the anti-Soviet policies of the APL were strongly criticized by the majority of the delegations in attendence. Albania thus, for all practical purposes, had by 1962 been expelled from the socialist commonwealth.

The rupture between Moscow and Tirana had the effect of consolidating the Sino-Albanian alliance. Albania now relied heavily on Peking for the diplomatic, economic, and military support it needed to survive. China found the support of a ruling Communist party most useful in its quarrel with the Soviets. The backing which Peking received from Tirana served to give an air of legitimacy to the emerging pro-Chinese faction within the world Communist system. The Albanians also provided China with bases both in Europe and at the United Nations from which to attack the USSR. Furthermore, Albania acted as a proxy through which China conducted its polemics with the Russians. In this latter capacity Tirana rendered a most valuable service until the Chinese and Soviets began to attack each other directly in 1963.

With the outbreak of open polemics between Moscow and Peking, the role of Albania in the Sino-Soviet rift began to decline. Though now overshadowed by China, Albania during 1963–64 continued its violent anti-Soviet campaign. Tirana's fury increasingly focused on Nikita Khrushchev,[77] the architect of the Soviet-Albanian break. The Albanians were especially resentful both of the Soviet dictator's efforts during the first months of 1964 to downgrade their importance in the Sino-Soviet conflict and of his move to convoke an international conference of

Communist parties to force them back into the fold or to expel them formally from the world Communist movement. By the autumn of 1964, the Albanian vilification of Khrushchev had reached such proportions that prospects for healing the Soviet-Albanian breach appeared dim without a change of leadership in either Moscow or Tirana.[78]

The APL hailed the ouster of Khrushchev on October 14, 1964, as a great victory for the Marxist-Leninists in their struggle against "modern revisionism." Tirana made it clear, however, that Khrushchev's successors would have to repudiate his policies to regain the loyalty of Albania. While there are indications that Tirana did not expect any significant changes in the Russian line following Khrushchev's removal, it initially muted its criticism of the new Soviet leaders to please the Chinese, who at this time were pursuing a rather cautious policy toward the USSR.[79]

Nevertheless, as far as the Soviets were concerned, the Albanians at this point were only of secondary importance. In the hope of paving the way for a rapprochement between Moscow and Peking, the Soviet government had invited the Chinese to send a delegation to participate in the forty-seventh anniversary celebration of the Bolshevik Revolution. During its brief stay in Moscow, the Chinese mission, headed by Chou En-lai, had conferred with Brezhnev and Kosygin in an attempt to iron out the differences that had arisen within the Communist camp. These conversations, however, ended in failure, since neither side was apparently willing to compromise.[80]

The position of the new Soviet leaders was also made clear to the Albanians in early November 1964. On November 10, in a broadcast commemorating the nineteenth anniversary of Soviet recognition of the PRA, Radio Moscow reaffirmed the Soviet position concerning peaceful coexistence, the Nuclear Test Ban Treaty, and the other issues that had become points of contention between the APL and the CPSU.

Convinced that there was no hope of reconciliation between the Soviet "revisionists" and the "Marxist-Leninists," the Albanians on November 13 resumed full-fledged polemics with Moscow with the publication of a scathing critique of Palmiero Togliatti's political "Testament." In a brief commentary appended to the article, the editors of the Albanian party daily *Zeri i Popullit* noted that they had delayed printing this commentary until they had been able to evaluate the policies of Khrushchev's successors. They had now concluded that Brezhnev and Kosygin had become partisans of the ultra-revisionist line of Togliatti, and this fact posed an even greater threat to world Communism than did the views of Khrushchev and Tito.

Enver Hoxha summed up the APL position concerning the new

Soviet rulers in his November 28, 1964, address to the nation when he observed:

The fall of Khrushchev . . . does not mark the end of Khrushchevian revisionism or modern revisionism as a whole. . . . There have not been
liquidated along with [Khrushchev] . . . the policies and socio-economic
roots of Khrushchevian revisionism. . . . Therefore the [Albanian] Party of
Labor, like all revolutionaries, has no illusions and should have none in this
regard.[81]

The Albanians further expressed their defiance of the Kremlin by putting on display during the national holiday celebrations in late November several surface-to-air missiles.[82] This was the first indication that Albania possessed such weapons. It appears this gesture was primarily intended to raise the people's morale and perhaps to warn would-be aggressors that Albania had a greater capacity for self-defense than they might have calculated.

The Moscow-Tirana rupture had profoundly affected Albania's international position between 1961–64. During this period Albania had become a base for Chinese propaganda operations in Europe, the Middle East, and Africa. Albania also served as a mecca for delegations from the pro-Peking "Marxist-Leninist" parties of Europe and Asia.

Tirana now also began to expand its diplomatic contacts with the non-Communist world. On the eve of the Soviet-Albanian split, the PRA had formal diplomatic relations with twenty-three states.[83] By 1964 this figure had risen to thirty. Between 1960–64, the number of states with which Albania maintained economic ties had increased from sixteen to twenty-five.[84] While it remained constant in its opposition to United States "imperialism," Yugoslav "revisionism," and Greek "monarcho-fascism," the PRA did make an effort to improve its relations with such states as Austria, France, Ghana, Italy, Libya, Morocco, and Turkey. During 1964 both Italy and France upgraded their legations in Tirana to embassies.

Although Albania's relations with the non-Communist world had shown signs of improvement, its ties with the Soviet Union and the East European party-states remained tense.[85] As a consequence of Rumania's independence movement, relations between Bucharest and Tirana took a turn for the better with the resumption of relations on the ambassadorial level in 1963. The Rumanians were also perhaps mainly responsible for a move to restore Albania to membership in the Communist camp in January 1965.[86]

It appears that in addition to its desire to accommodate the independent-minded Rumanians, the USSR was not averse to making a gesture to heal the breach with Tirana in order to determine whether any shift in

Albanian policy was in the offing.[87] Accordingly, Albania received an invitation through Poland to attend the January meeting of the Political Consultative Committee of the Warsaw Pact. Tirana wasted no time in rejecting this overture, while at the same time reaffirming its membership rights in the Warsaw Pact and establishing the conditions for its active participation in the affairs of the organization.[88] There was no real advantage to be gained by Albania's reassuming an active membership in the WTO at this time. Indeed, to have done so might have limited Tirana's freedom somewhat and strained its relations with Peking.

Not unexpectedly, the Albanians (along with the Chinese) bitterly condemned the March 1–5, 1965, Moscow Communist consultative meeting. Tirana had previously set forth the prerequisites, including extensive bilateral negotiations with the USSR, which would have to be fulfilled before it would participate in any international conference.[89] Furthermore, the APL had no intention of attending any gathering where its views were bound to be condemned. As long as the Sino-Albanian alliance remained firm, prospects for an Albanian rapprochement with the Soviet camp continued to be dim, unless some kind of face-saving formula was forthcoming from Moscow. There is no evidence to indicate that the Soviets were in any mood to oblige the Albanians on this score.

Chinese-Albanian relations during 1965 appear to have been strengthened by Chou En-lai's visit to Albania (March 27–30), the conclusion of an economic and technical assistance pact for the period of Albania's Fourth Five-Year Plan on June 8, and the development of two new anti-Soviet propaganda themes.

While Chou's stopover in Albania, following his attendance at the funeral of Georghiu-Dej, was essentially a courtesy visit, it did serve as an opportunity to whip mass enthusiasm for the Peking-Tirana alliance. It also offered the Albanian rulers a chance to make a high-level plea for more generous Chinese aid to help underwrite the Fourth Five-Year Plan.

The details of the Chinese aid program were hammered out in Peking between April 26 and June 8, 1965.[90] The length of the negotiations and the fact that the precise terms of the agreement were not officially disclosed seemed to indicate the existence of some disagreement between the two states. On the basis of statements made by the leadership at the Fifth Congress of the APL, it would appear that the Albanians were somewhat disappointed in the amount of aid they had been promised by the hard-pressed Chinese.

Despite the differences that may have arisen between them, Albania and China did present a united front in the international arena. While in

Tirana, Chou had revealed the formation of a worldwide anti-imperialist front, headed by China and Albania, and appealed for support—particularly among the Afro-Asian and Latin American peoples. He also set forth the doctrine that "to carry on a true fight against the American imperialists is the main criterion for distinguishing the "Marxist-Leninists" from the "modern revisionists."[91]

From this statement it followed that the Vietnam policy of the party-states would be used as a measure of their doctrinal purity. Especially after the inauguration of the U.S. bombing of North Vietnam in early 1965, Peking and its Albanian ally repeatedly lambasted the Soviets on the grounds that they had betrayed the national liberation war of the Vietnamese people and thereby aided the imperialists by withholding economic and military aid as well as by advocating a negotiated settlement to the conflict.[92] The Vietnam issue in the mid-1960s was elevated to a position of prime importance in the Sino–Soviet-Albanian quarrel.

Although there were no significant overt signs of tension between Peking and Tirana, rumors of an impending Sino-Albanian rift began to circulate throughout Europe in early 1966.[93] There was undoubtedly some unhappiness in Tirana over the amount of Chinese aid and the implied suggestion that Albania put greater emphasis on the development of the agricultural sector of the economy. Yet, when one examines the activities of the Albanians during this time, it is clear that Tirana did not make any major move which could be interpreted as anti-Chinese in nature. In fact, both in word and deed, Albania gave every indication of being a strong partisan of China.

In February 1966 the APL formally rejected an invitation tendered by Poland to meet with representatives of the European and Asian party-states to formulate a coordinated policy to aid the Communist forces in the Vietnam war. The Albanian refusal was based on the failure of the Soviet and East European parties to repudiate their anti-Albanian policies and on Tirana's dissatisfaction with the position of the pro-Soviet camp concerning the Vietnam issue.[94]

Albania's diplomatic relations with the USSR and Eastern Europe continued tense. In late January 1966, Poland, after just having resumed ties with Tirana at the ambassadorial level, ordered the expulsion of the Albanian ambassador for engaging in subversive activities.[95] At the same time the PRA rejected a second Soviet offer to resume commercial relations.[96] The APL announced in late March that it had turned down a Soviet invitation to attend the Twenty-third Congress of the CPSU on the grounds that "there are no ties between the Albanian Party of Labor and the Soviet revisionist leadership on either a party or a state basis." The Albanians also made clear their anger at the anti-Chinese letter circulated among the East European Communist parties in February 1966.[97]

Meanwhile Tirana sought to lay to rest the rumors concerning the state of its relations with Peking. On March 19, 1966, *Zeri i Popullit* published a lengthy article dealing with the development of Albania's foreign trade. It was emphasized that Albania was grateful for the economic assistance it had received from China and that prospects were favorable for continued growth in Sino-Albanian trade.[98] The Peking-Tirana alliance was further enhanced by the visits of Mehmet Shehu to China (April 28–May 12, 1966) and Chou En-lai to Albania (June 24–28, 1966). The theme of Sino-Albanian solidarity was emphasized during both these exchanges.

Tirana, however, did make an attempt to improve ties with its neighbors. There was a slight thaw in Yugoslav-Albanian relations during the spring of 1966. Following the ouster of Vice President Rankovic in July and the official disclosure of the maltreatment of the Albanian population of Kosovo-Metohija, Tirana resumed full-scale polemics against Yugoslavia.[99] Greek-Albanian affairs took a slight turn for the better with the conclusion of a trade agreement in March,[100] but with the seizure of power by the Greek military junta in April 1967 the old animosity between Athens and Tirana returned.

Despite the fact that it had diplomatic relations with thirty-five nations and commercial ties with forty in 1966,[101] Albania was still virtually isolated within the world Communist system. This condition was graphically demonstrated when only four ruling parties (the Chinese, North Korean, North Vietnamese, and Rumanian) sent delegations to the Fifth Congress of the APL. Most of the twenty-six foreign parties represented at the Congress were pro-Chinese "Marxist-Leninist" splinter groups.[102]

In the section of his speech to the Congress devoted to foreign affairs,[103] Hoxha reaffirmed the primacy of Albania's ties with China, endorsed the domestic policies of Mao and the Chinese Cultural Revolution, denounced the "holy alliance" of "American imperialism" and "Soviet revisionism" which sought to establish its hegemony throughout the world, and urged the formation of a "bloc" to combat the forces of revisionism in the Communist camp. While the APL Secretary expressed satisfaction at the progress registered in Albania's relations with China, North Vietnam, North Korea, Cuba, and Rumania, he noted that there could be no change in Tirana's posture toward the other members of the Communist system until they had abandoned "the anti-Albanian line of the Soviet revisionist leadership."

The proceedings of the Fifth Congress of the APL provided convincing evidence of the solidarity of the Sino-Albanian alliance. By the beginning of 1967, Peking and Tirana appeared to be drawing even closer together. Most of the impetus for this development seems to have come from China, whose prestige had been tarnished by the Indonesian debacle and the growing independence of the Asian Communist parties. Albania now assumed increasing importance as the only ruling party member of the pro-Peking faction of the world Communist movement. Furthermore, as the political infighting associated with the Chinese Cultural Revolution became more acute, the Maoist faction sought to enhance its position by obtaining the endorsement of the APL and the other Marxist-Leninist groups. For their part, the Albanians attempted to capitalize on this situation by pressing the Chinese to make more definite commitments for the defense of Albania. It is also interesting to note that the Soviets during 1967, sensing perhaps that China's internal problems and the closure of the Suez Canal would render it difficult for Peking to fulfill its economic promises to Albania, launched an ambitious propaganda campaign in the hope of undermining the Sino-Albanian relationship.

United by their common revolutionary experiences and their isolation within the Communist system, however, China and Albania markedly increased their personal exchanges throughout 1967. Two high-ranking Albanian delegations, one headed by Defense Minister Beqir Balluku and the other by Prime Minister Mehmet Shehu, toured China during January–February and October–November respectively. The pattern of their visits was similar. Balluku and Shehu both endorsed the Cultural Revolution, the Red Guard movement, and Mao's general line. Both traveled outside of Peking to campaign for the Chinese leadership. It would therefore appear that one of the major purposes of these visits was to convince the Chinese masses that Mao enjoyed wide support within the Communist movement.[104] The dispatch of a Red Guard delegation to Albania in June was probably intended as much for domestic considerations as for the promotion of Sino-Albanian friendship.[105]

Albania's role as a base for pro-Chinese propaganda continued to grow in importance. By 1967, the Chinese had constructed several powerful transmitters outside Tirana to spread more effectively their message to Europe, the Middle East, and Africa.[106] In addition, the PRA harbored several Marxist-Leninist parties in exile. Among the most vocal of these were the Polish Communist Party and the All Union Communist Bolshevik Party (Soviet).[107]

With the hardening of the Peking-Tirana alliance, the Albanian leaders adopted a more militant stance in the international arena. Albania merely dismissed the Karlovy Vary Conference in April 1967 as a "meeting of degenerate parties."[108] Tirana naturally supported the Arabs in the Six-Day War, but condemned the Soviet Union for having sold them out.[109] The PRA castigated Rumania for establishing diplomatic relations with West Germany,[110] Yugoslavia for committing genocide in Kosovo-Metohija,[111] Bulgaria for conducting subversive activity in Tirana,[112] and Greece for abandoning constitutional government.[113] When in March the United States made a modest gesture to improve the diplomatic climate existing between Washington and Tirana by lifting the ban on travel for American citizens in Albania, the Albanian regime responded by declaring their country off limits to Americans.[114]

The most violent Albanian rhetoric, however, was reserved for the USSR. In November 1967, on the occasion of the Fiftieth Anniversary of the Bolshevik Revolution, Tirana issued an appeal for a new Russian revolution to depose the current leadership.[115] Despite the violently anti-Soviet stance adopted by the PRA, Moscow during most of 1967 sought to weaken the bonds between Peking and Tirana by subjecting Albania to a low-keyed but persistent propaganda offensive. The Soviets first reminded the Albanians of the historic ties between their two nations[116] and next attempted to convince Tirana that Peking lacked the ability to provide Albania with the economic or military assistance it required to survive.[117] Moscow apparently went as far as to offer Albania the protection of the Warsaw Pact should it find itself confronted with an invasion from Greece.[118] Although Tirana did not succumb to these Soviet blandishments, it evidently began to give serious thought to the improvement of its defense posture in view of its deteriorating relations with its neighbors.

In August 1967 there were unconfirmed reports that the Chinese were constructing a system of missile bases in Albania.[119] Since there is evidence that the Albanians already possessed at least a small quantity of surface-to-air missiles,[120] it is not unlikely that they may have requested additional weapons of this type, and perhaps of more sophisticated types, as the leadership became increasingly apprehensive over potential Soviet, Greek, or Yugoslav moves against the country. Given the nature of the Soviet anti-Chinese propaganda line in Albania during 1967, it would have been logical for Peking to agree to provide Albania with at least token quantities of the military hardware it may have sought.

It was perhaps to allay the fears of the Albanian rulers that Deputy Defense Minister Wang Shu-sheng was dispatched to Albania in late September at the head of a Chinese-Albanian Friendship Society delegation. Simultaneously, a high-ranking Albanian mission, led by Mehmet

Shehu, traveled to China to participate in the eighteenth anniversary celebration of the Chinese People's Republic. While in China, Shehu may have received additional formal assurances of support for Albania. The Sino-Albanian communiqué issued at the conclusion of the Prime Minister's visit contained the promise that "should anyone dare to attack Albania, the Chinese people will definitely provide powerful backing for the Albanian people."[121]

Thus, during the latter part of 1967 there were indications that the PRA was again becoming increasingly sensitive to its isolation and its vulnerability to attack—especially from its neighbors. This concern may have stemmed from a fear that the Greeks and Yugoslavs, with Soviet blessings, might seek to capitalize on the confusion which had arisen within Albania as the Ideological and Cultural Revolution intensified by moving against the country. This fear, of course, could also have been manufactured to rally the masses behind the regime and the Ideological and Cultural Revolution. Be that as it may, with the Albanian leadership restive and with the Soviets making an effort to undermine Tirana's confidence in China, Peking was under pressure at this time to provide tangible proof of its support for its Albanian ally.

Beyond their public statements, the actual response of the Chinese to Albanian appeals for aid is uncertain. Some circumstantial evidence hints that Tirana may have been rather disappointed in what did receive from Peking. During the first four months of 1968 there was a decline of slightly over fifty percent in the incidence of Chinese materials appearing in the Albanian press. In addition, high-ranking political and cultural representatives from Peking were notably absent during the celebration of the five hundredth anniversary of the death of Skenderbeg, the Albanian national hero, in January.[122] Yet these factors can be explained. The drop in press coverage may derive largely from the fact that Sino-Albanian personal exchanges returned to their normal level after the peak activity in 1967. The absence of the usual Chinese delegation at the Skenderbeg commemoration was probably due either to domestic considerations related to the Chinese Cultural Revolution or to a feeling that the Chinese presence might have detracted from the national or historical character of this event.

Indeed, there is more than sufficient evidence to sustain the view that the Sino-Albanian alliance had not deteriorated during January–August 1968. The Albanians continued to endorse the policies of the Chinese Cultural Revolution, including the purge of the backers of Liu-Shao-chi.[123] They also persisted in following Peking's line on such foreign policy issues as the draft treaty on nuclear non-proliferation,[124] the Vietnam peace talks, and related matters. Albania turned a deaf ear to the continued efforts of the Soviets to wean her away from Peking, and her relations with her neighbors and the European party-states remained cool. In July there was another flare-up between Bulgaria and Albania following the expulsion of the Albanian ambassador and several members of his staff. Tirana reciprocated and subsequently blasted the Zhivkov regime, thus fomenting hostilities between these states on the eve of the invasion of Czechoslovakia.[125]

During the spring of 1968, Tirana had begun to show more than a passing interest in the activities of the Dubcek regime. By early May the Albanians had concluded that the new leadership consisted of "bourgeois, Slovak nationalist, and fascist elements" whose "ultra-revisionist policies would result in the restoration of capitalism."[126] As the difficulties between the Czechoslovaks and the Soviets mounted, Tirana viewed the struggle between Prague and Moscow as a civil war of the revisionist forces which would end in the eventual destruction of the revisionist heresy and the inevitable triumph of Marxism-Leninism.[127]

While the extent to which the Albanians believed their own propaganda is uncertain, it is clear that Tirana was both surprised and frightened by the Soviet-led invasion of Czechoslovakia on August 21, 1968. The APL bitterly condemned the Soviet action as well as Dubcek's "ultra-revisionist" policies which had invited it, and took the position that this episode represented the culmination of the "revisionist" line which the Soviet leaders had sought to impose on the world Communist movement at the Twentieth Congress of the CPSU.[128]

The PRA's response to the Czechoslovak incident was threefold in nature. It formally withdrew from the Warsaw Pact, attempted to improve its ties with Yugoslavia and Rumania, and appealed to Peking for support.

Albania's withdrawal from the Warsaw Pact on September 13[129] was primarily a propaganda gesture, since Tirana had not participated in the work of the organization since 1961. The PRA by its action hoped to underscore its contention that the WTO had been transformed into an agency of Soviet imperialism. While Albania may have previously been willing to remain in the WTO to keep alive its claim to membership in the Socialist Commonwealth, it now may have felt that its continued participation in this organization could provide the USSR with an excuse to intervene in its affairs.

The APL had halted polemics with Yugoslavia a week before the Soviet intervention into Czechoslovakia. It appears that the Albanian leaders were eager to forge a front with the Yugoslavs, and perhaps with the Rumanians, to discourage any potential Soviet action against the three dissident Balkan Communist states. While there is no evidence to suggest that Moscow ever seriously considered such a course of action, the Albanians were anxious to cover all contingencies and possibly to score a few propaganda points at the expense of Moscow and Sofia. For these reasons, the Albanians charged in late September 1968[130] that Bulgaria had become a staging ground for Warsaw-Pact forces. Since the Albanian accusations have never been proven, Tirana apparently used this stratagem in the hope of cementing its ties with Belgrade and Bucharest, both of which were not on the best of terms with Bulgaria. Albania's efforts, however, did not produce the desired results. The Albanian-Yugoslav rapprochement came to an end in early November 1968 when Tirana resumed hostilities following the outbreak of new difficulties between the Yugoslav government and the Albanians of Kosovo-Metohija.[131] Rumania, which found itself subjected to heavy pressure from the Kremlin, was in no position to respond favorably to the Albanian overture.

In his announcement of Albania's withdrawal from the Warsaw Pact, Prime Minister Shehu had invited the Chinese to endorse this action. On September 17, 1968, Peking responded by lavishly praising the Albanians for leaving the WTO and warning any would-be aggressors that should they "dare to touch even a hair of Albania, they will meet with none other than total, disgraceful, and inevitable defeat."[132]

Eight days later a high-ranking Albanian delegation headed by Defense Minister Balluku and Politburo member Adil Carcani departed for China. Balluku remained in China only until October 9.[133] His presence served mainly to emphasize the solidarity of the Sino-Albanian alliance. He probably also discussed with his hosts Albania's military situation in the light of conditions now prevailing in Eastern Europe. The rest of the mission, under the leadership of Carcani, remained in China until November 20, 1968, by which time they had concluded two new economic agreements. According to Hoxha, these pacts established the basis for Chinese aid to Albania during the Fifth Five-Year Plan (1971–75). Peking agreed to provide Tirana with an interest-free loan to underwrite the construction of thirty major industrial projects.[134] The nature and timing of these treaties points to the fact that they were intended to raise the morale of the Albanians and provide further evidence of China's concern for the welfare of its allies.

There were probably similar motivations behind the Albanian visit in late November 1968 of the Chinese military delegation headed by General Huang Yung-cheng, Chief of Staff of the People's Liberation Army.[135] While Peking appears to have increased somewhat its military aid to Albania in the aftermath of Czechoslovakia, it was primarily concerned with improving the defensive capabilities of the Albanian military forces.[136] It should also be noted that the Chinese had begun to update and strengthen Albania's defenses prior to 1968. Despite rumors to the contrary,[137] China does not seem to be inclined to transform Albania into an offensive base. Albania's main value to Peking, at least for the time being, remains as a propaganda center.[138]

Without question the most significant development in Albania's international relations during the 1960s was the formation of the Sino-Albanian alliance. As the decade drew to a close, this union continued firm, as both parties persisted in their hardline anti-Soviet, anti-revisionist policies. During 1969 Tirana staunchly backed Peking in its border clashes with the USSR,[139] joined with China in condemning the June 5 Moscow meeting of the world Communist parties,[140] and enthusiastically endorsed the program of the Ninth Congress of the Chinese Communist Party.[141] "To promote the revolutionary militant friendship between the two peoples of China and Albania," Radio Peking in June inaugurated a regular program of broadcasts in the Albanian language.[142] After some initial difficulties, it would appear that China has for the most part kept the economic promises it had made to Albania. The Sino-Albanian alliance meets the specific needs of both partners. Albania, however, by having become so heavily dependent on China, could find herself in a difficult position should there be any radical changes in Peking's foreign policy.

There seems to be little likelihood that Soviet Albanian relations will improve, at least during the early 1970s. The Albanians were severely jolted by the Soviet intervention in Czechoslovakia, and as late as the summer of 1969 they kept up a steady anti-Soviet propaganda barrage on this issue.[143] In December 1968, Shehu had denounced the Brezhnev Doctrine and compared it to Mussolini's view of limited Albanian sovereignty in the 1930s.[144] It was clear by the end of the 1960s that closer Albanian-Soviet ties were incompatible with the Sino-Albanian alliance.

Of the East European states, only Yugoslavia and Rumania in recent years have shown an interest in improving their relations with Tirana.[145] Yugoslav-Albanian ties will continue to be influenced by the Kosovo question and the state of Belgrade's relations with Peking. The nature of Albanian-Rumanian relations will largely reflect the degree of independence which Bucharest enjoys in the Soviet camp. So long as the regimes in control in 1970 remain in power, the prospects for an improvement in Tirana's relations with Greece and Bulgaria are dim.

Although the Albanians would like to strengthen their ties with Western Europe and the developing nations, progress in this area has been hindered by Tirana's difficulty in expanding trade and by its desire, for ideological reasons, to keep contacts with non-Communist states to a minimum. While Albania's attitudes and policies toward the non-Communist world may be modified during the 1970s, there would seem to be small probability of any improvement of U.S.–Albanian relations in the near future.

10

East European Relations
With the USSR

Vernon V. Aspaturian

10. East European Relations with the USSR

Vernon V. Aspaturian

By the late 1950s, Eastern Europe,* in the eyes of most Americans had been reduced to little more than an amorphous grey blob destined to languish as a permanent appendage to the Soviet Union. It seemed as if sixty million people divided among more than half-dozen nationalities had been suddenly and irrevocably stripped of their proud histories, deprived of their national identities, and shorn of their cultural individualities. They became part of an expanding Soviet or Communist empire. With almost indecent unanimity, the outside world forgot the national identities of these countries, and for more than a decade they were almost universally consigned to oblivion as Soviet "satellites," "captive states," "slave states," or vassal states. Submerged under a thick layer of Communist ideology, subjected to repeated social convulsions, reduced to abject political subordination, ruthlessly plundered of their natural resources, and languishing under Soviet military occupation, the countries of Eastern Europe were insulated from contact with the outside world, and their cruel fate seemed to be permanently and irreversibly sealed.

Communist regimes, cast from a common ideological and organizational mold in Moscow, and in some instances actually prefabricated in advance, were imposed upon a region of diverse nationalities, languages, religions, and legacies, as the great capitals of Eastern Europe literally suffocated under the ugly smog of uniformity which blew in from the East.

---

* For purposes of this chapter only, Eastern Europe is defined to include Poland, Czechoslovakia, Hungary, Rumania, Bulgaria, Yugoslavia and Albania and to exclude East Germany, Finland, Greece and the Baltic Countries.

Yet beneath this deceptive cloud of synthetic homogeneity, the peoples and nations of Eastern Europe managed to preserve and cherish their national individualities, which had been obscured but not snuffed out by the Soviet occupation. Even the manner in which Communist regimes were foisted upon the countries of Eastern Europe reflected a pale outline of national individuality. In Albania and Yugoslavia, the Communist regimes represented a curious fusion between alien and indigenous elements. While the ideology of the regimes was imported from Moscow, their organizational base was rooted in a native guerrilla movement which gave their Communist systems a distinctive national flavor. In Czechoslovakia, the Communist party enjoyed substantial, but not majority, electoral support and thus was by no means a completely alien force. The Communist regimes established in Poland, Bulgaria, Rumania, and Hungary, on the other hand, were purely alien in character, conveniently uncontaminated by indigenous influences, and supported almost entirely by the bayonets of the Red Army.

These variations in the relative indigenousness of Communist regimes in Eastern Europe were to have profound but uneven impact upon their evolving relationship with the Soviet Union. Yugoslavia, of course, broke away from the Soviet orbit as early as 1948, and a new nationalistic, or at any rate autonomous, form of Communism assumed shape alongside the spuriously universal Communism of Moscow. Titoism was in effect the forerunner of what was characterized for a time as "polycentric" Communism as opposed to the monolithic Communism of the Stalinist era. What was ultimately significant about Titoism was not its doctrinal substance, but its form—the idea of a pluralistic Communist universe of autonomous nations and states, starting from a common point of departure, but charting different roads to socialism or Communism in response to the pressures, demands, and needs of local constituencies and not the dictates of Moscow.

Ideology and Self-Interest in Soviet Hegemonic Policy

The relationship between the Soviet Union and Eastern Europe which emerged after World War II was shaped by a complex of factors which almost defy comprehensive analysis. History, geography, culture, language, religion, psychological attachments, national character, and ideology have all played a role in shaping both the direction and configuration of the relationship. The impact of these factors has varied considerably in uneven and changing proportions in Soviet relations with the individual countries of Eastern Europe, and this fact has contributed enormously to the differentiation evident in the developing relations between Moscow and the different countries of Eastern Europe. Some of these factors have served to bind the countries of Eastern Europe to Moscow, while others have served to alienate them. And it is not always a simple matter to sort out and disentangle the contradictory and converging forces which operate to influence and shape the attitudes of individual countries toward the Soviet Union.

Soviet interest in Eastern Europe, of course, has its origins in the pre-Bolshevik period. History and geography alone would be sufficient to guarantee a special role for Moscow in this region. Historically, the area has been a buffer zone between Russia and other major powers of Central Europe for many centuries, and for the past two hundred years Russia has sought to assert a dominant influence in the region. Indeed, there are some observers who suggest that history and geography alone are sufficient to explain the subjugation of Eastern Europe by Moscow after World War II. Yet the specific character and form of the subordination suggest that other factors have been equally influential.

The responses and reactions of the various countries of Eastern Europe to the Russian interest in the area have varied widely over time from one country to another—so have the perceptions and images about Russia in the region. Many of these attitudes and perceptions were shaped by the events and circumstances of nineteenth century European diplomacy. Less than two hundred years ago, all of the nationalities of Eastern Europe (except the Serbs of Montenegro and the Poles, who were ruled from Moscow) were languishing under Ottoman or Hapsburg domination. The conditions of their subjection, liberation, and independence were thus to shape national attitudes toward Russia for many decades. The Soviet state, as the successor of the Russian state, inevitably inherited to some degree both the enemies and friends of its Tsarist predecessors. While the advent of Communism in Russia served to compound and intensify traditional hatreds and fears, it also served in some degree to alienate those nations that were traditionally friendly.

Although both history and geography ineluctably impelled the Soviet Union to assert its dominance and influence in Eastern Europe, the precise nature and configuration of the relationship that emerged owes its character neither to history, language, and culture, nor to the strategic and security imperatives of geographical propinquity, but rather is to be found in the Bolshevik Revolution and the history of the relationship between the Communist Party of the Soviet Union (CPSU), and the world Communist movement, of which the prewar Eastern European Communist parties were an integral part.

The Soviet interest in Eastern Europe thus reflects the dual character of the Soviet Union as both a Great Power and the center of an ideological movement with ecumenical pretentions. And this dichotomous interest of Moscow in Eastern Europe has always confused external observers and statesmen who have sought to discern the motives that prompted the Soviet Union to establish a sphere of influence in Eastern Europe in the precise form that it assumed. Was Stalin motivated by a purely traditional and natural impulse to enhance the security of the Soviet/Russian state, or was the Soviet presence in Eastern Europe motivated by ideological imperatives? A correct perception was an indispensable prerequisite for an accurate and realistic projection of future Soviet behavior. If Stalin was acting on the basis of *primarily* security interests, then one might assume that the Soviet sphere of influence in Eastern Europe constituted a terminal exercise in Soviet imperialist or hegemonic policy in Europe, with which it was possible to reach an accommodation. If the Soviet move into Eastern Europe was motivated *primarily* by ideological interests, then it could be assumed that Eastern Europe was to be used as a springboard for the further extension of Soviet power and Communist systems in accordance with Moscow's unilaterally assumed ideological mission. If such were the case, then Europe and the world would be plunged into a prolonged and protracted ideological conflict that might be marked by turmoil, revolutions, repression, counterrevolutions, civil wars, local conflicts, and even general war.[1]

When the Soviet Union established its sphere of influence in Eastern Europe after World War II, Soviet state interests and ideological interests were conveniently and logically largely in tandem. The establishment of a Soviet bloc simultaneously satisfied the historic and strategic necessity of a security belt and the convenience of a springboard for the further Communization of Europe in accordance with the self-imposed mission assumed by Moscow. Increasingly, however, these two purposes of the Soviet presence in Eastern Europe have been rendered incompatible, and as the Soviet role and position in the international Communist movement has been challenged from within and eroded by the obstacles and hazards from without, Moscow has been forced to reexamine the basic premises of its presence in Eastern Europe.

One resolution of these periodic collisions of Moscow's dichotomous interests was the Soviet invasion and occupation of Czechoslovakia in August 1968. By resorting to force, the Soviet leaders signified their determination to maintain a sphere of influence in Eastern Europe in the traditional hegemonic power sense, even though it further erodes the credibility and effectiveness of the Soviet state as the center of an ideological movement. The Soviet occupation thus does not imply that Communism is once again "monolithic"; rather it proves the opposite. Neither does it signify a militant resurgence of "world Communism" as a motive force in Soviet behavior, but rather signifies the full flowering of the Soviet state as a traditional imperialistic state, whose influence and role in the world is determined not by the attractiveness of its ideology but by the enormity of its power and its determination to employ it in its self-interest. In subordinating ideological interests, norms, and goals to Soviet state interests, needs, and requirements, the Soviet Union not only has tended to confirm Peking's charge that Moscow's behavior is solely determined by the interests of the Soviet "revisionist clique": by its outrageous violation of the principle of "proletarian internationalism," the Soviet Union has further subverted whatever remained of the underlying theoretical basis of the world Communist movement and system.[2] This strongly suggests that the Soviet sphere in Eastern Europe has lost whatever utility it might have had as an ideological springboard for the Communization of Europe.

The Perversion of "Proletarian Internationalism" Into Soviet Imperialism

Although the interests of the Soviet Union as a Great Power in Eastern Europe now overshadow whatever residual ideological interests it might retain in the area, the consequences of the tension and conflict between the dual interests of Moscow in Eastern Europe have left their imprint and continue to condition Soviet policy in Eastern Europe. Hence, to an extraordinary degree, the process whereby the traditional interests of Russia contended with the ideological interests of the Soviet Union for priority in Eastern Europe is prologue to the current situation.

The sphere of influence established by the Soviet Union in Eastern Europe after World War II was no ordinary or traditional retinue of vassal or client states subordinated to Soviet power out of strategic, foreign-policy, economic, or simply power considerations. It was not sufficient that the countries of Eastern Europe were reduced to abject political submission or economic control, with foreign policies subordinated to those of Moscow or with resources plundered and carted away to the East. The entire region was at the same time ideologically, politically, and socio-economically homogenized. Internal orders were violently and forcibly refashioned to imitate those of the Soviet Union. Dictatorships of the proletariat were proclaimed in all countries; Marxism-Leninism was installed as the ruling and exclusive ideology; the Communist party unilaterally asserted a monopoly on all political power; the economy was nationalized, and collectivization was set into motion in the countryside; constitutions and formal institutions of government were introduced that were often shameless copies of the originals in Moscow; and all countries were forced to embark upon an identical political, economic, and social "road to socialism" in a patent attempt to force these countries through the same internal convulsions traversed by the Soviet Union. Stalin was elevated to a godlike figure as the leader of the Communist orbit, the Soviet Union was invested with the directorship of the movement, while organizationally, Soviet political and ideological control was coordinated through the Cominform. Economic exploitation was facilitated through the infamous Molotov Plan (Council of Mutual Economic Assistance), while Soviet occupation troops remained to enforce Soviet decisions.

It seemed as if the countries of Eastern Europe were being readied for absorption into the USSR as new union republics, as were the three hapless Baltic states only a few years earlier. In short, the Communization of Eastern Europe went beyond the traditional manner in which Great Powers established and maintained a sphere of influence for strategic and economic reasons; instead of being the terminal definition of a sphere of influence, the Sovietization of Eastern Europe seemed but a prelude to the further expansion of Communism beyond its new periphery. Communism was an ideology of universalist pretensions, not simply a vehicle for the establishment of a Russian Empire in new guise, although that is precisely how it turned out eventually. And the USSR was no ordinary Great Power, but a multi-national nucleus of a future world Communist state. Communist parties of varying magnitude existed in Western Europe that were no less eager than their Eastern European counterparts to be hoisted into power with the aid of Soviet bayonets. With Stalin's death in 1953, however, events were set into motion which ultimately deprived the Soviet Union of its universalist messianic character, trimming its dimensions to that of an arrested universal state in embryonic form seeking a new social stability as a terminal multi-national commonwealth.

The entire history of the Soviet relationships, first with foreign Communist parties, then with Communist states, and then with rivals for leadership (for example, with China), has been determined by two essentially contradictory purposes: (1) serving the interests of foreign constituencies (furthering world revolution, relating to party-states and China); or (2) reflecting the interests of internal constituencies (survival as a state, promotion of national interests, advancement of Soviet elites). The first purpose is inherently self-abnegative, since it demands that the interests of the Soviet Union's internal constituencies be subordinated to the interests of external constituencies, while the second is subversive to internationalism, since it gives higher priority to internal needs than to external obligations.

Tension between these two conflicting sets of demands was inevitable and not capable of easy resolution. One purpose was bound to subordinate the other. Either the Soviet state was to become an expendable instrument of the international proletariat or the Communist movement would be reduced to a creature supinely responsive to the demands of the Soviet state. This contradiction was resolved by adjusting the interests and behavior of the movement and foreign Communist parties to those of the Soviet state, and from 1928 to 1953, foreign Communist parties, even after they assumed power in their own countries, remained instruments rather than partners of the Soviet Union.

As long as the Soviet Union was the only Communist state, it could be rationalized that good Communists everywhere should display first loyalty to the only fatherland of the proletariat. Loyalty, however, was not founded on the inherent moral superiority or priority of interests of the Soviet proletariat over all others, but on the basis that as the only country ruled by a proletariat, class interests dictated highest loyalty to the base and center of the world revolutionary movement. This is the principle known as "proletarian internationalism." The refusal of Marshal Tito and other satellite leaders to place the interests of the Soviet state above those of their own Communist states and to act as Moscow's subservient agents of plunder and exploitation in the name of "proletarian internationalism," resulted in Tito's expulsion and the wholesale liquidation of satellite leaders who displayed signs of wavering loyalty.

Redefining "Proletarian Internationalism": The Erosion of Soviet Primacy

When Stalin died in March 1953, the dominance of the Soviet Union in the Communist system appeared fixed and permanent and the primacy of its interests established and assured. Stalin's death, however, unleashed internal divisions among his successors and thus created opportunities for other Communist states to stir and come back to life. The struggle for power unleashed in Moscow by Stalin's death, however, was grave cause for anxiety. Amorphous factional groupings assumed shape in satellite capitals corresponding to those in the Kremlin. The more inconclusive the struggle in Moscow, the greater the apprehension in Eastern Europe. The Communist world entered a period of turmoil and confusion. Direction from Moscow became contradictory, inconsistent, wavering, and hesitant. Surviving anti-Stalinists in satellite countries were emboldened to move and challenge their own Stalinist leaders left in the wake of Soviet confusion. Satellite leaders were soon drawn into the vortex of the Kremlin intrigues as pawns—not as pawns of Moscow, but as pawns of factional groupings in the struggle for power.

As the internal controversy became more acute, uncertain, and incapable of resolution on the basis of the internal factional balance, Kremlin factions reached out into their empire for incremental support. Communist leaders were once again about to become power constituencies, starting first with China and then with Yugoslavia, the most powerful and the most independent. Khrushchev apparently perceived factional capital in associating his interests with Peking's, and he thus called for the readjustment of relations with China. He also, about this time, may have perceived an advantage in seeking a rapproachment with Yugoslavia. We can date the beginnings of the subversion of Soviet primacy in the Communist world to Khrushchev's opportunistic maneuvers in using China and Yugoslavia against his factional rivals.[3] Presumably, both Mao and Tito would demonstrate their gratitude by supporting Khrushchev and his faction in turn. For the next three years, both China and Yugoslavia were to play significant roles both in shoring up Khrushchev at home and in his dealings with the Eastern European satellite states.

The Twentieth Party Congress constitutes a major watershed in the evolution of Soviet relations with the rest of the Communist world. Locally responsive Communists like Wladyslaw Gomulka and Imre Nagy were catapulted into power in Poland and Hungary by powerful internal pressures which were set into motion by the revelations of the Twentieth Party Congress. The demolition of Stalinism at home could only result in the progressive disintegration of Stalinist structures in Eastern Europe, which had been erected in response to the dictates of Moscow. The internal effects in China, Yugoslavia, and Albania were minimal, since they were governed largely by indigenous Stalinist regimes, particularly China and Albania.

The Polish and Hungarian "Octobers" were the immediate and most serious consequences of de-Stalinization, and the demands both events placed upon the Communist system as then organized threatened to reduce it to ruins. Nationalism of the Soviet variety could no longer be obscured, and nationalism of the smaller states could no longer be denied by the smoke screen of proletarian internationalism. The year 1956 thus inaugurated the gradual dissolution of proletarian internationalism into its constituent proletarian or Communist nationalisms. This process unfolded gradually and pragmatically in response to situations and events, and it falls into several distinct phases of development.

The role of the Soviet Union underwent discrete modification with each successive stage in the continuing evolution of the system and movement. Five distinct phases are discernible in the Soviet Union's relationship to the Communist universe of states and parties during the period 1956–70:

1. A short phase covered the period from the Twentieth Party Congress to the World Conference of Communist Parties in November

1957. During this period, the Soviet Union was clearly a crippled leader, mauled and bruised as a consequence of its de-Stalinization program. Split and divided at home, with its prestige tarnished and its power tattered and ragged, using both Belgrade and Peking as crutches, it hobbled from one capital to another, seeking to preserve its authority. The primacy of Soviet interests in Eastern Europe was subdued but by no means subordinated as a search began for a process which would substitute a consensus of all Communist states (a "socialist commonwealth") for the Soviet national interest as the main criterion of proletarian internationalism.

2. The November 1957 conference marks the end of the first phase and the beginning of the second, which lasted until the Twenty-second Party Congress of the CPSU in October 1961. As a crippled leader unable to assert its former primacy, the Soviet Union was soon challenged by China, which suddenly made an attempt to introduce Chinese interests as the chief input into the calculus of proletarian internationalism by making successive demands upon the Soviet Union, upon the system, and then upon the movement itself. Khrushchev's excommunication of China's echo, Albania, at the Twenty-second Party Congress, signaled a successful Soviet quashing of the Chinese bid for primacy and an attempted reassertion of positive Soviet leadership in Eastern Europe and over Western parties.

3. The third phase, which was abruptly terminated by Khrushchev's ouster in October 1964, left the Soviet Union stranded as a residual leader of European or Western Communism, a patron of the "bourgeois nationalist" states in Asia and Africa, and a global partner/rival with the United States. Moscow had, in effect, surrendered control of the Asian party-states (except for Mongolia), while Peking systematically endeavored to establish itself as the leader of Eastern Communism. The period covered by the third phase, 1961–64, is packed with events and developments of signal importance, among which are the Cuban Missile Crisis, the Sino-Indian Border War, the Test-Ban Treaty, and the open dispute with Peking. Each of these developments marked a definite escalation in the Sino-Soviet hegemonial conflict and a correspondingly growing assertion of independence by the Eastern European countries, which took advantage of the Sino-Soviet conflict to expand their latitude of independent action.

4. The fourth phase was ushered in with the sudden removal of Khrushchev from his posts of authority in October 1964. During this period, the Communist countries of Eastern Europe not only assumed virtually complete control over their internal affairs, but in some instances started to assert limited areas of independence in foreign policy, not only with respect to attitudes toward China but in relations with the

non-Communist countries as well. This was most conspicuously evident in the case of Rumania, whose foreign policy has deviated from that of Moscow more distantly than that of any other Eastern European Communist state still technically within the Soviet orbit.

5. The occupation of Czechoslovakia by the military forces of the Soviet Union and four of its Warsaw-Pact allies inaugurated the fifth phase in the evolution of the relationship between Moscow and Eastern Europe. The most conspicuous characteristic of this phase, as noted earlier, is the unambiguous emergence of Soviet security and national interests as the paramount factor in Soviet behavior. In the past, Moscow was largely successful in correlating or identifying its state interests with its ideological interests to the satisfaction of the overwhelming majority of Communists throughout the world. Although the Soviet leaders once again attempted to justify their invasion of Czechoslovakia in ideological terms, the action provoked condemnation not only in Western capitals and in the dissident Communist states (Yugoslavia, Peking, and Albania), but also prompted public denunciation by the leadership of the French and Italian Communist parties, and, most importantly, evoked for the first time the open repudiation of its act by a Warsaw-Pact ally and Communist state in good standing, Rumania. Ironically, but realistically, the strongest support for the Soviet action came from those Communist states whose interests were independently served by the invasion (Poland and East Germany) or who were beholden to the Soviet Union (Cuba, Bulgaria, Hungary), and those non-Communist states dependent upon Moscow for diplomatic, military, or economic assistance (Egypt, Syria, Iraq, and others). Curiously enough, the reaction of the Johnson Administration was remarkably mild, also on grounds of perceived self-interest. Thus, for the first time, worldwide reaction to a major Soviet action was determined not only on ideological or moral grounds, but on grounds of overt self-interest as well. Poland and Cuba, for example, frankly conceded that their behavior and reaction was determined by raison d'etat rather than by ideology.[4]

The Ideological Pluralization of Eastern Europe

The Soviet occupation of Czechoslovakia thus foreshadows new realignments in the world Communist movement and, most importantly, new cleavages and alignments in Eastern Europe. Whereas in the past conflicts of interest among Communist states were articulated as doctrinal conflicts, it is likely not that conflicts of interest and ideological differences may be expressed independently of one another as well as be intertwined. Even in the absence of basic ideological conflicts, differences among Communist states over territorial frontiers, treatment of minorities, economic and trade matters, administrative and institutional implementation of ideological principles, and external relations and attitudes toward individual Communist and non-Communist states will probably become more manifest. Moscow can be expected to counter these tendencies, and individual instances may succeed, but it appears that basic trends have been set into motion that will continue to express themselves in greater diversity internally and more variation in foreign policy.

Thus, Eastern Europe today, after more than two decades of Communist rule, represents an interesting kaleidoscope of ideological deviations and sociopolitical development within a broad common philosophical and institutional framework.[5] This diversity, however, remains diversity with a given ideological, social, and historical context. All Eastern Europe states remain "Marxist-Leninist" states; all share a common ideological point of departure; all bear the same birthmarks, which remain ineradicably "Stalinist," "Soviet," and "Russian," although each has attempted to surmount and compensate for its stigmata in different ways.

The diversity which has characterized the Communist world since 1956 is usually referred to as "polycentrism" to distinguish it from the "monocentrism" of the Stalinist era. While the term has gained general currency, it is somewhat awkward, since the notion of many centers of Communism is not only an inaccurate description but a logical absurdity. While China and the Soviet Union might conceivably consider themselves as rival Communist "centers," most of the Communist states are not centers of anything. A more descriptive term might be pluralistic Communism. Because of this common ideological framework which has resulted in the establishment of a common sociopolitical system with its peculiar pattern of institutional and political interpenetration, domestic politics in individual Communist states has been, and continues to be to some degree, intimately connected with Communist interstate relations. Institutionally, this pattern of political interpenetration has been expressed through the Cominform (1947–56), multilateral and bilateral conferences of Communist party representatives, the Warsaw Pact Organization (since 1955), and Comecon (since 1949). Although these institutions were initially established to legitimize and facilitate unilateral Soviet penetration and control of smaller Communist states in the guise of multilateral interpenetration, in later years the pattern assumed a more authentic interpenetrative character, with other Communist states and leaders demanding a voice in the determination of Soviet internal politics and foreign policy. As noted earlier, this reverse pattern of penetration was set into motion by Khrushchev when he sought the assistance of Mao and Tito against his internal factional rivals.

The divisive and corrosive factional squabbles in the Kremlin after Stalin's death, the kowtowing to Peking in 1954, and the apologies in Belgrade the following year, all combined to undermine Soviet prestige and authority in the Communist universe. Uncertainty and hesitation in Moscow encouraged arrogance in Peking, insolence in Belgrade, and dissidence in Eastern Europe.

The direction of political penetration, flow of demands, and the resolution of conflicts in the Communist system and movement underwent systematic and fundamental alteration, as the unilateral right of Moscow to intervene in the affairs of other states was successively defied, subdued, and challenged. Up to Stalin's death, the thrust of political penetration and flow of demands in the Communist system moved in one direction only, from the center to the periphery. Since Stalin's death, and with accelerated momentum after 1956, the equilibrium of demands has been substantially and progressively altered. First Peking in 1954, then Yugoslavia in 1955, and Poland in 1956, made demands upon the Soviet Union which were met and have since been repeated by other Communist states. The demands of the Nagy regime in Hungary in 1956 were such that they could be met only at the risk of permitting the system to disintegrate, and so they were forcibly denied. By 1958, the Soviet Union was bombarded with demands, trivial and serious, from all directions. While Moscow continued to make its own demands upon other Communist states, they were more limited and less coercively executed. The balance in the flow of demands, however, was radically upset during the years 1957–61, as demands flowing in from the periphery gradually exceeded those flowing outward from the center, and a new political equilibrium started to assume shape in both the Communist world and Eastern Europe.

As the Eastern European states continued to assert the priority of their own national interests in one area after another in their dealings with the USSR, it was virtually axiomatic that, as they succeeded in resisting or trimming the demands made upon them by Moscow, they would reverse the flow of demands. The Council of Mutual Economic Aid, for example, which was originally conceived to facilitate the economic plundering of Eastern Europe by Moscow, was reorganized to control and arrest Soviet exploitation. No sooner had this happened than it was converted into a vehicle for draining economic resources from the Soviet Union to the Eastern European countries, as demands were made in Moscow for restitution, reparations, economic assistance, and commercial autonomy. Soon Eastern European states asserted the right to receive economic assistance from and engage in profitable commercial transactions with capitalist countries.

Economic demands upon the Soviet Union spilled over into the political and ideological realms, as individual states demanded and received greater internal autonomy. Soviet-modeled institutions were, in many cases, dissolved or modified, while Soviet-type ideological controls over the arts, sciences, professions, education, and information media were renounced in accordance with the local demands of each state, and the Cominform itself was abolished in response to these demands. The extent to which these demands were successfully asserted depended in large measure upon the power and leverage exercised in individual cases. No overt attempt was made to organize joint or concerted action in making demands upon Moscow until 1961, when China and Albania forged an anti-Soviet factional alliance. Up to that time, only the Soviet Union enjoyed the luxury of mobilizing other parties and states against another member of the Communist confraternity.

While it was Tito's defection in 1948 that pointed the way and Stalin's death in 1953 that created the opportunity, it was the denunciation of Stalin by Khrushchev in 1956 at the Twentieth Party Congress that gave initial impetus to pluralistic Communism, and it was the Sino-Soviet split, the détente with the United States (as a consequence of the Limited Nuclear Test Ban Treaty signed in July 1963), and Khrushchev's sudden and unceremonious ouster in October 1964 that created new opportunities and successively accelerated the fragmentation of the Communist bloc and the autonomization of internal regimes. The Sino-Soviet conflict enabled the smaller states of Eastern Europe to play the two Communist giants against one another, and thus afforded them the opportunity to develop greater autonomy *within* the Communist movement as both Peking and Moscow bid for their favor and support in their rivalry for leadership within the Communist movement. First Albania succeeded in using China to separate herself from Soviet paternalism, and then Rumania offered herself as a "neutral" mediator between Russia and China while simultaneously enlarging her own freedom of action.

If the Sino-Soviet conflict created the opportunity for the smaller Communist countries to expand their latitude of freedom from Soviet influence within the Communist world, the Test-Ban Treaty of July 1963 and the Soviet-American détente provided the further opportunity to expand their freedom of action *outside* the Communist world. The Soviet-American détente served to diminish both the U.S. threat to Moscow and the Soviet threat to the West and thus contributed to the progressive erosion of both NATO and the Warsaw Pact Organization. The expansion of internal autonomy spilled over into the realm of foreign policy in April 1964 when Rumania announced what amounted to a virtual declaration of independence. Her leaders refused to subordinate their economic development of the central coordination and planning of the bloc's Council of Mutual Economic Assistance and supinely accept its dictate that Rumania concentrate on agricultural development and spurn industrialization.

The Emergence of Interpenetrative Politics in the Soviet Bloc and the "Brezhnev Doctrine"

Khrushchev's ouster in October 1964 afforded dramatic illustration of the degree to which Soviet unilateral political penetration was giving way to interpenetration. Prominent Communist leaders of both ruling and nonruling parties openly complained that Khrushchev was removed without prior consultation or discussion with other Communist states and parties in accordance with the principle of "proletarian nationalism." Although Moscow initially rebutted these complaints as unwarranted intrusion into Soviet domestic affairs, the Soviet leaders later implicitly conceded that theoretically, at least, Soviet internal affairs were properly subject to the same kind of collective scrutiny as they had persistently maintained was the case with the domestic affairs of other Communist states.

The unexpected and controversial dismissal of Khrushchev thus accelerated even more rapidly the trends towards independence started in 1956 and widened even further the opportunities to exercise autonomy which the Sino-Soviet conflict and the Soviet-American détente had created. For the first time, Communist leaders in Communist countries and non-Communist countries demanded and received an explanation for a purely domestic Soviet decision. This represented a further development in the reverse flow of demands from the periphery to the center in the Communist world. Up to then, only Moscow exercised the right to interfere and intervene in the factional squabbles of other party-states, while changes in Moscow were immune to outside scrutiny and intervention. Khrushchev's removal signaled the rupturing of this immunity, as party leaders in Eastern Europe and in the West asserted demands for an explanation of what was normally a purely internal affair of the Soviet Union. The chorus of demands and criticisms which descended upon Khrushchev's detractors and successors resulted, first, in arresting what appeared to be a systematic design to downgrade and degrade Khrushchev by subjecting him to verbal abuse and invective in accordance with standard Soviet ritual, and, second, in accepting the demands for a detailed explanation of the sudden change in Soviet leadership.

These demands and the Soviet response may have established the precedent that other Communist leaders have a right to be informed of factional debates and differences in the Soviet hierarchy and a further right to be consulted in advance concerning changes in policy or person-nel. Implied in this demand is the threat to repudiate the leadership and policies of Moscow if decisions of this character are taken without such participation. A similar demand, together with an implied corresponding threat, was actually formulated by Italian Communist leader Palmiro Togliatti in his so-called testament of September 1964, issued shortly before his death. The Italian leader demanded, no less, that the Soviet leaders permit greater public visibility of the factional and policy differ-ences among Soviet leaders so that other Communist leaders might not be caught by surprise:

It is not correct to refer to the socialist countries (including the Soviet Union) as if everything were always going well in them. . . . The worst is to give the impression that everything is going well, while suddenly we find ourselves faced with the necessity of referring to difficult situations and ex-plaining them. . . . Some situations appear hard to understand. In many cases one has the impression there are differences of opinion among the leading groups, but one does not understand if this is really so and what the differences are. Perhaps it could be useful in some cases for the socialist countries also to conduct open debates on current problems, the leaders also taking part. Certainly, this would contribute to a growth in the authority and prestige of the socialist regime itself.[6]

However, no sooner had the Soviet leaders tacitly conceded that Moscow's internal affairs were subject to collective scrutiny than Ru-mania defied the entire principle that individual Communist states had to defer to the demands of the collective in shaping their internal and external policies. Rumania in the year following Khrushchev's ouster refused to accept a Soviet demand through the Warsaw Pact Organiza-tion that all of the Pact countries adopt uniform rules on military conscription, and instead she reduced the military obligation of her conscriptees to below the suggested level. In 1966, Rumania issued her first independent call for the dissolution of all military blocs and in the same year demanded that Moscow not employ nuclear weapons without consulting the other members of the Warsaw Treaty Organization. At the same time, Bucharest questioned the right of Moscow to select the Commander of the Warsaw-Treaty forces and suggested that the right to make this decision be rotated among the other members.[7] The same year saw Rumania concluding a number of important commercial arrange-ments with Western countries, which reduced her trade with the Soviet Union to about thirty percent of the total by 1968, thus further reducing Moscow's capability to take punitive action.

Beginning in 1964 and continuing to the present, the Rumanian leaders refused to condemn Red China and side with Moscow in the Sino-Soviet split and adopted a policy of pursuing friendly relations with *all* countries, including the United States. In apparent pursuance of this policy, Rumania has served as a diplomatic conduit between Washington and Hanoi; established normal diplomatic relations with West Germany; refused to condemn Israel as the aggressor in the Six-Day War; continued to maintain diplomatic relations with Israel while the other Communist countries, including Yugoslavia, severed theirs; and voted independently of the Soviet bloc on a number of issues in the United Nations.

During the first half of 1968, Rumania's defiance of the Soviet Union accelerated and was no doubt encouraged by developments in Prague. As the Czechoslovaks expanded their area of internal freedom, Bucharest expanded hers in foreign policy, and the two processes appeared to feed back upon one another. Thus, in rapid-fire order, Rumania withdrew from the Budapest Consultative Conference of Communist Parties (March 1, 1968), and a week later, at the Sofia meeting of the Warsaw-Pact powers, she refused to sign the "unanimous" declaration endorsing the draft treaty against the spread of nuclear weapons sponsored by Moscow and Washington. Rumania's objections to the draft treaty were similar to those raised by West Germany and other NATO powers, but she also demurred on grounds that it represented another infringement on the sovereignty of the smaller non-nuclear powers by Russia and America. This declaration marked the first time that a document of this character was issued without the signature of all the members of the Warsaw Pact, although the meeting was sufficiently important to attract all the party chiefs, premiers, foreign ministers and defense ministers of the seven allied powers.[8]

This was followed by Bucharest's refusal to participate in the Dresden Conference of Warsaw Powers and its crude threat to intervene in Czechoslovakia (March 23–24, 1968).[9] She similarly refused to participate in the Warsaw Meeting of the Alliance (Prague also refused to attend) on July 14–15, 1968, which issued an even more threatening ultimatum to the Dubcek regime, while Warsaw-Pact forces were deliberately delaying their departure from Czechoslovak territory, although their summer military exercises (which Rumania refused to join) had been completed.[10] During this period, Rumanian leaders publicly encouraged the Czechoslovak reformers, and at the height of the crisis, President Ceausescu offered to lend his personal presence in Prague in a joint gesture of defiance. Dubcek prudently declined the offer, but after the Cierna and Bratislava meetings with the Soviet leadership, Ceausescu followed Tito to Prague in a display of solidarity. To Moscow, it would seem that the prewar Little Entente was being resurrected as a hostile grouping of Communist states in its erstwhile placid garden of client and vassal states. After the Soviet intervention, Rumania continued its gestures of defiance: she condemned the invasion, demanded that all Communist states be masters of their own affairs, vowed never to allow Warsaw-Pact forces on Soviet territory, placed the entire country on the alert, and threatened to actively resist any possible Soviet encroachment on its sovereignty.

This pattern of interpenetrative politics in the Communist world is ideologically legitimized by the principle of "proletarian internationalism," whose most recent operational manifestation is the so-called "Brezhnev Doctrine," which, in effect, declares that certain internal state matters are not shielded by the doctrine of state sovereignty but are the legitimate concern of the entire "socialist commonwealth."[11] Despite its outrageous implications, the "Brezhnev doctrine," like the "multilateral" invasion of Czechoslovakia, represents a sort of progress over previous Soviet policy. The "Brezhnev doctrine" legitimizes the right of the collective "socialist community" to intervene in the affairs of any individual socialist state, including the Soviet Union. This is surely an advance over the previous practice of "proletarian internationalism," which gave to Moscow a sort of monopolistic guardianship over the Communist movement, entitling it to unilaterally intervene, with or without consultation.

Thus, although the "Brezhnev doctrine" was enunciated by Moscow primarily to provide Soviet intervention in Czechoslovakia with an ideological fig leaf in the form of multilateralism, "multilateral" intervention in the affairs of small Communist states may logically lead to multilateral *demands* for intervention in Soviet affairs. Although Peking has condemned the "Brezhnev doctrine," the Chinese leaders have been insisting since about 1957 that they have a right under the doctrine of "proletarian internationalism" to call attention to Soviet doctrinal errors and to even rectify matters if necessary in the interests of world socialism.[12] While the Soviet leaders have rejected this particular Chinese impertinence and have sought protection behind the shield of "state sovereignty," it should be noted that the "Brezhnev doctrine" would not only assert a right to collective intervention in Chinese affairs, but also provide a basis for *legitimating a demand* that the Soviet Union accept collective intervention, although in practice, such an intervention remains remote.[13]

De-Stalinization and Desatellitization: Processes of Diversification or Dissolution?

Before the Soviet invasion and occupation of Czechoslovakia, the countries of Eastern Europe could be grouped into four distinct categories in reference to their relationship to the Soviet Union: (1) Yugoslavia, an independent, virtually "neutralist" and "nonaligned" Communist state that exercised complete sovereignty in its domestic and foreign policy; (2) Albania, an independent, anti-Soviet (anti-revisionist) Communist state, ideologically allied to but not under the control of China or any other Communist state; (3) the Warsaw-Pact countries of Poland, Czechoslovakia, Bulgaria, East Germany, and Hungary, which are residual satellite states, or, more properly, client states of Moscow;[14] (4) Rumania, a dissident and noncooperative member of the Warsaw Pact and the Comecon, a "neutral" in the Sino-Soviet conflict, and quasi-independent in its foreign policy. After the invasion of Czechoslovakia, both Yugoslavia and Rumania were further alienated from Moscow and the bloc, Albania formally withdrew from the Warsaw Pact, and Czechoslovakia was returned to vassalage, while Poland was forced into greater dependence on the Soviet Union and, like East Germany, was threatened with de facto diplomatic isolation. The alignments in Eastern Europe now coincided more closely with the national self-interests of individual Communist states rather than with ideological affinities. Thus, the three Communist states that were openly opposed to and hostile to the occupation of Czechoslovakia represent three *doctrinally* different regimes. Albania is a neo-Stalinist Communist state, and Yugoslavia is a "liberal" Communist state, while Rumania is doctrinally very close to Soviet orthodoxy. In foreign policy, Yugoslavia is "neutralist" and "nonaligned" and Rumania is a Warsaw Pact member, while Albania is allied to Moscow's rival, Peking. Yet all three are engaged in informal and indirect consultations in their opposition to any attempt by the Soviet leaders to apply the "Brezhnev doctrine" to their countries.

The current ideological diversity and political cleavages in Eastern Europe are the consequences of two distinct but closely interrelated and often confused processes—de-Stalinization and desatellitization. Although both concepts are defined in terms of a reaction against the starting point of each process and hence by now have assumed a more positive character in each case, it might still be useful to employ these terms in spite of their etymological obsolescence and inappropriateness. De-Stalinization refers primarily to the dismantling of Stalinist institutions and practices in domestic life, and it originally closely followed the de-Stalinization taking place in the Soviet Union itself. Desatellitization refers to the process whereby the individual countries of Eastern Europe gradually reasserted their autonomy and independence from Soviet control, a process that is still continuing. Both processes have contributed to the process of substantively transforming the principle of "proletarian internationalism" from a doctrine justifying unilateral Soviet penetration into the sociopolitical systems of other Communist states into one justifying multilateral and reciprocal intervention, or interpenetration.

Desatellitization has been a universal phenomenon, but de-Stalinization has not involved all countries. At a certain stage of development the
two processes came into conflict, since some countries asserted their
independence in order to retain certain Stalinist institutions and norms
or to resist their complete dismantling. In Albania, for example, desatellitization has resulted in the intensification of Stalinist norms rather than
greater internal liberalization. De-Stalinization was also resisted in varying degrees in Rumania, Bulgaria, and Czechoslovakia, although it had
recently been almost completely repudiated in Czechoslovakia. De-Stalinization is, in effect, a process of internal liberalization, a process that
has progressed at varying tempos in Eastern Europe, sometimes faster
and sometimes slower than in the Soviet Union itself. The two most
independent countries of Eastern Europe reflect opposite tendencies
with reference to Stalinism, with Yugoslavia the most distant in its
departure from Stalinist doctrines and Albania the least.

The terms "de-Stalinization" and "desatellitization" are thus no longer
entirely accurate in describing the manifold transformations taking place
in Eastern Europe. Both processes, it is now clear in retrospect, were but
transitional episodes in the drive for greater autonomy internally and
greater independence in foreign policy. In the case of de-Stalinization,
the process had moved into the phase of de-Sovietization in some
countries and could eventuate even in de-Communization, whereas desatellitization might logically result not only in withdrawal from the Soviet
alliance and neutralization, but eventually culminate in a reversal of
alliances. Either development would affect the balance of power between
East and West, and both taken together could alter the balance irreversibly. All of these fears and hazards, which were repeatedly and candidly
expressed by Moscow, Warsaw, and East Germany, congealed to trigger
the Soviet occupation of Czechoslovakia.

It is not always easy to determine which of the two processes—internal autonomy or independence in foreign policy—is perceived by the
Soviet leadership as posing the greatest danger to its interests. Undoubtedly the Soviet leaders are sharply divided on this point, as they are on
many others, and it is also quite possible that the relative danger of the
threat of each process varies over time and from one country to another.
The Soviet leadership might thus tolerate varying degrees of autonomy
and independence, which would in turn depend upon their perception of
the strategic importance of the country concerned or upon the reliability
and prudence of its leadership, which further involves an intuitive
calculation of the historical images of Russia prevailing in each country.
The two processes pose distinct, if not entirely unrelated, sets of dangers

and risks for Moscow, which seem to coincide not only with the two main purposes of the Soviet presence in Eastern Europe but also with the two major factional cleavages in the Soviet leadership. Thus growing internal autonomy directly challenges the ideological values and norms of the Soviet system and indirectly threatens the security of the Soviet State, while independence in foreign policy directly erodes Soviet power in world affairs and indirectly constitutes a challenge to Soviet ideological goals and values. Concomitantly, some Soviet leaders, especially those who are ideologically conservative, are most likely to be disturbed by deviations and departures from the Soviet system, while others might be agitated more by the degree of independence asserted in foreign policy, and still others might find both processes equally unpalatable and any combination of the two downright intolerable. Aside from factors such as inertia, factional paralysis, and the impact of cumulative developments, these conflicting perceptions of the "main" danger may account for the extraordinary self-restraint exercised by Moscow towards Rumania's growing independence in foreign policy and her intolerance of developments in Czechoslovakia.

While the Soviet leaders have accommodated and adjusted to the impulse of the Eastern European states to manage their own affairs, as long as they remain "socialist," the absence of any common or universal criteria of what constitutes "socialism" since Khrushchev's denunciation of Stalin in 1956 has created a wide area of ambiguity which has caused anxiety in Moscow and inspired boldness and innovation in Eastern European capitals. What started out as "de-Stalinization" was soon legitimized in the doctrine of "separate roads to socialism," but it quickly became evident that the "separate roads" doctrine created both logical possibilities and practical opportunities for subverting and displacing the social orders inspired and established by the Soviet Union. Thus was born the Soviet equivalent of the "falling dominoes" theory: de-Stalinization leads to "separate roads," which proliferate into various "national deviations," which may in turn inspire "modern revisionism," which is but a prelude to "social democracy" that quickly degenerates into "bourgeois democracy" and the "restoration of capitalism."

Soviet Options Before the Invasion of Czechoslovakia: Lost Opportunities

It is now apparent in retrospect that the Czechoslovak Crisis confronted the Soviet leaders with their moment of truth in Eastern Europe: to intervene or not to intervene? Either course would have produced unpalatable and distasteful consequences. Clearly the Soviet Union had reached an important crossroads in its relationship with Eastern Europe.

Before the intervention in Czechoslovakia, the Soviet position in Eastern Europe had been clearly slipping in response partly to the apparent erosion of NATO and the diminution of the U.S. threat to the Communist system. Either the Soviet empire was on the verge of dissolution as Rumania virtually seceded from the Warsaw alliance and Czechoslovak liberalization appeared to be irresistible and threatening to infect all of Eastern Europe, or it was on the brink of a fundamental transformation. The transformation of relationships could have assumed one of three forms:

1. The Warsaw Pact and the Comecon could be converted to an authentic socialist "commonwealth of nations," in which the individual members would be allowed a wide latitude of internal deviation from the Soviet norms of socialism, exercise greater freedom, and engage in trade and cultural relations with the West, while remaining tightly bound to the Soviet Union in a purely defensive alliance. Such a transformation would presuppose a continuation and expansion of the détente, a tacit disavowal of ideological agressiveness in foreign policy, and give greater form and shape to the new commonwealth as a purely regional association, in which the interests of the smaller members would no longer be sacrificed to those of the Soviet Union in the name of the bogus principle of "proletarian internationalism" or subordinated to purely Soviet "Great-Power diplomacy" in its dealings with the United States or Communist China. The chief objections to such a transformation before August 1968 were that it threatened to isolate East Germany, render Poland even more dependent upon Russia vis à vis West Germany, and deprive the Soviet Union of some useful levers and pressures in dealing with the German problem, the United States, and Communist China.

2. The spontaneous *devolution* of the Warsaw Pact, the Comecon, and other multilateral organizations might occur; they could be replaced with a series of bilateral and trilateral agreements. The Soviet Union could make periodic ad hoc adjustments to the situation, allowing the natural interests of each state to more or less shape its internal development and its individual relationship with the Soviet Union and with the outside world. Soviet leaders would have to forego the compulsion to force every Eastern European state to take a policy stand on each and every facet of Moscow's global foreign policy or to allow the Soviet leaders to determine ideological orthodoxy on internal matters. In matters remote to the interests of the smaller states (for example, U.S.–Soviet competition in such countries as Africa and Latin America), they would be permitted to remain uninvolved. Global policy would be properly the province of the Global Powers and not of their client or

allied states. The United States, for example, has learned to live with some of its allied and client states who are reluctant or even opposed to becoming involved in America's global enterprises. Czechoslovakia's internal innovations and Rumania's semi-independent foreign policy were clearly the prototypes of the kinds of behavior the Soviet leaders would have to live with in this kind of arrangement. Moscow would rely upon a common ideology, intersecting interests, the prudence and good sense of the smaller countries, and the reservoir of goodwill towards Moscow that would flow from such a policy to become the foundations of a new relationship. Under these conditions, the relationship of the individual member states with the Soviet Union could vary considerably, as would their relations with one another. The artificiality of imposed "fraternal" relations would be replaced by something more uncertain but perhaps more durable and natural.

The Soviet leaders found this second alternative to be clearly unacceptable, and the invasion of Czechoslovakia was the immediate consequence. A choice of this alternative would involve all of the hazards of the first alternative and furthermore undermine the foundations of the existing sociopolitical structure at home through Moscow's implicit legitimization of all changes taking place in Czechoslovakia and those that might take place elsewhere. The possible feedback effects into the Soviet Union were apparently too much to contemplate.

3. The Soviet Empire could be reconstituted as a "sphere of influence" or domination. Wherever and whenever necessary, naked force and fear would replace reliance on the shibboleths of ideology, pliable local leaders, and a common social system, in order to preserve Soviet control. This would clearly require a partial restoration of Stalinesque hegemonic controls in Eastern Europe. But the restoration of Stalinist controls in Eastern Europe would inevitably run the risk of their recrudescence at home. Just as the liberalization of Communism in Czechoslovakia threatened to infect the Soviet Union itself, the reappearance of Stalinist practices in Eastern Europe would probably encourage residual Stalinists in Soviet society to agitate for similar measures at home.

The Soviet leaders apparently opted for this third alternative as a temporary stop-gap device, more as a *threat* to impose Soviet military controls in all Eastern Europe rather than as a full-fledged policy. But in the process of selecting this option, even on a temporary basis, they may have effectively foreclosed the other two. It would seem that the Soviet Union by its action in Czechoslovakia has not only expended whatever might have remained of the reservoir of goodwill associated the historical, cultural, and ideological associations of the past, but it has reduced its options to only two: preserving its position by force, threat, and periodic intervention or allowing its control of Eastern Europe to completely disintegrate. For the moment, the Soviet Union has enhanced the credibility of its determination to use its immense power to control its immediate environment, but simultaneously it has restored its reputation for diplomatic perfidy, impetuous brutality, and psychological insecurity. Not only the Communist world, but the Communist states of Eastern Europe seem irrevocably split. Although there is no discernible military threat in sight from any quarter in Europe, the Soviet Union in 1970 is in military occupation of no less than four Eastern European countries (Poland, East Germany, Hungary, and Czechoslovakia). Albania has unilaterally withdrawn from the Warsaw Pact as a result of the Czechoslovak crisis, while Rumania refuses to allow Warsaw-Pact forces to maneuver on its territory and refuses to participate in their exercises elsewhere. Yugoslavia has never belonged to the Warsaw Pact, and at the height of the Czechoslovak crisis it announced its determination, together with Rumania, to resist by armed force any attempt on the part of Russia to occupy her territories.

The liberalization in Czechoslovakia has been arrested and is being reversed. Soviet leaders have announced not only their intention to keep Soviet troops on the Czechoslovak–West German frontier indefinitely, but are also imposing their dictates on purely internal Czechoslovak affairs, and they have refused to allow Prague to expand its trade relations outside the Soviet bloc. Like Hungary, Czechoslovakia has been retroverted from clientage to vassalage. While the initial reaction in the other countries of Eastern Europe was fear and apprehension combined with outrage and shame, they have been given notice that Moscow will not hesitate to reduce its fraternal allies to vassalage if the Soviet Union disapproves of their internal and external policies. Nevertheless, as the initial shock wears off and the Czechoslovaks continue their passive resistance and active noncooperation, the people of Eastern Europe are likely to become more restive than quiescent. Disturbances might even spread among disaffected and alienated Soviet intellectuals, scientists, and students. The moral position of Polish party First Secretary Gomulka has been probably irretrievably damaged since August 1968 when he stabbed his defenseless neighbor Czechoslovakia in the back with neither justification nor provocation. Poland, as a consequence, has been more tightly riveted to dependence upon the Soviet Union; it has become completely surrounded by states under Soviet military occupation, and its people have become even more thoroughly alienated from Moscow. It may be that Gomulka sold his country's honor mainly to gain a tactical advantage over his internal rival, General

Moczar, and in return for a mess of potage established a precedent for a future Soviet military occupation of Poland in the guise of "multilateral" action.

The Soviet military occupation of Czechoslovakia ushers Soviet relations with Eastern Europe into a new transitional phase—a phase of Soviet military control. This new phase is Stalinesque, but it should not be confused with the earlier Stalinist period. During the Stalin era, Moscow relied not only upon the Soviet military presence, but upon a common ideology, upon the reliability and servility of the local Communist party, and, most importantly, upon the prestige of Soviet power and Stalin's charisma. This is no longer even residually the case in Rumania, Yugoslavia, Albania, and Czechoslovakia (in spite of the occupation). Communist parties in Eastern European countries will continue to pay greater and greater attention to national needs rather than Soviet dictates and interests, although the danger of a desperate Soviet intervention has increased. But interventionism itself is a wasting asset and cannot be sustained indefinitely, and thus the Soviet military occupation of Czechoslovakia simultaneously signifies a Soviet determination to reintensify its control, but at the same time, risks contracting its range of control.

Thus, for the immediate future, we can expect the Soviet leaders to limit the necessity for intervention by both warnings and inducements. The fragmentation of national interests in the Soviet bloc demonstrated by the Warsaw-Pact invasion of Czechoslovakia makes it imperative for the Soviet leaders to formulate separate policies towards each country tailored to the peculiarities of each set of relationships. And increasingly these policies will be shaped by factors such as ideological loyalty, mutual interests, demands and claims, the range of levers and pressures available, and the degree of importance each Eastern European country has to Soviet interests. Soviet leaders may thus further de-ideologize their dealings with Eastern European countries, recognizing that bloc unity can no longer function as a credible operative norm of behavior, and this is bound to result in the cynical manipulation of differences among Eastern European countries by Soviet policy.

Among other functions, the Communist subsystem of states ("socialist commonwealth") also served as a conflict-resolving and conflict-containing mechanism, and as long as the entire Communist bloc was confronted by an overriding common threat and motivated by a common higher purpose, these local conflicts could be subordinated to a higher mission in the name of bloc unity. But, just as the weakening of NATO in the face of a receding Soviet threat has resulted in the revival of temporarily submerged local conflicts (the Greek-Turkish dispute over Cyprus, for example), the erosion of the Soviet bloc in Eastern Europe threatens to unleash the latent conflicts in Eastern Europe which antedate the advent of Communism. Many Eastern European states have serious territorial claims against one another and against the Soviet Union. Some of these are purely historical in character, while others represent the failure to correlate political frontiers with ethnographic boundaries, while still others are reflections of incompleted processes of national unification or arrested demands for national self-determination. With respect to Poland and Rumania, sensitive territorial issues may become an increasingly overt factor in their relations with Moscow. Soviet leaders may have to pay more or risk more as the case may be in individual instances. This also probably means that Moscow may pay greater attention to latent conflicts between individual countries (the Rumanian-Hungarian dispute over Transylvania, for example) in the calculation of its policies as it searches for new levers and pressures to exert its will in Eastern Europe.

The Soviet leaders are still confronted with the awesome alternatives of dissolution or transformation, but their range of options as far as transformation goes are now severely limited. The audacious attempt to transform a collection of vassal states into an ideological commonwealth of socialist states bound together by a common ideology and common sociopolitical system has failed. The primary reason for the failure was the inability of the Soviet system to transform itself and adapt itself to the transformations taking place in Eastern Europe. In 1970 it is clearer than ever that the fate of the Soviet system is irrevocably tied to the nature of the Soviet relationship to Eastern Europe.

Eastern Europe and the Soviet Future: Transformation or Dissolution?

Soviet leadership, by its invasion of Czechoslovakia and its enunciation of the "Brezhnev doctrine," in effect, has conceded that the Soviet system in its existing form cannot be preserved while its extensions are being dismantled and revamped in Eastern Europe. Eastern Europe came into being as an ideological and sociopolitical appendage of the Soviet system; now alterations in the appendage threaten to extend themselves into Soviet society. This may be the case, irrespective of Soviet policy. The reinstitution of Stalinist controls in Eastern Europe would probably result in their reappearance at home; to allow internal innovations in Eastern Europe would be to legitimize the raising of similar issues in the Soviet Union. To permit the Eastern European states to break away from Soviet control would probably plunge the USSR into a new "time of troubles," marked by collective paranoia, insecurity, instability, and even fragmentation. And this at a time when the Chinese danger looms on the Eastern horizon while the West German "revanchists" are becoming more insidious and clever in their approach to Eastern Europe.

In the short run, the Soviet leaders will continue to call the tune in Eastern Europe, but in the long run, the shape of the Soviet future will be determined by events in Eastern Europe. The currents of both nationalism, nurtured by two decades of oppressive Soviet control, and modernization, accelerated by two decades of Communist transformations, are forces which the Soviet leadership can no longer domesticate. Unlike Stalin and Lenin, who were young, vigorous, powerful, and ruthless personalities perhaps capable of successfully surmounting such forces, the Soviet leadership in 1970 is made up largely of aging, unimaginative, and fumbling leaders whose future is severely circumscribed by nature. The Soviet Union is on the brink of a massive generational shift in power, which will probably take place during the decade of the seventies. Unlike the 1970 leadership, the new generation of leaders will be largely a product of the post-Stalinist era. They will not be psychologically crippled nor morally corrupted by the cruel Stalinist legacy; neither will they be ideologically committed to the residual corpse of Stalinist mythology, nor will they be obligated by self-interest to preserve and perpetuate the Soviet system in the form in which they inherit it. This new leadership, while it may be conditioned by the specter of the Chinese threat, will not be conditioned by the fears and anxieties of the Stalinist era. Thus it may be more receptive to innovations at home and in Eastern Europe and be more flexible in its relationships. How this next generation of Soviet leaders will repudiate or reaffirm the Soviet past and present remains an enigma, but the shift in generational leadership will create new opportunities and possibilities.

The key to Soviet survival is thus no longer simply the transformation of its relationship with Eastern Europe but its own internal transformation. Upon the next crop of Soviet leaders will fall the burden of avoiding, on the one hand, the reimposition of totalitarian controls at home that would accompany a resurrection of Soviet hegemonic control in Eastern Europe, and, on the other, avoiding being plunged into a new period of internal instability and insecurity that would be unleashed by a successful Eastern European revolt against Soviet domination. And the key to this transformation is to de-universalize Soviet ideology and redefine the legitimacy of the Soviet system so that it rests upon purely domestic foundations and requires no external props for support.

But as Marxism-Leninism is de-universalized by objective events, if not by Soviet fiat, the Soviet Union must resign itself to becoming a terminal multinational state rather than the nucleus of a future universal Communist state. This will require that it search for a new equilibrium between the dominant Russian nation and the other Soviet nationalities, and demonstrate that their national interests, aspirations, and identities are better served as parts of a multinational commonwealth rather than as independent nation-states.

Whatever course the Soviet Union may take, as time goes on, the ideological bond of Communism will continue to erode, and Eastern European countries will become more European and less "Communist." In 1970, everywhere in Eastern Europe, in stark contrast to the Soviet Union, Communism appears as a thin, almost transparent veneer, ready to be shed the moment the climate is felicitous. Fundamental and far-reaching transformations are still imminent in Eastern Europe, and, perhaps at least through the 1970s, these changes will take place in the name of Communism while simultaneously subverting it. While similar changes may also take place in the Soviet Union, the necessity or desire to disavow Communism as an ideology may not be nearly as intense. Only its de-universalization may be required. After all, Soviet society and Marxism-Leninism are Russian creations and thus are not as incompatible with Russian nationalism as they are with the nationalisms of non-Soviet countries. It must be remembered that whereas the Communist system is an indigenous Russian phenomenon, in Eastern Europe it is an alien, imported system imposed from the outside by force. Thus while Communism and nationalism may be fused into a "Soviet patriotism" in the Soviet Union, this is by no means an assured amalgam in Eastern Europe.

Communism is now irrevocably associated with Russian and/or Soviet imperialism, domination, and control, and while this may have a minimal vitiating effect in countries traditionally pro-Russian, it may simultaneously be a barrier to its complete acceptance, assimilation, and adaptation in the traditionally anti-Russian countries of Eastern Europe. At least the 1970s must pass before permanent trends are conclusively discernible, when a new generation of leaders and citizens make their appearance in both the Soviet Union and Eastern Europe.

11

East European Relations With the West

Wolfgang Klaiber

11. East European Relations With the West

Wolfgang Klaiber

In this modern world of mass communications and transport, the field of international relations has grown into a multitude of interactions between states, carried on at various levels from government to the private citizen. The objectives of international relations have diversified. In addition to the age-old objectives of diplomacy, governments spend millions of dollars each year in efforts to improve the image of their countries abroad via radio and television, newspapers and magazines, public displays and artistic performances, as well as through foreign aid. To a large extent, international relations has become the art of "winning friends and influencing people," reflecting the political phenomenon of the twentieth century that man—the common man—is the center of this universe.

This art has become the more important as two conflicting ideo-political systems—that of the Communist East and that of the capitalist West—have sought to influence the allegiance and political development of the "Third World." They also, for that matter, have sought to influence each other, particularly in Europe.

The Legacy of World War II

The termination of the Second World War left Europe divided into two ideologically hostile camps. The Soviet Union extended its political and military control over Eastern Europe and imposed Communist governments upon the several countries in the area ruled by agents of Moscow. The United States, meanwhile, maintained and bolstered its forces in Western Europe in order to ward off further Soviet expansion. Two alliance systems came into being—NATO in the West and the

Soviet bloc in the East (formalized as the Warsaw Pact in 1955)—and they still endure in 1970. Germany, divided into East and West pending a peace treaty, symbolizes this division of Europe and embodies the major international problems still outstanding in that part of the world.

This legacy continues to impose the basic parameters which govern the conduct of international relations and condition the policy objectives of European nations on both sides of the ideological divide. Each side is tied by a special relationship (based on different criteria) to a super power; each side has formed its own economic bloc; each has built tremendous military establishments, fearing aggression from the other; and each seeks to influence and change the other side, if not toward its own image, then toward its own politico-strategic interests.

And yet, there have been phenomenal changes in the conduct of Europe's international relations over the past twenty years. Under Stalin, the doctrine of the inevitability of war between Communism and capitalism, together with Western declarations of intent to "liberate" the captive nations, helped to isolate Eastern Europe behind an impenetrable "Iron Curtain." During the remainder of Stalin's life, save for some trade, there was scarcely any interaction between Eastern and Western Europe—only radio waves and propaganda-laden balloons could penetrate the Iron Curtain. The United States, for its part, sought to restrict the trade policies of its West European allies to the effect that no goods of any strategic value would be made available to the Soviet bloc.

With Stalin's death, a new era opened in Europe's international relations. Khrushchev abrogated the doctrine of the inevitability of war and proclaimed the necessity of peaceful coexistence between the two ideological blocs.[1] In 1955, the Geneva summit meeting of the Big Four (U.S., U.K., France, and the Soviet Union) failed to settle any of the major European problems leftover from the Second World War, but it created a "spirit" that helped to thaw some of the frigid attitudes on both sides of the Iron Curtain and raised the possibility of improving relations between East and West. This spirit dissipated in the brutal suppression of the Hungarian revolt, but it never evaporated completely. Trade through the Iron Curtain increased from a trickle to a slow but steady flow as West Europeans narrowed their definition of "strategic" goods. Poland received U.S. agricultural aid in recognition and as encouragement of the defiance of the Soviet Union which it demonstrated in the accession of Wladyslaw Gomulka to the party leadership and his embarkation on a "Polish road to Communism."

Intermittent crises in Europe or involving West European powers in conflict with the USSR (Berlin in 1958 and 1961, the Middle East in 1956), alternated with attempts at détente and mutual understanding between East and West (such as East-West disarmament conferences and the meeting between Khrushchev and Eisenhower at Camp David). Neither side gave way on issues in conflict between them. Cold war continued to prevail in Europe; yet some communication had been reestablished between East and West, and the international environment was improved thereby.

It was after the Cuban Missile Crisis that the Soviet Union began to seek genuine détente with the United States in Europe, as well as in other parts of the world. The Limited Nuclear Test Ban Treaty was signed in 1963, and the "hot line" was established to connect the White House with the Kremlin, in order to make the world safer from destruction.

During the détente period, East-West relations improved rapidly in Europe. The Soviet Union had announced an ambitious economic development program at the Twenty-Second CPSU Congress in October 1961, which was aimed at overtaking the United States in production and consumption by 1980. Within less than two years, however, it became amply clear not only in the Kremlin but also in the "satellite" capitals that the economic growth of the Soviet bloc was declining. Poor harvest yields throughout the bloc in 1963 compounded the decline in industrial growth and forced the Soviets to import wheat from the United States and Canada. The realization of the Soviet Union's ambitious economic goals would require not only decentralizing economic reforms, but also large-scale technological help from the West.

Détente, economic reform, de-Stalinization, and East European nationalism conspired with the eruption of the Sino-Soviet ideological conflict to erode the unity of the Soviet bloc during the 1960s. Albania withdrew from the Soviet bloc to join the Chinese side. Rumania, in the first in a long series of more or less ostentatious departures from Soviet policy, rebelled against Khrushchev's plan to integrate the economies of the bloc countries into a supra-national Comecon structure.

The breakdown of the "monolith" helped the image of Communism in the West generally and of the Soviet bloc particularly and increased opportunities for East-West interactions. Western businessmen were eager to find new markets in the East, and Western governments perceived new policy options that might eventually lead to the bridging of the ideological divide. The East European governments, for their part, appeared to be gaining increasing freedom of maneuver in the international realm, at least in those areas of foreign policy where their interests did not conflict with those of the Soviet Union.

The major problems of Europe, particularly the German problem, still were not solved. Both sides appeared to feel, however, that they could coexist on the basis of the political and territorial status quo—the mutual recognition by the United States and the USSR of each other's sphere of influence, the continuing division of Germany, and the inviolability of existing frontiers in Europe. Basically, this was the status quo the Soviet bloc sought to legitimize and the West sought to change. Ironically, on the one hand, détente between East and West was possible only on the basis of the mutual (if only tacit) recognition of the status quo, and, on the other hand, détente would inevitably generate movement to change the status quo.

During the détente of the 1960s, the "Iron Curtain" was lifted and "bridge building" policies brought movement across the ideological divide. French policy-makers (under General de Gaulle) envisioned a future Europe "from the Atlantic to the Urals," a Europe of fatherlands no longer divided. West Germany launched an *"Ostpolitik"* designed to isolate East Germany within the Soviet bloc through rapprochement with the other East European Communist states in the hope that somehow this would speed the day of reunification. On both sides of the continent, the relevance of the military alliance systems (NATO and the Warsaw Pact) to the security of Europe came under debate, and the search for independence (personified by France in the West and Rumania in the East) strained the respective alliance structures. Increasing political, economic, and cultural interactions between East and West were weaving ties of interdependence and providing the foundation for this further evolution in Europe's international relations.

East-West Governmental Interactions

During the "Khrushchev era" the state of East-West relations can be said to have evolved from one of mutual disdain to one of outward respect accompanied by expectations of mutual gain. This evolution is reflected in the increase of intergovernmental interactions aimed at establishing contacts and reaching agreement on cooperation.

Illustrative of this new trend is an increasing number of high-level ministerial visits exchanged between the Soviet bloc countries and the West. Thus, in December 1963, Belgium's Foreign Minister Henri Spaak traveled to Poland, and the Polish Foreign Minister Adam Rapacki returned his visit in February 1965. The visit by Czechoslovakia's Foreign Minister Vaclav David to France in November 1964 was the first one made by a Foreign Minister of that country to the West since the Czechoslovak Communist Party gained control. In September 1965, Polish Premier Josef Cyrankiewicz went to France for discussions with President de Gaulle, and the French President returned the visit in September 1967. Bulgaria's Deputy Premier Stanko Todorov voyaged to

TABLE 1

Governmental Interactions Between the Soviet Bloc Countries and the U.S., U.K., West Germany, France, and Italy

Type of Interaction	Bulgaria	Czechoslo-vakia	East Germany	Hungary	Poland	Rumania
Ministerial Visits						
1957–60	1	1	1	0	9	0
1961–64	4	2	0	1	8	8
Trade Missions						
1957–60	2	3	2	3	4	2
1961–64	10	5	2	7	14	14
Trade Agreements						
1957–60	1	3	5	2	8	2
1961–64	14	6	2	8	17	16

SOURCE: Foreign Policy Research Institute, *Changing Trends in East Central Europe and Implications for U.S. Security* (Philadelphia: University of Pennsylvania Foreign Policy Research Institute, 1967), II, 321–26.

Great Britain and France in February 1965. Italy's President Guiseppe Saragat came to Warsaw for a three-day stay in October 1965. In March 1968, Paris was host to Hungary's Premier Jeno Fock and Foreign Minister Janos Peter. President Nixon's visit on August 2, 1969, to Bucharest established a new precedent for U.S. foreign policy. These are only some of the top-level East-West personal contacts which helped to improve and intensify the relations between East and West.

Table 1 gives a partial numerical indication of the increase in East-West governmental interactions in two consecutive four-year periods (1957–60 and 1961–64) at the beginning of the new trend in East-West relations which has accelerated since 1964. These figures cover only the governmental interactions between the Soviet bloc and the major Western countries, but they are representative of the intensification of relations between the bloc and other West European countries as well. The large increase in the number of trade missions exchanged and trade agreements concluded between the countries of the Soviet bloc and the West provided the basis for a rapid growth of trade and other trans-bloc economic cooperation.

East-West Economic Interactions

Since 1960, the quantitative volume of East-West trade has increased very significantly, although (except for Rumania and Bulgaria) the basic patterns of trade flow have remained virtually unchanged. For the West European countries, trade with the Soviet bloc amounts to only three to five percent of their total world trade. As for the East European coun-

Soviet Bloc Trade with OECD Europe as Percent of Total World Trade
(In Millions of U.S. Dollars)

	1958		1962		1964		1965		1966		1967	
	OECD	%	OECD	%	OECD	%	OECD	%	OECD	%	OECD	%
Bulgaria	65.9	9	169.1	10	243.6	12	349.2	15	501.9	18	480.6	16
Czechoslovakia	413.8	14	519.9	12	635.2	12	759.4	14	879.8	16	852.9	15
DDR	699.2	20	695.9	15	887.5	16	1010.3	17	1096.5	17	1106.8	16
Hungary	274.7	21	366.8	16	509.5	18	549.4	18	632.9	20	696.1	20
Poland	614.2	27	794.0	23	836.7	20	968.6	21	1114.2	23	1205.6	23
Rumania	158.4	17	406.0	23	488.9	23	560.3	26	662.0	28	959.4	33
USSR	1012.5	12	1706.8	13	1759.8	11	1983.9	12	2093.0	12	2510.4	14

NOTES: Table includes all Organization for Economic Cooperation and Development countries except the United States, Canada, Japan, and Finland. Statistics have been drawn from the following sources: International Monetary Fund and International Bank for Reconstruction and Development, *Direction of International Trade, 1958–62* (New York: United Nations Secretariat, Statistical Office, 1962); OECD, *Foreign Trade: Series C Trade by Commodities, 1964, 1965, 1966, 1967* (Paris: OECD); *Statistisches Jahrbuch der Deutschen Demokratischen Republik, 1968* (East Berlin: Staatsverlag der Deutschen Demokratischen Republik, 1968).

tries, the relative proportions of their trade with the West are greater, but only Rumania and Bulgaria have doubled the percentage of their total trade conducted with the West. (See Table 2.) The Soviet Union remains the most important single trading partner of East European countries.

Under Communism, trade with the West has posed special problems for the East European countries. Their currencies are not convertible, even within the Soviet bloc (let alone in the West.) Thus, unable to buy Western currencies, their trade with the West is constrained by what they can sell on the world market. East European manufactures, however, are so inferior to those of the West in quality and design as to make their marketing potential in hard-currency areas very low. With the exception of East Germany and Czechoslovakia, East European exports to the West are predominantly composed of agricultural goods and raw materials, which are, for the most part, already in short supply in the Soviet bloc.

Thus, the very fact that East-West trade has risen so sharply during the last ten years is significant. This would not have been possible without the adoption of policies in the West which facilitated trade with the East. Among the more consequential of these policies was the extension of long-term credits to East Europeans for the purchase of production plants. (These plants presumably would pay for themselves in exports to hard-currency areas.) This policy of extending long-term credits unfolded in 1964, and it represents an interesting undeclared reversal of the Berne Agreement, signed in 1961 by seven of the largest creditor nations in the West, which limited credits to no more than five years.[2]

Another more recent development promising long-range benefits to Eastern Europe's industrial development and trade is the growing number of joint production and marketing agreements between Eastern and Western Europe. Beginning in 1964, these agreements mushroomed into a network of East-West interdependence, involving research, investment, and licensing, as well as a "division of labor" in production and sales.[3]

Among the numerous examples that could be cited are the automobile plants built in Bulgaria, Poland, Rumania, and the Soviet Union under license by Fiat and Renault, some of which have already begun to turn out cars. A Dutch manufacturer (*Vereinigde Maschinefabriken V.W.F.*) has signed a co-production agreement with the East German government, calling for joint endeavors in technical development and marketing in their respective countries, as well as abroad. A British-Czechoslovak deal provided for co-production of automatic textile machinery to be sold in world markets. Hungary agreed with the West

German Krupp enterprises to cooperate in the production of controlled machine tools, and a West German typewriter manufacturer concluded an agreement with Bulgaria for joint production. Poland and Great Britain have come to terms on the joint manufacture of boat engines, and Italy and Czechoslovakia have created a joint stock company which will sell pumps on the world market.[4] The list of such joint production and marketing agreements, already very long, continues to grow even after the invasion of Czechoslovakia.

Thus, the development of East-West economic interactions has gone far beyond what mere trade statistics can show. Trends now in progress are certain to gather momentum in the future. Both sides are reaping economic profits from these interactions; and a retardation or reversal of this trend would have detrimental consequences which neither side would wish to contemplate.

East-West Tourism

One way for East European countries to earn some of the foreign exchange they require for the purchase of Western capital and consumer goods is tourism. This, undoubtedly, has been the prime motivation for the liberalization of travel to and from the Soviet bloc countries and for the huge investments those governments have made in service facilities. By 1965, contrary to Communist ideology and propaganda, tourists from capitalist countries were without a doubt the most privileged people in Eastern Europe. Only in the visa department were the tourists from the Soviet bloc ahead of those from the West: most of the East European countries agreed to abolish visas for their respective tourists, but Western visitors could obtain visas at almost any border crossing or airport. In all other aspects Western tourists had the advantage; they could buy the local currency at much more favorable rates[5] and were given preferred treatment at hotels and other service establishments. Local citizens fared the worst, often being deprived of their hotel rooms in order to accommodate affluent capitalists.[6]

As indicated on Table 3, each year the number of Western tourists has increased. They arrive in cars, campers, and on trains and planes, showing off their affluence and taxing the service facilities available in East European countries. Space problems forced the Communist regimes to allow their citizens to put up Western visitors in their houses,[7] a step they would undoubtedly have preferred to avoid in view of the high potential of "ideological contamination." Some private enterprise had to be reestablished to supplement the capacity of state-operated services. Arrangements had to be made with Western automobile manufacturers

TABLE 3

Western Tourists to Eastern Europe
(Selected Countries)

	Bulgaria	Czechoslovakia	DDR	Hungary	Poland	Rumania
Austria						
1958	6,003[b]			25,327[b]	2,053	247[a]
1963	14,706	15,338	561	86,875	2,871	8,779
1967	30,615	312,696	3,095	115,348	13,763	23,144
Belgium						
1958	823[b]			1,193[b]	1,030	69[a]
1963	2,075	2,998	1,630	1,853	1,563	1,956
1967	10,589	10,410	4,327		6,481	4,295
France						
1958	3,612[a]			5,590[b]	5,608	1,033[a]
1963	9,415	10,228	2,048	8,407	11,802	3,446
1967	41,741	40,255	9,979	16,914	37,341	23,326
West Germany						
1958	9,839[b]			9,909[c]	37,105	23[a]
1963	26,533	5,314		31,772	54,042	11,076
1967	128,579	248,415		87,977	31,588	65,868
Italy						
1958	1,705[b]			1,758[b]	760	62[a]
1963	3,825	3,554		4,808	2,215	
1967	18,562	30,765	904	20,317	11,568	15,777
Netherlands						
1958	467[a]			1,283[b]	1,335	
1963	1,638	1,723	527	2,167	1,633	
1967	10,423	28,395	3,698		7,450	5,933
Switzerland						
1958	992[a]			1,238[b]	666	7[a]
1963	2,196	857		2,117	945	509
1967	8,638	13,926	998		3,740	5,845
United Kingdom						
1958	1,133[b]			2,944[b]	3,325	46[a]
1963	8,806	5,999	2,294	5,733	10,016	2,034
1967	27,122	24,921	4,984	13,278	29,406	10,977
United States						
1958	3,318[b]			3,433[b]	7,829	583[a]
1963	4,471	6,185	229	9,620	9,859	2,513
1967	12,766	35,276	7,589	29,299	21,418	11,630

NOTES: (a) 1959, (b) 1960, (c) 1961. Statistics have been drawn from the following sources: United Nations, *Statistical Yearbook, 1959, 1964, 1968* (New York: United Nations); International Union of Official Travel Organizations, *International Travel Statistics, 1962* (London: The British Travel Association, 1962); *Statistisches Jahrbuch der Deutschen Demokratischen Republik,* 1966 and 1968 (East Berlin: Staatsverlag der Deutschen Demokratischen Republik, 1966 and 1968).

and gasoline suppliers for service stations in Eastern Europe. All this for the citizens of the despised capitalist countries who had money to spend.

At the same time, it became increasingly difficult for East European regimes to keep their own people from traveling to the West. Lack of foreign currency was an increasingly inadequate excuse for such restrictions. By the mid-1960s, East European governments were granting visas to their citizens for travel to the West and issuing limited amounts of foreign currency—or, alternatively, requiring guarantees that the Western hosts would furnish the expenses involved.[8] In this way, a great many East Europeans came to the West and, presumably, got a good look at the difference between capitalism and Communism.

In line with this increasing tourist flow, agreements were concluded with Western countries for the exchange of newspapers and magazines. Judging by the limited number of issues circulated in East European countries, the intent was obviously to provide Western visitors with their own kind of reading materials. But Western papers were also sold at street kiosks in the major cities, probably in order to build a good image of East European regimes in the eyes of Western tourists.

Effects Upon Politics in Eastern Europe

During this relatively short time span of increasing East-West interactions—that is, during the 1960s—one could note some significant changes in the structure and process of East European political systems, as well as in their relations with each other and with the Soviet Union. Though these changes came far short of transforming the Communist political systems, they revealed the forces at work and the weakening of the regimes' resistance to change. They also portended a gradual but liberalizing evolution for the future.

It should be mentioned at the outset of this discussion that the growing interactions between East European countries and the West were neither singly, nor probably primarily, responsible for the changes to be highlighted below. The problems, endemic to Communist political systems, which these regimes tried to solve, were quite sufficient in themselves to generate forces of change. But the growing network of East-West relations created an environment conducive to change in Eastern Europe and generated forces which helped to speed the transition.

The Domestic Impact. Perhaps the most significant single change in Eastern Europe has been the economic reform and the debate which preceded its enactment. The primary impetus for this reform probably came from indigenous forces which came increasingly into play after the publication of Yevsei Liberman's article in *Pravda* (September 9, 1962) and which removed the doctrinal fetters from the rigidly centralized economic system developed under Stalin's totalitarian tutelage.

The problems arising out of the Stalinist economic system were so great as to make one wonder how reform could be avoided. The quality of domestic manufactures was so low that many of them could not even be sold on the home market.[9] Hoarding of scarce resources by enterprises to ensure the fulfillment of future compulsory production quotas was straining the national budget and impairing economic growth. Managerial inefficiency and the general apathy of the proletariat contributed greatly to a prevailing sluggishness in productivity. Investment returns decreased alarmingly, partly because of a rising rate of uncompleted projects.[10]

These were only a few among many complaints, the cumulative effects of which could be observed in a declining growth rate throughout the Soviet bloc.[11] The problems were endemic to the highly centralized Communist economic system which placed quantitative output ahead of all other indicators of economic development and left enterprise managers no room or incentive for individual initiative, in keeping with the prevailing ideological tenet that the state should own and control all aspects of national life. Liberal-minded economists challenged these ideological foundations of the Communist economic system, contending among other things that centralized control and compulsory planning were not only unnecessary but also counterproductive.[12] Conservative *apparatchiks,* on the other hand, tried to defend the existing system, arguing that it was basically sound and suffered only from faulty implementation of centrally issued directives.

Most interesting in this debate was the clearly discernible influence of the West. It could be seen in the declared aspiration to improve the quality, design, and efficiency of production so as to make East European manufacturers competitive on world markets.[13] Frequent exhortations by party leaders and economists to learn from and adopt Western management and production techniques presented a striking and refreshing change from the prevailing propaganda output which so consistently distorted and condemned capitalism and its ways, revealing a grudging recognition that only by emulating capitalist techniques could Communism hope to compete and catch up with the West in economic performance.[14] Finally, outstanding foreign loan obligations and the need for increased trade were cited as factors lending greater urgency for economic reform.[15]

The above were among the visible indications of Western influences on the process of reforming East European economies. Other influences are more obscure and can, therefore, be only inferred. For instance, the high rate of propaganda output seeking to minimize or neutralize the conspicuous affluence of Western tourists in Eastern Europe betrays the impact of the Western standard of living on East European populations whose incomes have been increasing faster than consumer goods appear on the market. This can also be seen in the almost fourfold rise in Eastern Europe's import of consumer goods from the West between 1962 and 1966 (from $66 million to $240 million).[16] Then, also, the increasing contacts between East European managers, researchers, scientists, and their Western counterparts must have had a liberalizing effect and helped to generate pressures for change.

As a United Nation's observer has noted, "Experience in both West and East tends to confirm that big and dynamic industries can successfully develop only if they duly observe the requirements of technical and economic progress. Consequently, industrial managements are called upon to cope with increasingly similar sets of problems."[17] This observation is reflected in the economic reforms which several East European countries enacted between 1965 and 1967. It must be stressed here that each individual East European country has forged its own economic reform program and, as a result, there are great variations in scope. At the same time, the implementation process has been impeded in some countries by incompetent apparatchiks of Stalinist persuasion. Thus, any attempt at generalization is a hazardous undertaking. Nevertheless, keeping in mind these caveats, it will be useful to highlight some of the *more or less* common denominators of these economic reforms and to assess their implications for political change in Eastern Europe.[18]

In general, the reforms legislated in most of the Soviet bloc countries reflect the recognition that centralized control, planning, and distribution of production has hindered more than helped the overall performance of the Communist economies.[19] Central-plan indices were reduced to give enterprise managers greater scope for individual initiative. Profitability became the key index of enterprise performance. This meant, among other things, that the enterprises must plan their production and investments according to the prevailing and anticipated demand, and that they must sell the goods they produced. It meant also that the state would no longer absorb the costs of production for low-quality goods rotting in warehouses. An interest rate was imposed on the production resources of the enterprises to stimulate their efficient utilization and discourage hoarding. State-owned banks were given greater discretion in the dispensation of investment funds and foreign currency; the criteria for lending money hinged on the prospects of the profitability of the project in question.

The income of the managers and, to a lesser extent, of the workers, could vary greatly with the profitability of the enterprise in the new economic system, for after several compulsory assessments for investment, taxation, and social services were fulfilled, the rest of the profits would be distributable according to fixed schedules to the working staff of the enterprise. Inevitably, this would lead to profit motivations in production plans at the enterprise level and bring additional pressures to bear on the central decision-making process for liberalization.

In the early stages, it probably would be too much to expect the East European regimes to let free-market forces govern the economic process. However, it has been widely recognized that, if the profitability criterion of the new economic system is to be workable, the price of goods must be geared to the costs of production, if not to demand. This has led to efforts to find out the true cost of production and to far-reaching price changes, new endeavors which promise to commercialize both domestic and foreign trade. Some new economic models have introduced a threefold price-determination mechanism, which leaves the price of some goods entirely at the discretion of the producer, imposes a ceiling on others, and puts the price of still other goods in the hands of the central state organs.[20]

As the various economic reforms have been implemented, the East European regimes have delegated some of their control functions to lower echelons. This amounts to a curbing of state power over the production units and, conversely, an increase of technocratic influence upon the state. It bespeaks a rationalization of the management process which, under the outdated Stalinist system, used to be largely governed by ideological and political criteria. In those states where decentralization has progressed the furthest (Hungary and Czechoslovakia), there have been visible spillover effects upon the trade unions, the legislature, and the intellectual strata, which the regimes have found increasingly difficult to contain.

Other developments in Eastern Europe's Communist polities bespeak departures from the ideologically conditioned and Soviet-imposed systems. In order to keep pace with the growing demand for consumer goods and services, East European countries have lifted some of their restrictions on private artisans, even to the point that they can borrow money for materials and tools.

Social scientists have been given the green light in Eastern Europe.[21] Regimes are paying increasing attention to public opinion polls on a variety of issues. To be sure, they may be seeking new ways to manipulate the participation of their peoples in the political, economic, social, and cultural processes, and new ways to educate the "Communist man." But this, too, reflects a recognition of past failures and the need for change. More importantly, it reflects a greater responsiveness to the opinions and aspirations of the citizens.

It is noteworthy that most of the East European regimes have stopped jamming Western radio broadcasts. (Since 1964, only Bulgaria has continued jamming on a regular basis.) This has been accompanied in some of the East European countries by a demand for more objective reporting and news. In a sense, consciously or unconsciously, East European regimes have initiated an attempt to compete with Western media in the news department—an attempt to close the "credibility gap."[22]

Many other developments could be mentioned, but they would unduly enlarge the scope of this discussion. In perspective, they are small steps in a long evolutionary process which, if it continues, will eventually transform these Communist political systems. So far, the trend has carried Eastern Europe from "totalitarian" to "authoritarian" political processes, with a great deal of diversity entering into the evolution.

Impact on the Bloc System. The diversification of East European Communist political systems has had a detrimental impact upon the cohesion of the Soviet bloc, particularly in the economic realm. It will be remembered that in 1962 Soviet Premier Khrushchev tried to integrate the Soviet bloc's economic organization, the Council for Mutual Economic Assistance, into a supra-national framework which the USSR could dominate. In 1963 this project foundered on the open resistance of the Rumanian regime, probably tacitly supported by some other East European leaderships.[23] When Khrushchev's successors revived this effort in 1968, they found that the diversity of East European economic structures and processes had made the economic integration of the bloc virtually impossible in the immediate future.[24]

Each bloc regime appears to have its own blueprint for Comecon integration; each is making its own demands and conditions for intensifying collaboration in the Comecon, seeking to maximize its advantages and minimize those of the other bloc countries. The differences have been impossible to reconcile. Rumania and Hungary, citing different reasons, have openly opposed a supra-national structure for the Comecon. Rumania, which has made very little progress in domestic decentralization, objects to any infringement upon its "sovereignty" which a supra-national (Soviet-dominated) structure would inevitably impose,[25] while Hungary argues, in line with its decentralized economic model, that enterprises should be free to deal directly with each other with a minimum of central direction.[26] The Polish and Bulgarian regimes have not addressed themselves directly to this question in public, but Czechoslovakia was, at least until Husak's assumption of the party leadership, disposed toward Hungary's predilections.[27] The Soviet Union and East Germany have been the only two vigorous proponents of Comecon supra-nationalization.[28]

Currency convertibility has been another stumbling block on the way to Comecon integration. Hungary and Poland have regarded it as a sine qua non for further progress in this respect.[29] It has been opposed by East Germany on the ground that most of the Comecon countries have not yet developed a rational cost-accounting and pricing mechanism that could provide a common denominator for *commercial* (as opposed to barter) trade.[30] The Soviet Union (the kingpin of the argument) has also dragged its feet on this issue. For, should the ruble become convertible on world markets, the East European regimes would have greater flexibility in their trade options, and they would in all probability shift some of their trading patterns from the East to the West and the Third World, thus reducing their dependence on the Soviet Union for raw materials and other commodities.

In these arguments, not only the national advantage, but also the freedom to deal with countries outside the Soviet bloc (in hard-currency areas) was a vital consideration. The rationalization of economic processes has combined with nationalistic orientations to stifle the integration of Soviet bloc economies under a supra-national roof. As of May 1969, Comecon stands about where it stood in 1964; the *aim* of making the Soviet ruble convertible *within the bloc's trade area* was reaffirmed in Moscow,[31] revealing the fact that the Comecon Bank had not yet managed to become the clearinghouse for bloc trade. This is regarded by some of the bloc countries as the prerequisite for monetary convertibility in world markets.

The obstacles facing Soviet policy objectives regarding Comecon integration bespeak a growing autonomy of East Europeans from Moscow's control. This autonomy has grown most visibly during the détente period, when East-West interactions so markedly have increased. One should caution, however, against overstressing the role of the West in promoting this evolution of Soviet-East-European relations, for the options opened up by East-West interactions are still quite limited, and East European countries continue to depend primarily on the Soviet Union for their national income. Other factors, such as the Sino-Soviet dispute and the de-Stalinization drive initiated under Khrushchev, are at least equally responsible.

The marked improvement in East-West relations has helped to create an atmosphere in which East European governments (as well as those of the West) are less apprehensive about aggression from the West. To this extent, they tend to feel less dependent on the Soviet Union. By the

mid-1960s, only East Germany and Poland expressed in any way convincingly their fears of West German "militarism and revanchism,"
based in part on Bonn's outstanding claims regarding reunification and
the Oder-Neisse line, and dramatized by the fact that West Germany
was the strongest military power in Western Europe.

This lessening dependence of East European countries on the Soviet
Union for their national security is reflected in a growing disinterest in
the Warsaw Pact. Since 1965, repeated calls for strengthening the
Warsaw Pact have betrayed the inadequacy of the East European response from the Soviet point of view. Soviet attempts at reorganizing the
Warsaw Pact into a supra-national structure have failed.[32] Rumania
pointedly reduced its forces, and when, in 1968, Bucharest took steps to
improve its national defense posture, it was to counter a military threat
from the Soviet Union, not from the West. Similarly, in 1966, the
reinitiation of the Soviet bloc's offensive for an all-European security
system, which would lead to the liquidation of both NATO and the
Warsaw Pact,[33] received a spontaneous response in Bucharest more
enthusiastic than the Kremlin might have wished. Nicolae Ceausescu's
assertion that "military blocs and the existence of military bases and of
. . . troops on the territory of other states is one of the barriers in the
path of collaboration among peoples"[34] was not well received in Moscow, where the Soviet leadership maintained that NATO, the only
pernicious military organization in Europe, must be abolished first.

None of the other East European regimes has tried to outpace Soviet
policy-makers as conspicuously as Rumania has done in promoting
European security and the liquidation of military alliances. Nevertheless,
the Rumanians are not alone in wanting a European security system.
Indeed, Hungary's foreign policy has been more assiduously, if less
conspicuously, aimed at this goal,[35] and the Czechoslovaks have not
been too far behind in this endeavor.

The German Problem at the Center of European Stability

No discussion of East-West relations would be complete without
treating the German problem, which not only symbolizes the division of
Europe, but is also the most important single obstacle to the bridging of
the gulf. On both sides, divided Germany has more or less successfully
sought the allegiance of its allies to its basic goals: West Germany has
depended on its NATO allies to support its claim as sole representative
of all German people (including those of the DDR), its goal of reunification, and its contention that the Polish-German border is still open to
negotiation. East Germany has been counting on its allies in the Warsaw
Pact to support its claim to separate statehood and its contention that

West Berlin is a separate political entity on East Germany's territory.

In large part, the conflict between the two Germanys has focused on the problem of recognition. Each has sought to isolate the other to the maximum extent possible. West Germany proclaimed the "Hallstein Doctrine," which declared that Bonn regarded the diplomatic recognition of East Germany as an unfriendly act punishable by a severance of relations. (Thus, in 1957 when Yugoslavia recognized East Germany, West Germany broke its diplomatic relations with that country; they were, however, resumed in 1968.) Similarly, East Germany has sought to keep its allies from recognizing West Germany without first exacting Bonn's unconditional concessions to East Berlin's vital claims.

On balance, West Germany has been the more successful of the two. Until April 1969, only the fourteen Communist countries of the world had accorded diplomatic recognition to East Germany.[36] Between 1963 and 1964 Bonn obtained the agreement of Bulgaria, Hungary, Poland, and Rumania to establish permanent reciprocal trade missions; to the consternation of East Berlin, Bonn made no concessions at all.[37] In January 1967, Rumania established diplomatic relations with West Germany,[38] provoking the East German leadership to frantic diplomatic efforts to keep Hungary, Czechoslovakia, and Bulgaria (all of them were similarly inclined) from following the Rumanian example. Nevertheless, in September 1967, Czechoslovakia caught up with its neighbors by exchanging trade missions with West Germany.[39]

The fact that diplomatic relations are no longer a prerequisite to normal economic, social, and cultural intercourse between nations must surely be counted among the more interesting phenomena of the post–World War II era. West Germany has consistently ranked among the East European Communist countries' most important Western trading partners, long before permanent trade missions were established. As Table 4 shows, more than half of East Germany's trade with Western Europe has been with West Germany. Even more striking is the fact that over the past few years, on the average, two hundred thousand Yugoslav workers have been employed in West Germany's booming economy, while no diplomatic relations exist between these two countries. And West German tourists have been by far the most numerous single national contingent in Eastern Europe's tourist boom.

All of these relationships have developed steadily even while the East European propaganda machines continued to brand West German "militarism and revanchism" as the bug-bear of European détente and security. Indeed, except for the fact that West Germany has refused to make any concessions on its outstanding claims leftover from the Second World War, these relationships have given the Communist anti-FRG

TABLE 4

DDR's Trade with FRG

Country Traded with:	West Berlin		West Germany, not including West Berlin		West Germany, including West Berlin	
	In millions of U.S. $	% of Trade with OECD	In millions of U.S. $	% of Trade with OECD	In millions of U.S. $	% of Trade with OECD
1958	—	—	—	—	401.4	57
1962	81.2	12	294.6	42	375.8	54
1964	109.1	12	372.9	42	482.0	54
1965	123.3	12	391.8	39	551.1	51
1966	132.4	12	474.1	43	606.5	55
1967	120.7	11	437.5	40	558.2	51

NOTES: Table includes all Organization for Economic Cooperation and Development countries except the United States, Canada, Japan, and Finland. Statistics have been taken from *Statistisches Jahrbuch der DDR, 1968* (East Berlin: Staatsverlag der Deutschen Demokratischen Republik, 1968) and OECD, *Foreign Trade: Series C Trade by Commodities, 1958–1967* (Paris: OECD).

propaganda a hollow ring. The evident willingness of several East European regimes to establish diplomatic ties with West Germany leads one to question the strength of these countries' "fraternal" (political and ideological) ties to East Germany and the genuineness of the animosities they have so vociferously proclaimed toward the West German regime.

In view of the manifest benefits which the East Europeans already enjoy in their economic and cultural relationships with West Germany, one is hardput to attribute to economic reasons alone their willingness to normalize their relations with the FRG, which runs counter to Soviet policy and has created conflict between them and the DDR regime. One plausible explanation seems to be that the East Europeans are getting tired of the status quo (particularly where the German question is concerned) and the fetters it has placed on their freedom of political maneuver in Europe.

While, on the whole, West Germany has outscored East Germany in the confrontation, it has not been able to achieve any of its goals connected with the German problem. It has not been able to promote a better political life for the East German people; the *Ostpolitik* stopped making headway after the diplomatic breakthrough with Rumania; and reunification is no closer at hand than it ever was—indeed, one might well say that its prospects looked better in 1960 than in 1969. There is little question but that West Germany's limited foreign policy success regarding the German problem (abetted by East Germany's economic success at home) has generated resistance to any rapprochement within

East Germany's ruling group. During the 1960s, an East German political nationalism came into being. It is clearly visible at the official level (through leadership speeches and the propaganda output), and there are some observers who say that it has gained a foothold among the populace—indeed, the West German Ministry of All-German Affairs fears that this is the case.[40]

Time and changing circumstances have a way of eroding doctrines, habits, and beliefs. Until 1965, the West German Government refused to have any relations with East Germany on the ministerial level, fearing that such intercourse would be interpreted as recognition of the DDR regime. Officially, East Germany was called *Mitteldeutschland* (Middle Germany, implying the claim to the prewar German territory which Poland inherited), or simply the *Sowietzone* (Soviet zone), to reflect the fictitious nature of the DDR's "sovereignty" as well as the FRG's refusal to recognize the de facto existence of two separate German states. With the creation of the "Grand Coalition" in 1966 (composed of the major political parties, the CDU-CSU [Christian Democratic Union-Christian Socialist Union] and the SPD [German Social Democratic Party]), however, this rule was less strictly applied, and newspapers began referring to East Germany as the "DDR" (German Democratic Republic).

By 1969, political sentiment for the recognition, in some form, of East Germany was visibly growing in Bonn's political circles. It was incorporated into the political platform of the Free Democratic Party of Germany (FDP) and had widespread support in the Social Democratic Party (SPD).[41] Even Chancellor Kiesinger (leader of the CDU) would no longer foreclose official talks with the DDR aimed at mutual recognition. But by 1969, the East German policy line had hardened on the German problem to the extent that official circles in West Germany feared that negotiations would prove fruitless. One factor contributing to this hardening of the East German line was the Czechoslovak Crisis of 1968. Nevertheless, at the time of this writing, a unilateral West German recognition of East Germany was no longer unthinkable, if only because the trend in the political thinking in the Bonn government appeared to have shifted toward the point of view that communication, even fruitless communication, was better than no communication at all. Additional impetus to this trend derived from the breakdown of the effectiveness of the Hallstein Doctrine (Syria, the United Arab Republic, Cambodia, and South Yemen had established diplomatic relations with the DDR).

Should West Germany give even only tacit recognition to the DDR— or simply drop its opposition to other countries recognizing the DDR— and agree to the finality of the Oder-Neisse line as well as to the nullity of the 1938 Munich Agreement, a new set of variables would enter into

East-West European relations. East European regimes would be less constrained by East German objections to normalizing relations with the FRG, which most of them have indicated their desire to do, and the scare propaganda of West German revanchism would lose much of its credibility. This eventuality may have liberalizing implications for both the domestic and foreign politics of Soviet bloc countries.

The Invasion of Czechoslovakia and its Portent for East-West Interactions

The preceding discussion has illustrated that East-West interactions have introduced centrifugal forces into the domestic and intra-bloc politics of East European Communist systems. On the domestic level, the several Communist regimes have been more or less apprehensive about these forces and have tried to neutralize them through propaganda, persuasion, and some concessions to popular demands. In Czechoslovakia, this effort did not suffice to forestall the ouster of the Stalinist Novotny regime and the rise of popular ferment that was eventually to bring Soviet forces (accompanied by military contingents of four other Warsaw-Pact countries) into the country for an indefinite occupation. The events leading to occupation and the analysis of the Czechoslovak drama are presented in chapters 6 and 10. The objective here is simply to make an assessment of the impact of the invasion on East-West relations.

It should be stated at the outset that East-West interactions were probably not primarily responsible for the political turmoil which ousted the Czechoslovak "old guard" from power. They may have been a catalyst in the process. The problems that gave rise to the political turmoil in Czechoslovakia were endemic to the Communist system. Economic stagnation, intellectual ferment, and a tradition of democracy combined with de-Stalinization in opposition to an outdated, incompetent, Stalinist leadership. Czech domination over Slovaks only aggravated these problems. The opposition to Novotny's ruling group came into the open in 1963; it succeeded in toppling him in 1968.

The political process which unfolded in Czechoslovakia after Novotny's ouster was not only more intimately related to that of Western political systems, but it also bore a much greater affinity to the Western way of life and gave greater freedom for interaction at all levels with individuals, groups, enterprises, and governments of the West. This growing affinity between Czechoslovakia and the countries of the West —particularly with West Germany—was subsumed under the progressive erosion of the Communist party's control over the life of Czechoslovak society, which threatened the stability of the surrounding orthodox regimes and thus prompted Warsaw Pact military action against Czechoslovakia.

In the aftermath of the invasion, the orthodox propaganda machines of the Soviet bloc stressed the need for unity against Western imperialism, which, allegedly, had softened up the Czechoslovak Communist system from within. East Germany's Walter Ulbricht went so far as to urge that the Soviet bloc countries cease their interactions with the West and rely on the resources of the socialist countries for their economic development needs on grounds that their ties with the West had made them dependent on imperialist powers and susceptible to capitalist exploitation.[42] None of the other bloc leaderships, however, would follow Ulbricht's advice, and even East Germany did not practice what Ulbricht preached.[43]

As Table 5 shows, the number of contacts between the Soviet bloc countries and the West grew, rather than diminished, during the months following the invasion of Czechoslovakia. This continuing rise in East-West contacts indicates a predominant feeling on both sides of the ideological divide that détente and cooperation must continue for the sake of peace and security.[44] To the West Europeans, the marked improvement in East-West relations which had developed during the 1960s was too important to be sacrificed to the feeling of consternation over the moral depravity the Soviet leadership had displayed in its relations with one of its allies. As for the East Europeans, this growing number of East-West contacts seemed to indicate that the influence of

TABLE 5

East-West Interactions

	1968 July	Aug.	Sept.	Oct.	Nov.	Dec.	1969 Jan.
Bulgaria	10	10	3	8	8	3	4
Hungary	9	6	5	11	20	11	22
Poland	25	14	15	19	21	14	22
USSR	18	13	8	14	15	7	24
DDR	1	—	—	1	1	2	1
Subtotal	63	43	31	53	65	37	73
Czechoslovakia	26	26	27	33	51	29	18
Rumania	10	7	34	43	30	31	35
Total	99	76	92	129	146	97	126

NOTE: The figures in this table represent the counted total number of each Soviet bloc country's interactions reported in Radio Free Europe, *East-West Contacts, A Monthly Survey* (New York: Free Europe, Inc.) for the months listed, exclusive of contacts with Western Communist parties and international organizations. The table reflects all kinds of contacts, regardless of their immediate or potential significance, including exhibits, conferences, ministerial visits, trade and specialization agreements, and the like.

the West on their Communist systems, which their propaganda machines decried so vehemently, was not an unmanageable threat. For economic as well as security reasons, it was essential to keep open the lines of communication and contacts.

Portents for the Future of East-West Relations

The growing East-West interaction patterns since 1960, accompanied by domestic decentralization and liberalization, are trends prodded by seemingly irreversible forces and, therefore, likely to continue in the years ahead. At the same time, it seems prudent to point out that the flow of events has been known suddenly to halt, reverse, or change the direction of trends, and to turn the "unthinkable" into reality. Present leaderships may fall or fade away, and those which replace them may opt for different policy orientations. There may be new, as yet unforeseeable, crises in Eastern Europe, more upsetting than the one through which Czechoslovakia is still passing in 1970, which might force trends in Eastern Europe and East-West relations off their course. Many more imponderables could be listed. For the present purpose, however, we shall assume that trends will remain stable and that "what's past is prologue."

The progressive improvement of East-West relations witnessed during the 1960s would not have been possible without a tacit recognition among the governments of both East and West of two separate spheres of super-power influence, of the inviolability of the borders between East and West, and of the integrity of the political systems on both sides —the essential elements of the political and territorial status quo in Europe. Among the ironies of modern international relations in Europe is the fact that the improvement of international relations has been eroding this status quo in several important respects.

The cohesion of the Soviet bloc has been weakening during the period of détente, as has been that of the Atlantic Alliance. On both sides of the ideological divide, popular demands for higher standards of living have taxed the national resources and the policy-making ingenuity of governments. Increasingly, East and West Europeans have sought in political, economic, and cultural cooperation the way to the solution of this problem. As East-West contacts grow, the common interests of Europeans increasingly overshadow the divisive ones. Governments and peoples on both sides have sought in various ways to bridge their differences and to form new affiliations with each other.

The military aspect of Europe's security needs seems to be receding, leaving greater scope for political solutions. Neither side is willing or able to spend an inordinately large part of its gross national product on armaments. As the 1970s mark their beginning, it is perhaps not too optimistic to say that the nations of Europe (as opposed to the super powers) fear their security less threatened by each other than they have at any time in this century. It is equally true that European nations today are more preoccupied with their own economic betterment and that they have more to gain by collaboration and more to lose from war than has ever been the case before.

In this light, it is perhaps not surprising that the idea of a European security conference (such as proposed by the Warsaw Pact summit meeting in Budapest in March 1969) has received more than passing attention in Europe. Even in the ideational stage, this proposal has helped to legitimize the expansion and intensification of bilateral, trans-bloc contacts, as well as the notion that the international political status quo of Europe is no longer sacrosanct. As cross-national images and political processes become de-ideologized, new visions of Europe attract the imagination of Europeans, reflecting the inherent instability of a continent divided. On both sides, the hegemony of super powers (which continues to exist in the Soviet bloc much more so than in the West) is under challenge, and their ability to impose policies upon their respective allies is gradually diminishing as Europeans continue building their bilateral and multilateral trans-bloc relationships.

The political status quo in Eastern Europe has fallen prey to erosive forces on several fronts. Preoccupied with the management of increasingly complex economic and social processes (which have been aggravated rather than solved by ideology), the Communist regimes have come to allow greater influence and freedom of maneuver to the managerial elites and scientific intelligentsia of their countries. The flow of information is becoming less restrictive, both from within and from abroad. Group pressures are beginning to influence the political process, and although the ruling Communist parties have by no means given up their "leading role" in their societies, they are now less privileged and more subject to legitimacy constraints than they were during the early years of Communist rule. The imperative of mass participation in the productive processes of the state has forced East European regimes to make political concessions to their peoples.

These and other changes that have been mentioned in the preceding pages add up to a process of assimilation between Eastern and Western political systems, an evolution which, if it continues, will narrow the politico-ideological gulf in Europe. East European Communist systems have only recently embarked on this road of evolution toward a political process in which coercion and repression no longer serve as the substitute for broad popular consensus.

The progress of this evolution will, in the last analysis, determine the future shape of Europe. The experience of Czechoslovakia in August 1968 leads one to the conclusion that the best hope for Eastern Europe lies in gradual change which allows time and room for adjustment both in Moscow and in other bloc capitals. For years, perhaps for decades to come, therefore, one can anticipate the perpetuation of special communities of interest in the East as well as the West, based on common values and political beliefs. Gradually, however, as the political evolution of the Soviet bloc countries continues and converges with that of the West, these values and beliefs will merge and narrow the ideological gulf that still divides East and West in Europe.

Although the trend seems clear and no one would want to reverse it, the shape of Europe in the future cannot yet be foretold. Too many dreams compete for the imagination of Europeans; too many problems remain as yet unsolved. But in all of these dreams there are several important common denominators: collaboration between East and West is essential for socio-economic development and security, the political environment in which this collaboration takes place will continue to improve, and the eventual elimination of Europe's division is presaged. Out of these dreams may yet arise the dawning of a new age in Europe.

12
Conclusions
Peter A. Toma

12. Conclusions

Peter A. Toma

In the USSR the transmutation of Marxism into Soviet utopianism produced a state dictatorship built on the traditions of the oldest police state in Europe and a social climate of Russian mysticism of power dating back to the Byzantine Empire. This political system (called Soviet totalitarianism), which might have been suitable for achieving a certain developmental goal in a backward country ruled by tsarist despotism, after World War II was grafted onto several East European countries under Stalinist coercion.

Soviet satellitization of Eastern Europe was achieved primarily through three factors: Soviet military occupation, the destruction of the old political and social structure by the Nazis, and the ineptitude or naivité of the so-called democratic leaders in coalition governments. Although the anti-Nazi resistance movement in Eastern Europe was quite widespread, it failed to effect a genuine social revolution anywhere but in Yugoslavia. In other parts of Eastern Europe, the goals and aspirations of the resistance fighters were entirely different from those delivered to them via the baggage train of the Soviet Army. Because Soviet totalitarianism was alien to European tradition, it was never deeply rooted in any East European country and therefore had to be sustained by the use of terror. The Yugoslavs, who fought for and built their own independence during World War II, in 1948 once again freed themselves from vassalage. The rest of the Soviet satellites, however, continued to pay tribute to Stalinism. Consequently, the people in these countries developed a kind of schizophrenic personality. The youth lived in an atmosphere of double morality; the workers followed a double consciousness; the peasants, constantly fearing collectivization, maintained a double standard; and the intelligentsia paid lip-service to the dogma while at the same time promoting traditional values.

The Stalinist aim to destroy the last vestiges of the old social order and bourgeois morality—which separated the USSR from Europe proper —failed in spite of the use of police terror. On the contrary, as soon as the collective leadership in Soviet Russia replaced the Stalinist cult of personality, nationalism became the most popular centrifugal force in the Communist states of Europe as well as in the Soviet Union. After 1953, the new elites were very much in need of mass support and loyalty to achieve economic efficiency in their own country. Thus a new social mobilization was launched which stimulated the national aspirations and ambitions, not only of the new elites, but of the multitudes in a heterogenous Eastern Europe as well. The result was the legitimization of post-Stalinist national Communism as a direct reaction to the disintegrating Stalinist dictatorship. The same national Communism was also responsible for the breaking up of world Communism as a monolith and the transformation of Poland, Hungary, East Germany, Czechoslovakia, Bulgaria, and, to a great extent, Rumania from Stalinist satellites into nation-states with limited sovereignty. When this happened in the late sixties, some historians were convinced that the Soviet Union could still exert enough influence over certain geographic areas in Europe without employing its obsolete ideological weapons.

Since the USSR in 1970 is behaving more like a major power and less like a revolutionary nucleus of world Communism, it is conceivable that the Soviet leaders derive their loyalty from the East European elites through defense nationalism rather than Communist internationalism. The new Communist elites of the Warsaw-Pact countries are, in fact, national Communists fighting against party intellectuals (revisionists) whose disillusionment with Soviet utopianism and disenchantment with the imperialistic policy of the Soviet Union led to a reexamination of Marxist theories in the light of humanism and democracy. Several critics go so far as to predict that the Soviet state will disintegrate into anarchy in less than two decades. While the Soviet regime is, according to some prognosticators, charting a course of self-destruction, European Communist states are becoming more European and less Communist. This trend becomes even more evident when we consider that the Soviet leadership, either under the Stalinist monolith or defense nationalism, has failed to provide satisfactory models of social behavior for European Communist states under its influence. The prescriptive Stalinist totalitarian model and the Brezhnevist mobilization model have proved to be too rudimentary for European needs. Thus, probing and experimentation with new ideas and policies in Communist Europe can be viewed both as a courageous act, involving risk-taking in political survival, and as a political game with neither rules nor precedence.

Trends in Economic Modernization

In the area of economics, experimentation with new models is permitted (in some cases even encouraged) within certain bounds by the Soviet and European Communist rulers. Consequently, all Communist countries in Europe with the exception of Albania have experimented with one type of economic reform or another. The models vary from that of Yugoslavia, where the Soviet influence is nil, to those of Hungary, Czechoslovakia, East Germany, Bulgaria, Poland, and Rumania, where Soviet influence is exercised in varying degrees.

Rumania. Although Rumania's annual economic growth rate is one of the largest in the world (from 1961 to 1968, 13.2 percent), in contrast to other Communist countries in Europe, the country still lacks a blueprint for economic reforms. The reason for this seems obvious when we consider that in economic development Rumania is still lagging behind Hungary and Poland. Under Khrushchev, Rumania was denied the option to develop its industrial base under Soviet auspices. Thus Rumania chose to continue with Stalinism without support from the Soviet Union in order to create a modern industrial potential to balance its agricultural and raw-material economy. Rapid industrialization, however, was not necessarily the best method for the development of Rumania's backward economy. The cost of industrialization is just beginning to reveal itself in agricultural developments and consumer-goods production.

Among the Warsaw-Pact countries, Rumania is at the bottom in per capita income. The high accumulation of industrial production has resulted in a very low living standard. For this reason, Rumanian First Secretary Nicolae Ceausescu at the party congress in 1969 emphasized the necessity for improving the agricultural sector of the Rumanian economy. Yet the directives of the 1971–75 plan and the guidelines for 1976–80 plan clearly indicate the priority given to industry over agriculture—the emphasis remains on the leading role of heavy industry.

Since the Rumanian party leaders are far more susceptible to the national interest than to the dictates of Marxist ideology, prospects for economic efficiency in the long run are much better in Rumania than in other Warsaw-Pact countries. However, Rumania's ambitions for achieving a complex, many-sided and balanced economy, with an increase in labor productivity and a reduction in the costs of production, will hardly be accomplished without radical economic reforms.

Poland. In Poland, where economic reforms were proposed immediately after the bloodless revolution of October 1956, no major changes in the technique of planning and management were undertaken until recently. On the contrary, the blueprint for a new Polish economic model, prepared by the Economic Council, caused a reaction in the party and government which led to the strengthening rather than the weakening of centralized control of the Polish economy. None of the proposals submitted by the Economic Council, such as the abolition of wage and price controls, the introduction of Workers' Councils, and other features of a market economy, were ever implemented.

By 1959 the Economic Council had become moribund, and most of its members were stripped of power and influence. From 1956 to 1959, the central planners in Poland prevented any fundamental economic reforms. It is true, though, that in 1965, after Poland had experienced some economic difficulties, the Central Committee of the United Polish Workers' Party approved a new program of economic reforms. However, the program never got off the ground because the dogmatists and the hardliners in the party procrastinated long enough to block its implementation. As it happened, many of the economic reformers were Polish Jews, and after the Six-Day War in June 1967, under the guise of a "Zionist plot," the dogmatists shelved the proposed economic reforms once again.

A third attempt was made to introduce economic reforms in 1969, when the expense of witch-hunting and economic mismanagement became known to the party leaders. In order to fulfill the 1966–70 Five-Year Plan, the Polish treasury had to find one hundred billion zlotys for investment purposes. Such examples of waste were directly attributed to the command-type economy. Thus, the party leadership decided at the Fifth Congress to use 1969–70 as a transition period for the reconstruction of the Polish national economy. Although at this writing the precise blueprint for economic reform in Poland has yet to be produced, there is no doubt that the new model will embrace the principles of a market economy based on the profit motive, self-management, competition among enterprises, planning from below rather than above, and a greater independence in determining prices and wages.

The new model, slated for January 1971, will be a drastic departure from the previous plan. Its aims are to improve efficiency in industrial production and to increase the standard of living. How successful this model will prove depends on how much risk-taking the party leadership will be willing to take in order to achieve economic efficiency, even if it means losing some of its own power. There exists also the possibility that before the 1971 program gets underway, some diehard reactionaries may once again foil the efforts of the reformists, just as they did twice before.

Bulgaria. In Bulgaria economic reforms date back to May 1964, when the new system of planning and management—originally proposed by the rehabilitated Professor Petko Kunin a year earlier—was put to a test through micro-economic experiments. By 1965, almost one-third of all major industrial establishments in Bulgaria were involved in these experiments. Although the new system fell short of Professor Kunin's expectations, nevertheless, it did contain two significant ingredients of the market economy: the profit motive and the profit sharing. Inasmuch as the earlier experiments proved to be successful, Bulgaria continued with additional economic reforms during the late sixties. At this writing, the new economic system, which encompasses all of the Bulgarian economy, follows some centralized planning combined with indirect controls at the factory and trust levels. This applies to the regulation of prices, wages, taxation, the compulsive character of planned indices, the establishment of priorities in economic development, and so forth. Hence, more than five years after the introduction of the new economic system, the Bulgarian enterprises have little or no effect on the determination of prices and wages, have little authority in shaping the profile of production or managerial prerogatives, and cannot determine freely the use of their profits or the incentives for raising labor productivity or the extent of their competition. The Bulgarian party leaders are among the most loyal supporters of the Kremlin, and they are determined to maintain party control over the economy, even if it means sacrificing the future success of economic efficiency in Bulgaria.

The DDR. A similar attitude to economic planning and management prevails in the German Democratic Republic (DDR). The New Economic System (NOS), introduced in 1963, is a pragmatic yet arbitrary model which has always been under a strict control by the elite of the Socialist Unity Party (SED). The approach to the NOS is one of organizational efficiency rather than one of incentives in labor productivity and improved standard of living. Thus, the concept of a free market is negated in the DDR by the concept of the dictatorship of the proletariat. Nevertheless, East Germany managed to introduce a series of reform measures which were responsible for the so-called "economic miracle," making the DDR the most prosperous country in the Communist system. Among the reform measures were the transfer of fundamental economic decisions to industrial associations (VVB); the use of interest rates, subsidies, profits, and depreciation rates; a more flexible price and wage system; the development of "partnership councils"; and a greater utilization of the banking system.

Unlike some other countries in Communist Europe, East Germany does not feel the strong pressure from the reformists seeking economic modernization for the purpose of attaining political pluralization. Walter Ulbricht's economic model has other aims: first, to make the party-controlled economy function more efficiently; and, second, to prevent the rise of a vocal opposition in the party and government which might develop because of economic deficiencies.

Czechoslovakia. Whereas in Poland, East Germany, and Bulgaria economic reforms developed gradually—step-by-step—in Czechoslovakia, the new economic model was instituted suddenly, without prior experimentation. The Czechoslovak model was to be implemented in two stages. The first stage, beginning on January 1, 1966, was to create incentives to discover material and labor reserves on the enterprise level. The second stage, beginning January 1, 1967, was to provide the solution for the problems of investments and the development of enterprises. This implied a decentralization of economic decision-making on such issues as wages, prices, and assortment of products. The managers of enterprises were to be given latitude to regulate employment as well as to establish their own wage rates.

As in Poland, the party elite in Czechoslovakia was hesitant to carry out the promises as conveyed in the blueprint for the new economic model. Nevertheless, by early 1967, some progress had been achieved. The wholesale price system was finally realized but with a disastrous result. During 1967 wholesale prices increased by thirty percent instead of nineteen percent, thus defeating one of the major goals of the reforms, specifically, the elimination of inefficient and marginal producers. Consequently, every enterprise showed a profit, regardless of its efficiency standards. Enterprises were free to employ additional workers at a higher rate of pay. The result was an inflationary economy with the consumers at the mercy of the dictates of the producers. Since the inflationary trend could be checked only by strict price control, the new economic model lost its effectiveness, and Czechoslovakia was left with no choice but to return to the former centralized system. During 1966–67, of course, the Novotny regime made every effort to make the new economic model falter. At the same time, however, Novotny's attitude to the reforms contributed to his own downfall because the disgruntled reformists became staunch allies with Novotny's political opponents in seeking his ouster in 1968.

Under Dubcek, Czechoslovakia initiated a search for the improvement and revitalization of economic reforms. Those reformists who had joined with the Dubcek forces in 1967 were assigned the task of preparing a new blueprint for facilitating economic management in Czechoslovakia. This task was twofold: first, to improve economic efficiency in the country, and, second, to expand the process of democratization of the society. Consequently, recommendations for strengthening the economic situation in Czechoslovakia included several far-reaching objectives: to abolish the existing system of universal, impenetrable protectionism of enterprises; to provide the enterprises with a genuine freedom of decision-making; to de-bureaucratize the central management; to eliminate the administrative monopoly and establish free competition among the enterprises; to free the price system from the existing subjectivism and adjust it to the demands of the market; to rationalize the income policy; to create a natural atmosphere for making investments more effective; and to set up a socialist market economy, suitably combined with central planning.

In order to gain approval for these recommendations, the proponents fought hard against the dogmatists in the party and state bureaucracy. Until August 21, 1968, reformists in the Dubcek regime were willing to take great risks to stimulate and encourage economic efficiency in Czechoslovakia. Economic reforms were made conditional upon political pluralization, and the role of the party dictatorship was seriously questioned. Because the ruling elite in Czechoslovakia went too far, according to the Kremlin leaders, the armies of the Warsaw-Pact countries forced the Dubcek regime to give up its liberal program. In 1970, Czechoslovakia is adhering to a pragmatic economic system with strict administrative controls initiated and supervised by hardline party bureaucrats. The ambitious reforms, formulated in the spring of 1968, have been intentionally and harshly ignored.

On the basis of the preceding discussion it is possible to formulate the following hypothesis. In countries where economic reforms have been initiated from below, through pressure exerted by reformists and intellectuals, the models have failed to succeed. However, in countries where economic reforms have been introduced by the party elites, that is, initiated from above, the models have been successful, primarily because they have received much-needed support from deeply entrenched party bureaucrats.

Hungary. A good example of the latter situation is Hungary. Compared to other European Communist countries, Hungary was one of the late arrivals to join the club of the economic pragmatists. On January 1,

1968, Hungary introduced the New Economic Mechanism (NEM). Unlike in Czechoslovakia, in Hungary the party organized conferences, debates, and seminars in many cities and villages with the basic aim of selling the idea of the reform to the masses. For two years the Hungarian Socialist Workers' Party (HSWP) busily prepared itself for this task.

With the exception of Yugoslavia, in 1970, Hungary has the most liberal blueprint for economic planning and management in Communist Europe. It encompasses both industry and agriculture. Although central direction under the NEM remains in the hands of the party, economic leadership in the enterprises is in the hands of experts and managers. Thus, party decisions affecting the enterprises are guided to a great extent by the point of view of economists rather than ideologists. Hungary is trying to achieve a harmonious blend of the socialist plan and the laws of the market. Similarly, the necessity of political control by the party is identified with the role of harmonizing the interest between the management and the working people. Again, with the exception of Yugoslavia, party influence on economic decision-making is imposed less in Hungary than in other socialist countries experimenting with new economic models. In spite of many far-reaching reform measures, the party and government still decide wage increases, prices on certain consumer goods, restrictions on foreign trade, the size of capital investments and revenue distribution, tax policies, interest rates on credit, allocation of natural resources, and technical development in major segments of the economy. What has actually changed, then, is not so much the party and government's direction of the economy, but the means applied by the party dictatorship to achieve its ends. The Hungarian NEM is more consumer-oriented than any of the other models among the Warsaw-Pact countries. The emphasis in Hungary is not so much on producing commodities as it is on selling them, because through sales the enterprises create the incentives for profit-sharing.

In 1969, the Hungarian NEM produced the most significant changes in the sphere of foreign trade. Exports to non-socialist countries were twice as high as imports. Industrial production increased by three percent, and the nominal wages also increased by three percent. The consumer's price index increased by two percent. Thus, the results of the reform during the first two years have been favorable. Nevertheless, in 1970 Hungary is contemplating introducing the following changes in the NEM: a stricter economy in enterprise labor, a reduction of surplus labor, an increase in average wages, a relaxation in the categories of profit-sharing, a reduction of the rate of state subsidies, an increase in the development of services, and an increase in the imports of consumer goods. So far, the greatest difficulties for the NEM have been in the area of agriculture. Problems of transportation, packaging, and refrigeration of agricultural products, as well as supply bottlenecks due to monopolies are a great hinderance to economic efficiency in agriculture. The Hungarian economists are optimistic, however. They believe that in five or six years time most of the problems will be resolved so as to ensure a balanced economy.

Yugoslavia. The economic system in Yugoslavia, which is a mixture of public ownership, state regulation, and private entrepreneurship, in 1970 is undergoing a convergence to market socialism. Whereas in the Warsaw-Pact countries the key issue is how much decentralization in economic decision-making can be permitted without impairing the role of the party dictatorship, in Yugoslavia the most vital question is how much central planning can be tolerated without damaging the efficiency of the free-market system. The dispute which exists in many European Communist states between the reformists and the bureaucratic centralists was encountered and resolved in Yugoslavia in the early sixties. Since 1965, Yugoslavia has been embarked upon economic reforms which resemble more the advanced Western nations than her ideological Communist neighbors. Many Yugoslav reformists today are of the opinion that neither the state nor the party has a place in determining the operation of the free-market mechanism.

In 1970, the Yugoslav economic system is based on the concept of self-management supported by such autonomous units as Communes, Workers' Councils, and the *Sindikat* (trade union). The state's share in the profits of the self-managing enterprises is minimal; so is the state's subsidy to the less-efficient enterprises. Competition among the enterprises is high, which encourages speedy modernization. In 1969, for example, Yugoslavia permitted the establishment of customs-free zones in six ports for warehousing and economic cooperation with foreign enterprises. This type of legislation is designed to accelerate the modernization of Yugoslav industry. Economic reforms in Yugoslavia are fast approaching market socialism, which promises continued modernization of the industry and a pluralization of the Yugoslav society.

The final test determining the effectiveness of the Yugoslav model and subsequently the other socialist economic models in Europe will depend on whether the superstructural institutions (controlled by the party) will permit micro-economy to lead macro-economy. Decentralization and self-management are not enough to foster an attitude of free entrepreneurship and market orientation at all levels of the economic organization in the state. In countries belonging to the Comecon and the Warsaw

Pact, the ultimate decisions of decentralization and pluralization are not made solely by the national party elites, but also by the leaders in the Kremlin.

Since Soviet interests in Communist Europe vary from country to country, not every Comecon state will go through the same economic development at the same time. In states where the Soviet interpretation of loyalty and security is greater than in other states, we can expect an accelerated process of economic modernization. Two important issues which will have a bearing on the future of economic reforms in Communist Europe are how fast modernization develops in the USSR and how soon that country moves from subsistence economy to pleasure economy.

After the summer of 1968, the Soviet Union decided to revive its Stalinist principle of "proletarian internationalism." The trend in Eastern Europe, however, has been toward "Communist nationalism." Should this trend continue, in spite of Soviet efforts, it could eventually lead to a repetition of the 1957–61 period when the economic demands upon the Soviet Union, flowing inward from the European periphery, exceeded those flowing outward from the Kremlin, forging a new relationship between the USSR and the countries of Communist Europe. These economic demands spilled over into the sociopolitical areas, which led to greater autonomy of East European states. Thus, it is reasonable to assume that the future of economic reforms and political pluralization in Communist Europe is not solely dependent upon Soviet interests in Europe.

An examination of the history of the Sino-Soviet rift reveals some cause for optimism in the future relations of East European countries with the Soviet Union. While relations between China and the USSR continue to deteriorate, it can be assumed that the Soviet Union will once again be willing to pay the price for the support of the Warsaw-Pact countries. In addition, strong influence is being exerted on the leaders of the Kremlin by the party elites in the non-ruling European countries. The Italian, French, and other Communist parties consider economic reforms and pluralization in European party-states vital to their own interests. It would appear, therefore, that in spite of the display of naked force in Czechoslovakia in 1968, the insecure psychological position of the Soviet Union today can be stabilized only by strengthening the multilateral and reciprocal ties with the East European countries. Provided Soviet leaders will follow a rational dictum of the Soviet national interest, we can expect separate future policy formulations toward each East European country tailored to meet the peculiarities of each set of relationships. Thus, in the future, Soviet leaders will have to take into account not only ideological loyalties, but also the various demands and claims arising from domestic pressures and the mutual interests of a pluralistic Eastern Europe.

Soviet Policy and the West

Regardless of whether Soviet policies are favorable or unfavorable to the individual interests of East European countries, they do have a serious impact on the rest of the world. Soviet action in Czechoslovakia in 1968, for example, changed the course of relations between the East and the West and caused an intensification of the cold war. The invasion and occupation of Czechoslovakia created anxiety and further division in the world Communist movement and, in general, was responsible for a serious setback in internal cooperation and in the pursuit of world peace. Some pessimists looked upon the invasion as an act of desperation coming from a major power that is incapable of leadership in its sphere of influence. On numerous occasions the Soviet regime was charged by critics in the U.S. and abroad with becoming too nationalistic, static, and bureaucratized to a point reminiscent of prewar fascist movements. Professor Zbigniew Brzezinski of Columbia University, for example, stated it this way in *Die Zeit* (Hamburg), October 3, 1969, "Degeneration into social fascism, rather than evolution toward social democracy, may thus loom on the horizon as the more likely immediate prospect for the Soviet Union." Thus, by pursuing an irrational policy of subordinating the national interests of the East European countries, the Soviet Union is only helping to feed nationalism in Communist Europe, a fact which could encourage the Soviet decision-makers in the future to commit an even more disastrous blunder than the one committed on August 21, 1968.

In order to induce rational, instead of irrational, policy-making in the Soviet Union, it is imperative for the West, not necessarily under the leadership of the United States, to initiate a stronger program of cooperation with the Communist states in Europe. International cooperation, both in the economic and the cultural fields, is a fertile area for easing tension between East and West and for developing trust. Such assimilation between Eastern and Western political systems, as exhibited by the Yugoslav experiment, can also be realized elsewhere in Eastern Europe. This would necessitate, however, a policy for the West to improve relations in every European Communist country unilaterally, including the Soviet Union. The lesson learned from the tragic Czechoslovak experience should be a constant reminder to the West to proceed gradually, with caution and patience. On the other hand, it would be a mistake to pursue a policy vis-a-vis pluralistic Communist Europe which would be designed to strengthen regional cooperation of the Warsaw-Pact and Comecon nations. The national aspirations of individual East European states must be respected and promoted wherever and whenever possible.

Notes

CHAPTER 2. THE SOCIALIST REPUBLIC OF RUMANIA

1. An English version of the "Statement" is contained in William E. Griffith, *Sino-Soviet Relations, 1964–1965* (Cambridge, Mass.: M.I.T. Press, 1967), pp. 269–96.
2. Speech by Nicolae Ceausescu in *Scinteia* (Bucharest), June 10, 1969.
3. The most comprehensive account of the "takeover" in Rumania is contained in Ghita Ionescu, *Communism in Rumania, 1944–1962* (London: Oxford University Press, 1964), pp. 71–143.
4. Stephen Fischer-Galati, *The New Rumania: From People's Democracy to Socialist Republic* (Cambridge, Mass.: M.I.T. Press, 1967), pp. 93–103.
5. A good account of the origins of the Rumanian Communist Party will be found in Ionescu, *op. cit.,* pp. 1–21.
6. Fischer-Galati, *op. cit.,* pp. 14–15. See also Nicolae Ceausescu's speech delivered on the occasion of the Rumanian Communist Party's forty-fifth anniversary on May 7, 1966, published in *Scinteia* (Bucharest), May 8, 1966.
7. Fischer-Galati, *op. cit.,* pp. 18–28.
8. The proceedings of the conference are in *Scinteia* (Bucharest), October 18–22, 1945.
9. On these points consult Ionescu, *op. cit.,* pp. 147–218.
10. Most edifying evidence is contained in *Documents Concerning Right Wing Deviation in the Rumanian Workers' Party* (Bucharest: Rumanian Workers' Party Publishing House, 1952), pp. 3–85. An analytical interpretation of the events leading to the crisis of 1952 and of the crisis itself will be found in Fischer-Galati, *op. cit.,* pp. 38–43.
11. John Michael Montias, *Economic Development in Communist Rumania* (Cambridge, Mass.: M.I.T. Press, 1967). Pp. 1–38 provide an excellent analysis of these problems.
12. Fischer-Galati, *op. cit.,* pp. 44–67.
13. See Gheorghiu-Dej's speech on the ninth anniversary of the "liberation" of Rumania in *Scinteia* (Bucharest), August 23, 1953.
14. Montias, *op. cit.,* pp. 38–53.

15. Ionescu, *op. cit.,* pp. 219–87.
16. Fischer-Galati, *op. cit.,* pp. 50–52.
17. Ionescu, *op. cit.,* pp. 255–87 contain a particularly lucid discussion of these problems.
18. A minute analysis of the events of 1957 will be found in Fischer-Galati, *op. cit.,* pp. 66–68.
19. *Ibid.,* pp. 68–77.
20. On Comecon and related matters consult Montias, *op. cit.,* pp. 187–230.
21. The best study on Rumanian military policy and politics is by Robin Alison Remington, *The Changing Soviet Perception of the Warsaw Pact* (Cambridge, Mass.: Center for International Studies, M.I.T., 1967), pp. 36–43. See also *Pravda* (Moscow), May 27, 1958.
22. Ionescu, *op. cit.,* pp. 240–52.
23. Montias, *op. cit.,* pp. 53–79, 203–205.
24. Ionescu, *op. cit.,* pp. 301–309.
25. *Ibid.,* pp. 321–25.
26. *Ibid.,* pp. 309–15.
27. Fischer-Galati, *op. cit.,* pp. 79–80.
28. *Ibid.,* pp. 80–82.
29. *Scinteia* (Bucharest), March 9, 1963.
30. Fischer-Galati, *op. cit.,* pp. 103–109.
31. *Ibid.,* pp. 112–14.
32. *Statutes of the Romanian Communist Party* (Bucharest: Editura Politica, 1965).
33. Jan F. Triska, ed., *Constitutions of the Communist Party-States* (Stanford: Hoover Institution, 1968), p. 378.
34. Ceausescu's principal speech at the Congress may be found in *Scinteia* (Bucharest), July 20, 1965.
35. Fischer-Galati, *op. cit.,* pp. 114–15.
36. The most valuable source of information on these matters is the two-volume collection of Ceausescu's writings and speeches: Nicolae Ceausescu, *Romania pe Drumul Desavirsirii Constructiei Socialiste* (Rumania on the Road of Completion of Socialist Construction) (Bucharest: Editura Politica, 1968).
37. Comparative foreign trade statistics are provided in Central Statistical Board, *Statistical Pocket Book of the Socialist Republic of Romania, 1968* (Bucharest: n.p., 1969), pp. 297–315.
38. A summary statement of Rumania's foreign policy was made by Ceausescu in July on the occasion of a meeting of the Grand National Assembly. See Ceausescu, *op. cit.,* 2: 412–64.
39. *Ibid.,* p. 415.
40. *Scinteia* (Bucharest), December 7, 1967.
41. Radu Constantinescu, "Why Patrascanu Was Rehabilitated," *East Europe* 17, no. 8 (1968), pp. 6–9.
42. The principal source of information for developments in this period is *Scinteia* (Bucharest), which provides complete texts of all significant speeches and meetings.
43. *Scinteia* (Bucharest), August 21–September 10, 1968.
44. Consult the "Theses of the Central Committee of the Rumanian Communist Party Concerning the Tenth Congress of the Party," *Scinteia* (Bucharest),

May 31, 1969, and the proceedings of the Congress in *Scinteia,* August 6–13, 1969.

45. A comprehensive statement of Rumania's foreign policy is contained in *Scinteia* (Bucharest), June 10, 1969.

46. Consult Ceausescu's major address delivered at the Plenary Session of the Central Committee of the Rumanian Communist Party in *Scinteia* (Bucharest), December 14, 1969.

47. Important data on Rumania's economic position and relations with foreign countries are found in Ceausescu's speech referred to in note 46.

CHAPTER 3. THE POLISH PEOPLE'S REPUBLIC

1. For a perceptive analysis of the Polish intelligentsia, see Janusz Zarnowski, *O inteligencji polskiej lat miedzywojennych* (Warsaw: Wiedza Powszechna, 1965).

2. *Polska Ludowa: Slownik encyklopedyczny* (Warsaw: Wiedza Powszechna, 1965), pp. 160–61.

3. Glowny Urzad Statystyczny, *Rocznik Statystyczny: 1966,* 26, section 1 (1966), p. 35.

4. *Kurier Polski* (Warsaw), organ of the Democratic Alliance (S.D.), June 22, 1966.

5. KTT, "Kuchnia polska: Pomowmy o Pieniadzach," *Kultura* (Warsaw) 3, no. 42 (October 17, 1965), p. 12.

6. Adam Sarapata, "Stratification and Social Mobility in Poland," in Institute of Philosophy and Sociology, Polish Academy of Sciences, *Empirical Sociology in Poland* (Warsaw: Polish Scientific Publishers [PWN], 1966), pp. 39–40.

7. Joseph R. Fiszman, *Teachers in Poland as Transmitters of Socio-Political Values,* Office of Education, Bureau of Research, Final Report, Project No. S-417 (Washington, D.C.: U.S. Department of Health, Education, and Welfare, October 1969), p. 244.

8. Zygmunt Skorzynski, *Miedzy praca a wypoczynkiem: Czas "zajety" i czas "wolny" mieszkancow miast w swietle badan empirycznych* (Wroclaw: Zaklad Narodowy im. Ossolinskich for the Institute of Philosophy and Sociology, Polish Academy of Sciences, Workshop for Research on Mass Culture, 1965), p. 72.

9. See, for example, the regular matrimonial advertisement columns appearing in the Warsaw daily, *Kurier Polski,* official organ of the Democratic Alliance (*Stronnictwo Demokratyczne, S.D.*). Prior to World War II this group operated under the name of Democratic Club and was an organization representing the liberal intellectual and academic elite, but in 1970 it is designed to politically represent the class of private entrepreneurs within the Front of National Unity.

10. See Andrzej Sicinski, ed., *Spoleczenstwo polskie w badaniach ankietowych Osrodka Badania Opinii Publicznej przy Polskim Radiu i TV: Lata 1958–1964: Przeglad zebranych materialow* (Warsaw: Panstwowe Wydawnictwo Naukowe, 1966).

11. Fiszman, *op. cit.,* p. 176.

12. *Ibid.,* p. 191.

13. E.G., "Problemy i dyskusje: Czy stan normalny?" *Stolica* (Warsaw) 23, no. 20 (May 19, 1968), p. 14.

14. *Kultura* (Warsaw), May 28, 1966.
15. See Fiszman, *op. cit.*, as well as Mikolaj Kozakiewicz, *Swiatopoglad 1000 nauczycieli: Sprawozdanie z badan ankietowych* (Warsaw: Panstwowe Zaklady Wydawnictw Szkolnych, 1961).
16. Czeslaw Milosz, *Native Realm: A Search for Self-Definition,* tran. from the Polish by Catherine S. Leach. (Garden City, N.Y.: Doubleday & Co., 1968), pp. 32–33.
17. Zbigniew Kwiatkowski, *Bylem niemilczacym swiadkiem* (Warsaw: Iskry, 1965), p. 269.
18. See Adam Sarapata, "Social Mobility," *Polish Perspectives* (Warsaw, English language edition) 9, no. 1 (January 1966), pp. 18–27.
19. Speech by Deputy Dyzma Galaj (United Peasant Alliance) in Parliament *(Sejm)*, as reported in *Zycie Warszawy,* November 11, 1966, p. 4.
20. Janusz Skarzynski, "Zrodlo konfliktu," *Polityka* (Warsaw), May 28, 1966.
21. Tadeusz Nowacki, "Milicja czy regularne wojsko?" *Kultura* (Paris), no. 5/260, May 1969, p. 123.
22. Konstanty Grzybowski, "Roma locuta . . . ," in *Oredzie biskupow polskich do biskupow niemieckich: Materialy i dokumenty,* 2nd ed. (Warsaw: Polonia, 1966), p. 121.
23. Wladyslaw Gomulka, "Speech . . . delivered at Session of All-Polish Committee of the Front of National Unity, January 14, 1966," *ibid.,* p. 197.
24. See letter from the Metropolitan Curia and Editor's response in *Polityka* (Warsaw), May 28, 1966.
25. Speech by Andrzej Werblan at the 12th Plenary Session of the Central Committee of the United Polish Workers' Party, as reported in *Trybuna Ludu* (Warsaw), daily organ of the Central Committee of the PZPR, July 11, 1968, pp. 3–4.
26. *Polityka* (Warsaw), May 28, 1966.
27. *Ibid.*
28. For an elaborate discussion on the relationship between "legal consciousness" and "socialist consciousness," see Grzegorz Leopold Seidler, "Marxist Legal Thought in Poland," *Slavic Review* 26, no. 3 (September 1967), pp. 382–94. Profesor Seidler is the former rector of Maria Curie-Sklodowska University at Lublin.
29. Harry M. Geduld, ed., *The Rationalization of Russia* (Bloomington: Indiana University Press, 1964), p. 71.

CHAPTER 4. THE PEOPLE'S REPUBLIC OF BULGARIA

1. The evolution of Bulgarian affairs from 1944, when the Communist party came to power, to the mid-1950s is adequately presented in *Bulgaria,* a handbook edited by L. A. D. Dellin (New York: Praeger, 1957); Robert L. Wolff, *The Balkans in Our Time* (Cambridge, Mass.: Harvard University Press, 1956); and the two volumes edited by Stephen D. Kertesz, *The Fate of East-Central Europe: Hopes and Failures of American Foreign Policy* (1956) and *East-Central Europe and the World: Developments in the Post-Stalin Era* (1962), both published in Notre Dame, Indiana, by University of Notre Dame Press. The latter volume covers developments to 1961.

    Brief surveys of events to the mid-1960s are included in J. F. Brown, *The New Eastern Europe: The Khrushchev Era and After* (New York:

Praeger, 1966) and Richard F. Staar, *The Communist Regimes in Eastern Europe: An Introduction* (Stanford, Calif.: The Hoover Institution, 1967). Official Bulgarian accounts include *Istoriia na Bulgariia,* 2nd rev. ed., vol. 3 (Sofia: Nauka i izkustvo, 1964) and *Kratka istoriia na Bulgariia,* 2nd rev. ed. (Sofia: Nauka i izkustvo, 1966), both written by historians in the Bulgarian Academy of Sciences; *Materiali po istoriia na Bulgarskata Komunisticheska Partiia, 1925–1962 g.* (Sofia: Bulgarska Komunisticheska Partiia, 1964); and articles on Bulgarian subjects in *Kratka Bulgarska Entsiklopediia,* vol. 1 (Sofia: Bulgarska akademiia na naukite, 1963).

For additional references, see M. Pundeff, *Bulgaria: A Bibliographic Guide* (Washington: Library of Congress, 1965; reprinted by Arno Press, N.Y., 1968), and "Bulgaria" in *Southeast Europe: A Bibliographic Guide,* ed. by Paul L. Horecky (Chicago: The University of Chicago Press, 1969).

2. *Materiali, . . . 1925–1962 g., op. cit.,* p. 388.
3. For additional **known** details of his life, see M. Pundeff, "Todor Zhivkov: Bulgaria's Loyal **Pragmatist**," in *Leaders of the Communist World,* ed. by **Rodger** Swearingen (New York: Free Press [Macmillan], 1970).
4. S. S. Biriuzov, *Sovetskii soldat na Balkanakh* (Moscow, 1963), pp. 194, 288.
5. The change was formalized at the Sixth Congress of the Bulgarian Communist Party in March 1954, which was still dominated by Chervenkov. The effects of the purge, which, according to party sources, had eliminated 92,500 members, were still felt: at the congress the party had 455,251 members (including 87,109 probationary members) as against the 496,000 it had at the Fifth Congress in 1948. See *Materiali . . . 1925–1962 g., op. cit.,* pp. 352–54; *Materiali po istoriia na Bulgarskata Komunisticheska Partiia, 9 septemvri 1944–1960 g.* (Sofia: Bulgarska Komunisticheska Partiia, 1961), p. 73.
6. *Materiali . . . 1925–1962 g., op. cit.* (1964 edition), pp. 359–60.
7. *Ibid.,* pp. 390–91.
8. Zhivkov led the Bulgarian delegations to the Moscow conferences of Communist parties in 1957 and 1960, the Twenty-First Congress of the Soviet Communist Party in 1959, and other meetings in Moscow, and accompanied Khrushchev on his trip to the United Nations in 1960. Everywhere he echoed his mentor's views.
9. *Ibid.,* pp. 494–95.
10. For the changes through June 1965, see *Directory of Bulgarian Officials* (Washington: U.S. Department of State, 1965).
11. *Spravochnik na propagandista i agitatora, 1967* (Sofia: Bulgarska Komunisticheska Partiia, 1967), p. 23.
12. For brief biographies, see the respective volumes of *Kratka Bulgarska Entsiklopediia, op. cit.*
13. The lists of the members of these bodies are in the sources cited in notes 10 and 11 above.
14. *Rabotnichesko Delo* (Sofia), December 27, 1968.
15. *Ibid.,* December 28, 1968.
16. See note 10.
17. *Materiali, . . . 1925–1962 g., op. cit.* (1964 edition), p. 237.
18. In the Politburo-secretariat circle, Avramov, Tsolov, and Tsanev are also

men of obvious importance and must not be overlooked. Avramov's Soviet credentials are impeccable: the son of a Bulgarian Communist leader who worked in the USSR, he spent three years (1938–41) in the Soviet Union and was parachuted into Bulgaria to work with the wartime guerrilla movement. Tsolov is entrusted with economic planning on both the national and the international scale. Tsanev, a lieutenant-general, has charge of military affairs.

19. Interview with Austrian journalists, *Neues Oesterreich* (Vienna), July 17, 1965, quoted in *East Europe,* September 1965, pp. 37–38. The few known details are summed up in Norbert Bornemann, "Die Verschworung in Bulgarien," *Osteuropa* (Stuttgart), September 1965, pp. 616–19. Since the men involved had records as guerrilla fighters during the war years, it has been speculated that they were nationalistically motivated by resentment of Zhivkov's excessive subservience to the Soviet Union and were seeking a pro-Yugoslav orientation.

20. *Kratka Bulgarska Entsiklopediia,* vol. 1, p. 321; B. Spasov and A. Angelov, *Durzhavno pravo na Narodna Republika Bulgariia,* 2nd. rev. ed. (Sofia: Nauka i Izkustvo, 1968), p. 66.

21. *Statisticheski spravochnik na NR Bulgariia, 1968* (Sofia: Tsentralno Statistichesko Upravlenie pri Ministerskiia Suvet, 1968), pp. 2, 7.

22. The party has grown vastly in size since 1944, when it had only 25,000 members. Within the first six months after coming to power, it swelled to 250,000 and 496,000 at the Fifth Congress in 1948. The growth, according to party sources, came in large measure from the influx of "opportunist, alien, careerist, and in some areas hostile elements," that is, old-regime bureaucrats, minor fascists, and multitudes of career-seekers. The purge of Titoists eliminated nearly 100,000, but the ranks were quickly replenished. At the Sixth Congress (1954), the party had 455,251 members; at the Seventh (1958), 484,255; at the Eighth (1962), 528,674; at the Ninth (1966), 611,179. Of the last number, 38.4 percent were workers, 32.4 percent white-collar intelligentsia, and 29.2 percent peasants. (*Materiali, op. cit.* [1964 edition], pp. 257, 326, and Staar, *op. cit.,* p. 39.)

23. A Commission on the People's Councils of the National Assembly, established in 1965 as part of Zhivkov's program of fostering the "development of socialist democracy" and augmenting the role of the legislature, also has a function in this area. The commission is one of ten established since 1958. (Spasov and Angelov, *op. cit.,* p. 222.)

24. *Ibid.,* pp. 394–403.

25. *Ibid.,* pp. 417, 422–26.

26. *Ibid.,* pp. 436–49.

27. *The Trial of Traicho Kostov and His Group* (Sofia, n.p., 1949); Traicho Kostov, *Izbrani statii, dokladi, rechi* (Sofia: Bulgarskata Komunisticheska Partiia, 1964). The party also made Kostov posthumously "Hero of Socialist Labor."

28. Texts in *Rabotnichesko Delo* (Sofia), July 25, 26, and 27, 1968.

29. Michael Costello, "The July Plenum: Political Considerations," *Radio Free Europe Report,* Bulgaria/13, August 19, 1968, pp. 9–10.

30. The congress will presumably be convened in November 1970, when the new constitution is also likely to be finished and presented. A commission of seventy-eight members chaired by Zhivkov was established by the

National Assembly in March 1968 to prepare the constitution for the twenty-fifth anniversary of the regime in 1969, but this deadline was not met. (*Rabotnichesko Delo* [Sofia], March 16 and May 16, 1968; September 9, 1969.) The constitution will presumably proclaim that Bulgaria has completed the transition from capitalism to socialism and that it is constructing the mature socialist society which is the preliminary stage to Communism. Accordingly, the title of People's Republic is likely to be changed to Socialist Republic as was done in the Czechoslovak and Rumanian constitutions of 1960 and 1965, respectively.

31. Texts, *ibid.,* November 30 and December 1, 1968. Zhivkov's speech is available in English translation in *A Further Broadening of Socialist Democracy,* published in Sofia by Sofia Press in 1968. The resulting regulations are in *Durzhaven Vestnik* (Sofia), no. 60, August 1, 1969.

32. *Rabotnichesko Delo* (Sofia), December 28, 1968.

33. *Ibid.,* July 4, 1969.

34. *Materiali . . . 1925–1962 g.* (1964 edition), p. 385.

35. *Kratka Bulgarska Entsiklopediia, op. cit.,* vol. 3 (1966), p. 100.

36. The 1961–80 projection envisaged the commencement of the construction of the Communist society in the USSR and the "more or less simultaneous" transition of all socialist states to Communism in this period. The Bulgarian Communists adopted a similar projection for 1961–80.

37. Zhivkov's report in *Osmi kongres na Bulgarskata Komunisticheska Partiia; stenografski protokol* (Sofia: Bulgarskata Komunisticheska Partiia, 1963), especially pp. 46, 84.

38. Zhivkov's report to the Ninth Congress, *Rabotnichesko Delo,* November 15, 1966. For absolute figures in the various categories of industrial and agricultural production, see *Statisticheski godishnik na Narodna Republika Bulgariia, 1968* (Sofia: Tsentralno Statistichesko Upravlenie pri Ministerskiia Suvet, 1968), pp. 117–226.

39. *Rabotnichesko Delo* (Sofia) November 15, 1966, and *Statisticheski godishnik, 1968, op. cit.,* for absolute figures for 1966 and 1967.

40. *Rabotnichesko Delo* (Sofia), May 10, 1968.

41 *Ibid.,* February 23, March 29, and April 2, 1967.

42. *Ibid.,* April 25–29, 1967.

43. M. Pundeff, "The Bulgarian Academy of Sciences," *East European Quarterly,* September 1969, pp. 371–86.

44. Its statute is in *Izvestiia na Prezidiuma na Narodnoto Subranie* (Sofia), no. 6, January 19, 1962.

45. The functions of the Committee are detailed *ibid.,* no. 79, October 2, 1962, and *Durzhaven Vestnik* (Sofia), no. 48, June 21, 1963.

46. Cf. Krustanov's annual report for 1961 in *Spisanie na Bulgarskata akademiia na naukite* (Sofia), no. 1–2, 1962, pp. 3–17.

47. K. Bratanov, "Bulgarskata nauka," *Slaviani* (Sofia), June 1969, p. 2; A. Obretenov, *Kulturnata revoliutsiia v Bulgariia* (Sofia: Bulgarskata Komunisticheska Partiia, 1968), p. 101. The institutes and such existing in 1966 are listed (with addresses, directors, subunits, and regular publications), in *Nauchni uchrezhdeniia v Bulgariia, 1966; spravochnik* (Sofia: Bulgarska akademiia na naukite, 1967).

48. The first decade of cooperation under the agreement with the Soviet Academy of Sciences is reviewed in *Voprosy Istorii* (Moscow), no. 12,

1968, pp. 159–66. As an index of the scientific exchange with the USSR, which far exceeds all other exchange and cooperation programs, annually some three hunderd Bulgarian scholars work in Soviet institutions and two hunderd Soviet scholars work in Bulgarian institutions.

49. Text in *Izvestiia . . . ,* (Sofia), *op. cit.,* no. 92, October 17, 1959.

50. Excerpts in *Rabotnichesko Delo* (Sofia), March 17, 1967.

51. Translation of the resulting law in Peter John Georgeoff, *The Social Education of Bulgarian Youth* (Minneapolis: University of Minnesota Press, 1968), pp. 169–76. On the reform in the context of educational change in the bloc, see M. Pundeff, "Schulsystem und Schulreformen in Osteuropa," *Osteuropa* (Stuttgart), July-August 1963, pp. 482–94; English text in *Eastern Europe in the Sixties,* ed. Stephen Fischer-Galati (New York: Praeger, 1963), pp. 26–51.

52. *Kratka Bulgarska Entsiklopediia* 1: 372–74. For a translation of the chart of organization of the educational system on p. 373, see Georgeoff, *op. cit.,* p. 16.

53. *East Europe,* November 1962, pp. 31–33, quoting speeches by Zhivkov and Education Minister Nacho Papazov.

54. *Narodna Prosveta* (Sofia), no. 1, 1967, pp. 3–8; see also *ibid.,* no. 2, 1967, pp. 3–59, and *Uchitelsko Delo* (Sofia), January 11, 1967.

55. *Statisticheski godishnik, 1968, op. cit.,* p. 349.

56. For data, see M. Pundeff, "The University of Sofia at Eighty," *Slavic Review,* September 1968, pp. 438–46. For the organization of the institutions of higher learning and their majors, see *Spravochnik na kandidat-studentite* (Sofia: Nauka i Izkustvo, annual).

57. P. Avramov, *Bulgarskata Komunisticheska Partiia i formirane na sotsialisticheskata inteligentsiia* (Sofia: Bulgarskata Komunisticheska Partiia, 1966), p. 274.

58. In addition to the Komsomol for the age group of fourteen to twenty-eight, the Party sponsors the so-called Young Septembrist Pioneer Organization for the nine-to-fourteen age group, which has Little Chavdar Detachments for children in the first and second grade. The names are selected to relate to the September 1944 seizure of power, the Pioneer Organization in the USSR, and the Chavdar Brigade in the wartime underground movement. (*Kratka Bulgarska Entsiklopediia,* 2: pp. 177–80.)

59. Georgeoff, *op. cit.,* pp. 66–102. Georgeoff has concentrated on the general eight-grade schools.

60. Kotsev's statement is in *Narodna Prosveta* (Sofia), no. 8, 1967, pp. 3–8. The report on specific problems by the deputy minister of education, Bistra Avramova, also noted rises in use of alcohol and in juvenile delinquency, more than fifty percent of the crimes being committed by Komsomol and Pioneer members. (*Ibid.,* pp. 9–30.)

61. The essential texts were published in the national press during December 1967. For references and analysis, see Michael Costello, "The Bulgarian Youth Discussion: Consequences, Initiatives, and Implications," *Radio Free Europe Report,* Bulgaria/3, February 13, 1968.

62. *Rabotnichesko Delo* (Sofia), January 11–14, 1968.

63. *Ibid.,* July 30, 1969.

64. See the report on the conference of Bulgarian historians to deal with the

"ravages of Stalinism," *Istoricheski Pregled* (Sofia), no. 2, 1963, pp. 142–49.

65. *Istoriia na Bulgariia, op. cit.,* note 1 above.

66. Illustrative of the new adulation is the fact that an imposing monument is planned in the center of Sofia to honor Asparukh as "the founder of the Bulgarian state." (*Rabotnichesko Delo* [Sofia], April 9, 1968.)

67. See, for example, M. Voinov, "Kum vuprosa za bulgarskata narodnost v Makedoniia," *Istoricheski Pregled* (Sofia), no. 5, 1966, pp. 61–72.

68. See, for example, the article of Professor Emil Georgiev in *Rabotnichesko Delo* (Sofia), February 8, 1969.

69. I. Vandov, "Patriotizmut i nashata suvremenna khudozhestvena literatura," *Novo Vreme,* no. 7, 1968, pp. 65–74.

70. For the details of the "Bulgarian Writers' Revolt," see *East Europe,* March 1958, pp. 15–23.

71. Todor Zhivkov, *Izkustvoto, naukata i kulturata v sluzhba na naroda; rechi, statii i dokladi* (Sofia: Bulgarski Pisatel, 1965), 1: 421–24.

72. The regulations governing the committee are in *Durzhaven Vestnik* (Sofia), no. 94, December 3, 1963.

73. The proceedings of the congress are in *Purvi kongres na bulgarskata kultura, 18 mai–20 mai 1976 g.* (Sofia: Nauka i Izkustvo, 1967). The congress adopted a statute on the organization and tasks of the committee (Text, *ibid.,* pp. 419–23.) The developments surrounding the congress are analyzed by Emil Popoff, "Bulgaria's Literary 'Mini-Thaw,'" *East Europe,* February 1968, pp. 19–23.

74. *Rabotnichesko Delo* (Sofia), February 6, 1968.

75. *Ibid.,* May 21, 1968.

76. Reviewed in *The New Yorker,* January 25, 1969, pp. 101–103.

77. Details of the developments of the first dozen of years after 1944 and the general Law on Religious Denominations of 1949 are given in D. Slijepcevic, *Die bulgarische orthodoxe Kirche, 1944–1956* (Munich: n.p., 1957), and A. A. Bogolepov, *Tserkov' pod vlast'il kommunizma* (Munich: n.p., 1958). For an English translation of the law, see *The Church and State Under Communism* (Washington, D.C.: U.S. Government Printing Office, 1965), part 2, pp. 23–26.

78. In addition to leading the church, Kiril has been exceptionally productive as a scholar in the field of Bulgarian church history in the nineteenth century. For this aspect of him, see I. Doens, "Patriarch Kiril, Kirchenhistoriker Bulgariens," *Oesterreichische Osthefte* (Vienna) 7, no. 4 (1965), pp. 322–31.

79. Interview with a Bulgarian journalist, *Slaviani* (Sofia), March 1969, pp. 18–19.

80. *NR Bulgariia i religioznite izpovedaniia v neia* (Sofia: Sinodalno Izdatelstvo, 1966), p. 15. The twelfth diocese is formed by the Bulgarians residing in North and South America and Australia and has its seat in New York. In Bulgaria, there are, 3,720 churches and chapels and 123 monasteries with 232 monks and 289 nuns. The church has also a monastery on Mount Athos and churches in Moscow, Bucharest, Budapest, Vienna, and elsewhere.

81. The progress in the commission's work is reported by its chairman, Metro-

politan Iosif of Varna and Preslav, in *Dukhovna Kultura* (Sofia), nos. 6–7, 1968, pp. 1–5.

82. *NR Bulgariia i religioznite izpovedaniia v neia, op. cit.,* p. 23; N. Mizov, *Isliamut v Bulgariia* (Sofia: Bulgarskata Komunisticheska Partiia, 1965), p. 195.

83. On the Catholics, see K. Drenikoff, *L'Eglise Catholique en Bulgarie* (Madrid: n.p., 1968). The plight of the Protestants is reflected in the account of Haralan Popoff, *I Was a Communist Prisoner* (Grand Rapids, Mich.: Zondervan, 1966). Popoff was one of the fifteen pastors tried and sentenced to prison terms in 1949. On the postwar treatment of the Jews and the mass exodus to Israel in 1948–49, see Peter Meyer, ed., *The Jews in the Soviet Satellites* (Syracuse, N.Y.: Syracuse University Press, 1953), pp. 557–629.

84. Text in *Bulgarska Komunisticheska Partiia v rezoliutsii i resheniia na kongresite, na plenumi i na Politbiuro na TsK na BKP, 1956–1962* (Sofia: Bulgarskata Komunisticheska Partiia, 1965), pp. 166–72.

85. Texts, *ibid.,* pp. 665–95, and *Spravochnik na aktivista* (Sofia: Bulgarskata Komunisticheska Partiia, 1966), pp. 478–80 and 544–48.

86. A complete report of the survey is provided in *Protsesut na preodoliavaneto na religiiata v Bulgariia; sotsiologichesko izsledvane,* ed. by Zh. Oshavkov (Sofia: Bulgarskata akademii na nankite, 1968). A preliminary report appeared in *Religion und Atheismus Heute; Ergebnisse und Aufgaben marxistischer Religionsoziologie,* ed. O. Klohr (East Berlin, 1966), pp. 81–92.

87. *Rabotnichesko Delo* (Sofia), April 18, 1968.

88. *Naruchnik na Agitatora* (Sofia), no. 12, June 1967, pp. 62–64.

89. Paul Lendvai, *Eagles in Cobwebs: Nationalism and Communism in the Balkans* (Garden City, N.Y.: Doubleday, 1969), p. 255. An experienced journalist, Lendvai provides interesting observations of the Bulgarian scene under Zhivkov, including Zhivkov's reactions to the plot in 1965 on pp. 255–323.

CHAPTER 5. THE GERMAN DEMOCRATIC REPUBLIC

1. For a penetrating and balanced political biography of Walter Ulbricht, see *Ulbricht: A Political Biography,* by Carola Stern (New York: Frederick A. Praeger, 1965).

2. Klaus-Eberhard Murowski, *Der Andere Teil Deutschlands* (Munich: Gunter Olzog Verlag, 1967), p. 68.

3. Kurt Erdmann, "Verfassungskommission eingesetzt," *SBZ-Archiv* (East Berlin) 17, nos. 23–24 (December 1967), pp. 361–63.

4. For a detailed and comprehensive analysis of the constitutional foundations of the DDR as originally established in 1949, and subsequently modified, see Ernst Richert, *Macht Ohne Mandat,* 2nd ed. (Cologne: Westdeutscher Verlag, 1963), pp. 36–104. Karl Loewenstein also points up these main features in his "Reflections on the Value of Constitutions in Our Revolutionary Age," reprinted in *Comparative Politics: A Reader,* edited by Harry Eckstein and David E. Apter (New York: The Free Press [Macmillan], 1963), pp. 153–54, especially.

5. Elmer Plischke, *Contemporary Governments of Germany,* 2nd ed. (Boston: Houghton Mifflin Company, 1969), p. 195.

6. Ernst Richert, *Das Zweite Deutschland: Ein Staat, der nicht sein darf* (Gutersloh: Sigbert Mohn Verlag, 1964), pp. 64–67.

7. Erdmann, *op. cit.,* p. 362.

8. Jean Edward Smith, *Germany Beyond the Wall* (Boston: Little, Brown and Company, 1969), pp. 245–72, furnishes a full text of the new constitution, as may also be found in *Documents of Major Foreign Powers: A Sourcebook,* edited by Louise W. Holborn, John H. Herz, and Gwendolen Carter (New York: Harcourt, Brace & World, Inc., 1968), pp. 257–69. Constitutional references throughout this analysis will be to Smith's version. No basic differences exist between the two translations of the constitution's first official printing in *Neues Deutschland* (East Berlin) on March 27, 1968. Nowhere does Smith's analysis of "the people, politics and prosperity" of East Germany, however, include a rigorous analysis of the constitution, so conveniently appended to his work.

9. Smith, "Constitution of the German Democratic Republic" in *Germany Beyond the Wall, op. cit.,* "Preamble," p. 245.

10. *Ibid.,* Article 1, p. 246.

11. *Ibid.,* Article 8, p. 248.

12. *Ibid.,* Article 2, p. 246.

13. *Ibid.,* Article 9, p. 248.

14. *Ibid.,* Article 6, p. 247.

15. Holborn, *et al., op. cit.,* p. 257.

16. Smith, *op. cit.,* Preamble and Articles 1, 18, 23, and 25, pp. 245, 246, 251, 253, and 254, respectively.

17. State Secretariat for West German Affairs, *Democracy in the GDR: Power Relations and Social Forms in the Socialist State of the German Nation* (Dresden: Verlag Zeit im Bild, 1968), p. 57.

18. Smith, *op. cit.,* Articles 45 and 48, pp. 259–60.

19. Plischke, *op. cit.,* p. 181.

20. Werner Rietschel, *State and Society* (Dresden: Verlag Zeit im Bild, 1968), pp. 3–4.

21. Smith, *op. cit.,* p. 257.

22. *Ibid.,* Articles 9 and 47, pp. 249 and 259, respectively.

23. *Ibid.,* Articles 49 and 50, p. 260.

24. *Ibid.,* Article 65, p. 263.

25. *Ibid.,* Articles 56, 57, 58, 59, and 60, pp. 261–62.

26. *Ibid.,* Articles 61, 62, 63, 64, and 65, pp. 262–63.

27. Bundesministerium fur gesamtdeutsche Fragen, *Der Staatsapparat der "Deutschen Demokratischen Republik,"* 4th ed. (Bonn: n.p. 1969), pp. 6–9. These committees are: External Affairs; National Defense; Constitutional and Judicial Affairs; Industry, Building, and Commerce; Land and Forestry; Trade and Supply; Budget and Finance; Labor and Social Policy; Health; Public Instruction; Culture; Youth; Citizen's Petitions; Rules; Mandate Review; and the Inter-Parliamentary Group. Almost every committee has a chairman, one or more deputy chairmen, a recorder, and a variable number of members ranging from six for the Rules to thirty-four for Industry, Building, and Commerce.

28. *Ibid.,* p. 3. More detailed professional profiles of the Presidium's membership are furnished in *Die Volkskammer der Deutschen Demokratischen*

Republik, op. cit., pp. 226, 417, 273, 348, 235, 271, 439, 492, and 511, respectively.

29. *Ibid.,* p. 4.
30. *Ibid.,* p. 10. The expanded political profiles of the State Council's membership were obtained from *Die Volkskammer, op. cit.,* pp. 580, 559, 226, 328, 226, 488, 273, 217, 235, 281, 294, 311, 359, 424, 428, 448, 487, 489, 517, 533, 544, 549, and 561, respectively.
31. Smith, *op. cit.,* pp. 263–64.
32. Smith, *op. cit.,* pp. 264–65.
33. *Ibid.,* p. 265.
34. *Ibid.,* p. 264.
35. *Ibid.,* Article 73, pp. 264–65.
36. Bundesministerium, *Der Staatsapparat, op. cit.,* p. 11.
37. Prasidium der Volkskammer, *Die Volkskammer der Deutschen Demokratischen Republik: 5. Wahlperiode* (East Berlin: Staatsverlag der Deutschen Demokratischen Republik, 1967), pp. 580, 329, 253, 354 (Scheibe and Hoffmann unlisted), 426, 224, and 559, respectively.
28. Bundesministerium fur gesamtdeutsche Fragen, *Der Parteiapparat der "Deutschen Demokratischen Republik,"* 3rd ed. (Bonn: n.p., 1969), pp. 1–9.
39. Karl Loewenstein, *op. cit.,* p. 155.
40. *Ibid.*
41. Smith, *op. cit.,* p. 266.
42. The 1968 Constitution completely omits the old constitution's requirement that a motion of nonconfidence could only be posed to the Chamber if one-fourth of the Chamber's membership signed it and that it had to be carried by at least an absolute majority of the members to be effective. See Plischke, *op. cit.,* p. 198.
43. For an analysis of these and other parliamentary requirements, as well as those corresponding features of presidential systems, consult "Analysis of Political Systems," by Douglas V. Verney, reprinted in *Comparative Politics: A Reader,* edited by Harry Eckstein and David E. Apter, *op. cit.,* pp. 175–91.
44. Consideration of the kinds of specific responsibilities articles 78 and 79 assign to the Council of Ministers further confirms this general observation. They are few in number, vague in definition, and implementary rather than truly executive in scope and power. See Smith, *op. cit.,* pp. 265–66.
45. Bundesministerium, *Der Staatsapparat, op. cit.,* p. 12.
46. These positions include, by way of illustration, finance, interior, culture, defense, building, traffic, justice, health, foreign affairs, prices, school construction, science and technology, post and telegraph, heavy industry, chemical industry, light industry, mining, electronics, foreign trade, and electronic technology.
47. Bundesministerium, *Der Parteiapparat, op. cit.,* pp. 5–9.
48. Bundesministerium, *Der Staatsapparat, op. cit.,* pp. 16–25. Concentrically moving beyond the Chairman, the First Deputy Chairman, the Deputy Chairmen without Portfolio, Deputy Chairmen with Portfolio, and the ordinary ministers, two further zones of administrative activity are encountered, best classified under the headings of state-secretaries and secretariats, exercising modest but distinctive jurisdictions, and so-called central state organs attached to the Council of Ministers, of which there are six and

twenty-nine bodies, respectively. The SED also controls about ninety-five percent of the one hundred positions available in these two administrative spheres combined.

49. *Ibid.,* p. 27.
50. Bundesministerium, *Der Parteiapparat, op. cit.,* pp. 4–7.
51. Smith, *op. cit.,* pp. 262, 264, 269, 265, and 268, respectively.
52. Bundesministerium fur gesamtdeutsche Fragen, *Die SED: Historische Entwicklung, Ideologische Grundlagen, Programm und Organization* (Bonn: n.p., 1967), p. 84.
53. Bundesministerium, *Der Parteiapparat, op. cit.,* pp. 5–9.
54. Eckart Fortsch with Rudiger Mann, *Die SED* (Stuttgart: W. Kohlhammer Verlag, 1969), pp. 57. Also see Bundesministerium, *Der Parteiapparat, op. cit.,* pp. 10–14. Among these sections, by way of illustration, are to be found specialized groups dealing with cadre affairs, party organs, party finance, agitation, propaganda, press, sports, sciences, culture, security, health, youth, women, trade, agriculture, construction, light industry, unions, and international contacts. Agitation, women, security, party work, foreign policy, and ideology are among the topics of commission-level attention.
55. Fortsch, *op. cit.,* pp. 112–13.
56. *Ibid.,* pp. 113–14.
57. *Ibid.,* p. 114.
58. *Ibid.*
59. *Ibid.*
60. *Ibid.,* p. 58.
61. *Ibid.,* pp. 58–59.
62. *Ibid.,* p. 115.
63. *Ibid.,* pp. 121–22.
64. *Ibid.,* pp. 122–23.
65. *Ibid.,* p. 124.
66. *Ibid.,* pp. 124–26.
67. *Ibid.,* p. 66.
68. *Ibid.,* 11, 29 and 67.
69. *Ibid.,* pp. 47–48.
70. *Ibid.,* pp. 49–54.
71. *Ibid.,* p. 54.
72. Bundesministerium, *Der Parteiapparat, op. cit.,* p. 23.
73. Fortsch, *op. cit.,* pp. 34–43.
74. In this connection, consult *Parteien im Blocksystem der DDR,* by Roderick Kulbach and Helmut Weber (Cologne: Verlag Wissenschaft und Politik, 1969), and *LDP und NDP in der DDR: 1949–1958* (Cologne: Westdeutscher Verlag, 1965).
75. Fortsch, *op. cit.,* pp. 132–41.
76. *Ibid.,* pp. 29–30.
77. *Ibid.,* pp. 30–33.
78. Smith, *op. cit.,* pp. 112–13.
79. *Ibid.,* pp. 84–88.
80. *Ibid.,* pp. 89–94. Smith's observations have been revised, updated, and recalculated on the basis of 1968 figures taken from the *Statistisches Jahrbuch 1969 der Deutschen Demokratischen Republik,* 14th ed. (East Berlin:

Staatsverlag der Deutschen Demokratischen Republik, 1969), issued by the Staatliche Zentralverwaltung fur Statistik.

81. *Ibid.,* p. 102. Also consult Konstantin Pritzel, *Die Wirtschaftsintegration Mitteldeutschlands* (Cologne: Verlag Wissenschaft und Politik, 1969), p. 124, as well as Staatliche Verwaltung fur Statistik, *op. cit.,* p. 39. Differences in the 1950 figures are apparent between Smith and the Staatliche Verwaltung, possible due to a recalculation by the latter agency in its 1969 *Jahrbuch* as compared to the 1967 edition used by Smith.

82. *Ibid.,* p. 101.

83. *Ibid.,* p. 102.

84. *Ibid.,* pp. 102, 108, and 114–22.

85. *Ibid.,* pp. 108–10.

86. *Ibid.,* p. 109.

87. *Ibid.,* p. 95.

88. Fritz Schenk, *Das Rote Wirtschaftswunder* (Stuttgart: Seewald Verlag, 1969), pp. 126–92.

89. *Ibid.,* pp. 85–89.

90. *Ibid.,* pp. 92–100. Also, see Smith, *op. cit.,* pp. 97–99.

91. *Ibid.,* pp. 109–10.

92. *Ibid.,* pp. 110–11.

93. *Ibid.,* pp. 111 and 114–15.

94. *Ibid.,* pp. 115–17.

95. *Ibid.,* pp. 117–20.

96. Pritzel, *op. cit.,* pp. 129–32.

97. Schenk, *op. cit.,* pp. 121–22.

98. *Ibid.,* p. 124. Schenk's analysis is taken from Michael von Berg, "Die Wirtschaft der DDR," *Neue Zurcher Zeitung* (Zurich), August 16–17, 1968. Refigured for all years in terms of 1967 prices, according to *Statistisches Jahrbuch, 1969, op. cit.,* the reinvestment figures for the years 1960, 1961, 1962, 1963, 1964, 1965, 1966, 1967, and 1968, respectively, are (in billions of marks): 16.0, 16.3, 16.7, 17.0, 18.7, 20.4, 22.0, 24.0, and 26.5. Of the total reinvestment figure for 1968 (an estimate), industry was the recipient of about 47.5 percent; construction 4.0 percent; agriculture 15.5 percent; transportation, post, and telephone systems about 9.2 percent; trade 4.7 percent; miscellaneous production 0.6 percent; social and cultural activities 1.5 percent; and a category of miscellaneous non-productive sectors received 17.0 percent. See pp. 44–48, and following table, in *Statistisches Jahrbuch, 1969, op. cit.*

99. *Ibid.*

100. Pritzel, *op. cit.,* p. 242.

101. *Ibid.,* p. 176.

102. The 1968 figures, surveyed again in the 1969 *Statistisches Jahrbuch,* only further confirm this observation. In fact, in both exports and imports, DDR trade with the USSR was six times the trade with West Germany, while trade with Poland, not to mention with Czechoslovakia, exceeded that with West Germany in exports and nearly did so in imports. (*Statistisches Jahrbuch, 1969, op. cit.,* pp. 298–99.)

103. Schenk, *op. cit.,* pp. 123–25.

104. The Institute for Strategic Studies, *The Military Balance: 1969–1970* (London: The Institute for Strategic Studies, 1969), pp. 12–13.

105. Pritzel, *op. cit.*, p. 234.
106. *Ibid.*, pp. 234–35.
107. *Ibid.*, p. 235.
108. Thomas M. Forster, *The East German Army* (New York: A. S. Barnes and Company, 1968), pp. 77–78.
109. *Ibid.*, pp. 78–90.
110. Joachim Nawrocki, "Auf Mission in Moskau: Willi Stoph, Ministerprasident der DDR ist fur die Sowjets ein zaher Gesprachspartner," *Die Zeit* (Hamburg) 24, no. 29 (July 18, 1969), p. 2.
111. Frank Henning, "Genosse X: Spekulationen um Ulbrichts Nachfolger," *Christ und Welt* (Cologne) 22, no. 28 (July 11, 1969), p. 4.
112. Fortsch, *op. cit.*, p. 16.

CHAPTER 6. THE SOCIALIST REPUBLIC OF CZECHOSLOVAKIA

1. On the Bulgarian program of economic reform through the preparatory Permanent Commission on the New Economic System of Managament, see *Rabotnichesko Delo* (Sofia), December 23, 1966, p. 1; also *ibid.*, December 4, 1967, p. 1. On the first major step toward implementing the Hungarian New Economic Model (especially resolution of the Hungarian Economic Council on profit-allocation for enterprises) see *Nepszava* (Budapest), April 16, 1967, p. 1, and *Nepszabadsag* (Budapest), April 19, 1967, p. 1. On Rumania's economic reform plans see N. Ceausescu's speech to the party's Central Committee in *Scinteia* (Bucharest), December 25, 1966, p. 1 (trans. in part in *East Europe,* February 1967, pp. 23–28). On the Polish new Five-Year Plan (1966–70 targets) see *Trybuna Ludu* (Warsaw), November 20, 1966, p. 1. On the Czechoslovak New Economic Model for its Five-Year Plan, see *Rude Pravo* (Prague), October 28, 1966, p. 1. The best evaluation of the Model to date is Vaclav Holesovsky, "Prague's Economic Model," *East Europe,* February 1967, pp. 13–16. On the East German economic system see the following articles in *Problems of Communism:* Ilse Spittman, "East Germany: The Swinging Pendulum," July/August 1967, pp. 14–20; Dorothy Miller and Harry Trend, "Economic Reforms in East Germany," March/April 1966, pp. 29–36; and Hans Apel, "Economic Reforms in East Germany: A Comment," May/June 1966, pp. 59–62. On Soviet economic reforms, see *Problems of Communism:* Keith Bush, "The Reforms: A Balance Sheet," July/August 1967), pp. 30–41; Theodore Frankel, "Economic Reform: A Tentative Appraisal," May/June 1967, pp. 29–41.
2. Emil Durkheim, *The Division of Labor* (Glencoe, Ill.: The Free Press of Glencoe [Macmillan], 1949).
3. Ota Sik, *K Problematice socialistickych zboznich vztahu* (*The Problems of Commodity Relations in a Socialist Economy*) (Prague: Akademie Ved, 1967), especially Part II.
4. Hadley Cantril, *The Pattern of Human Concern* (New Brunswick, N.J.: Rutgers University Press, 1965).
5. Bruce Sievers, "The Divided Nations: International Integration and National Identity," in Jan F. Triska, *Communist Party–States: Comparative and International Studies* (Indianapolis and New York: Bobbs-Merrill, 1969), pp. 160–88.

6. See, for example, Sandor Szalai, "Statistics, Sociology and Economics of Research in Hungary," *Social Sciences Information,* December 1966.

7. *IV Sjezd Svazu Ceskoslovenskych Spisovatelu* (Praha: Ceskoslovensky spisovatel, 1968), p. 141.

8. Gaetano Mosca, *The Ruling Class* (New York: McGraw-Hill, 1939), pp. 404–405.

9. Robert Dahl and Charles Lindblohm, *Politics, Economics, and Welfare* (New York: Harper, 1963), pp. 171–72.

10. See the controversial Josef Mnacko, *The Taste of Power* (New York: Praeger, 1967).

11. For comparison with the Soviet built-in resistance to change, see Yevsei Liberman, "The Soviet Economic Reform," *Foreign Affairs,* October 1967, p. 62.

12. See the discussions, "Progress and Ideology in the USSR" and "Whither Russia" in *Problems of Communism,* January/February 1966, and especially Zbigniew Brzezinski, "The Soviet Political System: Transformation or Degeneration," *ibid.,* pp. 1–15. Other good articles in *Problems of Communism* are: Frederick C. Barghoorn, "Changes in Russia: The Need for Perspectives," May/June 1966, pp. 39–42; Boris Meissner, "Totalitarian Rule and Social Change," November/December 1966, pp. 55–61; Jayntanuja Bandyopadhyaya, "The Changes Ahead," January/February 1967, pp. 41–44; Sidney Hook, "Fifty Years After," March/April 1967, pp. 76–79; Alexander Bregman, "The USSR and Eastern Europe," May/June 1967, pp. 50–51; Merle Fainsod, "Roads to the Future," July/August 1967, pp. 21–23; and Arrigo Levi, "The Evolution of the Soviet System," *ibid.,* pp. 24–29. See also Albert Perry, *The New Class Divided* (New York: Macmillan, 1966). For a dissenting voice, see Jeremy R. Azrael, *Managerial Power and Soviet Politics* (Cambridge: Harvard University Press, 1966), especially the introduction and the conclusion.

13. In both cases, in developing and also in developed nations, it is thus the clientele which determines the elite's attitude toward the function and structure of the party. In this respect the Bolshevik formula makes the party fit well into the developing society, while the Marxian prescription lacks overall interpretation and application to fit it into modern developed society without new Lenins. Marxism has never been creatively translated into modern industrial society. I doubt that, after the Soviet occupation of Czechoslovakia, it ever will.

14. Norman Kogan, "Italian Communism, the Working Class and Organized Catholicism," mimeographed paper (University of Connecticut, 1965), p. 5. See also Giorgio Galli, *Il bipartismo imperfetto: Communisti e democristiani in Italia* (Bologna: Societa editrice il Mulino, 1966).

15. Giorgio Amendola, "Ipotesi sulla riunificazione," *Rinascita* (Rome), November 28, 1956, pp. 8–9, cited by Kogan, *op. cit.,* p. 9.

16. See Seymour M. Lipset, *Political Man* (Garden City, N.Y.: Doubleday, 1960); Karl W. Deutsch, "Social Mobilization and Political Development," *American Political Science Review* (September 1961), pp. 493–514; Daniel Lerner, *The Passing of Traditional Society* (New York: The Free Press [Macmillan], 1958); David E. Apter, *The Politics of Modernization* (Chicago and London: University of Chicago Press, 1965); Gabriel A. Almond and James S. Coleman, eds., *The Politics of the Developing Areas* (Prince-

ton: Princeton University Press, 1960), pp. 17–26; Bruce M. Russett with Robert Bunselmeyer *et al., World Handbook of Political and Social Indicators* (New Haven: Yale University Press, 1964), pp. 261ff.

17. Dennis C. Pirages, "Socioeconomic Development and Political Access in the Communist Party–States" in Jan F. Triska, ed., *Communist Party–States: Comparative and International Studies* (Indianapolis and New York: Bobbs-Merrill, 1969), pp. 249–81.

18. Vernon V. Aspaturian, "Soviet Foreign Policy," in *Foreign Policy in World Politics,* ed. Roy C. Macridis (Englewood Cliffs, N.J.: Prentice-Hall, 1958), pp. 169–75.

19. "Political Development and Political Decay," *World Politics,* April 1965, pp. 386–430.

20. Clement H. Moore, "Symposium on the Evolution of Established One-Party Systems: Statement of Purpose" mimeographed paper (Berkeley: University of California, 1967).

21. James Bourgart in a research memo to the author, Stanford, Institute of Political Studies, fall 1968.

22. Bozidar Bogdanovic, *Politika* (Belgrade), October 31, 1967.

23. Predrag Vranicky, *Knjizevne Novine* (Belgrade), October 14, 1967.

24. Bogdanovic, *ibid.*

25. Zbigniew Brzezinski, *op. cit.,* p. 15.

26. This discussion is based on Harold Guetzkow, "Structured Programs and their Relation to Free Activity within the Inter-Nation–Simulation" in *Simulation in International Relations: Developments for Research and Teaching* (Englewood Cliffs, N.J.: Prentice Hall, 1966), pp. 110–15.

27. James H. Billington, "Force and Counterforce in Eastern Europe," *Foreign Affairs* 47, no. 1 (October 1968), p. 31.

28. Erik H. Erikson, *Childhood and Society* (New York: Norton, 1950); Leonard Doob, *Patriotism and Nationalism: Their Psychological Foundations* (New Haven, Conn.: Yale University Press, 1965).

29. Lucien Pye, *Politics, Personality, and Nation Building* (New Haven, Conn.: Yale University Press, 1962); Sidney Verba and Lucien Pye, *Comparative Political Culture* (Princeton: Princeton University Press, 1965).

30. Karl W. Deutsch, *Political Community at the International Level* (New York: Doubleday, 1954); Bruce M. Russett, *Community and Contention: Britain and America in the Twentieth Century* (Cambridge, Mass.: M.I.T. Press, 1963).

31. Sievers, *op. cit.,* p. 30.

32. "Yet developments in the People's Democracies could, and probably will, affect to a considerable degree the course of events in the Soviet Union." (Bregman, *op. cit.,* pp. 50–51.)

CHAPTER 7. THE HUNGARIAN PEOPLE'S REPUBLIC

1. Quoted in Robert E. Sherwood, *Roosevelt and Hopkins* (New York: Harper & Row, 1948), p. 852.

2. Quoted in United Nations, General Assembly, *Report of the Special Committee on the Problem of Hungary* (New York: United Nations, 1957), p. 57.

3. For a more detailed account of the Rakosi era and subsequent develop-

ments, see Bennett Kovrig, *The Hungarian People's Republic* (Baltimore: Johns Hopkins Press, 1970).

4. See Bela A. Balassa, *The Hungarian Experience in Economic Planning* (New Haven: Yale University Press, 1959), pp. 31–35.

5. On the Kremlin's role in the New Course, see Paul Kecskemeti, "Limits and Problems of Decompression: The Case of Hungary," *The Annals* 317 (May 1958), pp. 97–106, and Ferenc A. Vali, *Rift and Revolt in Hungary* (Cambridge: Harvard University Press, 1961), chapters 8–13, *passim*.

6. Imre Nagy, *On Communism: In Defence of the New Course* (London: Thames and Hudson, 1957), p. 194.

7. *Ibid.*, p. 24.

8. See I. L. Halasz de Beky, *A Bibliography of the Hungarian Revolution* (Toronto: University of Toronto Press, 1963).

9. See Gyula Borbandi, "Istvan Bibo: Hungary's Political Philosopher," *East Europe* 13, no. 10 (1964), pp. 2–7, and Istvan Bibo, *Harmadik Ut* (London: Magyar Konyves Ceh, 1960).

10. Zoltan Komocsin, "The Class Approach and Internationalism," *World Marxist Review* (Prague) 11, nos. 10/11 (1968), p. 7. Cf. Janos Molnar, *Ellenforradalom Magyarorszagon 1956-ban* (Budapest: Akademia kiado, 1967), p. 240.

11. Revai's last-ditch defense of the old regime appeared in the party daily *Nepszabadsag* (Budapest) March 7, 1957.

12. *Fiqyelo* (Budapest), May 27, 1958, cited in Zbigniew K. Brzezinski, *The Soviet Bloc* (New York: Praeger, 1961), p. 143.

13. Istvan Varga, "The Report of the Committee of Economic Experts," *Kozgazdasagi Szemle* (Budapest) 4, no. 10 (1957), pp. 997–1008, and 4, no. 12 (1957), pp. 1231–47.

14. Kozponti Statisztikai Hivatal, *Magyar statisztikai zsebkonyv, 1968* (Budapest: Statisztikai Kiado Vallalat, 1968), p. 72.

15. *Nepszabadsag,* February 23, 1964.

16. Sandor Kiss, "Hungarian Agriculture Under the NEM," *East Europe* 17, no. 8 (1968), p. 11.

17. Michael Gamarnikow, "Political Patterns and Economic Reforms," *Problems of Communism* 18, no. 2 (1969), pp. 13–14.

18. Rezso Nyers, "Problems of Our Economic Planning System," *Tarsadalmi Szemle* (Budapest) 20, no. 7 (1965), pp. 10–29.

19. *Nepszabadsag* (Budapest), May 29, 1966.

20. *Nepszabadsag* (Budapest), February 2, 1969.

21. See Barnabas A. Racz, "Assessing Hungary's Economic Reforms," *East Europe* 17, no. 12 (1968), pp. 2–9.

22. Dr. Gyorgy Kalman, "The Function of Legal Instruments in the New System of Economic Planning," *Tarsadalmi Szemle* (Budapest) 23, no. 1 (1968), pp. 70–77.

23. *Magyar Nemzet* (Budapest), March 23, 1969.

24. Sandor Gaspar, "Trade Union Problems in Hungary," *World Marxist Review* (Prague) 11, no. 6 (1968), p. 10.

25. *Ibid.*, p. 9.

26. *Nepszava* (Budapest), July 7, 1968. Cf. Michael Gamarnikow, "New Trends in East European Trade Unionism," *East Europe* 28, no. 6 (1969), pp. 18–19.

27. Jozsef Bognar, "Principles of Foreign Trade in the New Economic Mechanism," *New Hungarian Quarterly* 8, no. 26 (1967), p. 168.

28. *Nepszabadsag* (Budapest), April 24, 1969.

29. Komocsin, *op. cit.,* p. 8.

30. *Ibid.*

31. *Ibid.* The fluctuations since 1919 in the party's attitude toward nationalism are analyzed in an unpublished paper by Andrew C. Janos, "Nationalism and Communism in Hungary" (Berkeley: University of California, 1968).

32. Cf. Francois Fejto, "Hungarian Communism," in William E. Griffith, ed., *Communism in Europe* (Cambridge: M.I.T. Press, 1964), p. 214, and Gyorgy Mate, "Thoughts on the Evolution of Our Party's Composition," *Tarsadalmi Szemle* (Budapest) 19, no. 2 (1964), pp. 33–42.

33. Aladar Mod, "Social Stratification in Hungary," *Tarsadalmi Szemle* (Budapest) 22, no. 5 (1967), pp. 15–33. Another analyst stressed that the "critical support" of the party remains that of the industrial workers and that therefore this support has to be assured above any other. (Ferenc Kovacs, "Debate on the Concept of the Working Class," *Tarsadalmi Szemle* (Budapest) 23, no. 1 [1968], pp. 70–77.)

34. Maria Markus and Andras Hegedus, "The Chief Tendencies of the Development of Marxist Sociology in Socialist Countries," *Kortars* (Budapest) 12, no. 12 (1968), excerpted in *East Europe* 28, no. 2 (1969), p. 29.

35. See Istvan Friss, "Class Struggle, State, Party, and Social Development," *Kortars* (Budapest) 12, no. 10 (1968), pp. 1599–1609.

36. Komocsin, *op. cit.,* p. 9.

37. Janos Kadar, "Statement at the November 24 Meeting of the Central Committee," *Tarsadalmi Szemle* (Budapest) 22, 12 (1967), p. 25.

38. *Nepszabadsag* (Budapest), June 9, 1968. Cf. "The Function of Literature and Art in Our Society," *Tarsadalmi Szemle* 21, nos. 7/8 (1966), pp. 29–58.

39. See Otto Bihari, "Hungary's New Electoral Law," *New Hungarian Quarterly* 8, no. 26 (1967), pp. 94–104.

40. *Nepszabadsag* (Budapest), January 28, 1967.

41. Gaspar, *op. cit.,* p. 8.

42. *Magyar Nemzet* (Budapest), March 13, 1969.

43. See Sandor Szalai, "Restratification of a Society," *New Hungarian Quarterly* 7, no. 23 (1966), pp. 24–33, and Andras Hegedus, *A szocialista tarsadalom strukturajarol* (Budapest: Akademia kiado, 1966).

44. Karoly Nagy, "The Impact of Communism in Hungary," *East Europe* 28, no. 3 (1969), p. 14.

45. See Ferenc Pataki, "Sociology and the Question of Upbringing," *Tarsadalmi Szemle* (Budapest) 23, no. 11 (1968), pp. 72–82.

46. In 1967, non-socialist countries sent 498,565 visitors to Hungary and received 143,030 Hungarians, representing a manifold increase over 1960 and earlier years. (Hitvatal, *Magyar statisztikai zsebkonyv, 1968, op. cit.,* p. 123.)

47. Dr. Dezso Kalocsai, "On the Social Roots of Individualism," *Tarsadalmi Szemle* (Budapest) 21, no. 6 (1966), pp. 104–14.

48. Jozsef Lukacs, "The International Conference in Budapest on the Sociology of Religion," *Tarsadalmi Szemle* (Budapest) 23, no. 6 (1968), pp. 82–89.

49. See Peter Veres, "Alienation: A Hungarian View," *East Europe* 14, no. 3 (1965), pp. 23–26.

50. Agnes Havas, "Nationalistic Influences on Our Children," *Tarsadalmi Szemle* (Budapest) 22, no. 3 (1967), pp. 97–111.

51. Gabor Czako, "Twenty-year-Old Morality," *Kortars* (Budapest) 12, no. 11 (1968), pp. 1729–42. The author, noting a widespread dichotomy in moral upbringing between the official materialism of the educational system and a religious family environment, deplores that the battle against Christian ideology began before an alternate socialist morality had been elaborated; his survey found that fifty-nine percent of the respondents were simply ignorant of the content of this new "morality."

52. Radio Szulofoldunk (Radio Fatherland), June 7, 1969.

53. Miklos Veszpremi, "A Threatening Generation?" *Elet es Irodalom* (Budapest) 20, no. 19 (1969), p. 5.

54. See Tibor Petho, "Modern Forms of Cooperation in the Danube Valley," *New Hungarian Quarterly* (Budapest) 8, no. 27 (1967), pp. 10–16.

55. *Magyar Hirlap* (Budapest), October 26, 1968.

56. *News From Hungary* (Free Europe Committee, Inc. [FEC]), July 11, 1969.

57. *Magyar Nemzet* (Budapest), March 16, 1958, cited in Sandor Kiss, "Soviet Troops in Hungary," *East Europe* 13, no. 10 (1964), p. 13.

58. Komocsin, *op. cit.,* p. 8.

CHAPTER 8. THE FEDERAL SOCIALIST REPUBLIC OF YUGOSLAVIA

1. In the wake of the war, Yugoslavia had lost 1,700,000 out of a total estimated population of 16,000,000. Twenty-five percent of the population was homeless, and in Belgrade forty percent of the housing was rendered unusable. At the end of the war not a single railroad was in operation, and the merchant marine shrank from 410,000 gross registered tons to 55,000; the damages to industry were on a comparable scale. George W. Hoffman and Fred Warner Neal, *Yugoslavia and The New Communism* (New York: Twentieth Century Fund, 1962), pp. 86–87.

2. ". . . given the price system, one dinar invested in Slovenia was almost three times as productive as a dinar invested in Serbia, and a dinar invested in Croatia was twice as effective as a dinar invested in Macedonia." (Joseph T. Bombelles, *Economic Development of Communist Yugoslavia* [Stanford, Calif.: The Hoover Institution, 1968], p. 154.)

3. These terms are used by Yugoslavs to designate those who stand for more authoritarian forms of Communism.

4. The term "etatism" has been used in Yugoslavia to describe the type of social order in which the state's interests override all individual claims. The era of Stalin is frequently described as "etatist."

5. The party plenum which acted on the dismissal of Rankovic met on the Island of Brioni on July 1, 1966.

6. Tito stated: "One of the basic obstacles is at the top of our League of Communists, that is, in the leadership bodies. . . . There is no place in the Communist League for those who are not carrying out its instructions. They should get out. . . . Obstructionists have created confusion . . . used by class enemies and various chauvinistic and nationalistic elements." (*The New York Times,* February 26, 1966, p. 1.)

7. Few journals in Yugoslavia were banned. One famous case is that of *Perspektive* in Ljubljana in 1965. At times specific issues of publications have

been banned. This has affected such journals as *Praxis* (Zagreb) and *Delo* (Ljubljana).

8. The intellectuals usually published their views in *Praxis* (Zagreb) or *Gledista* (Belgrade). The replies from political figures appeared in *Socijalizam* (Belgrade) or *Komunist* (Belgrade), both organs of the League.

9. Article 39 states: "Freedom of thought and determination shall be guaranteed." (*The Constitution of the Socialist Federal Republic of Yugoslavia,* Secretariat for Information of the Federal Executive Council, Belgrade, 1963.)

10. *The New York Times,* April 8, 1967, p. 4.

11. Veli Deva, The Secretary of Kosmet League, accused the Serbian chauvinists of many sins, including being against the League because "it gives many rights to the Albanians and Turks." (*Politika* [Belgrade], November 15, 1968.)

12. *The New York Times,* June 10, 1968, p. 14.

13. The program of the Seventh Congress is found in *Yugoslavia's Way: The Program of the League of Communists,* translated by Stoyan Pribichevitch (New York: All Nations Press, 1958).

14. Ilija Jukic, "Tito's Last Battle," *East Europe* 16 (April 1967), p. 9.

15. The Socialist Alliance of Working People of Yugoslavia (SAWP) is a mass organization which seeks to incorporate all Yugoslavs who are in a fundamental position of support. They need not espouse the principles of Communism, but membership in the Alliance is the minimum necessary for minimal political participation.

16. "Man Bites Dog and Now What?" *Economist* 221 (December 10, 1966), p. 1132.

17. *Ibid.*

18. *The New York Times,* August 26, 1968, p. 16.

19. This is the first time that the Army organization has been treated as a separate entity and allowed to select its own representatives. Previously, they were named by the central party organs.

20. Paul Shoup observes in his book, *Communism and the Yugoslav National Question* (New York: Columbia University Press, 1968), p. 275, that the 1963 Central Committee had nineteen Croat representatives for a population of 4,293,860 million, while Montenegrins with a population of 513,833 held fourteen seats.

21. *Borba* (Belgrade), March 13, 1969, p. 1.

22. *The Times* (London) March 13, 1969, p. 1.

23. Budislav Soskich, "Democratic Centralism in the Draft of the New Statute of the LCY," *Socijalizam* (Belgrade), no. 12, December 1968.

24. Milija Komatina, "On the Eve of the Public Discussion on the LCY Statute: New Norms for a New Practice," *Komunist* (Belgrade), October 24, 1968, p. 6.

25. "President Tito on Economic Reform," *Yugoslav Facts and Views,* no. 1 (September 10, 1965), p. 2.

26. *Ibid.*

27. Speech over TV–Belgrade, reported by *The New York Times,* January 10, 1966, p. 7.

28. *Yugoslav Facts and Views* no. 52 (March 16, 1969), p. 13.

29. "What is Stoppage of Work?" *Yugoslav Trade Unions* 8 (December, 1968) p. 9.
30. "All-Out Comrades," *Economist* 224 (September 16, 1967), p. 16.
31. See statements by Milorad Mandic, *Nedeljne Informativne Novine,* October 29, 1967; Vladimir Bakaric, *Vjesnik* (Zagreb), October 26, 1967 and Veljko Vlahovic, *Borba* (Belgrade), October 27, 1967.
32. *Nedeljne Novosti* (Zagreb), December 29, 1968, p. 7.
33. In the fall of 1968, after the events in Czechoslovakia, the League opened up its membership to young people. A study conducted in Zagreb during 1967 when a representative sample of 4,915,000 Croatian young people revealed that: twenty-five percent had a great desire to join the League; twenty-nine percent had a desire to join the League; twenty-three percent were undecided; twelve percent would not join the League; and four percent would not join the League under any circumstances. This study was published in Zagreb under the auspices of the Youth League and the League of Communists of Croatia by Pavle Novosel, Faculty of Political Science at Zagreb University.

CHAPTER 9. THE PEOPLE'S REPUBLIC OF ALBANIA

1. For a summary and analysis of developments during this period see Nicholas C. Pano, *The People's Republic of Albania* (Baltimore: Johns Hopkins, 1968), pp. 45–87.
2. For discussions of the Albanian Constitution of 1950 see Kemal Aly Vokopola, "Albania," in Vladimir Gsovski and Kazimierz Grzybowski, eds., *Government, Law and Courts in the Soviet Union and Eastern Europe* (New York: Praeger, 1959), 1: pp. 181–98; Stavro Skendi, ed., *Albania* New York: Praeger, 1958, pp. 66–72); Dhimo M. Dhima, *Kushtetuta e Republikes Popullore te Shqiperise,* botim e dyte (*The Constitution of the People's Republic of Albania,* 2nd edition) (Tirana: Ministria e Aresimit dhe Kultures, 1960), pp. 51–120. For the text of the 1950 Constitution see *Constitution of the People's Republic of Albania* (Tirana: the Albanian Committee for Cultural Relations and Friendship with Foreign Countries, 1964). Hereafter cited as *Constitution of the P.R.A.*
3. *Constitution of the P.R.A.,* Articles 2–4, 41, 42.
4. *Ibid.,* Article 21.
5. *Ibid.,* Article 41.
6. *Ibid.,* Articles 57–60.
7. *Ibid.,* Articles 61–69.
8. *Ibid.,* Articles 71–78.
9. *Ibid.,* Articles 79–90.
10. The best detailed and documented account of the development of the Soviet-Albanian rift is William E. Griffith, *Albania and the Sino-Soviet Rift* (Cambridge, Mass. The M.I.T. Press, 1963). Also useful is Harry Hamm, *Albania—China's Beachhead in Europe* (New York: Praeger, 1963).
11. See, inter alia, Hasan Banja, *Industrializimi socialist dhe perspektivat e tij ne Pesevejcarin e IV (Socialist Industrialization and Its Prospects During the Fourth Five Year Plan)* (Tirana: Naim Frasheri, 1967), pp. 11–66.
12. Prior to the Soviet-Albanian break, the NSSR and the East European Com-

munist states had promised to supply Albania with credits of $132–$135 million for the period 1961–65.

13. *Vjetari Statistikor i R.P.Sh., 1965 (Statistical Yearbook of the People's Republic of Albania, 1965)* (Tirana: Drejtoria e Statistikes, 1965), p. 315. Total Albanian imports in fact dropped in value from $81,078,000 in 1960 to $70,742,000 in 1963. (*Ibid.*)

14. Enver Hoxha, *Fjala e mbylljes ne plenumin e K.Q. te P.P.Sh. mbi forcimin e metejshem te punes ideologjike te Partise per edukimin komunist te punonjesve (Closing speech at the Plenum of the C.C. of the APL on the Further Strengthening of the Ideological Work of the Party for the Communist Education of the Workers)* (Tirana: Naim Frasheri, 1964); Ramiz Alia, *Raport "Mbi forcimin e metejshem te punes ideologjike te Partise per edukimin komunist te punonjesve" (Report on the Further Strengthening of the Ideological Work of the Party for the Communist Education of the Workers)*, Tirana: Naim Frasheri, 1964.

15. *The Washington Post*, May 2, 1965.

16. *Ibid.*

17. *Zeri i Popullit* (Tirana), March 12, 1965.

18. For useful summary accounts of these developments see "Bourgeois Influences in Albania," *East Europe* 14, no. 9 (1965), 27–28; *The Washington Post*, July 7, 1965.

19. See, for example, *Zeri i Popullit* (Tirana), July 7, 1965; Radio Tirana, October 23, 1965.

20. Radio Tirana, July 15, 1965.

21. *Zeri i Popullit* (Tirana), October 28, 1965.

22. Radio Tirana, February 10, 1966.

23. For the development of the "back to the masses movement" see *Zeri i Popullit*, February 9–24, 1966.

24. *Bashkimi* (Tirana), February 26, 1966.

25. The text of this document appeared in *Zeri i Popullit* (Tirana), March 6, 1966.

26. *Ibid.*

27. *Ibid.*

28. Radio Tirana, March 7, 1966.

29. Radio Tirana, March 17, 1966. This move reversed the action taken by the party in June and December of 1965 when it created three new ministries. (*Ibid.*, June 23, 1965; December 28, 1965.)

30. *Historia e Partise se Punes te Shqiperise* (Tirana: Naim Frasheri, 1968), p. 448. Hereafter cited as *Historia e P.P.Sh.*

31. Radio Tirana carried the text of the most important of the Shehu and Hoxha speeches on July 5 and 8, 1966, respectively.

32. See *Historia e P.P.Sh.*, p. 447.

33. *Vjetori Statistikor i R.P.Sh., 1966 (Statistical Yearbook of the People's Republic of Albania, 1966)* (Tirana: Drejtoria e Statistikes, 1967), p. 23.

34. *Zeri i Popullit* (Tirana) June 18, 1966.

35. *Ibid.*, July 2, 7, 1966.

36. Radio Tirana, September 15, 1966. This ministry was restored without fanfare in March 1969.

37. *Zeri i Popullit* (Tirana), September 7, 1966.

38. In his September 13 address to the People's Assembly, for example, Mehmet

Shehu observed that the growth of bourgeois influences in Albania had rendered it imperative that the APL implant a "high [level] of revolutionary consciousness" among the people. Among the abuses he demanded be eradicated were fraudulent reporting of quota fulfillment, mass indifference to administrative malfeasance, misuse of state property, aversion to hard work, and cronyism in the conduct of party and state business. (Radio Tirana, September 14, 1966.)

39. The proceedings of the Fifth Congress received extensive coverage in *Zeri i Popullit* (Tirana), November 1–9, 1966, and on Radio Tirana, November 1–9, 1966. The major documents of the Congress are found in *Kongresi i Peste i Partise se Punes te Shqiperise, 1–8 Nendor 1966 (The Fifth Congress of the Albanian Party of Labor, 1–8 November 1966)* (Tirana: Naim Frasheri, 1966). For a summary and interpretation see *Historia e P.P.Sh.*, pp. 449–78.

40. *Zeri i Popullit* (Tirana), November 2, 1966.

41. *Ibid.,* November 6, 1966.

42. For details see *ibid.,* November 8, 9, 1966, and *Kongresi i Peste i Partise se Punes, op. cit.,* pp. 392–93, 399–402.

43. *Zeri i Popullit* (Tirana), November 2, 1966. Another source of imbalance in the APL was the fact that women accounted for only 12.5 percent of its membership in 1966. (*Ibid.*) The results of the campaign during 1961–66 to redress the composition of the party were not overly impressive. The membership of the APL in 1961 was comprised of laborers, thirty percent; collectivized peasants, twenty-four percent; white-collar workers, forty-two percent; and others, four percent. (*Kongresi IV i Partise se Punes se Shqiperise* [*The Fourth Congress of the Albanian Party of Labor*] Tirana: Naim Frasheri, 1961, p. 121.)

44. Between 1961–66, the increase in membership of the APL (12,668) was more than double the increase between 1956–61 (5,015). This situation stemmed mainly from the desire of the leadership to enlarge the party base in order to create more support at the grass roots for the regime in the troubled period following the Soviet-Albanian break in 1961. It is interesting to note that of the APL members expelled between 1961–66, eighteen percent had been admitted during this period. (*Zeri i Popullit* [Tirana], November 2, 1966.) Since Hoxha expected every Communist to serve as a model for the masses during the Ideological and Cultural Revolution, he has stressed quality rather than quantity in recruiting.

45. By 1966, ninety percent of the farmland in Albania had been collectivized, and eighty percent of the farmers were employed in the socialist sector of agriculture. (*Zeri i Popullit* [Tirana], November 6, 1966.)

46. *Zeri i Popullit* (Tirana), January 2, 1967.

47. For the text of this address see *ibid.,* February 6, 1967.

48. *Ibid.*

49. See for example *ibid.,* February 8–28, 1967.

50. For a discussion of this phase of the revolution see the *New York Times,* March 3, April 2, 1967. For opposition to the wall newspapers campaign the report of BTA (Tirana), April 11, 1967, is useful. Unlike their Chinese model, the Albanian wall newspapers were exclusively a tool of the leadership to promote the revolution.

51. For collections of these letters see, inter alia, *Qe Shqiperia te mbetet per*

jete keshtjelle e pamposhtur e socializmit dhe e komunizmit (That Albania May Always Be an Indestructible Citadel of Socialism and Communism) (Tirana: Naim Frasheri, 1967); *Nuk ka liri te vertete shoqerore pa emancipimin e plote te gruas (There Can Be No True Social Freedom Without the Full Emancipation of Women)* (Tirana: Naim Frasheri, 1967); *Lufta kunder zakoneve prapanike dhe besimeve fetare—shprehje e luftes se klasave (The Struggle Against Backward Customs and Religious Beliefs —the Hope of the Class War)* (Tirana: Naim Frasheri, 1967); *Ne shekuj do te perjetesohen emrat e bijave dhe bijve te ketij trualli (The Names of the Sons and Daughters of This Land Shall Be Immortalized for Centuries)* (Tirana: Naim Frasheri, 1968), While most of these letters to Hoxha were undoubtedly "inspired" by pressure from local officials, it does appear that many were spontaneous affirmations of support for the ideals of the revolution.

52. At the Fifth Congress it had been announced that approximately 90 percent of the land under cultivation had been collectivized. (*Zeri i Popullit* [Tirana], November 6, 1966). By June 1967 this figure had risen to 98.6 percent. (*Ibid.,* June 21, 1967).

53. Radio Tirana, April 30, 1967.

54. See *Bashkimi* (Tirana), June 18, 20, 1967.

55. Women in 1967 comprised forty-two percent of the Albanian labor force. (*Ibid.,* June 18, 1967).

56. For reports on this development see the *New York Times,* July 12, 1967; *Christian Science Moniter,* July 14, 1967. For an analysis see *Shqiptari i Lire* (New York), September-October, 1967.

57. Ismail Hoxha, "Mbi disa ceshtje te punes per edukimin aresimor, kultural e estetik te rinise" ("Some Problems Concerning the Work for the Pedagogical, Cultural and Esthetic Education of Youth"), *Nendori* (Tirana), 14 (September 1967), 10–12.

58. *Zeri i Popullit* (Tirana), September 15, 1967.

59. *Gazeta Zyrtare* (Tirana), November 22, 1967.

60. Radio Tirana, October 21, 1967. Hoxha on this occasion reaffirmed the leading role of the party in the management of the economy and condemned the "revisionist" Soviet and Yugoslav economic decentralization schemes.

61. The congress was rescheduled to meet in 1968, but was not convened until April 1969.

62. *Zeri i Popullit* (Tirana), March 10, 1968. For a collection of articles dealing with this phase of the revolution see *Per revolucionarizmin e metejshem te shkolles sone (For the Further Revolutionization of Our Schools)* (Tirana: Naim Frasheri, 1968). For a discussion of developments in Albanian education during the 1960s see John I. Thomas, *Education for Communism: School and State in the People's Republic of Albania* (Stanford, Calif.: The Hoover Institution, 1969), pp. 40–120.

63. *Zeri i Popullit* (Tirana), March 10, 12, 1968. After extensive public hearings, it was expected that the commission would make recommendations for the reform of the Albanian school system.

64. Radio Tirana, April 11, 1968. For a collection of articles dealing with this phase of the revolution see *Kontrolli i plote i klases punetor i sherben forcimit te diktatures se proletariatit (The Full Control of the Working*

Class Serves to Strengthen the Dictatorship of the Proletariat) (Tirana: Naim Frasheri, 1968).

65. See, inter alia, *Drita* (Tirana), April 11, May 12, May 19, 1968. *Zeri i Popullit* (Tirana), July 2, October 31, 1968.
66. *Zeri i Popullit* (Tirana), December 27, 1968.
67. Radio Tirana, April 24, 1969.
68. *Zeri i Popullit* (Tirana), April 25, 1969.
69. See especially *Zeri i Popullit* (Tirana) and *Bashkimi* (Tirana) during July and August. Also revealing is Sevo Tarifa, "The Class Struggle Is One of the Principal Moving Forces of Our Society," *Rruga e Partise* (Tirana) 15 (August 1968), 77–87 (Joint Publications Research Service, microfiche no. 46801 [Washington, D.C.: U.S. Government Printing Office, November 5, 1968]).
70. For the Sixth Plenum and its aftermath see *Zeri i Popullit* (Tirana) October 11, December 6, December 26, 1968.
71. The average annual rate of increase over the previous year in Albanian industrial production was 1966–12 percent, 1967–12.8 percent, 1968–19 percent. (Radio Tirana, February 7, 1967); *Zeri i Popullit* (Tirana, June 3, 1969). Albanian industrial production was scheduled to increase by 12.4 percent in 1969. (Radio Tirana, January 15, 1969).
72. Albanian agricultural output in 1968 was 28 percent greater than in 1965. (Albanian Press Agency [ATA] [Tirana], November 29, 1968).
73. For two contrasting interpretations of this aspect of the Revolution see Ahmmad il Drrha, "Mission to Albania," *Nea Politeia* (Athens), December 1–5, 1968 (Joint Publications Research Service, microfiche no. 47411 [Washington, D.C.: U.S. Government Printing Office, February 7, 1969]); E. V., "Visit to Albania," *Octobre* (Tirana) 4 (November-December 1968) (Joint Publications Research Service, microfiche no. 47118 [Washington, D.C.: U.S. Government Printing Office, December 7, 1968]).
74. For a more detailed account see Peter R. Prifti, *Albania's "Cultural Revolution,"* M.I.T. Center for International Studies, Series, no. C/68–9 (Cambridge, Mass., September 1968), pp. 5–14.
75. For a detailed discussion and analysis of the Soviet-Albanian conflict during 1960–61 see Griffith, *op. cit.,* pp. 35–143. For a more general overview see Pano, *op. cit.,* pp. 111–57.
76. For the Albanian position on this issue see *Zeri i Popullit* (Tirana), June 6, 13, 1962. The Soviets maintained that the Albanians had withdrawn their representative from the Comecon Secretariat and ceased paying their membership dues in December 1961. They further noted that the PRA closed down the headquarters of the Warsaw-Pact mission in Tirana in January 1962. (TASS [Moscow], December 20, 1962; Radio Moscow, September 13, 1968.)
77. The Tirana city council in April insultingly revoked the honorary citizenship it had granted Khrushchev in 1959. (Radio Tirana, April 17, 1964). The Soviet leader was also accused of complicity in a plot to assassinate Stalin. (*Ibid.,* May 24, 1964.) *Zeri i Popullit* (Tirana) published lengthy and bitter attacks on Khrushchev and his policies on June 12, 13, and 14.
78. The Albanians rejected on October 6 an invitation to participate in the preliminary planning for the proposed world Communist conference. (*Zeri i Popullit* [Tirana], October 6, 1964.)

79. Radio Tirana, October 15, 17, 20, 1964; *Zeri i Popullit* (Tirana), November 1, 7, 8, 1964.
80. New China News Agency (Peking), November 13, 14, 20, 1964.
81. Radio Tirana, November 29, 1964.
82. *Zeri i Popullit* (Tirana), November 30, 1964.
83. Radio Tirana, November 8, 1959.
84. *Ibid.*, April 2, 1964.
85. Albania, for example, was the only party-state not invited to participate in the celebration of the forty-seventh anniversary of the Bolshevik Revolution. The Soviet government sent only perfunctory greetings to the Albanian people on the occasion of the country's national holidays in late November, and only Rumania of the European party states sent a delegation to take part in the Albanian celebration.
86. On this point see Robin Alison Remington, *The Changing Soviet Perception of the Warsaw Pact*, M.I.T. Center for International Studies Series, no. C/67–24 (Cambridge, Mass., 1967), pp. 125–26.
87. In "early" 1965 the Soviets had expressed a willingness to resume commercial relations with Albania. Tirana never responded to this overture. (Radio Moscow, June 30, 1967.)
88. Radio Tirana, February 3, 1965.
89. *Zeri i Popullit* (Tirana), February 16, March 18, 1965.
90. Radio Tirana, April 9, 1965. The Soviets maintain that the final details were not worked out until Shehu's visit to Peking in April-May 1966. (Radio Moscow, June 15, 1969.) It appears that the value of the Chinese credit for the Fourth Five-Year Plan amounted to $214 million. (*Zeri i Popullit* [Tirana], July 28, 1966.) For a general discussion of these issues see Jan S. Prybyla, "Albania's Economic Vassalage," *East Europe* 18, no. 1 (January 1967), 9–13.
91. Radio Tirana, March 29, 1965.
92. See, inter alia, *Zeri i Popullit* (Tirana), April 20, June 27, December 30, 1965.
93. *New York Times,* February 12, 1966; *Christian Science Monitor,* February 21, 1966.
94. Radio Tirana, February 12, 1966; *Zeri i Popullit* (Tirana), July 20, 1966.
95. Radio Warsaw, February 23, 1966. In addition to distributing propaganda material, the Albanian ambassador had granted a diplomatic passport to a Polish Stalinist, Kazmierz Mihal, who made his way to Tirana, where he organized the "Marxist-Leninist" Polish Communist Party.
96. Radio Moscow, June 30, 1967.
97. *Zeri i Popullit* (Tirana), March 22, 1966. In his speech to the Congress, Brezhnev noted that the USSR was prepared "to do everything possible" to improve relations with Albania. (TASS [Moscow], March 29, 1966.) On May 10 *Zeri i Popullit* (Tirana) printed a lengthy critique which left no doubt that prospects for a Soviet-Albanian rapprochement were not at all favorable.
98. It was also noted that Albania was encountering difficulty in expanding trade with capitalist countries because outside of minerals and foodstuffs there was little demand for Albanian goods.
99. *Zeri i Popullit* (Tirana), August 31, 1966.
100. *New York Times,* April 1, 1966.

101. *Zeri i Popullit* (Tirana), May 1, November 2, 1966.
102. *Kongresi i Peste i Partise se Punes, op. cit.,* pp. 3–6.
103. *Zeri i Popullit* (Tirana), November 2, 1966.
104. The Chinese information media provided extensive coverage of the activities of these and other Albanian delegations.
105. The Chinese coverage of this trip bears this out. See New China News Agency (Peking) dispatches, June 22, July 10, August 2, 1967.
106. Radio Tirana, December 23, 1967. The Chinese-built facilities apparently began their operations during 1966. (*Ibid.,* November 27, 1966.)
107. The Polish group was established in 1966 and the Soviet organization in 1967.
108. Radio Tirana, April 13, 1967.
109. *Zeri i Popullit* (Tirana), June 11, 1967.
110. *Ibid.,* February 8, 1967.
111. Radio Tirana, March 31, 1967.
112. Albania Press Agency (ATA) (Tirana), July 24, 1967.
113. *Zeri i Popullit,* September 15, 1967.
114. *New York Times,* March 14, 1967; *Shqiptari i Lire* (New York), March–April 1967.
115. Albanian Press Agency (ATA) (Tirana), November 8, 1967.
116. Radio Moscow, May 10, 11, 22, 24; July 10, 1967.
117. *Ibid.,* March 11, April 7, June 30, July 13, 1967.
118. *Zeri i Popullit* (Tirana), September 15, 1967.
119. Radio Prague, August 3, 1967 (quoting *Paris Jour* of the same date). The Czechoslovaks maintained that the Chinese action was designed to convince both the USSR and the Western powers that China's military influence and potential were not limited to the Far East. This, however, does not seem to have been the major Chinese concern at this point.
120. It is believed by some intelligence specialists that construction of a small defensive missile network extending from Durres to the Greek frontier had been initiated as early as 1962. (*Christian Science Monitor,* June 12, 1969.)
121. New China News Agency (Peking), October 14, 1967. Shehu, for his part, had elevated the acceptance of Mao's Cultural Revolution (and by implication the Albanian Revolution) to the status of a test of "Marxist-Leninist" orthodoxy when he observed that "the attitude [of a Communist party] toward China's Great Proletarian Cultural Revolution is a touchstone for distinguishing Marxist-Leninists from revisionists and genuine revolutionaries from counter-revolutionaries." (*Ibid.*)
122. On these points see Peter R. Prifti, "Albania Gets the Jitters," *East Europe* 18, no. 1 (January 1969), pp. 11, 13, n. 6; and Prifti, *op. cit.,* pp. 14–19. Prifti also feels that the Albanians were somewhat disturbed by the course the Cultural Revolution had taken.
123. *Zeri i Popullit* (Tirana), January 25, 1968.
124. The Albanian delegate, who was one of only four who voted against this item in the UN political committee, argued that it was designed to prevent China from developing a nuclear arsenal. (*New York Times,* June 13, 1968.)
125. For the Bulgarian version see Bulgarian Press Agency (Sofia), July 22, 1968; and for the Albanian rejoinder, *Zeri i Popullit* (Tirana), July 24, 1968.

126. Radio Tirana, May 6, 1968.
127. *Zeri i Popullit* (Tirana), July 24, 1968.
128. *Ibid.*, September 22, 23, 1968.
129. Radio Tirana, September 13, 1968.
130. *Zeri i Popullit* (Tirana), September 24, 1968.
131. *Ibid.*, November 5, 1968.
132. *Ibid.*, September 19, 1968.
133. New China News Agency (Peking), October 9, 1968.
134. *Zeri i Popullit* (Tirana), December 22, 1968.
135. For coverage of this visit see *ibid.*, November 27–December 3, 1968.
136. On this point see *The Daily Telegraph* (London), August 21, 1969 and the *Christian Science Monitor,* December 11, 1968, July 12, 1969.
137. Czechoslovak Press Agency (CTK) (Prague), December 13, 1968.
138. In addition to their extensive broadcast facilities in Albania, the Chinese have established a school to train youthful revolutionary agitators from Europe and the Middle East. (*The Daily Telegraph* [London], August 22, 1969.)
139. *Zeri i Popullit* (Tirana), March 4, 1969, August 14, 1969.
140. *Ibid.*, May 28, 1969.
141. New China News Agency (Peking), April 4, 10, May 22, 1969.
142. *Ibid.*, June 6, 1969.
143. Radio Tirana, August 10, 11, 14, 18, 1969.
144. *Ibid.*, December 2, 1968.
145. *Christian Science Monitor,* March 22, 1969, April 28, 1969.

CHAPTER 10. EAST EUROPEAN RELATIONS WITH THE USSR

1. Assumptions concerning Soviet intentions and motives in occupying Eastern Europe played a decisive role in the genesis and evolution of the "cold war." For various interpretations, see the standard work on the evolution of Soviet relations with Eastern Europe, Zbigniew Brzezinski, *The Soviet Bloc,* second edition (Cambridge, Massachusetts: Harvard University Press, 1967); Christopher Lasch, "The Cold War Revisited and Revisioned," *The New York Times Magazine,* January 14, 1968; Arthur Schlesinger, Jr., "Origins of the Cold War," *Foreign Affairs,* October 1967; Adam B. Ulam, *Expansion and Co-existence: A History of Soviet Foreign Policy, 1917–1967* (New York: Praeger, 1968), especially chapter 8.
2. After the conclusion of the Test-Ban Treaty in July 1963, an official Chinese statement charged: ". . . The Soviet leaders seek only to preserve themselves and would leave other people to sink or swim. They have repeatedly said that so long as they themselves survive and develop, the people of the world will be saved." (Chinese statement of August 14, 1963, *Peking Review,* no. 33, August 16, 1963.)
3. Vernon V. Aspaturian, "The Genesis of the Sino-Soviet Conflict," in R. C. Macridis, ed., *Modern European Governments* (Englewood Cliffs, N.J.: Prentice-Hall, 1968), pp. 202–44.
4. Castro conceded that the Soviet action was "illegal," but nevertheless supported it on grounds of self-interest:

   What are the factors that created the necessity for a step which unquestionably entailed a violation of legal principles? . . . what cannot be denied here is that the sovereignty of the Czechoslovak State was violated. . . . And the violation was, in fact, of a flagrant nature. . . . Not the slightest trace of legality exists. Frankly, none whatever.

5. For an accounting of the diversity in institutions, policies and tendencies developing in Eastern Europe, cf. the following: Ghita Ionescu, *The Politics of the European Communist States* (New York: Praeger, 1967); H. Gordon Skilling, *The Governments of Communist East Europe* (New York: Crowell, 1966); Kurt London, *Eastern Europe in Transition* (Baltimore: The Johns Hopkins Press, 1966); and J. Triska, *The World Communist System* (Stanford, Calif.: Stanford Studies of the Communist System, 1964). For an analysis of the sources of diversity, see R. V. Burks, *The Dynamics of Communism in Eastern Europe* (Princeton, N.J.: Princeton University Press, 1961).

6. Complete text published in *The New York Times,* September 5, 1964. Khrushchev's ouster seriously affected the internal factional equilibrium in a number of Eastern European countries, particularly in Czechoslovakia, Hungary, and Poland, whose policies were closely aligned with those of Khrushchev. Brezhnev and Kosygin, for example, scurried to the Polish border to explain the ouster to an irritated Gomulka; see *The New York Times,* October 26, 1964. For a survey of the general reaction of Eastern European capitals to Khrushchev's ouster, see *The New York Times,* November 8, 1964. For Prague's reaction to the ouster, see *The New York Times,* November 1, 1964; for the reaction of the French Communist Party, see *L'Humanite* (Paris) October 22, 1964.

7. Excerpts from Ceausecu's speech in *The New York Times,* March 14, 1966. The Rumanian leader, in this speech, also condemned past Soviet interference in the affairs of the Rumanian Communist Party and Rumanian internal affairs and expressed resentment at the manner in which Bessarabia was annexed by Moscow.

8. *Pravda* (Moscow), March 5, 7, and 9, 1968, and *The New York Times,* March 2, 8, and 9, 1968.

9. Harry Schwartz, *Prague's 200 Days* (New York: Praeger, 1969), pp. 117–19, for details on the discussions of the Dresden Conference.

10. The Five Powers dispatched a joint letter to the Czechoslovak leadership on July 18, 1968, which warned:

The frontiers of the socialist world have moved to the center of Europe, to the Elbe and Sumava Mountains [i.e., to the Western Czechoslovak borders]. . . . And we shall never agree to have these historical gains of socialism, independence and security of our peoples endangered. We shall never agree to have imperialism, using ways peaceful and nonpeaceful, gouge a gap from the inside or from the outside in the socialist system and alter the correlation of forces in Europe in imperialism's favor. . . . Each of our parties is responsible not only to its working class and its people, but also to the international working class and the world Communist movement, and we cannot evade the obligations following from this. . . . That is why we believe that the decisive rebuff to the anti-Communist forces and the decisive efforts for the preservation of the socialist system in Czechoslovakia are not only your but also our task. (*Pravda* [Moscow] July 18, 1968.)

11. The so-called "Brezhnev Doctrine" (sometimes also called the "Socialist Commonwealth Doctrine," was first enunciated in an article by Sergei Kovalev in *Pravda* (Moscow), September 25, 1968:

> There is no doubt that the peoples of the socialist countries and the Communist Parties have and must have freedom to determine their country's path of development. However, any decision of theirs must damage neither socialism in their own country nor the fundamental interests of the other socialist countries nor the worldwide workers' movement, which is waging a struggle for socialism. This means that every Communist Party is responsible not only to its own people but also to all the socialist countries and to the entire Communist movement. Whoever forgets this in placing sole emphasis on the autonomy and independence of Communist Parties lapses into one-sidedness, shirking his internationalist obligations. . . . The sovereignty of individual socialist countries cannot be counterposed to the interests of world socialism and the world revolutionary movement.

See also Brezhnev's speech to the Polish Party Congress on November 12, 1968 (*Pravda* [Moscow], November 13, 1968.)

12. The issue of mutual interference arose publicly in June 1963, when Chinese embassy personnel illegally distributed the Chinese letter of June 14, 1963, criticizing Soviet policy. After a number of protests failed to stop the distribution, several Chinese embassy officials were expelled for engaging in illegal activities. Peking complained as follows:

"Since Soviet establishments and personnel can do, and have always done this in China, why cannot the Chinese establishments and personnel do the same in the Soviet Union? What justification has the Soviet Government to lodge a protest with the Chinese Embassy in the Soviet Union in this connection? What justification has it to demand that the Chinese Government recall the said Chinese personnel?" (See *The New York Times,* June 30, 1963, for a text of the Chinese statement.)

Moscow angrily retorted that the Chinese embassy officials "were conducting themselves in the Soviet Union as though they were still in one of the provinces of China," and went on to say: "The attempts on the part of the Chinese to represent the matter as though such norms [i.e. international law and Soviet law] as respect by one socialist state for the laws and regulations of another socialist state and its sovereignty have no force in the relations between socialist states are contrary to Leninist principles." (*Pravda* [Moscow], July 5, 1963.) The Soviet statement to the Chinese denied that Soviet personnel would disseminate Soviet literature in contravention to Chinese laws, but the Chinese retorted that there were no such restrictions and none would be invoked and demanded reciprocity.

And on August 21, 1963, *Pravda* further charged that Peking was arrogating to itself the right to represent the true interests of the Soviet people: "The CPR leaders attempt to present matters as though their statements, which are aimed at undisguised interference in the internal affairs of other socialist countries, specifically the Soviet Union, are dictated allegedly by a sense of 'proletarian international duty. . . .' It must be said that no imperialist state has yet gone so far as to assert that it and not the Soviet Government represents the Soviet Union in international affairs or to speak in the name of the Soviet people. . . . If any government . . . began to assume that it, and not the government of another state, expressed the will of the people of the latter state, chaos and confusion would reign in international affairs. . . . In the statement of the representative of the CPR Government, the claim to determine for the Soviet people what furthers their interests and what does not, what ensures their security and what does not, grows to simply fantastic proportions."

A few days later, the Soviet jurist, G. Tunkin, asserted that the Chinese leadership was even claiming a right to represent the USSR in international affairs: "The leaders of the CPR have gone even farther in their policy of flouting the norms of international relations than imperialist governments permit themselves to go. The Chinese leaders have gone so far as to assert insolently that they, not the Soviet Government, represent the Soviet Union in international affairs." (F. Kozhevnikov, "On That Which is Obligatory For All—Position of the Chinese Leadership From Standpoint of International Law," *Izvestiia* (Moscow), August 24, 1963. See also G. Tunkin, "State Borders and Peaceful Coexistence," *Izvestiia* (Moscow), August 27, 1963.

13.   There was just a touch of sweet irony in the Chinese assertion of their right to behave in the Soviet Union as if it were a Chinese province on grounds that "proletarian internationalism" transcended the ordinary restrictions and artificialities of such a bourgeois concept as sovereignty. The Chinese were demanding nothing less than the exercise of extraterritorial rights on Soviet soil similar to those demanded by Stalin with respect to Yugoslavia in 1948, and essentially on the same grounds. It may be recalled that when Tito and Kardelj complained about the activities of Soviet personnel on Yugoslav soil in contacting individuals and organizations outside ordinary administrative and legal channels, Moscow retorted as follows: "Soviet workers are politically mature people and not simple hired laborers, who have no right to be interested in what is happening in Yugoslavia. It is only natural for them to talk with Yugoslav citizens, to ask them questions and gain information, etc. One would have to be an incorrigible anti-Soviet to consider these talks as attempts to recruit people for the intelligence service. . . . It must be emphasized that Yugoslav comrades visiting Moscow frequently visit other cities in the USSR, meet our people and freely talk with them. In no case did the Soviet Government place any restrictions on them. . . . According to the Yugoslav scheme, information about the Party and State can only be obtained from the leading organs of the CC of the CPY or from the Government. . . . It may be asked now: Why should Soviet Communists in Yugoslavia have fewer rights than Yugoslavs in the USSR?" (Soviet letter of May 4, 1948, to the Yugoslav Central Committee, in *The Soviet-Yugoslav Dispute,* [London: Royal Institute of International Affairs, 1948], pp. 40–41.

Although the Soviet-Yugoslav and Soviet-Chinese situations are comparable, they are by no means symmetrical in their effects. What is interesting in both situations is the shameless manner in which Moscow manipulates the principles of "sovereignty" and "reciprocity" to its advantage even when the Soviet Union must reverse its position. Thus, in 1948, the Soviet Union condemned the Yugoslavs for invoking "sovereignty" and demanded "reciprocity" on Soviet terms, while in 1963, the Soviets were invoking "sovereignty" and denying that "reciprocity" had any applicability in the situation. In 1948, Moscow wanted the right to freely conduct its activities on Yugoslav territory, whereas such a "right" was of no advantage to Yugoslavia; in 1963, Moscow wanted to exclude Peking's personnel from conducting its activities on Soviet soil and saw no advantage in gaining or preserving a similar "right" on Chinese territory. Thus, the "Brezhnev Doctrine" emerges as little more than an earlier Chinese interpretation of "proletarian internationalism."

Tito, however, remains consistent. In March 1969, he denounced the "Brezhnev Doctrine," as he earlier resisted Soviet attempts to infringe upon Yugoslav sovereignty: "In the name of the alleged higher interests of Socialism, attempts are made to justify even the open violation of the sovereignty of a socialist country and the adoption of military force as a means of preventing independent socialist development." Predictably, Peking also condemned the doctrine as fascist and imperialist: " 'Limited sovereignty' in essence means that Soviet revisionism can encroach upon the sovereignty of other countries and interfere in their domestic affairs at will, and even send its aggressor troops into the territory of these countries to suppress the people there, while the people invaded have no right to resist aggression and safeguard their own sovereignty and independence. This is an out-and-out fascist 'theory.' . . . The fascist theories of the Soviet revisionist renegade clique are of the same kind as the tsars' imperialist ones created to invade other countries. . . . Didn't the Soviet revisionist new tsars behave in just this manner in Czechoslovakia? . . . They have also applied these measures to Asia, turning the People's Republic of Mongolia into their colony, and making further attempts to encroach upon China's territory. The recent Soviet revisionists' extending of their claws to intrude into China's sacred territory of Chenpao Island is a major revelation of their frenzied aggressive ambitions and social-imperialist nature." (*Jenmin Jihpao* [Peking], March 17, 1969.)

Kommunist (Moscow), on April 21, 1969, apparently stung by the chorus of denunciation, denied the existence of "some kind of doctrine called the 'limited sovereignty' of the socialist countries," while simultaneously reaffirming it. In any event, Moscow assured Yugoslavia in September 1969 that the "Brezhnev Doctrine" was not applicable to her, but an ominous dispatch by Victor Louis (a Soviet citizen with Secret Police connections) from Moscow reported that the Soviet leaders were contemplating a Soviet preventive attack on China's nuclear installations in the name of the "socialist commonwealth doctrine." (*The New York Times,* September 18, 1969.)

14. East Germany, the only divided national state in Eastern Europe, was actually under full Soviet military occupation, while Poland and Hungary were under partial Soviet occupation, and Bulgaria was and remains supinely servile. East Germany's status was improved by the Czechoslovak occupation, while the autonomy of Poland and Hungary was seriously compromised.

CHAPTER 11. EAST EUROPEAN RELATIONS WITH THE WEST

1. See Khrushchev's report to the Twentieth CPSU Congress, translated in *Current Soviet Policies,* Vol. 2: *The Documentary Record of the 20th Communist Party Congress and its Aftermath,* ed. Leo Gruliow (New York: Praeger, 1957), pp. 29–37.

2. Among the long-term credits extended by Western countries to Eastern Europe were the following: a British loan to Czechoslovakia for a fertilizer plant (twelve years); a French loan of $350 million to the USSR (ten years); a French loan to Rumania (seven years). Even the U.S. Government (a laggard in this respect) authorized a seven-year loan guarantee to Rumania for the purchase of a steel mill. See J. F. Brown, *The New Eastern Europe: The Khrushchev Era and After* (New York: Praeger, 1966), p. 225.

3. *The Economic Survey of Europe: The European Economy in 1967,* prepared by the Secretariat of the Economic Commission for Europe (New York: United Nations, 1968), chapter 2, "Recent Economic Developments in Eastern Europe and the Soviet Union," p. 80.

4. See Gyorgy Adam, "New Features of East-West Economic Relations," *Gazdasag* (Budapest), November 1967, translated in Radio Free Europe, *Hungarian Press Survey,* no. 1885.

5. For instance, beginning in May 1964, the Czechoslovak regime offered Western tourists korunas at four times the official exchange rate. In January 1965, this rate was reduced to a little over twice the official exchange. It required an obligatory purchase (of $4.00 in 1964 and $3.00 in 1965) for every day's stay in Czechoslovakia. (*East Europe,* March 1965, p. 42.) Similarly, Poland offered Western tourists zlotys at six times the official rate. (*East Europe,* August 1965, p. 52.) Bulgaria offered its currency for foreign exchange at seventy percent over par. (*East Europe,* April 1965, p. 32.)

6. Such incidents are probably legion. They have provided material for both complaint and satire in Eastern Europe. See, for instance, "There's Always Room for Dollars," by Tamas Pinter, translated in *East Europe,* March 1968, pp. 26–28, from *Eletes Irodalom* (Budapest), December 2, 1967.

7. For a Czechoslovak regulation on this issue, see *East Europe,* August 1965, p. 33.

8. In 1965, Czechoslovakia lifted the requirement that Western hosts furnish guarantees to pay expenses for its citizens desiring to visit Western countries and allowed Czechoslovaks to purchase $100 per year in hard currency at five times the official rate. (*East Europe,* May 1965, p. 41.) However, before the year was out, the regime claimed that it was short of foreign currency, and the offer was suspended. (*East Europe,* September 1965, p. 43).

9. Thus the Hungarian regime launched sales at discount prices to rid the warehouses of low-quality goods. (Radio Free Europe, *Hungarian Background Report,* November 17, 1965.) The Bulgarian Ministry of Internal Trade discontinued purchases from 160 enterprises because of their substandard production. (*Rabotnichesko Delo* [Sofia], August 1, 1963.) The USSR cancelled several orders of Czechoslovak engineering products for reasons of their low quality and obsolescence. (*East Europe,* December 1965, p. 37.)

10. As Walter Ulbricht complained to an East German Central Committee Plenum: "While in the years 1951 to 1955 a growth in national income of 21 billion marks was achieved with an investment volume of 32 billion marks, . . . in 1961 to 1964, investments of 66 billion marks brought a growth of national income of only 10.7 billion marks." (Quoted by George Bailey, "East Germany: The Plan Collapses," *The Reporter*, April 20, 1967, p. 21.) In Bulgaria, between 1959 and 1962 capital investments had risen by 38 percent, while unfinished projects had grown by 108 percent. (Ivan Mironov, "The Efficient Use of the Basic Turnover Funds of Material Incentive," *Ikonomicheska Misal* [Sofia], no. 5, 1964, translated in Radio Free Europe, *Bulgarian Press Survey*, no. 542.)

11. See J. F. Brown, *op. cit.*, p. 291.

12. Among the many examples that could be cited from the economic debates in Eastern Europe, see P. Kunin, "The Systematic Development of the National Economy According to Plan and the Principle 'From Each According to his Abilities, to Each According to his Work,' Under Socialism," *Novo Vreme* (Sofia), December 12, 1963, translated in Radio Free Europe, *Bulgarian Press Survey*, no. 503; Istvan Fris, "The Plan and the Market," *Tarsadalmi Szemle* (Budapest), November 1966, translated in Radio Free Europe, *Hungarian Press Survey*, no. 1766. For an excellent general comparative discussion of the economic reform debate in Eastern Europe, see J. F. Brown, *op. cit.*, pp. 75–132, and articles treating individual countries in *Problems of Communism*, January/February to November/December 1966.

13. In East Germany, for instance, the essential goal of the economic reform was to achieve the world's highest standard of production (i.e. *Hochstniveau*). See Walter Ulbricht's speech to the Fifth SED Central Committee Plenum, *Neues Deutschland* (East Berlin) February 5, 1965.

14. Ulbricht held America's du Pont de Nemeurs as an example for East Germany to follow. (*Ibid.*) In Czechoslovakia, the study of Henry Ford's production techniques was recommended. (*East Europe*, January 1967, p. 47.) Rumanians came to the U.S. to study management. (*East Europe*, May 1967, p. 48.)

15. Jeno Fock, "On Some Timely Questions Connected with Economic Development," *Tarsadalmi Szemle* (Budapest), October 1965, translated in Radio Free Europe, *Hungarian Press Survey*, no. 1651.

16. *Economic Survey of Europe, 1967, op. cit.*, p. 77.

17. *Ibid.*, p. 81.

18. Judging by the scope of decentralization envisaged in the several East European economic reform programs, Hungary and Czechoslovakia are the two most progressive countries in the Soviet bloc. Czechoslovakia's reform program, however, has been in suspension since the invasion. East Germany and Bulgaria, next in this lineup, have delegated many of the formerly centralized planning, distribution, and control functions to the directorates of mammoth amalgamated enterprises, but left little freedom of maneuver to the component enterprises themselves. Poland and Rumania have made the least progress in decentralization of the six East European Soviet bloc countries.

19. For an excellent summary and evaluation of the economic reforms in the

Soviet bloc, see Gregory Grossman, "Economic Reforms: A Balance Sheet," *Problems of Communism,* November/December 1966.

20. For Bulgaria's price structure reform, see Radio Free Europe, *Bulgarian Situation Report,* December 14, 1965; for Czechoslovakia's, see Radio Free Europe, *Czechoslovak Background Report,* November 7, 1964; for Hungary's, see Decree No. 11/1967, *Magyar Kozlony* (Budapest), May 13, 1967, translated in Radio Free Europe, *Hungarian Press Survey,* no. 1822.

21. For East Germany, see "Late Bloomer: Sociology," *East Europe,* July 1965, p. 42. For Czechoslovakia, "Sociology Becomes Respectable," *East Europe,* June 1964, p. 47, and "Sociologists at Work," *ibid.,* August 1964, p. 32. Knowledgeable Western scholars judge Polish sociology to be among the most advanced in Eastern Europe. In Hungary, former Premier Andras Hegedus developed an interest in sociology and has made several perceptive contributions, some perhaps more candid than the regime was prepared to tolerate. See "Former Premier Loses Editorial Post," *East Europe,* November 1965, p. 40.

22. In 1965, for instance, a Hungarian Politburo resolution urged a radical improvement in the dissemination of information, maintaining that ". . . if we do not speak of something in time, the enemy does it. As a result, reticence comes to amount to a political defeat. . . . Regime media should not recoil either from mentioning 'unfavorable' facts or from echoing differing views provided that they are accompanied by adequate explanations." (Radio Free Europe, *Hungarian Situation Report,* July 9, 1965.)

23. See Robert S. Jaster, "The Defeat of Khrushchev's Plan to Integrate Eastern Europe," *The World Today,* December 1963.

24. See David Binder, "Comecon Reported in Stalemate on Trade and Currency Issues," *The New York Times,* January 31, 1969.

25. Thus, Ceausescu told the Rumanian National Assembly on November 29, 1968: "We cannot in any case agree . . . to investing this organization [Comecon] with suprastate prerogatives and the creation of certain supranational economic bodies. This would hurt the sovereignty and independence of the states. . . ." (*Scinteia* [Bucharest], November 30, 1968.)

26. Reszo Nyers, somewhat rhetorically, put it this way to the Hungarian National Assembly: "In our view the following questions arise and require an answer in the present phase of development: should we continue to develop international production cooperation chiefly in the framework of interstate agreements, or base it more on the economic interests of the enterprises?" (Hungarian Press Agency [MTI] [Budapest] December 19, 1968.)

27. See Marcel Brozik, "For a Direct Participation of Enterprises in Cooperation with CEMA," *Rude Pravo* (Prague), April 22, 1969.

28. Binder, *op. cit.*

29. Thus, Hungary's chief delegate to Comecon, Antal Apro, has argued for a convertible Comecon currency and an international bank for economic cooperation, "so as to cope better with the financial and credit relations among the CMEA states and carry out banking activity not only among the CHEA states but also in the sphere of international economic cooperation." (Radio and Television Interview, Budapest, December 28, 1968.) For a discussion of Poland's long-standing attitude on this issue, see Stefan Stolte, "Comecon Through Soviet Eyes," *Studies on the Soviet Union* 5, no. 3 (1966), p. 44.

30. Binder, *op. cit.*
31. Tad Szulc, "Soviet Bloc Agrees to Work Toward Mutual Convertibility of its Currencies," *The New York Times,* May 11, 1969.
32. This became apparent at the Bucharest Warsaw Pact summit in June 1966, and again at the Budapest summit in March 1969. See *The New York Times,* July 6, 1966, p. 12 and *The Washington Post,* March 19, 1969, p. A-1.
33. See Joseph Lelyveld, "Red Bloc Invites West Europeans to Security Talk," *The New York Times,* July 9, 1966. The text of the Warsaw Pact declaration on peace and security in Europe was published by TASS, July 8, 1966. Excerpts appeared in *The New York Times,* July 9, 1966, p. 6.
34. From excerpts in *The New York Times,* May 14, 1966, p. 4.
35. See, for instance, the speech by Janos Peter, Hungary's Foreign Minister, to the Political Academy of the Hungarian Party Central Committee, December 11, 1968, in which he said: "Our European policy is directed toward strengthening the peaceful coexistence and cooperation of European countries with different regimes through bilateral systems of alliance, thus paving the way toward the establishment of a new European security system." (Hungarian Press Agency [MTI] [Budapest], December 11, 1968.)
36. Since April 1969, Syria, Cambodia, the United Arab Republic, and the Republic of South Yemen have exchanged ambassadors with East Germany.
37. For the establishment of reciprocal trade missions between West Germany and Poland (March 1963), Rumania (October 1963), and Hungary (November 1963), see *East Europe,* December 1963, p. 40; for Bulgaria, see *East Europe,* April 1964, p. 32.
38. *The New York Times,* February 1, 1967.
39. *East Europe,* September 1967, p. 39.
40. See Welles Hangen, *The Muted Revolution: East Germany's Challenge to Russia and the West* (New York: Alfred A. Knopf, 1966), chapter 1, "Shaking the Temples of Certainty."
41. See *Neue Zuricher Zeitung* (Zurich), June 27, 1969 and April 19, 1966, respectively.
42. See Ulbricht's speech to the Ninth Central Committee Plenum, *Neues Deutschland* (East Berlin), October 25, 1968.
43. Thus, in June 1969, the DDR and France established a joint marketing firm for the French import of East German agricultural machinery. (*Frankfurter Rundschau* [Frankfurt], May 23, 1969.)
44. "Some five months after the invasion of Czechoslovakia, statements by official Eastern and Western European spokesmen have, in increasing numbers, supported a policy of qualified detente and cooperation among 'socialist' and 'capitalist' states as the only means of maintaining peace and providing a measure of security in Europe and the world." (Radio Free Europe, *East-West Contacts, A Monthly Survey,* January 1969.)

Bibliography

A SELECTED BIBLIOGRAPHY

The following list of recent scholarly books, primarily in the English language, is intended for the reader who desires further knowledge about the countries of Eastern Europe. Additional references, especially to articles, can be found in the footnotes.

BOOKS AND MIMEOGRAPHED PAPERS

Aczel, Tamas, ed. *Ten Years After*. New York: Holt, Rinehart, and Winston, 1967.

Adams, Arthur E. *An Atlas of Russia and East European History*. New York: Praeger, 1967.

Allen, Robert L. *Soviet Influence in Latin America*. Washington: Public Affairs Press, 1959.

―――. *Yearbook on International Communist Affairs*. Hoover Institution on War, Revolution and Peace: Stanford University, 1968.

Almond, Gabriel A. and James S. Coleman. *The Politics of the Developing Areas*. Princeton, N.J.: Princeton University Press, 1960.

Apel, Hans. *DDR: 1962; 1964; 1966*. West Berlin: Woltaire Verlag, 1967.

Apter, David E. *The Politics of Modernization*. Chicago and London: University of Chicago Press, 1965.

Armstrong, John A. *Ideology, Politics, and Government in the Soviet Union*. New York: Praeger, 1967.

Aspaturian, Vernon V. *The Soviet Union in the International Communist System*. Stanford, Calif.: Hoover Institution Studies, 1966.

Augstein, Rudolf. *Meinungen zu Deutschland*. Frankfurt/Main: Suhrkamp Verlag, 1967.

Avakumovic, Ivan. *History of the Communist Party of Yugoslavia*. Aberdeen, England: Aberdeen University Press, 1964.

Avramov, P. *Bulgarskata Komunisticheska Partiia i formirane na sotsialisticheskata inteligentsiia*. Sofia: Bulgarskata Komunisticheska Partiia, 1966.

Azrael, Jeremy R. *Managerial Power and Soviet Politics.* Cambridge: Harvard University Press, 1966.

Baade, Hans W., ed. *The Soviet Impact in International Law.* New York: Oceana, 1965.

Balassa, Bela A. *The Hungarian Experience in Economic Planning.* New Haven, Conn.: Yale University Press, 1959.

Banja, Hasan. *Establishment and Prospects of Development of Socialist Industry in the People's Republic of Albania.* Tirana: Naim Frasheri, 1968.

Benes, V. A. Gyorgy and G. Stambuk. *Eastern European Government and Politics.* New York: Harper and Row, 1966.

Beky, I. L. Halasz de. *A Bibliography of the Hungarian Revolution.* Toronto: University of Toronto Press, 1963.

Bergson, Abram. *Planning and Productivity Under Soviet Socialism.* New York: Columbia University Press, 1968.

Berciu, D. *Romania.* New York: Praeger, 1967.

Berrins, Alfred S. *The Two Faces of Coexistence.* New York: Speller, 1967.

Bibo, Istvan. *Harmadik Ut.* London: Magyar Konyves Ceh 1960.

Blumenfeld, Yorich. *Seesaw: Cultural Life in Eastern Europe.* New York: Harcourt, Brace, and World, 1968.

Bombelles, Joseph T. *Economic Development of Communist Yugoslavia.* Hoover Institution on War, Revolution and Peace: Stanford University, 1968.

Bromke, Adam, ed. *The Communist States at the Crossroads.* New York: Praeger, 1965.

Bromke, Adam and Philip E. Ureu, eds. *The Communist States and the West.* New York: Praeger, 1967.

Brown, J. F. *The New Eastern Europe: The Khrushchev Era and After.* New York: Praeger, 1966.

Brzezinski, Zbigniev K. *Alternative to Particion.* New York: McGraw-Hill, 1965.

————. *The Soviet Bloc: Unity and Conflict.* New York: Praeger, 1961.

Bundesministerium fur gesamtdeutsche Fragen. *Die SED: Historische Entwicklung, Ideologische Grundlagen, Programm und Organization.* Bonn: n.p. 1967.

————. *Der Parteiapparat der "Deutschen Demokratischen Republik."* 3rd edition. Bonn: n.p. 1969.

————. *Der Staatsapparat der "Deutschen Demokratischen Republik."* 4th edition. Bonn: n.p. 1969.

Burks, R. V. *Technological Innovation and Political Change in Communist Eastern Europe.* Santa Monica, California: RAND Memorandum (RM-6051-PR), 1969.

Burks, R. V., ed. *The Future of Communism in Europe.* Detroit: Wayne State University Press, 1968.

Burks, R. V. *The Dynamics of Communism in Eastern Europe.* Princeton, N.J.: Princeton University Press, 1966.

Byrnes, Robert F. *The United States and Eastern Europe.* Englewood Cliffs: Prentice-Hall, 1967.

Campbell, John C. *Tito's Separate Road.* New York: Harper and Row, 1967.

Campbell, Robert W. *Soviet Economic Power*. Boston: Houghton Mifflin, 1966.

Cantril, Hadley. *The Pattern of Human Concern*. New Brunswick: Rutgers University Press, 1965.

Cheng, Chu-Yuan. *Economic Relations Between Peking and Moscow, 1919–1963*. New York: Praeger, 1964.

Collier, D. S. *Western Policy and Eastern Europe*. Chicago: H. Regnery Company, 1966.

Collier, D. S. and K. Glaser. *Elements of Change in Eastern Europe*. Chicago: H. Regnery Company, 1968.

Cretzianu, Alexandre, ed. *Captive Rumania: A Decade of Soviet Rule*. New York: Praeger, 1956.

Dahl, Robert and Charles Lindblohm. *Politics, Economics, and Welfare*. New York: Harper and Row, 1963.

Dallin, Alexander, and Jonathan Harris, eds. *Diversity in International Communism*. New York: Columbia University Press, 1963.

Dallin, Alexander and T. B. Larson. *Soviet Politics Since Khrushchev*. Englewood Cliffs: Prentice-Hall, 1968.

Clissold, Stephen, ed. *A Short History of Yugoslavia*. Cambridge: Cambridge University Press, 1967.

Dedijer, Vladimir. *Tito*. New York: Simon & Schuster, 1953.

Dellin, L. A. D. *Bulgaria*. New York: Praeger, 1957.

Deutsch, Karl W. *Political Community at the International Level*. New York: Doubleday, 1954.

Dilo, Jani I. *The Communist Party Leadership in Albania*. Washington, D.C.: Institute of Ethnic Studies, Georgetown University, 1961.

Dinerstein, Herbert S. *Fifty Years of Soviet Foreign Policy*, Baltimore: Johns Hopkins Press, 1968.

Djilas, Milovan. *Conversations with Stalin*. New York: Harcourt, Brace, and World, 1968.

———. *The Unperfect Society: Beyond the New Class*. New York: Harcourt, Brace, and World, 1969.

Doernberg, Stefan. *Kurze Geschichte der DDR*. 3rd edition. East Berlin: Dietz Verlag Berlin, 1968.

Doob, Leonard. *Patriotism and Nationalism: Their Psychological Foundations*. New Haven: Yale University Press, 1965.

Dornberg, John. *The Other Germany*. New York: Doubleday, 1968.

Drenikoff, K. *L'Eglise Catholique en Bulgarie*. Madrid: n.p. 1968.

Dubs, Rolf. *Freiheitliche Demokratie und Totalitare Diktatur: Eine Gegenuberstellung am Beispiel der Schweiz und der Sowjetzone Deutschlands (DDR)*. Frauenfeld: Verlag Huber, 1966.

Durkheim, Emil. *The Division of Labor*. Glencoe, Ill.: Free Press of Glencoe (now Macmillan) 1949.

Dzyuba, Ivan. *Internationalism or Russification?*. New York: Humanities Press, 1968.

Erickson, Erik H. *Childhood and Society*. New York: Norton, 1950.

Fainsod, Merle. *How Russia is Ruled*. 2nd edition. Cambridge: Harvard University Press, 1963.

Farrell, Barry R., ed. *Political Leadership in Eastern Europe and the Soviet Union*. Chicago: Aldine, 1970.

Feiwel, George R. *The Soviet Quest for Economic Efficiency.* New York: Praeger, 1967.

──────. *New Currents in Soviet-Type Economies.* Scranton: International Textbook Company, 1968.

Filene, Peter G., ed. *American Views of Soviet Russia, 1961–1965.* Homewood, Ill.: Dorsey Press, 1968.

Fisher, Jack C. *Yugoslavia: A Multi-National State.* San Francisco: Chandler Publishing Co., 1966.

Fisher-Galati, Stephen, ed. *Eastern Europe in the Sixties,* New York: Praeger, 1963.

Fisher-Galati, Stephen. *Romania.* New York: Praeger, 1957.

──────. *The New Rumania: From People's Democracy to Socialist Republic.* Cambridge, Mass: The M.I.T. Press, 1967.

──────. *The Socialist Republic of Rumania.* Baltimore: Johns Hopkins Press, 1969.

Fiszman, Joseph R. *Teachers in Poland as Transmitters of Socio-Political Values.* Washington: U. S. Department of Health, Education and Welfare, Office of Education, Bureau of Research, Final Report, Project No. S-417, October 1969.

Fleron, Frederick J., ed. *Communist Studies and the Social Sciences.* Chicago, Ill.: Rand McNally and Company, 1969.

Floyd, David. *Rumania: Russia's Dissident Ally.* New York: Praeger, 1965.

Forster, Thomas M. *The East German Army: A Pattern of a Communist Military Establishment.* New York: A. S. Barnes and Company, 1968.

Fortsch, Eckhart. *Die SED.* Stuttgart: W. Kohlhammer Verlag, 1969.

Fromm, Erich, ed. *Socialist Humanism: An International Symposium.* New York: Doubleday, 1965.

Galli, Giorgio. *Il bipartismo imperfetto: Communisti e democristiani in Italia.* Bologna: Societa editrice il Mulino, 1966.

Gamarnikow, Michael. *Economic Reforms in Eastern Europe.* Detroit: Wayne State University Press, 1968.

Garvy, G. *Money, Banking and Credit in Eastern Europe.* New York: Federal Reserve Bank of New York, 1966.

Georgeoff, P. J. *The Social Education of Bulgarian Youth.* Minneapolis: University of Minnesota Press, 1968.

Gittings, John. *Survey of the Sino-Soviet Dispute.* Oxford: Royal Institution of International Affairs, 1968.

Goldman, Marshall T. *The Soviet Economy.* Englewood Cliffs: Prentice-Hall, 1968.

──────. *The Soviet Economy: Myth and Reality.* Englewood Cliffs: Prentice-Hall, 1968.

Gorlich, J. Wolfgang. *Geist und Macht in der DDR: Die Integration der Kommunistischen Ideologie.* West Berlin: Olten und Freiburg, 1968.

Great Britain, Central Office of Information. *Russia, China, and the West.* London: Her Majesty's Stationery Office, 1968.

Griffith, William E., ed. *Communism in Europe.* Cambridge, Mass: The M.I.T. Press, 1964.

Griffith, William E. *Sino-Soviet Relations, 1964–1965.* Cambridge, Mass.: The M.I.T. Press, 1967.

──────. *The Sino-Soviet Rift.* Cambridge, Mass.: The M.I.T. Press, 1964.

————. *Albania and the Sino-Soviet Rift.* Cambridge, Mass.: The M.I.T. Press, 1963.

Grub, Phillip and Karel Holcik, eds. *American-East European Trade: Controversy, Progress, Prospects.* Washington, D.C.: National Press, 1969.

Gruilow, Leo, ed. *The Documentary Record of the 20th Communist Party Congress and its Aftermath. Current Soviet Policies,* Vol. 2. New York: Praeger, 1967.

Grzybowski, Kasmierz. *The Socialist Commonwealth of Nations.* New Haven: Yale University Press, 1964.

Grzybowski, Konstanty. *Oredzie biskupow polskich do biskupow niemieckich: Materialy i dokumenty.* 2nd edition. Warsaw: Polonia, 1966.

Gsovski, Vladimir and K. Grzybowski. *Government, Laws, and Courts in the Soviet Union and Eastern Europe.* New York: Praeger, 1959.

Gyorgy, Andrew, ed. *Issues of World Communism.* Princeton, N.J.: D. Van Nostrand, 1966.

Hagen, Louis. *The Secret War for Europe: A Dossier of Espionage.* New York: Stein and Day, 1968.

Halperin, Morton H., ed. *Sino-Soviet Relations and Arms Control.* Cambridge, Mass.: The M.I.T. Press, 1967.

Hamilton, F. E. I. *Yugoslavia: Patterns of Economic Activity.* New York: Praeger, 1968.

Hamm, Harry. *Albania: China's Beachhead in Europe.* New York: Praeger, 1963.

Hammond, Thomas T. *Soviet Foreign Relations and World Communism.* Princeton, N.J.: Princeton University Press, 1965.

Hangen, Welles. *The Muted Revolution: East German's Challenge to Russia and the West.* New York: Knopf, 1966.

Hanhardt, Arthur M., Jr. *The German Democratic Republic.* Baltimore: Johns Hopkins Press, 1968.

Hardt, John P., ed. *Mathematics and Computers in Soviet Economic Planning.* New Haven: Yale University Press, 1967.

Hata, Ikuhiko. *Reality and Illusion.* New York: Columbia University Press, 1967.

Hegedus, Andras. *A szocialista tarsaldalom strukturajarol.* Budapest: Akademiai kiado, 1966.

Hoffman, George W. *The Balkans in Transition.* Princeton: Van Nostrand, 1963.

Hoffman, George W. and Fred Warner Neal. *Yugoslavia and the New Communism.* New York: Twentieth Century Fund, 1962.

Holborn, Louise W., John H. Herz, and Gwendolen M. Carter. *Documents of Major Foreign Powers: A Sourcebook on Great Britain, Germany, France, and the Soviet Union.* New York: Harcourt, Brace and World, 1968.

Hornsby, Lex. *Profile of East Germany.* New York: Harper and Row, 1966.

Howe, George M. *The Soviet Union.* London: MacDonald & Evans, 1968.

Hungarian Chamber of Commerce. *Handbook of Hungarian Foreign Trade.* Budapest: Kossuth Printing House, 1967.

Hulten, Kurt. *Iron Curtain Christians: The Church in Communist Countries Today.* Minneapolis: Augsburg Publishing House, 1967.

Hyland, William. *The Fall of Khrushchev*. New York: Funk and Wagnalls, 1968.

Institute for Strategic Studies. *The Military Balance: 1969–1970*. London: The Institute for Strategic Studies, 1969.

International Labour Office. *Worker's Management in Yugoslavia*. Geneva: La Tribune de Geneve, 1964.

Ionescu, Ghita. *Communism in Rumania, 1944–1962*. London: Oxford University Press, 1964.

————. *The Break-up of the Soviet Empire in Eastern Europe*. London: Penguin, 1965.

Ionescu, Ghita. *The Politics of the European Communist States*. New York: Praeger, 1967.

Istoriia na Bulgariia. 2nd revised edition. Sofia: Nauka i Izkustvo, 1964.

Jackson, George D. *Comintern and Peasants in East Europe*. New York: Columbia University Press, 1965.

Jacobs, Dan U., ed. *The New Communism*. New York: Harper and Row, 1969.

Jamgotch, Nish. *Soviet-East European Dialogue*. Stanford: Stanford University Press, 1968.

Juviler, Peter H., ed. *Soviet Policy-Making*. New York: Praeger, 1967.

Karcz, Jerzy F. *Soviet and East European Agriculture*. Berkeley: University of California Press, 1967.

Kase, Francis J. *People's Democracy*. Holland: Sijthoff (Leyden), 1968.

Kaser, Michael. *Comecon: Integration Problems of the Planned Economies*. New York: Oxford University Press, Royal Institution of International Affairs, 1967.

Kasneci, Lefter. *Steeled in the Heat of Battle: A Brief Survey of the History of the National-Liberation War of the Albanian People (1941-1944)*. Tirane: Naim Frasheri, 1966.

Kassoff, Allen, ed. *Prospects for Soviet Society*. New York: Praeger, 1968.

Kecskemeti, Paul. *The Unexpected Revolution*. Stanford: Stanford University Press, 1961.

Kennedy, Robert F. *Thirteen Days*. New York: Norton, 1969.

Kertesz, Stephen D., ed. *East Central Europe and the World*. Notre Dame: University of Notre Dame Press, 1962.

Kertesz, Stephen D., ed. *The Fate of East Central Europe: Hopes and Failures of American Foreign Policy*. Notre Dame: University of Notre Dame Press, 1956.

Klohr, O. *Religion und Atheismus Heute: Ergebnisse und Aufgaben Marxistischer Religionsoziologie*. East Berlin, 1966.

Kogan, Norman. Italian Communism, the Working Class and Organized Catholicism. Mimeographed paper. Storrs: University of Connecticut, 1965.

Kohler, Heinz. *Economic Integration in the Soviet Bloc: With an East German Case Study*. New York: Praeger, 1965.

Kolaja, Jiri. *Workers' Councils: The Yugoslav Experience*. New York: Frederick A. Praeger, 1966.

Kolkowicz, Roman. *The Soviet Military and the Communist Party*. Princeton, N.J.: Princeton University Press, 1967.

Kopp, Fritz. *Kurs auf ganz Deutschland?: Die Deutschland Politik der SED.* Stuttgart: Seewald Verlag, 1965.

Korbonski, Andrzej. *Politics of Socialist Agriculture in Poland: 1945–1960.* New York: Columbia University Press, 1965.

Kostov, Traicho. *Izbrani statii, dokladi, rechi.* Sofia: Bulgarskata Komunisticheska Partiia, 1964.

Kovrig, Bennett. *The Hungarian People's Republic.* Baltimore: Johns Hopkins Press, 1960.

Kovacs, Imre. *Facts About Hungary.* New York: Hungarian Committee, 1966.

Kozakiewicz, Mikolaj. *Swiatopoglad 1,000 nauczycieli: Sprawozdanie z badan ankietowych.* Warsaw: Panstwowe Zaklady Wydawnictwo Szkolnych, 1961.

Kozponti Statisztikai Hivata. *Magyar statisztikai zsebkonyv, 1968.* Budapest: Statisztikai Kiado Vallalat, 1968.

Kreig, Harold. *LDP und NDP in der "DDR": 1949–1958: Ein Beitrag zur Geschichte der Nichtsozialistischen Parteien und Ihrer Gleichschaltung mit der SED.* Cologne and Opladen: Westdeutscher Verlag, 1965.

Kulbach, Roderick and Helmut Weber. *Parteien im Blocksystem der DDR: Aufbau und Funktion der LDPD und der NDPD.* Cologne: Verlag Wissenschaft und Politik, 1969.

Kwiatkowski, Zbigniew. *Bylem niemilczacym swiadkiem.* Warsaw: Iskry, 1965.

Laqueur, Walter and Leopold Labedz, eds. *Polycentrism.* New York: Praeger, 1962.

Larson, Thomas B. *Disarmament and Soviet Policy, 1964–1968.* Englewood Cliffs, N.J.: Prentice-Hall, 1969.

Laslo, Ervin. *The Communist Theory in Hungary.* New York: Reidel Company, 1966.

Lendvai, Paul. *Eagles in Cobwebs: Nationalism and Communism in the Balkans.* New York: Doubleday, 1969.

Lerner, Daniel. *The Passing of Traditional Society.* New York: Free Press of Glencoe (Macmillan), 1958.

Littell, Robert. *The Czech Black Book.* New York: Avon Books, 1969.

Lipset, Seymour. *Political Man.* New York: Doubleday, 1960.

London, Kurt, ed. *Eastern Europe in Transition.* Baltimore: Johns Hopkins Press, 1966.

Lowenthal, Richard. *World Communism: The Disintegration of a Secular Faith.* New York: Oxford University Press, 1964.

Macartney, C. A. and A. S. Palmer. *Independent Eastern Europe.* New York: St. Martin, 1962.

Macesich, George. *Yugoslavia: The Theory and Practice of Development Planning.* Charlottesville: The University Press of Virginia, 1964.

Maerker, Rudolf. *Jugend im Anderen Teil Deutschlands: Schrittmacher oder Mitmacher?* Munich: Juventa Verlag, 1969.

Mayer, Peter. *Cohesion and Conflict in International Communism.* The Hague: Martinus Nijhoff, 1966.

Meissner, Boris. *Das Selbstbestimmungsrecht der Volker in Osteuropa und China.* Koln: Verlag Wissenschaft und Politik, 1968.

Merton, Robert K. *Social Theory and Social Structure.* Glencoe, Ill.: The Free Press (Macmillan), 1957.

Meyer, Peter. *The Jews in the Soviet Satellites.* Syracuse: Syracuse University Press, 1953.

Milosz, Czeslaw. *Native Realm: A Search for Self-Definition.* Translated from the Polish by Catherine S. Leach. New York: Doubleday, 1968.

Mizov, N. *Isliamut v Bulgariia.* Sofia: Bulgarskata Komunisticheska Partiia, 1965.

Mnacko, Ladislaw. *The Taste of Power.* New York: Praeger, 1967.

Molnar, Janos. *Ellenforradalom Magyarorszagon 1956-ban.* Budapest: Akademiai kiado, 1967.

Montias, John Michael. *Economic Development in Communist Rumania.* Cambridge, Mass.: The M.I.T. Press, 1967.

Moore, Clement H. *Symposium on the Evolution of Established One-party Systems: Statement of Purpose.* Mimeographed paper. Berkeley: University of California, 1967.

Moraca, Pero. *The League of Communists of Yugoslavia.* Translated by Bosko Milosavljevic. Belgrade: Medunarodna Politika, 1966.

Morgenthau, Hans J. *In Defense of the National Interest.* Chicago: University of Chicago Press, 1950.

Morris, Bernard S. *International Communism and American Policy.* New York: Atherton Press, 1966.

Morrison, James F. *The Polish People's Republic.* Baltimore: Johns Hopkins Press, 1968.

Mosca, Gaetano. *The Ruling Class.* New York: McGraw-Hill, 1939.

Murowski, Klaus Eberhard. *Der Andere Teil Deutschlands.* Munich: Gunter Olzog Verlag, 1967.

McNeal, Robert H., ed. *International Relations Among Communists.* Englewood Cliffs, N.J.: Prentice-Hall, 1967.

McVicker, Charles. *Titoism: Pattern for International Communism.* New York: St. Martin's Press, 1957.

Nagy, Imre. *On Communism: In Defense of the New Course.* London: Thames and Hudson, 1957.

Neal, Fred Warner. *Titoism in Action.* Berkeley and Los Angeles: University of California Press, 1958.

Nette, Wolfgang. *DDR Report.* Dusseldorf and Cologne: Eugen Diederichs Verlag, 1968.

Obretenov, A. *Kulturnata Revoliutsiia v Bulgariia.* Sofia: Bulgarskata Komunisticheska Partiia, 1968.

Osborne, R. H. *East-Central Europe: An Introductory Geography.* New York: Praeger, 1967.

Oshavkov, Zh, ed. *Protsesut na preodoliavaneto na religiiata v Bulgariia: sotsiologichesko izsledvane.* Sofia: Bulgarskata akademiia na naukite, 1968.

Pano, Nicholas, C. *The People's Republic of Albania.* Baltimore: Johns Hopkins Press, 1969.

Pejovich, Svetozar. *The Market-Planned Economy of Yugoslavia.* Minneapolis: University of Minnesota Press, 1966.

Papajorgji, Harilla. *The Development of Socialist Industry and Its Prospects in the People's Republic of Albania.* Tirane: Naim Frasheri, 1964.

Pirages, Dennis, C. *Socioeconomic Development and Political Change in the Communist System.* Mimeographed paper. Studies of the Communist System. Stanford, Calif.: Stanford University, 1966.

Planck, Charles R. *The Changing Status of German Reunification in Western Diplomacy. 1955–1966.* Baltimore: Johns Hopkins Press, 1967.

Plischke, Elmer. *Contemporary Governments of Germany.* 2nd Edition. Boston: Houghton Mifflin, 1969.

Popoff, Haralan. *I Was A Communist Prisoner.* Grand Rapids, Mich.: Zondervan, 1966.

Praesidium der Volkskammer der Deutschen Demokratischen Republik. *Die Volkskammer der Deutschen Demokratischen Republik. Wahlperiode.* Vol. 5. East Berlin: Staatsverlag der Deutschen Demokratischen Republik, 1967.

Prauss, Herbert. *Jugend in Mitteldeutschland: Tatsachen und Analysen.* Dusseldorf: Verlag Haus Atenberg, 1968.

Pritzel, Konstantin. *Die Wirtschaftsintegration Mitteldeutschlands.* Cologne: Verlag, Wissenschaft und Politik, 1969.

Prpic, George J. *Eastern Europe and World Communism.* University Heights, Ohio: John Carroll University, 1966.

Pryor, F. L. *The Communist Foreign Trade System.* Cambridge: Harvard University Press, 1963.

Pundeff, M. *Bulgaria: A Bibliographic Guide.* New York: Arno Press, 1968.

Pye, Lucien. *Politics, Personality, and Nation Building.* New Haven: Yale University Press, 1962.

Ramundo, Bernard A. *Peaceful Coexistence.* Baltimore: Johns Hopkins Press, 1967.

Richert, Ernst. *Die DDR-Elite oder Unsere Partner von morgen.* Reinbeck/Hamburg: Rowohlt Taschenbuch, 1968.

————. *Das Zweite Deutschland: Ein Staat, der nicht sein darf.* Gutersloh: Siegbert Mohn Verlag, 1964.

————. *Macht Ohne Mandat: Der Staatsapparat in der Sowjetischen Besatzungszone Deutschlands.* 2nd edition. Cologne and Opladen: Westdeutscher Verlag, 1963.

Rietschel, Werner. *State and Society.* Dresden: Verlag Zeit im Bild, 1968.

Roberts, Henry L. *Rumania: Political Problems of an Agrarian State.* New Haven: Yale University Press, 1951.

Ronchey, Alberto. *The Two Red Giants.* New York: Norton, 1965.

Rosser, Richard F. *An Introduction to Soviet Foreign Policy.* Englewood Cliffs, N.J.: Prentice-Hall, 1966.

Rostow, W. W. *The Dynamics of Soviet Society.* New York: Norton, 1967.

Russett, Bruce M. *Community and Contention: Britain and America in the Twentieth Century.* Cambridge, Mass.: The M.I.T. Press, 1963.

————. *World Handbook of Political and Social Indicators.* New Haven: Yale University Press, 1964.

Sarapata, Adam. *Empirical Sociology in Poland.* Institute of Philosophy and Sociology, Polish Academy of Sciences, Warsaw: Polish Scientific Publishers (PWN), 1966.

Schenk, Fritz. *Das Rote Wirtschaftswunder: Die zentrale Planwirtschaft als Machtmittel der SED-Politik.* Stuttgart-Degerloch: Seewald Verlag, 1969.

Schulz, Eberhard and Hans Dieter Schulz. *Braucht der Osten die DDR?* Opladen: C. W. Leske Verlag, 1968.

Seton-Watson, H. *The East European Revolution.* 3rd edition. New York: Praeger, 1956.

Shaffer, Harry G., ed. *The Communist World.* New York: Appleton-Century-Crofts, 1967.

Sherman, Howard J. *The Soviet Economy.* Boston: Little, Brown, 1969.

Shoup, Paul. *Communism and the Yugoslav National Question.* New York: Columbia University Press, 1968.

Sicinski, Andrzej, ed. *Spoleczenstwo polskie w badaniach ankietowych Osrodka Badania Opinii Publicznej przy Polskim Radiu i TV: Lata 1958–1964: Przeglad zebranych materialow.* Warsaw: Panstwowe Wydawnictwo Maukowe, 1966.

Sievers, Bruce. *The Divided Nations: International Integration and National Identity.* Mimeographed paper. Studies of the Communist System. Stanford, Calif.: Stanford University, 1966.

Singleton, F. F. *Background to Eastern Europe.* New York: Pergamon, 1965.

Sik, Ota. *K problematice socialistickych zboznich vztahu.* Prague: Ceskoslovenska akademie ved, 1967.

——. *Plan and Market Under Socialism.* White Plains: International Arts & Sciences Press, 1968.

Skendi, Stavro. *Twenty Years of Socialism in Albania.* Princeton, N.J.: Princeton University Press, 1967.

Skilling, H. Gordon, *Communism, National and International: Eastern Europe After Stalin.* Toronto: University of Toronto Press, 1964.

——. *The Governments of Communist East Europe.* New York: Crowell, 1966.

Slijepcevic, D. *Die bulgarische orthodoxe Kirche, 1944–1956.* Munich: n.p. 1957.

Smith, Jean Edward. *Germany Beyond the Wall: People, Politics and Prosperity.* Boston: Little, Brown, 1969.

Sokolovskii, V. D. *Soviet Military Strategy.* Englewood Cliffs, N.J. Prentice-Hall, 1963.

Sorel, George. *Reflections on Violence.* New York: Collier Books, 1961.

Spasov, B. and A. Angelov. *Durzhavno pravo na Narodna Republika Bulgariia.* 2nd revised edition. Sofia: Nauka i Izkustvo, 1968.

Spulber, Nicholas. *The Economics of Communist Eastern Europe.* London: Chapman and Hall, 1958.

——. *The State and Economic Development in Eastern Europe.* New York: Random House, 1966.

Staar, Richard F. *The Communist Regimes in Eastern Europe: An Introduction.* Stanford: The Hoover Institution, 1967.

Staatliche Zentral Verwaltung fur Statistik. *Statistiches Jahrbuch: 1969, der Deutschen Demokratischen Republik.* Vol. 14. East Berlin: Staatsverlag der Deutschen Demokratischen Republik, 1969.

State Secretariat for West German Affairs. *Democracy in the DDR: Power Relations and Social Forms in the Socialist State of the German Nation.* Dresden: Verlag Zeit Bild, 1968.

Statystyczny, Glowny Urzad. *Rocznik Statystyczny: 1966.* Warsaw: Wiedza Powszechna, 1965.

Stern, Carola. *Ulbricht: A Political Biography.* New York: Praeger, 1965.
Stojanovich, Radmila. *Marx and Contemporary Economic Thought.* New York: International Arts & Sciences Press, 1968.
Stokke, Baard R. *Soviet and East European Trade and Aid in Africa.* New York: Praeger, 1967.
Taborsky, Edward. *Communism in Czechoslovakia, 1948–1960.* Princeton: Princeton University Press, 1961.
Tatu, Michel. *Power in the Kremlin.* New York: Viking Press, 1969.
Thomas, John I. *Education for Communism: School and State in the People's Republic of Albania.* Stanford University: Hoover Institute Press, 1969.
Toma, Peter A. and Andrew Gyorgy, eds. *Basic Issues in International Relations.* Boston: Allyn and Bacon, 1967.
Tornquist, David. *Look East, Look West.* New York: Macmillan, 1966.
Triska, Jan, ed. *Communist Party-States: International and Comparative Studies.* New York: Bobbs-Merrill, 1969.
———. *Constitutions of the Communist Party States.* Hoover Institution on War, Revolution and Peace: Stanford University, 1968.
Ulam, Adam B. *Expansion and Coexistence.* New York: Praeger, 1968.
———. *Titoism and the Cominform.* Cambridge: Harvard University Press, 1962.
Vali, Ferenc A. *Rift and Revolt in Hungary.* Cambridge: Harvard University Press, 1961.
———. *The Quest for a United Germany.* Baltmore: Johns Hopkins Press, 1967.
Verba, Sidney and Lucien Pye. *Comparative Political Culture.* Princeton, N.J.: Princeton University Press, 1965.
Windsor, Philip and Adam Roberts. *Czechoslovakia 1968.* New York: Columbia University Press, 1969.
Woitzik, Karl-Heinz. *Die Auslandsaktivitat der Sowjetischen Besatzungszone Deutschlands: Organization, Wege, Ziele.* Mainz: Kase and Hoehler, 1968.
Wolff, Robert Lee. *The Balkans in Our Time.* New York: Norton, 1967.
Wolfers, Arnold. *Alliance Policy in the Cold War.* Baltimore: Johns Hopkins Press, 1959.
Zaninovich, M. George. *The Development of Socialist Yugoslavia.* Baltimore: Johns Hopkins Press, 1968.
Zarnowski, Janusz. *O inteligencji polskiej lat miedzywojennych.* Warsaw: Wiedza Powszechna, 1965.
Zhivkov, Todor. *Izkustvoto, naukata i kulturata v sluzhba na naroda; rechi, statii i dokladi.* Sofia: Bulgarski Pisatel, 1965.
———. *Osmi kongres na Bulgarskata Komunisticheska Partiia; stenografski protokol.* Sofia: Bulgarskata Komunisticheska Partiia, 1963.
Zinner, P. E., ed. *National Communism and Popular Revolt in Eastern Europe.* New York: Columbia University Press, 1947.
———. *Revolution in Hungary.* New York: Columbia University Press, 1962.

JOURNALS

ACTA Oeconomica. Budapest, Hungary.
Canadian Slavic Studies. Montreal, Quebec, Canada.
Czechoslovak Economic Papers. Prague, Czechoslovakia.
East Europe. New York, Free Europe Committee. (Ceased publication in January 1970.)
East European Quarterly. Boulder, Colorado.
East-West. Brussels, Belgium.
East-West Commerce. England, Foreign Correspondence Limited.
East-West Digest. England, Foreign Affairs Publishing Company.
International Affairs. Moscow, USSR.
New Times. Moscow, USSR.
New Trend. Prague, Czechoslovakia.
Praxis. Zagreb, Yugoslavia.
Problems of Communism. Washington, United States Information Agency.
Review of International Affairs. Belgrade, Yugoslavia.
Slavic Review. Seattle, Washington.
Socialist Thought and Practice. Belgrade, Yugoslavia.
Studies in Comparative Communism. Los Angeles, California.
Survey: A Journal of Soviet and East European Studies. London.
The New Hungarian Quarterly. Budapest, Hungary.
The New Yugoslav Law. Belgrade, Yugoslavia.
The Slavic and East European Journal. Madison, Wisconsin.
The Slavonic and East European Review. London, England.
World Marxist Review. Prague, Czechoslovakia.

Index

*(Index to Personal Names
appears on pages 410–13)*

INDEX TO PERSONAL NAMES